THE WORLD'S CLASSICS

UPANIṢADS

PATRICK OLIVELLE is the Chair, Department of Asian Studies, and Director, Center for Asian Studies, at the University of Texas at Austin, where he is the Professor of Sanskrit and Indian Religions. Among his recent publications are *The Saṃnyāsa Upaniṣads: Hindu Scriptures on Asceticism and Renunciation* (Oxford, 1992), *The Āśrama System: History and Hermeneutics of a Religious Institution* (Oxford, 1993), and *Rules and Regulations of Brahmanical Asceticism* (State University of New York Press, 1994).

THE WORLD'S CLASSICS

UPANIṢADS

Translated from the Original Sanskrit by

PATRICK OLIVELLE

Oxford New York
OXFORD UNIVERSITY PRESS
1996

Oxford University Press, Walton Street, Oxford OX2 6DP

Oxford New York
Athens Auckland Bangkok Bombay
Calcutta Cape Town Dar es Salaam Delhi
Florence Hong Kong Istanbul Karachi
Kuala Lumpur Madras Madrid Melbourne
Mexico City Nairobi Paris Singapore
Taipei Tokyo Toronto

and associated companies in
Berlin Ibadan

Oxford is a trade mark of Oxford University Press

First published as a Worldēs Classics paperback 1996

British Library Cataloguing in Publication Data
Data available

Library of Congress Cataloging in Publication Data
Upaniṣad. English.
Upanishads / translated from the original Sanskrit by Patrick Olivelle.
I. Olivelle Patrick. II. Title. III. Series.
294.5'9218—dc 20 BL 1124. 52. E5 1996
ISBN 0–19–282292–6

1 3 5 7 9 10 8 6 4 2

Typeset by Pure Tech India Ltd, Pondicherry
Printed in Great Britain by
BPC Paperbacks Ltd.
Aylesbury, Bucks

For Suman and Meera

PREFACE

EARLY in 1992, soon after the publication of my translation of the Saṃnyāsa Upaniṣads by Oxford University Press, New York, Catherine Clarke, the then editor of World's Classics, invited me to prepare a fresh translation of the so-called major Upaniṣads. For a variety of reasons, not the least of which was the difficulty of the task, I turned down her invitation. Not being content with taking no for an answer, she wrote to me again several months later renewing her invitation and noting the inadequacy of the existing translations. In a moment of weakness I accepted. Thanks to her persistence and after two years of intense work I am relieved and delighted that the translation is now complete. With the hard work behind me, what remains is the pleasant task of thanking the many individuals who gave generously of their time and in a variety of ways made this translation far better than it would otherwise have been. Catherine Clarke and her successor as editor, Susie Casement, gave me constant encouragement and wise counsel.

The one individual to whom I owe the deepest debt of gratitude and without whose advice and assistance this project would not have been completed is my colleague and friend Joel Brereton, who perhaps knows more about the Upaniṣads and the vedic literature than any other living scholar. He read closely my translations, notes, and introduction and provided me with detailed and lucid comments and suggestions. We spent five intense and cold wintry days in January 1995 in his house in Columbia, Missouri, discussing many difficult Upaniṣadic passages. If this translation has any merits, much of the credit should go to Joel.

In the autumn of 1993 I taught a graduate seminar on translating the Upaniṣads attended by my students Roger Conant, Don Davis, Robert Gooding, and Bill Rasmussen, as well as by my colleagues at the University of Texas, Richard Lariviere, Gregory Schopen, and Sagaree Sengupta. The seminar proved to be invaluable; my thanks to all of them. Steven Collins, Anne Feldhaus, and Gregory Schopen read the introduction and offered valuable comments. George Cardona and Madhav Deshpande shared their deep knowledge of Sanskrit grammar and phonetics with me and resolved several intractable problems. My debt to all previous scholars who have worked on the Vedas and the Upaniṣads is acknowledged in the numerous references to their works in the notes.

It is always the family that bears the brunt of a project such as this. My wife, Suman, not only provided comfort and encouragement but also proofread the entire manuscript. My daughter, Meera, was the model of patience as I stared at a computer screen for hours on end. They provided an environment of love and peace. To both this book is dedicated.

CONTENTS

LIST OF FIGURES

ABBREVIATIONS

AA	Aitareya Āraṇyaka, tr. Keith (1909).
AB	Aitareya Brāhmaṇa, tr. Keith (1920).
AU	Aitareya Upaniṣad.
AV	Atharva Veda, tr. W. D. Whitney, HOS 7–8, 1905.
BhG	Bhagavad Gītā, ed. and tr. W. G. P. Hill (London: Oxford University Press, 1928).
BS	Brahma Sūtra, tr. with Śaṃkara's commentary by G. Thibaut. 2 pts. SBE 34, 1890; SBE 38, 1896.
BU	Bṛhadāraṇyaka Upaniṣad.
CU	Chāndogya Upaniṣad.
HOS	Harvard Oriental Series, Cambridge, Mass.
Int.	Introduction to this volume.
IIJ	*Indo-Iranian Journal*.
IU	Īśā Upaniṣad.
JAOS	*Journal of the American Oriental Society*.
JB	Jaiminīya Brāhmaṇa, tr. Bodewitz (1973).
JRAS	*Journal of the Royal Asiatic Society*.
JU	Jaiminīya Upaniṣad, ed. Limaye and Vadekar (1958); ed. and tr. Ortel (1896).
KaU	Kaṭha Upaniṣad.
KeU	Kena Upaniṣad.
KS	Kāṭhaka Saṃhitā.
KsU	Kauṣītaki Upaniṣad.
LU	Les Upanishad, ed. L. Renou (Paris: Adrien-Maisonneuve, 1943–76).
MaU	Māṇḍūkya Upaniṣad.
MS	Maitrāyaṇīya Saṃhitā.
MtU	Maitrāyaṇīya (Maitrī) Upaniṣad, ed. and tr. J. A. B. van Buitenen (The Hague: Mouton, 1962).
MuU	Muṇḍaka Upaniṣad.
PU	Praśna Upaniṣad.
RV	Ṛg Veda, tr. K. F. Geldner. HOS 33–6, 1951–7.
SA	Śāṅkhāyana Āraṇyaka, ed. Keith (1909).
SB	Śatapatha Brāhmaṇa, tr. J. Eggeling. SBE 12, 26, 41, 43, 44, 1882–1900.

SBE	Sacred Books of the East, Oxford.
SILP	*Studies in Indian Literature and Philosophy: Collected Articles of J. A. B. van Buitenen*, ed. L. Rocher (American Institute of Indian Studies; Delhi: Motilal Banarsidass, 1988).
SU	Śvetāśvatara Upaniṣad.
TA	Taittirīya Āraṇyaka (Ānandāśrama Sanskrit Series, 36 (2 pts.). Poona: 1898).
TB	Taittirīya Brāhmaṇa (Ānandāśrama Sanskrit Series, 37 (3 pts.); Poona: 1898).
TS	Taittirīya Saṃhitā, tr. Keith (1914).
TU	Taittirīya Upaniṣad.
VS	Vājaseneyi Saṃhitā of the White Yajurveda. ed. A. Weber (Berlin: Ferd. Dümmler's Verlag, 1852).
WZKSA	*Wiener Zeitschrift für die Kunde Südasiens.*
ZDMG	*Zeitschrift der Deutschen Morgenländischen Gesellschaft.*

GUIDE TO THE PRONUNCIATION OF SANSKRIT WORDS

SANSKRIT words, including proper names, are printed here with diacritical marks. Sanskrit diacritics are simple and, with a minimum of effort, should enable the reader to pronounce these words properly. A general rule is that an 'h' after a consonant is *not* a separate letter but merely represents the aspirated version of a consonant. Thus 'bh' is pronounced somewhat as in a*bh*or', and 'ph' not as in '*ph*ysics but as in 'she*ph*erd'. The dental group of consonants (t, th, d, dh, n) are distinguished from the retroflex group indicated by a dot placed beneath (ṭ, ṭh, ḍ, ḍh, ṇ). The distinction in their pronunciation is somewhat difficult for the Western ear. The dentals are pronounced with the tip of the tongue placed behind the upper front teeth, and the sound is similar to the way these letters are pronounced in Romance languages such as French (e.g. toi, de). The English pronunciation of these letters is closer to the Sanskrit retroflex, but the latter is pronounced with the tip of the tongue striking the roof of the mouth further back. Thus 'ṭ' is somewhat like *t* in '*t*ry, and 'ḍ' is like *d* in *d*ental. The difference between the dental 'n' and retroflex 'ṇ' is very difficult for untrained ears to distinguish and is better ignored. The same applies to the palatal sibilant 'ś' and the retroflex 'ṣ'; both may be pronounced as *sh* in '*sh*ame'. 'ṃ' nasalizes the preceding vowel sound, as in French *bon*. 'ḥ', with a dot underneath and most frequently at the end of a word, is a pure aspiration and is to be distinguished from the consonant 'h'. In practice, the vowel sound preceding it is pronounced faintly; thus 'ḥ' of *bhuvoḥ* is pronounced like the *ho* in Soho when it is pronounced with the accent on the first syllable and the second shortened. Finally, an apostrophe before a word indicates an elided 'a', which is not pronounced.

Guide to the Pronunciation of Sanskrit Words

Pronounce Sanskrit	as in English
a	c*u*t
ā	f*a*r
i	s*i*t
ī	m*e*
u	p*u*t
ū	t*oo*
ṛ	*ri*sk
e	pr*ay*
o	h*o*pe
ai	s*igh*
au	*s*ound
c	*ch*urch
g	*g*ive
ṅ	a*n*ger
ñ	pu*n*ching

BIBLIOGRAPHY

Beall, I. F. (1986), 'Syntactical Ambiguity at Taittirīya Upaniṣad 2.1' *IIJ* 29: 97–102.

Bodewitz, H. W. (1973), *Jaiminīya Brāhmaṇa I, 1–65: Translation and Commentary with a Study Agnihotra and Prāṇāgnihotra* (Orientalia Rheno-Traiectina, 17; Leiden: E. J. Brill).

—— (1985), 'Yama's Second Boon in the Kaṭha Upaniṣad', *WZKSA* 29: 5–26.

—— (1986), 'Prāṇa, Apāna and other Prāṇa-s in Vedic Literature', *Adyar Library Bulletin*, 50: 326–48.

Böhtlingk, O. (1890), *Drei kritisch gesichtete und übersetzte Upanishad mit erklärenden Anmerkungen* (Berichte über die Verhandlungen der Königlichen Sächsischen Gesellschaften zu Leipzig, philologisch-historische Classe, 42: Leipzig).

—— (tr.) (1989a), *Bṛhadâraṇjakopanishad in der Mâdhjaṁdina-Recension* (St Petersburg: Kaiserliche Akademie der Wissenschaften).

—— (tr.) (1889b), *Khândogjopanishad* (Leipzig: Verlag H. Haessel).

Brereton, J. (1982), 'The Particle *iva* in Vedic Prose', *JAOS* 102: 443–50.

—— (1986), '*Tat Tvam Asi* in Context', *ZDMG* 136: 98–109.

—— (1988), 'Unsounded Speech: Problems in the Interpretation of BU(M) 1.5.10 = BU(K) 1.5.3', *IIJ* 31: 1–10.

—— (1990), 'The Upanishads', in Wm. T. de Bary and I. Bloom (eds.), *Approaches to the Asian Classics* (New York: Columbia University Press), 115–35.

—— (1991), 'Cosmographic Images in the Bṛhadāraṇyaka Upaniṣad', *IIJ* 34: 1–17.

—— (forthcoming), 'Yājñavalkya's Curse', in P. Thieme Festschrift.

Buitenen, J. A. B. van (1955), '*Vācārambhaṇam*', *Indian Linguistics*, 16: 157–62. Repr. in *SILP*, 13–24.

—— (1955), 'Notes on *Akṣara*', *Bulletin of the Deccan College Research Institute*, 17: 204–15. Repr. in *SILP*, 29–42.

—— (1957a), 'Studies in Sāṃkhya (II)', *JAOS* 77: 15–25. Repr. in *SILP*, 53–73.

—— (1957b), 'Studies in Sāṃkhya (III): *Sattva*', *JAOS* 77: 88–107. Repr. in *SILP*, 75–110.

—— (1958), '*Vācārambhaṇam* Reconsidered', *IIJ* 2: 295–305. Repr. in *SILP*, 121–34.

——(1959), '*Akṣara*', *JAOS* 79: 176–87. Repr. in *SILP*, 157–80.

——(1962), *The Maitrāyaṇīya Upaniṣad: A Critical Essay, with Text, Translation, and Commentary* (Disputationes Rheno-Trajectinae, 6; The Hague: Mouton).

——(1964), 'The Large Ātman', *History of Religions*, 4: 103–14. Repr. in *SILP*, 209–22.

—— (1968), 'The Speculations on the Name "Satyam" in the Upaniṣads', *Studies in Indian Linguistics* (M. B. Emeneau Volume), 54–61. Repr. in *SILP* 263–72.

——(1979), '*Ānanda*, Or All Desires Fulfilled', *History of Religions*, 19: 27–36. Repr. in *SILP*, 323–32.

Caland, W., and Henry, V. (1906), *L'Agniṣṭoma: Description complète de la forme normale du sacrifice de Soma dans le cult védique* (2 vols.; Paris: Ernest Leroux).

Cowell, E. B. (tr.) (1861), *The Kaushítaki-Bráhmaṇa-Upanishad with the Commentary of Śankaránanda* (Bibliotheca Indica; Calcutta: Baptist Mission Press).

Deussen, P. (tr.) (1897), *Sechzig Upanishad's des Veda* (Leipzig: F. A. Brockhaus). English tr. by V. M. Bedekar and G. B. Palsule. *Sixty Upaniṣads of the Veda* (2 vols.; Delhi: Motilal Banarsidass, 1980).

—— (1966), *The Philosophy of the Upanishads* (New York: Dover Publications; Repr. of 1906 edn.).

Edgerton, F. (1915), 'Studies in the Veda', *JAOS* 35: 240–6.

——(1965), *The Beginnings of Indian Philosophy: Selections from the Rig Veda, Atharva Veda, Upaniṣads, and Mahābhārata* (Cambridge, Mass.: Harvard University Press).

Emeneau, M. B. (1968–9), 'Sanskrit Syntactic Particles—*kila, khalu, nūnam*', *IIJ* 11: 241–68.

Erdosy, G. (1988), *Urbanisation in Early Historic India* (Oxford: British Archaeological Reports).

Ewing, A. H. (1901), 'The Hindu Conception of the Functions of Breath', *JAOS* 22: 251–308.

Faddegon, B. (1926), 'The Catalogue of Sciences in the Chāndogya-Upaniṣad', *Acta Orientalia*, 4: 42–54.

Falk, H. (1986a), *Bruderschaft und Würfelspiel: Untersuchungen zur Entwicklungsgeschichte des vedischen Opfers* (Freiburg: Hedwig Falk).

——(1986b), 'Vedisch *upaniṣád*'. *ZDMG* 136: 80–97.

Frenz, A. (ed. and tr.) (1968–9), 'Kauṣītaki Upaniṣad', *IIJ* 11: 79–129.

Geib, R. (1976), 'Food and Eater in Natural Philosophy of Early India', *Journal of Oriental Institute*, 25: 223–35.

Gonda, J. (1950), *Notes on Brahman* (Utrecht: J. L. Beyers).

—— (1954), 'Pratiṣṭhā', *Samjñāvyākaraṇam, Studia Indologica Internationalia*, 1: 1–37.

Gonda, J. (1955a), 'Reflections on *Sarva-* in Vedic Texts', *Indian Linguistics*, 16: 53–71.

——(1955b), 'Etymologies in the Ancient Indian Brāhmaṇas', *Lingua*, 5: 61–85.

—— (1965), '*Bandhu* in the Brāhmaṇas', *Adyar Library Bulletin*, 29: 1–29.

——(1966), *Loka: World and Heaven in the Veda* (Amsterdam: North-Holland).

——(1969), 'Āyatana', *Adyar Library Bulletin*, 23: 1–79.

——(1982), 'In the Beginning', *Annals of the Bhandarkar Oriental Research Institute* (Poona), 63: 43–62.

——(1986), *Prajāpati's Rise to Higher Rank* (Leiden: E. J. Brill).

Gren-Eklund, G. (1978), *A Study of the Nominal Sentences in the Oldest Upaniṣads* (Studia Indoeuropaea Upsaliensia, 3; Uppsala: Almquist & Wiksell).

Hamm, F.-R. (tr.) (1968–9), 'Chāndogyopaniṣad VI. Ein erneuter Versuch', *WZKSA* 12–13: 149–59.

Hanfeld, E. (1976), *Philosophische Haupttexte der älteren Upaniṣaden* (Freiburger Beiträge zur Indologie, 9; Wiesbaden: Otto Harrassowitz).

Hauschild, R. (1927), *Die Śvetāśvatara-Upaniṣad: Eine kritische Ausgabe mit einer Übersetzung und einer Übersicht über ihre Lehren* (Abhandlungen für die Kunde des Morgenlandes, 17.3; Leipzig).

——(1968), 'Saṃvarga-vidyā', in *Mélanges d'Indianisme à la mémoire de Louis Renou* (Paris: Éditions Boccard), 337–65.

Hertel, J. (1924), *Muṇḍaka-Upaniṣad. Kritische Ausgabe mit Rodarneudruck der Erstausgabe (Text und Kommentare) und Einleitung* (Indo-Iranische Quellen und Forschungen, 3; Leipzig: Verlag H. Haessel).

Hillebrandt, A. (1920), 'Weitere Bemerkungen zu den Upaniṣads', *ZDMG* 74: 461–3.

Hopkins, E. W. (1907), 'The Sniff-kiss in Ancient India', *JAOS* 28: 120–34.

Horsch, P. (1966), *Die vedische Gāthā- und Śloka-Literatur* (Berne: Francke Verlag).

——(1968), 'Buddhismus und Upaniṣaden', in J. C. Heesterman *et al.* (eds.), *Pratidānam: Indian, Iranian and Indo-European Studies Presented to Franciscus Bernandus Jacobus Kuiper on his Sixtieth Birthday* (The Hague: Mouton), 462–77.

Hume, R. E. (tr.) (1931), *The Thirteen Principal Upanishads*, 2nd edn. (Oxford: Oxford University Press).

Ickler, I. (1973), *Untersuchungen zur Wortstellung und Syntax der Chāndogyopaniṣad* (Göppingen: Verlag Alfred Kümmerle).

Insler, S. (1989–90), 'The Shattered Head Split and the Epic Tale of Śakuntalā', *Bulletin d'Études Indiennes*, 7–8: 97–139.

Jamison, S. (1986), 'Brāhmaṇa Syllable Counting, Vedic *tvac* "Skin", and the Sanskrit Expression for the Canonical Creature', *IIJ* 29: 161–81.

——(1991), *The Ravenous Hyenas and the Wounded Sun: Myth and Ritual in Ancient India* (Ithaca, NY: Cornell University Press).

Johnston, E. H. (1930), 'Some Sāṁkhya and Yoga Conceptions of the Śvetāśvatara Upaniṣad', *JRAS* 855–78.

Kaelber, W. O. (1989), *Tapta Mārga: Asceticism and Initiation in Vedic India* (Albany, NY: State University of New York Press).

Kane, P. V. (1962–75), *History of Dharmaśāstra*. I. 1 (1968), i. 2 (2nd edn., 1975), ii. 1–2 (2nd edn., 1974), iii. (1973), v. 1 (2nd edn., 1974), v. 2 (1962).

Keith, A. B. (ed. and tr.) (1909), *The Aitareya Āraṇyaka*, repr. 1969 (Oxford: Clarendon Press).

——(tr.) (1914), *The Veda of the Black Yajus School entitled Taittiriya Sanhita* (2 parts, HOS 18–19; repr. Delhi: Motilal Banarsidass, 1967).

——(tr.) (1920), *Rigveda Brahmanas: The Aitareya and Kauṣītaki Brāhmaṇas of the Rigveda* (HOS 25; repr. Delhi: Motilal Banarsidass, 1981).

Kuiper, F. B. J. (1960), 'The Ancient Aryan Verbal Contest', *IIJ* 4: 217–81.

Lienhard, S. (1978), 'On the Meaning and Use of the Word *Indragopa*', *Indologica Taurinensia*, 6: 177–88.

Limaye, V. P. and Vadekar, R. D. (eds.) (1958), *Eighteen Principal Upaniṣads* (Poona: Vaidika Saṁśodhana Maṇḍala).

Lüders, H. (1907), *Das Würfelspiel im alten Indien* (Abhandlungen der Königlichen Gesellschaft der Wissenschaften zu Göttingen, Philologisch-Historische Klasse 9. 2 Berlin).

——(1940a), 'Zu den Upaniṣads: I. Die Saṃvargavidyā', in *Philologica Indica: Ausgewählte kleine Schriften von Henrich Lüders* (Göttingen: Vandenhoeck & Ruprecht). 361–90.

——(1940b), 'Zu den Upaniṣads: II. Die Ṣoḍaśakalavidyā', ibid. 509–25.

Macdonell, A. A. (1898), *Vedic Mythology* (repr. 1974; Delhi: Motilal Banarsidass).

——and Keith, A. B. (1912), *Vedic Index of Names and Subjects* (repr. 1967, 2 vols.; Delhi: Motilal Banarsidass).

Mitchiner, J. E. (1982), *Traditions of the Seven Ṛṣis* (Delhi: Motilal Banarsidass).

Morgenroth, W. (1970), 'Die Lehre des Uddālaka Āruṇi', *Archiv Orientální*, 38: 33–44.

Müller, F. Max (ed.) (1879–84), *The Upanishads* (2 parts, SBE 1, 15; repr. 1981; Delhi: Motilal Banarsidass).

Oldenberg, H. (tr.) (1886–92), *The Gṛhya-Sūtras* (2 vols., SBE 29–30; repr. 1967; Delhi: Motilal Banarsidass).

Olivelle, P. (1991), 'Contributions to the Semantic History of *Saṃnyāsa*', *JAOS* 101: 265–74.

——(1992), *Saṃnyāsa Upaniṣads: Hindu Scriptures on Asceticism and Renunciation* (New York: Oxford University Press).

——(1993), *The Āśrama System: The History and Hermeneutics of a Religious Institution* (New York: Oxford University Press).

Oertel, H. (1896), 'The Jaiminīya or Talavakāra Upaniṣad Brāhmaṇa', *JAOS* 16: 79–260.

——(1897), 'Contributions from the Jāiminīya Brāhmaṇa to the History of the Brāhmaṇa Literature', *JAOS* 18: 15–48.

——(1937), *Zum altindischen Ausdrucksverstärkungstypus* satyasya satyam *'das Wahre des Wahren' = 'die Quintessenz des Wahren'* (Sitzungsberichte der Bayerischen Akademie der Wissenschaften, Philosophisch-historische Abteilung, 1937: 3; Munich: Verlag der Bayerischen Akademie der Wissenschaften).

Parpola, A. (1981), 'On the Primary Meaning and Etymology of the Sacred Syllable *ōm*', Proceedings of the Nordic South Asia Conference, *Studia Orientalia*, 50: 195–213.

Radhakrishnan, S. (tr.) (1953), *The Principal Upaniṣads* (London: George Allen & Unwin).

Rau, W. (1957), *Staat und Gesellschaft im alten Indien nach den Brāhmaṇa-Texten dargestellt* (Wiesbaden: Otto Harrassowitz).

——(1964), 'Versuch einer deutschen Übersetzung der Śvetāśvatara-Upaniṣad', *Asiatische Studien*, 17: 25–46.

——(1965), 'Versuch einer deutschen Übersetzung der Muṇḍaka-Upaniṣad', *Asiatische Studien*, 18–19: 216–26.

——(1970), *Weben und Flechten im vedischen Indien* (Akademie der Wissenschaften und der Literature. Abhandlungen der Geisten- und Sozialwissenschaftlichen Klasse 11; Wiesbaden: Steiner Verlag).

——(1971), 'Versuch einer deutschen Übersetzung der Kāṭhaka-Upaniṣad', *Asiatische Studien* 25: 158–74.

——(1973), *Metalle und Metallgeräte im vedischen Indien* (Akademie der Wissenschaften und der Literature. Abhandlungen der Geisten- und Sozialwissenschaftlichen Klasse 8; Wiesbaden: Steiner Verlag).

Renou, L. (1946), ' "Connexion" en védique, "cause" en bouddhique', in *Dr. C. Kunhan Raja Presentation Volume* (Madras: Adyar Library).

——(tr.) (1948), *Kauṣītaki Upaniṣad.* In *LU*, vi.

——(1953), 'Le Passage des Brāhmaṇa aux Upaniṣad', *JAOS* 73: 138 f.

—— (1955), 'Remarques sur la Chāndogya-Upaniṣad', in *Études védiques et pāninéennes*, (Paris: Éditions Boccard), i. 91–102.

—— and Silburn, L. (1949), 'Sur la notion de "Brahman"', *Journal Asiatique*, 7–46. Repr. in L. Renou, *L'Inde fondamentale: Études d'indianisme réunies et présentées par Charles Malamoud* (Paris: Hermann, 1978), 83–116.

Ruben, W. (1947), *Die Philosophen der Upaniṣaden* (Berne: A. Francke).

Salomon, R. (1981), 'A Linguistic Analysis of the Muṇḍaka Upaniṣad'. *WZKSA* 25: 91–105.

—— (1991), 'A Linguistic Analysis of the Praśna Upaniṣad', *WZKSA* 35: 47–74.

Senart, E. (tr.) (1930), *Chāndogya-Upaniṣad* (Paris: Société d'Édition 'Les Belles Lettres').

—— (tr.) (1934), *Bṛhad-Āraṇyaka-Upaniṣad* (Paris: Société d'Édition 'Les Belles Lettres').

Schmithausen, L. (1994), 'Zur Textgeschichte der Pañcāgnividyā', *WZKSA* 38: 43–60.

Sharma, A., and Young, K. K. (1990), 'The Meaning of *ātmahano janāḥ* in *Īśā Upaniṣad* 3', *JAOS* 110: 595–602.

Singh, M. (1994), *The Upaniṣadic Etymologies* (Delhi: Nirmal Publications).

Smith, B. K. (1989), *Reflections on Resemblance, Ritual, and Religion* (New York: Oxford University Press).

—— (1990), 'Eaters, Food, and Social Hierarchy in Ancient India: A Dietary Guide to a Revolution in Values', *Journal of the American Academy of Religion*, 58: 177–205.

—— (1994), *Classifying the Universe: The Ancient Indian* Varṇa *System and the Origins of Caste* (New York: Oxford University Press).

Sparreboom, M. (1985), *Chariots in the Veda* (Memoirs of the Kern Institute, 3; Leiden: E. J. Brill).

Sprockhoff, J. F. (1976), *Saṃnyāsa: Quellenstudien zur Askese im Hinduismus. I. Untersuchungen über die Saṃnyāsa-Upaniṣads* (Abhandlungen für die Kunde des Morgenlandes, 42.1; Wiesbaden: Franz Steiner).

—— (1979), 'Die Alten im alten Indien: Ein Versuch nach brahmanischen Quellen', *Saeculum*, 20: 374–43.

Thieme, P. (1951–2), 'Der Weg durch den Himmel nach der Kaushitaki-Upanishad', *Wissenschaftliche Zeitschrift der Martin-Luther-Universität Halle-Wittenberg*, 1: 3; *Gesellschafts- und sprachwissenschaftliche, ser.* 1: 19–36. Repr. Paul Thieme, *Kleiner Schriften* (Wiesbaden: Franz Steiner, 1984, ii. 82–99).

—— (1952), 'Brahman', *ZDMG* 102: 91–129. Repr. Paul Thieme, *Kleiner Schriften*, ii. 100–38.

Thieme, P. (tr.) (1965), 'Īśopaniṣad (= Vājasaneyi-Saṃhitā 40) 1–14', *JAOS* 85: 89–99. Repr. Paul Thieme, *Kleiner Schriften*, ii. 228–38.

—— (tr.) (1968a), *Upanischaden: Ausgewälte Stücke* (Stuttgart: Philipp Reclam).

—— (1968b), 'Ādeśa', in *Mélanges d'Indianisme à la mémoire de Louis Renou* (Paris: Éditions Boccard), 715–23.

Vogel, J. P. (1962), *The Goose in Indian Literature and Art* (Memoirs of the Kern Institute, 11. Leiden).

Weller, F. (1953), *Versuch einer Kritik der Kaṭhopaniṣad.* Deutsche Akademie der Wissenschaften zu Berlin, Institut für Orientforschung, 1.2. Berlin: Akademie Verlag.

Wezler, A. (1982), 'Zum Verständnis von Chāndogya-Upaniṣad 5.1.12.', *Studien zur Indologie und Iranistik*, 8/9: 147–68.

—— (1992), 'Sanskrit Prāṇabhṛt or What Supports What?' in A. W. van den Hoek, D. H. A. Kolff, and M. S. Oort (eds.), *Ritual, State and History in South Asia: Essays in Honour of J. C. Heesterman* (Leiden: E. J. Brill), 393–413.

—— (1993), 'On a Prose Passage in the Yuktidīpikā of Some Significance for the History of Indian Medicine', *Journal of the European Āyurvedic Society*, 3: 282–304.

Willman-Grabowska, H. (1927–8), *Les Composés nominaux dans le Śatapathabrāhmaṇa* (2 parts; Prace Komisji Orjentalistycznej Polskiej Akademji, Umiejetnosci. 12; Warsaw: W. Krakowie).

Witzel, M. (1984), 'Sur le chemin du ciel', *Bulletin d'Études Indiennes*, 2: 213–79.

—— (1987), 'On the Localisation of Vedic Texts and Schools', in G. Pollet (ed.), *India and the Ancient World: History, Trade and Culture before* AD. *650* (Orientalia Lovaniensia Analecta, 25; Leuven: Department Oriëntalistiek), 174–213.

—— (1989), 'Tracing the Vedic Dialects', in C. Caillat (ed.), *Dialectes dans les littératures Indo-aryennes* (Publications de l'Institut de Civilisation Indienne, 55; Paris: Éditions Boccard), 97–265.

Zysk, K. G. (1993), 'The Science of Respiration and the Doctrine of the Bodily Winds in Ancient India', *JAOS* 113: 198–213.

INTRODUCTION

THE Upaniṣads translated here represent some of the most important literary products in the history of Indian culture and religion, both because they played a critical role in the development of religious ideas in India and because they are valuable as sources for our understanding of the religious, social, and intellectual history of ancient India. The Upaniṣads were composed at a time of great social, economic, and religious change; they document the transition from the archaic ritualism of the Veda into new religious ideas and institutions. It is in them that we note for the first time the emergence of central religious concepts of both Hinduism and of the new religious movements, such as Buddhism and Jainism, that emerged not long after the composition of the early Upaniṣads. Such concepts include the doctrine of rebirth, the law of *karma* that regulates the rebirth process, and the techniques of liberation from the cycle of rebirth, such as mental training associated with Yoga, ascetic self-denial and mortification, and the renunciation of sex, wealth, and family life. Even though theoretically the whole of the vedic corpus is accepted as revealed truth, in reality it is the Upaniṣads that have continued to influence the life and thought of the various religious traditions that we have come to call Hindu. Upaniṣads are the vedic scriptures *par excellence* of Hinduism.

In translating and interpreting these ancient documents I have drawn on the most current philological, historical, and anthropological research available to me, research that provides glimpses into the social and intellectual world of the ancient Upaniṣads. Some of that research is presented in the notes and my debt to previous scholarship is thereby acknowledged. Much of it is implicit in the translation itself. In this introduction, I want to supplement and to organize the information scattered in the notes—information that will give the reader the social, religious, and cultural background of these documents, information without which much of what is said in them cannot be understood. Given the constraints imposed by the very nature of an introduction and the limits of space prescribed by the format of this series, it is impossible to explore fully that background. I have deliberately aimed these introductory remarks at non-specialist readers, knowing that the specialists can fend for themselves. My hope is that the information given here, although inadequate, will provide a sufficient background to appreciate these documents within their historical contexts. My task is complicated by the fact that the Upaniṣads translated here were composed over a period of about six centuries, a period which saw many and far-reaching social, economic, and religious changes. My emphasis will be on the early period, which produced some of the major Upaniṣads, including the Bṛhadāraṇyaka and the Chāndogya, although I will deal with some of the doctrines of the Sāṃkhya and Yoga traditions and with the monotheistic and devotional tendencies that underlie several later Upaniṣads.

In this Introduction I have avoided speaking of 'the philosophy of the Upaniṣads', a common feature of most introductions to their translations.[1] These documents were composed over several centuries and in various regions, and it is futile to try to discover a single doctrine or philosophy in them. Different theologians, philosophers, and pious readers down the centuries both in India and abroad have discovered different 'truths' and 'philosophies' in them. That has been, after all, the common fate of scriptures in all religions. Even in the future, that is an enterprise best left to the readers themselves, and the prudent translator will try and step aside and not get in their way.

The Social Background of the Upaniṣads

Modern scholarship has unveiled to some degree the distant and long-forgotten past of northern India. Prior to the middle of the second millennium BCE this region was probably populated by numerous groups of diverse ethnic and linguistic backgrounds. About most of them we know very little. About one group, however, we have a wealth of information unearthed by archaeologists early in the twentieth century. This group of people built an urban civilization along the Indus River (hence the name Indus

[1] For an eminently readable yet accurate, unbiased, and brief presentation of the main doctrinal themes of the Upaniṣads I refer the reader to Brereton 1990.

Valley Civilization); it lasted from around 2300 until the middle of the second millennium BCE and centred on the two major cities of Harappa and Mohenjo Daro.[2] This urban civilization died without exerting any noticeable influence on the civilizations that followed.

At about the time when the Indus Valley Civilization became extinct, according to the commonly accepted theory, there took place a relatively large migration of people from the west into the upper Indus valley.[3] They were a pastoral but militarily powerful people who called themselves *ārya* (literally, 'noble' or 'honorable'; whence the word Aryan). Modern linguistic studies have demonstrated that the language of these people, the language in which the ancient vedic literature including the Upaniṣads was written and which later came to be known as Sanskrit, belongs to a family of languages (generally referred to as Indo-European) that includes Greek, Latin, and most of the modern European and northern Indian languages, as well as the ancient and modern languages of Iran. This distribution of languages suggests that a related group of nomadic pastoral people migrated across Europe and towards the east, settling first in Iran and finally in northern India.

The Aryans who came into India first settled in the fertile land of the upper Indus tributaries (the area of present-day Punjab) but soon migrated farther east into the Ganges valley. Although the material culture of the Aryans was much inferior to that of the Indus Valley Civilization—urban culture, for example, would not rise again for another thousand years—they left

[2] For information about this civilization see B. and F. R. Allchin, *The Rise of Civilisation in India and Pakistan* (Cambridge: Cambridge University Press, 1982); Gregory L. Possehl (ed.), *Ancient Cities of the Indus* (Durham, NC: Carolina Academic Press, 1979); Gregory L. Possehl (ed.), *Harappan Civilization: A Contemporary Perspective* (New Delhi: Oxford University Press, 1982).

[3] The Aryan migration theory has been challenged recently by several archaeologists: see Colin Renfrew, *Archaeology and Language: The Puzzle of Indo-European Origins* (London: Jonathan Cape, 1987). Even though the migration theory possibly needs revisions and the Aryan migrations may have occurred at different times and at a much earlier period, I think the preponderance of evidence still supports the view that there was an Aryan migration into India in the second millennium BCE and that the language of the Veda reflects the language of those Aryans.

behind a vast corpus of literature, the Vedas, and for this reason the Aryan civilization from the time of the composition of the earliest Ṛgvedic hymns, probably in the last few centuries of the second millennium BCE, until about the fifth century BCE is known as the Vedic Civilization.[4]

The Aryans dominated the native populations across much of northern India. Their military prowess may have had many causes, but the horse and the horse-drawn chariots that they possessed must have been an important factor. The horse remained a central symbol of royal power in ancient India, and the horse-sacrifice that figures so prominently in the opening chapter of the Bṛhadāraṇyaka Upaniṣad became the primary ritual expression of that power. But their domination was not necessarily numerical. 'The evidence of widespread settlement in the Ganga Valley by the late 2nd millennium B.C.', Erdosy (1988, 101) points out, 'would suggest, that numerically the native population would have been overwhelmingly dominant.' It is this blend of indigenous and Aryan peoples that constituted vedic society.

The subjugated non-Aryans appear to have been by and large relegated to the lower class of an emerging quadripartite social structure: (1) the élite ruling cum military class generally referred to as Kṣatriya; (2) the hereditary priestly class of Brahmins; (3) the large group of peasants and artisans knows as Vaiśya; and finally (4) the Śūdra group, which included a motley array of people, including subjugated non-Aryans, servants, and slaves. These four social groups were called *varṇa* (lit. 'colour'), the first three consisting at least in theory of Aryans.

These groups were not as watertight as the later caste divisions of Indian society, and there appears to have been some mobility across the groups. The *varṇa* division of society, however, has remained from the vedic period until modern times the primary

[4] The best and the most accurate description of vedic society drawn from literary sources is Rau 1957. Accessible, though somewhat dated, studies on vedic religion and mythology are: Macdonell 1898; A. B. Keith, *The Religion and Philosophy of the Veda and Upanishads* (2 vols., 1925; Repr. Delhi: Motilal Banarsidass, 1989).

theological and theoretical conception of society in India,[5] and it underlies much of the discussion in the Upaniṣads. By the time of the latest hymns of the Ṛgveda, probably the early centuries of the first millennium BCE, the *varṇa* division of society had become theologically so central that a creation hymn (RV 10.90) depicts the emergence of the four classes from the mouth (Brahmin), arms (Kṣatriya), loins (Vaiśya), and feet (Śūdra) of a primeval man (*puruṣa*), whose sacrifice and dismemberment created the universe.

How much influence the non-Aryan religious and cultural traditions may have exerted on the dominant vedic culture has been a matter of much debate and controversy. That there must have been some influence is unquestionable; but to identify specific non-Aryan elements of vedic culture is, I believe, a nearly impossible and an altogether futile enterprise.[6] As Erdosy (1988, 101) has argued, the very durability of the social order that the Aryan migrants created indicates that the Aryans may have utilized and exploited the social divisions of the non-Aryan groups themselves. It is likely that the élites of these groups were co-opted into the Kṣatriya ruling class and that the Brahmin priestly class incorporated both Aryan and non-Aryan ritual specialists. The Aryans themselves soon lost any collective memory they may have had of having migrated from the west; none of the early vedic texts preserve any such memory.

The influence of the native peoples was probably most marked in the economic area. The Aryans, who had been nomadic cattle herders, adopted much of the economic system of the natives; the economy of the vedic society along the Ganges valley during circa 1000–600 BCE was by and large an agricultural one, although animal husbandry, especially cattle, continued to play an important role and cows were the symbol of wealth. Rice, a native cereal of the Ganges region, became their staple food. There is also evidence of crafts, especially pottery, textile, and metal work. The vedic texts themselves attest to the existence of

[5] For a fine discussion of the *varṇa* ideology and its use as the central classificatory principle, see Smith 1994.

[6] For a discussion of this issue, see Olivelle 1993, 68–9.

trade and traders.[7] The economy, however, was primarily agricultural and was based on villages; vedic society remained primarily village-based until about the sixth century BCE.

Beyond the villages and their internal organization, there were broader political units run by chieftains who ruled over many villages. 'Already in the 10th–7th centuries BC,' Erdosy (1988, 55) claims, 'we can see the presence of a two-tier hierarchy of settlements, and suggest that the largest centre existed to control the movement and processing of raw materials, exploiting its position at the boundary of two zones with distinct resources.' These chiefdoms were probably the largest political units during this period, controlling crafts and commerce, collecting taxes and tributes, and exercising military and judicial powers.

By the late vedic period these units had been sufficiently consolidated so that we can speak of the emergence of kingdoms and a monarchical form of government along the Ganges. By about the sixth century BCE, that is, during the period of the first Upaniṣads, many relatively large kingdoms had been created. Kings and royalty, as the Upaniṣadic evidence itself indicates, began to play an increasing role both in the political economy of northern India and in the area of religious thinking and institutions.

A major issue regarding late vedic society is urbanization. After the demise of the urban civilization of Harappa and Mohenjo Daro, northern Indian society was essentially village-based. The available archaeological and literary data indicate the rise of cities along the Ganges valley between the sixth and fourth centuries BCE.[8] The cities functioned as administrative, commercial, and military centres of the kingdoms. 'If the previous period's findings indicated a chiefdom,' writes Erdosy (1988, 116), 'here we may justifiably argue for the first emergence of a state level of political organization.' These relatively large realms facilitated commerce and travel, permitting not only the distribution of goods but also the dissemination of religious ideas and institutions.

7 See Rau 1957, 28.

8 The most recent and very readable study of the archaeological evidence for the emergence of cities and states in the Ganges valley in the sixth to fourth centuries BCE is Erdosy 1988.

It is, however, uncertain whether the urbanization of the Ganges valley occurred before or after the composition of the early prose Upaniṣads and what influence, if any, it had on the development of Upaniṣadic thought. The society and culture reflected in these documents, nevertheless, are far different from those of the early vedic period. At least some of the new ideas and institutions, especially asceticism and celibacy,[9] I believe, reflect, if not an urban environment, then at least one that is in the process of urbanization. The vast geography known to the Upaniṣads indicates the relative ease of travel and commerce across much of northern India. They refer to the Gandhāra region of the north-west and the Videha region of the south-east, two regions separated by over 1,600 kilometres. People travelled long distances not only to trade but also to acquire knowledge (BU 3.3.1). It is also interesting in this context to note that there are very few agricultural metaphors and images in the Upaniṣads, while examples derived from crafts such as weaving, pottery, and metallurgy are numerous. These crafts, of course, could appear in village life, but the dominance of craft metaphors at least suggests a milieu somewhat removed from the agricultural routine of villages. After a close reading of these texts, it appears to me that, by and large, their social background consists of court and crafts, rather than village and agriculture. The later verse Upaniṣads were certainly composed after the rise of urbanization and possibly even after the creation of the Maurya empire in the late fourth century BCE.

The Literary History of the Upaniṣads

The Upaniṣads, on the one hand, are portions of a large body of sacred texts collectively known as the Veda and are thus an integral part of the fundamental scriptures of most people we have come to call 'Hindu'; it is in this manner that the Upaniṣads have been transmitted through the centuries, and we should, therefore, consider their position within the broader vedic corpus. They are, on the other hand, documents composed and edited by indi-

[9] For a summary of how this new urbanization may have affected religious ideas and institutions, see Olivelle 1993, 55–8.

viduals at given moments in history and in specific geographical locations; we need to, therefore, look at the history of their composition.

The Upaniṣads within the Vedic Corpus

In the brief introductions to individual Upaniṣads I identify each as belonging to a particular branch of the Veda. The literature of the Veda was produced by and largely intended for Brahmins. Different families of Brahmins became specialists in different aspects of the many and complicated sacrifices that dominated their lives and thought. These specialized family traditions developed into the vedic 'branches' (*śākhā*, sometimes also translated as 'school') within which specialized ritual texts were produced and transmitted. The literary structure of the vedic corpus, therefore, mirrors the division of the priestly community into branches specializing in different aspects of the complex sacrificial ritual.[10]

The Veda is broadly divided into three sections: Ṛgveda, Sāmaveda, and Yajurveda, but in time a fourth, the Atharvaveda, came to be added to these three.[11] The first identity of a Brahmin is determined by his affiliation to one of these vedic traditions; I will explain below the different priestly functions associated with each. Further 'branching' of the vedic traditions took place as a result of numerous factors, including geographical location, ritual specialization, and doctrinal and ritual disputes.

Each of these vedic branches has as its foundational text a 'collection' (Saṃhitā) of verses or liturgical formulas[12] and a prose text (Brāhmaṇa) explaining the meaning of the liturgy (see Fig. 1). The Saṃhitā of each Veda is by and large common to all

[10] For a survey of this literature, see M. Winternitz, *A History of Indian Literature*, tr. S. Ketkar, vol. i (1927; repr. New Delhi: Oriental Books Reprint Corp., 1972); J. Gonda, *Vedic Literature* (Wiesbaden: Harrassowitz, 1975).

[11] The Atharvaveda is not directly connected with the vedic liturgical tradition and incorporates beliefs and rituals from traditions of healing and magic. Upaniṣads ascribed to the Atharvaveda are generally late and were probably composed as independent documents outside the vedic branches.

[12] The Saṃhitā of the Ṛgveda is in verse and contains, 1028 hymns divided into ten books; the Saṃhitā of the Sāmaveda consists mostly of Ṛgvedic verses set to music; and the Saṃhitā of the Yajurveda is in prose and contains formulas that are recited during a sacrifice.

ṚGVEDA	YAJURVEDA			SĀMAVEDA	ATHARVAVEDA
	Black (Kṛṣṇa)		**White** (Śukla)		
Ṛgveda Saṃhitā	Taittirīya Saṃhitā	Kāṭhaka Saṃhitā	Vājasaneyi Saṃhitā	Sāmaveda Saṃhitā	Atharvaveda Saṃhitā (Śaunaka)
Aitareya Brāhmaṇa	Taittirīya Brāhmaṇa		Śatapatha Brāhmaṇa	Talavakāra (Jaiminīya) Brāhmaṇa	Gopatha Brāhmaṇa
Kauṣītaki/Śāṅkhāyana Brāhmaṇa					Chāndogya Brāhmaṇa
Aitareya Āraṇyaka	Taittirīya Āraṇyaka				
Śāṅkhānaya Āraṇyaka					
Aitareya Upaniṣad	Taittirīya Upaniṣad		Bṛhadāraṇyaka Upaniṣad	Chāndogya Upaniṣad	Muṇḍaka Upaniṣad
Kauṣītaki Upaniṣad	Śvetāśvatara Up.	Kaṭha Upaniṣad	Īśa Upaniṣad	Jaiminīya-Upaniṣad-Brāhmaṇa	Praśna Upaniṣad
				Kena Upaniṣad	Māṇḍukya Upaniṣad

NB This chart is not comprehensive, and there are other vedic branches and texts, which are not included because they do not have extant Upaniṣads. The chart is intended only to indicate the position within the broader vedic corpus of the Upaniṣads translated or referred to in this book.

Fig. 1. The Upaniṣads within the Vedic Corpus

its branches, even though some may have their own recension of it, while each branch has its own Brāhmaṇa. The Brāhmaṇas were not the work of single authors, and periodic additions were made to them. These additions included esoteric material explaining the hidden meanings of ritual actions and words. Some of these esoteric sections of the Brāhmaṇas came to be called Āraṇyakas (texts that were to be recited in the wilderness outside the village), while others came to be called Upaniṣads. The distinction between these two groups of texts is not altogether clear, since both deal with similar material; some of the Upaniṣads, such as the Aitareya, are embedded within their respective Āraṇyakas, while others, such as the Bṛhadāraṇyaka (lit. 'Great Āraṇyaka'), are viewed as both Āraṇyaka and Upaniṣad. Cosmological and metaphysical topics generally occupy a more central position in the Upaniṣads, however, than in the Āraṇyakas, and the Upaniṣads are, by and large, later than the Āraṇyakas. Figure 1 illustrates the position of the early Upaniṣads within the framework of the vedic corpus.

The vedic texts, including the Upaniṣads, were composed and at first transmitted from generation to generation orally and within their respective vedic branches. The reader will observe, and I have frequently pointed out in the notes, the many instances where the oral nature of the Upaniṣads is manifest, as when the author uses deictic pronouns 'this' and 'this' to refer to his two eyes, or 'this (here)' and 'that (over there)' to refer to the earth (or something on earth) and the sun. The writing down of these documents did not take place for perhaps a thousand years, but the transmission was, none the less, very faithful—more accurate, I might add, than most manuscript traditions—and the priestly tradition developed many, often artificial, devices to ensure a faithful transmission.

Toward the last centuries BCE and certainly by the first centuries of the common era, the role of the sacrifice within religion and of the vedic branches within Brahmanical learning became less significant. Specialized traditions of learning (*śāstra*) came into existence, first Sanskrit grammar and then others such as religious law (Dharmaśāstra), political science (Arthaśāstra), and medicine, traditions that cut across vedic branches. Even within ritual and religious practice, Brahmanical thought came to consider the literature of all vedic branches, that is, the totality of the Veda, as authoritative over individuals in every vedic branch. The Upaniṣads themselves became somewhat detached from their respective vedic branches and became the common property of all Brahmins under the generic title 'Vedānta', meaning the end or conclusion and, in an extended sense, the essence of the Veda.

An early effort, probably within the first five hundred years of the common era, to make a systematic presentation of Vedāntic doctrines is the *Vedāntasūtra* (or *Brahmasūtra*) ascribed to Bādarāyaṇa.[13] The Upaniṣads came to be considered the section of the Veda containing salvific knowledge (*jñānakāṇḍa*), whereas the other sections contained information about rites (*karmakāṇḍa*). As the revealed source of knowledge, therefore, the Upaniṣads became the basic scriptural authority for most later Indian theological traditions.

Given the importance of these basic texts, numerous documents, often espousing sectarian viewpoints, were composed with the title 'Upaniṣad', and, at least among some segments of the population, they enjoyed the authority and sanctity attached to the Vedas; most of these late texts are ascribed to the Atharvaveda. Such Upaniṣads continued to be produced possibly as late as the sixteenth century CE and number in the hundreds. In the first half of the second millennium CE, furthermore, the early Upaniṣads were detached from the Brāhmaṇas of which they were a part and, together with these later Upaniṣads, gathered into collections; the number of Upaniṣads included in these collections varied according to the region, 52 being a common number in the north and 108 in the south.[14]

The Composition of the Upaniṣads

The second issue relating to the literary history of the Upaniṣads concerns their composition. Who were their authors? When and

[13] See *The Vedānta Sūtras of Bādarāyaṇa with the Commentary by Śaṅkara*, tr. G. Thibaut (2 parts; SBE 34, 38, Oxford: 189–96; repr. New York: Dover Publications, 1962).

[14] For an account of these collections, the translation of fifty into Persian (Oupnikhat) in 1656, and the European encounter with these collections, see Deussen 1966, 33–8. For a study on the date of late Upaniṣads and Upaniṣadic collections, see Sprockhoff 1976, 9–26, 277–95.

where were they composed?[15] These are difficult questions to answer, because the Upaniṣads have come down to us as anonymous documents and, apart from evidence internal to the texts themselves, no external evidence exists regarding their authorship or dates.

Authorship: The issue of authorship is complicated by the fact that some of the earliest and largest Upaniṣads—at least the Bṛhadāraṇyaka, the Chāndogya, and the Kauṣītaki—are anthologies of material that must have existed as independent texts before their incorporation into these Upaniṣads by an editor or a series of editors. Several such source texts are included in more than one Upaniṣad, leading us to believe that the editors at least partly drew upon a common stock of episodes and teachings.[16]

Some of this source material consists of dialogues, debates, and formal teachings by famous teachers of the time, who are identified. Prominent among these are Yājñavalkya (in the BU), Uddālaka Āruṇi (in the CU), Janaka, Pravāhaṇa Jaivali, Ajātaśatru, Śāṇḍilya, and Satyakāma Jābāla.[17] Many of these are, of course, Brahmins, who were not only priests but also the theologians and teachers within the social hierarchy of the time. It is, therefore, surprising that several prominent teachers of Upaniṣadic doctrines are presented as kings, or at least as belonging to the Kṣatriya class. The Kṣatriya contribution to Upaniṣadic thought has been an issue long debated among scholars. Many have gone so far as to claim that the creative and new elements of Upaniṣadic doctrines were the creation of Kṣatriyas.[18]

[15] These are, of course, historical questions. Theologically, the Vedas are considered by the Brahmanical tradition as revelation. The mainstream view is that they are without human or divine authors; they are self-existent knowledge (*veda* literally means 'knowledge') 'heard' by ancient seers (hence *śruti* or 'hearing' is another term for Veda). Others consider the Vedas to have been revealed by God.

[16] The episode relating to the disclosure of the doctrine of five fires is found in BU 6.2; CU 5.3–10; KsU 1.1–2; and elsewhere (see Bodewitz 1973, 110–23; Schmithausen 1994). Further, BU 6.1–3 corresponds to CU 5.1–10.

[17] For a study of these thinkers, see Ruben 1947.

[18] See e.g. Deussen 1966, 17–21; Horsch 1966, 427–41. Some scholars have explained the non-standard Sanskrit phrases occurring in some Upaniṣads as due to the influence of a hypothetical Kṣatriya dialect of Sanskrit.

The Upaniṣads themselves appear to lend support to such a view. They record numerous episodes where a Brahmin or a group of Brahmins who claim to be learned are worsted in debate by a Kṣatriya, who then goes on to teach a new doctrine to them. King Pravāhaṇa Jaivali, for example, claims that the famous doctrine of the five fires 'had never reached the Brahmins. As a result in all the worlds government has belonged exclusively to royalty' (CU 5.3.7). Similar episodes are narrated with reference to kings Aśvapati Kaikeya (CU 5.11–24), Ajātaśatru (BU 2.1), and others.

The relationship between the priestly and royal classes in ancient India was complex. At one level it was symbiotic; the co-operation between these two groups, in whose hands power was concentrated, permitted both to thrive. At another level, the two groups were rivals for power and prestige. The entire Brahmanical ideology of society and the science and practice of ritual were designed, on the one hand, to enhance Kṣatriya power and, on the other, to ensure the recognition by the Kṣatriyas that the source of their power was the Brahmin. It is naïve, therefore, to accept the literary evidence of the Upaniṣads regarding their Kṣatriya authorship at face value and as historical fact. Surely, these documents were composed and transmitted by Brahmins. Why, then, did they deliberately include episodes that placed them at a disadvantage *vis-à-vis* the royal class? There must have been political, religious, economic, and even literary reasons for including or creating these episodes. We must bear in mind that the Brahmin community itself was not a monolithic entity. The most we can say is that some segments of the Brahmanical community must have perceived it as advantageous to present doctrines they favoured as coming from the royal élite.[19]

This is not to deny, however, that the nobility surrounding the kings played a part in the intellectual and religious life of the time. Indeed, at a time not too distant from the early Upaniṣads, we have new religions such as Buddhism and Jainism rising in approximately the same geographic region of northern India, religions whose founders are considered to have come from the royal class. The doctrines of the devotional religions that became

[19] For a more extended discussion of this point, see Olivelle 1993, 61–2.

part of Brahmanism are also depicted as being taught by people belonging to that class, people such as Kṛṣṇa and Rāma who are viewed as incarnations of god Viṣṇu. What is important, however, is not whether a particular doctrine originated among the Kṣatriyas, but that the new religious climate in northern India, of which the Upaniṣads were a part, was created through the intellectual interaction among 'new thinkers' within both groups.

The early Upaniṣads also present at least two women, Gārgī Vācaknavī (BU 3.6, 8) and Maitreyī, the wife of Yājñavalkya (BU 2.4; 4.5), as participating in theological disputes and discussions. The fact that these women are introduced without any attempt to justify or to explain how women could be engaged in theological matters suggests the relatively high social and religious position of at least women of some social strata during this period.

Chronology: In spite of claims made by some,[20] in reality, any dating of these documents that attempts a precision closer than a few centuries is as stable as a house of cards. The scholarly consensus, well-founded I think, is that the Bṛhadāraṇyaka and the Chāndogya are the two earliest Upaniṣads. We have seen, however, that they are edited texts, some of whose sources are much older than others. The two texts as we have them are, in all likelihood, pre-Buddhist; placing them in the seventh to sixth centuries BCE may be reasonable, give or take a century or so.[21] The three other early prose Upaniṣads—Taittirīya, Aitareya, and

[20] See e.g. the precise dating of various Upaniṣadic thinkers by Ruben (1947): Śāṇḍilya, 670–640 BCE; Uddālaka Āruṇi and Yājñavalkya, 640–610 BCE; and Śvetaketu, 610–580 BCE.

[21] Much of the chronology of the Upaniṣads and of other ancient texts depends on the date of the Buddha's death. The generally accepted date of around 486 BCE has been challenged recently. Bechert's dating of 375–355 BCE ('The Date of the Buddha Reconsidered', *Indologica Taurinensia*, 10 (1981), 29–36) has been supported by Erdosy using archaeological data ('The Archaeology of Early Buddhism', in N. K. Wagle and F. Watanabe (eds.), *Studies on Buddhism in Honour of Professor A. K. Warder* (Toronto: University of Toronto Centre for South Asian Studies, 1993), 40–56. If the latter date is accepted, which I favour, then the dates of the early Upaniṣads should be pushed forward a century or so (see Witzel 1989, 241–51).

Kauṣītaki—come next; all are probably pre-Buddhist and can be assigned to the sixth to fifth centuries BCE.

The Kena is the oldest of the verse Upaniṣads and contains many of the themes, such as the search for the one god who is both the creator and the agent of liberation for humans, that recur in the four subsequent verse Upaniṣads. Of these, the oldest is probably the Kaṭha, followed by Īśā, Śvetāśvatara, and Muṇḍaka. All exhibit strong theistic tendencies and are probably the earliest literary products of the theistic tradition, whose later literature includes the Bhagavad Gītā and the Purāṇas. All these Upaniṣads were composed probably in the last few centuries BCE. Finally, we have the two late prose Upaniṣads, the Praśna and the Māṇḍūkya, which cannot be much older than the beginning of the common era.

Geography: The final issue regarding the composition of the Upaniṣads relates to the geographical areas where these documents were composed. The land known to the authors of the Upaniṣads was broadly northern India ranging from the upper Indus valley to the lower Ganges, and from the Himalayan foothills to the Vindhya mountain range. We can say with a great deal of confidence that they were all the product of the geographical centre of ancient Brahmanism, comprising the regions of Kuru-Pañcāla and Kosala-Videha, together with the areas directly to the south and west of these (see Fig. 2). It is much more difficult, however, to determine the geographical location of individual Upaniṣads. Several scholars have recently attempted to localize vedic branches and texts using evidence internal to the texts themselves. Although the results are not conclusive, this research is significant and is evidence of a growing realization that in interpreting ancient texts philology needs to be supplemented by the knowledge of the geographical region and the social context in which they were composed. I reproduce here some of the tentative conclusions of Witzel's (1987, 1989) important studies; the map (Fig. 2) shows both the important regions mentioned in the Upaniṣads and the areas in which some of the individual Upaniṣads may have been composed. In general, we find that the early texts of the vedic corpus were composed in the western and north-western regions, whereas the centre of

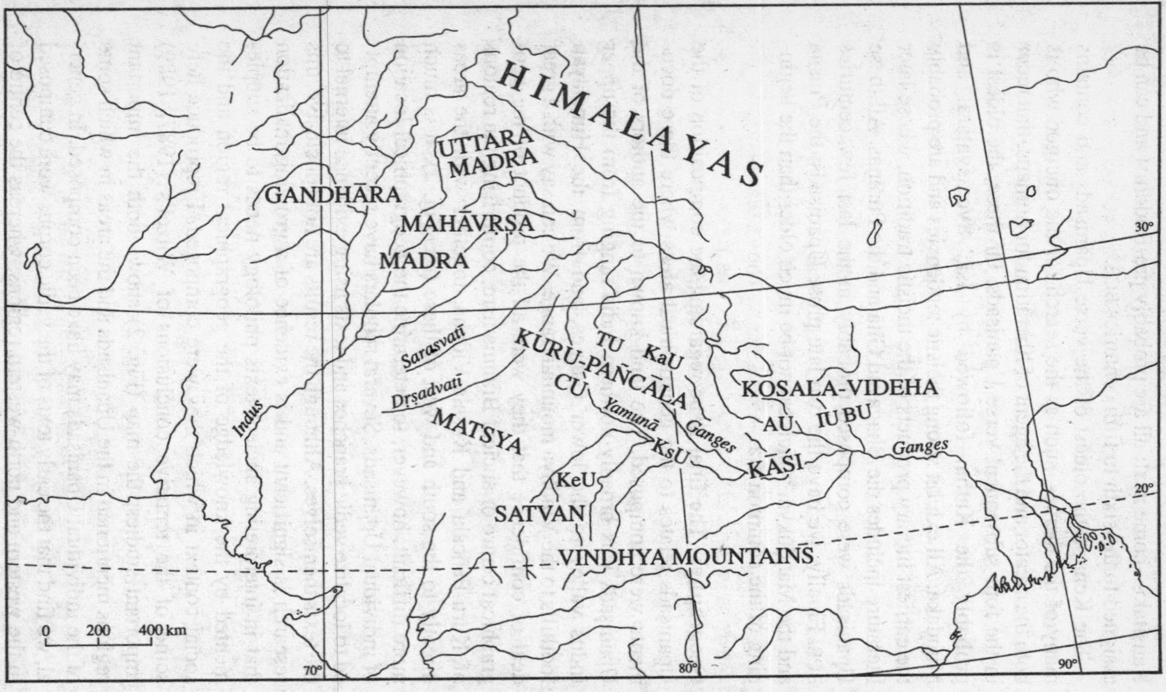

Fig. 2. Map of northern India: The Geography of the Upaniṣads

literary activity in the later vedic period shifts further east, mostly to the Kuru-Pañcāla region; some were composed even further east in the region of Videha.

In the case of the two oldest Upaniṣads, the BU and the CU, localization is complicated by the fact that they are compilations of pre-existing documents. On the whole, however, the centre of activity in the BU is the area of Videha, whose king, Janaka, plays a central role, together with Yājñavalkya, who appears almost as the personal theologian of the king. During the late vedic period the heartland of Brahmanism was the central region of Kuru-Pañcāla; the Kuru-Pañcāla Brahmins considered their land as the place where the best theological and literary activities were taking place. They must have viewed Videha as something of an unsophisticated frontier region. The entire setting of the third and fourth chapters of the BU was probably intended to show how Yājñavalkya defeated all the best theologians of Kuru-Pañcāla (BU 3.9.19), thus demonstrating not only the pre-eminence of Yājñavalkya but also the rising importance of Videha as a centre of learning.

The evidence for localizing the CU is more meagre,[22] but I think Witzel (1987, 194 n 74) is right in assigning 'a more Western than an Eastern location', probably somewhere in the western region of the Kuru-Pañcāla country. The great Kuru-Pañcāla theologian Uddālaka Āruṇi,[23] who is vilified in the BU, and Pravāhaṇa, the king of the Pañcāla region, play central roles in the CU.

Turning to the other early prose Upaniṣads, Witzel places the Kauṣītaki/Śāṅkhāyana branch of the Ṛgveda, to which the KsU belongs, in the western parts of the Kuru-Pañcāla country. There

[22] The hazard of internal evidence is demonstrated by a couple of examples relating to the CU. The reference to hail in the Kuru country (CU 1.10.1) and the reference to rivers flowing to the east and to the west (CU 6.10.1) may point to a geographical location in the northern Kuru region, where hail is common and the upper tributaries of the Ganges and the Indus flow towards the east and the west, respectively. But the meaning of the term for 'hail' is unclear; it probably means locust. And even the BU (4.8.9), a clearly eastern text, knows of rivers flowing in both directions; this may have been a bit of geographical knowledge commonly available to people at this time, irrespective of where they lived.

[23] He is explicitly identified as a Kuru-Pañcāla Brahmin in the SB 11.4.1.1–2, where he is said to have travelled in the northern regions trying to draw the Brahmins of that frontier region into debate.

is little evidence internal to the KsU itself that would help its localization. In chapter 4, however, Ajātaśatru, the king of Kāśi, which is somewhat to the east of the central Kuru-Pañcāla region, plays a central role. The TU and the AU are more difficult to locate. Witzel places the early portions of the AB in the north-western region around the Sutlej and the later portions, and hence possibly also the AU, further east in the Videha region. The early texts of the Taittirīya branch, such as the TS, were probably composed in the north-western region of Kuru-Pañcāla. The picture is less clear in the case of the later texts, including the TU, although a region somewhat to the north of the central Kuru-Pañcāla appears reasonable.

The later verse Upaniṣads are much more difficult to locate both because they hardly ever mention geographical locations and because they are less closely connected to the Brāhmaṇas of the respective vedic branches. The KeU belongs to the Talavakāra or Jaiminīya branch of the Sāmaveda. Although the early literature of the Jaiminīyas appears to have been composed in the Kuru-Pañcāla country, this vedic branch spread further south to the region where 'the rivers run north', that is, to what is today northern Madhya Pradesh and eastern Rajasthan. It was possibly in this region that the KeU was composed.

The KaU belongs to the lost Kāṭhaka Brāhmaṇa; without the latter it is impossible to determine the location of the former, which itself gives no geographical information. Witzel places the early literature of the Kāṭhaka branch in the eastern Punjab, near the River Beas, for it is here that, as the Kāṭhaka Saṃhitā states, the rivers flow westward. Whether this branch was still located in that region when the KaU, a somewhat late text, was composed is impossible to determine.

The IU, which comprises chapter 40 of the Vājasaneyi Saṃhitā of the White Yajurveda, likewise, contains no geographical information. However, both branches of the White Yajurveda were located in the region of Kosala and Videha, even though their early literature may have been composed in a more western region. The IU is certainly later than the BU, and it is very likely that it too was composed in that region. Since they do not form parts of larger vedic texts, it is impossible to locate the SU, MuU, PU, and MaU.

Vedic Rituals

Even though the Upaniṣadic authors sometimes speak vehemently against the vedic ritual, these documents are so closely connected with it that it is impossible to understand them without some knowledge of vedic ritual practice and vocabulary. Just like the Brāhmaṇas, the Upaniṣads seek to explain the hidden meanings and connections of ritual actions and words. Their authors were masters of the ritual and assumed a similar knowledge in their listeners.

By the time of the early Brāhmaṇas, approximately the eighth century BCE, the vedic ritual had developed into a highly complex and very expensive set of sacrifices requiring the services of an array of ritual specialists. These sacrifices included some that followed the liturgical calendar, for example, the daily fire sacrifice (*agnihotra*), the new- and full-moon sacrifices, the four-month sacrifices performed at the beginning of the three seasons (spring, rains, autumn), and the offering of first fruits at harvest time. Other sacrifices were offered for special reasons or on special occasions. Such are the two major sacrifices that occupy a central position in upaniṣadic thought, the horse sacrifice and the Soma sacrifice, as well as the anointing of a new king and the building of a fire-altar.

A sacrifice is offered by a man, a wealthy patron who in most cases must have been a Kṣatriya.[24] He is designated the *yajamāna*, a term generally translated as 'sacrificer'. This translation is somewhat misleading, because it is not the 'sacrificer' but the priests hired by him who actually perform the sacrifice. The *yajamāna* is the 'patron of the sacrifice', and it is on his behalf and for his benefit that the priests perform a sacrifice. Only a married man accompanied by his legitimate wife is eligible to become the patron of a sacrifice, indicating the centrality of marriage within the vedic ritual religion. The patron undergoes a sacrificial consecration called *dīkṣā* prior to a sacrifice; a man so consecrated is set apart from other people and has to

24 Theoretically, however, Brahmanical law permits any married male belonging to one of the three twice-born classes, i.e. Brahmin, Kṣatriya, and Vaiśya, to perform a sacrifice.

follow a stringent regimen until he takes the bath that signals the completion of the sacrifice.

The priests, on the other hand, are always Brahmins who have specialized knowledge of some aspect of the sacrificial performance. As I have already indicated in describing the division of vedic texts, there are three major classes of priests. The Hotṛ is a priest of the Ṛgveda and is responsible for all recitations. The Adhvaryu is a priest of the Yajurveda and is responsible for all sacrificial actions, including the preparation of the sacrificial ground, building the fire pits, killing and butchering the sacrificial animal, cooking the sacrificial offerings, and actually throwing the oblations into the ritual fire. The Udgātṛ is a priest of the Sāmaveda and is responsible for the singing. Each of these chief priests has several assistants. The Upaniṣads mention the Āgnīdhra, an assistant of the Adhvaryu, and Prastotṛ and Pratihartṛ, two assistants of the Udgātṛ. Besides these priests who actually perform the various rites connected with the sacrifice, there is another chief priest called Brahman, who sits silently to the south of the offertorial fire. He is supposed to be the most learned and to know the entire sacrificial performance. The Brahman is expected to set right any ritual mistakes made by the other priests.

The central feature of all vedic sacrifices, from the simplest to the most complex, is the ritual fire. All offerings are made in the fire, and it is believed that as the fire consumes the offering, the gods themselves partake of it. The Sanskrit term *agni* is, at one and the same time, the ritual fire and the fire god, who is regarded as the mouth of the gods, for it is through the medium of the fire that the gods partake of the sacrificial offerings.

During a vedic sacrifice, normally three ritual fires were used: the householder's fire (*gārhapatya*), the southern fire (*anvāhāryapacana* or simply *dakṣiṇāgni*), and the offertorial fire (*āhavanīya*). These fires are placed in the hollow of fire pits of different shapes. The householder's fire is located in the west; the southern fire is somewhat to the south and east of it; and the offertorial fire is directly to the east of it (see Fig. 3). At the beginning of the sacrifice, the householder's fire is lit first, using a fire newly produced by churning the fire-drills (see BU 1.4.6n). After that the other two fires are lit using coals from the

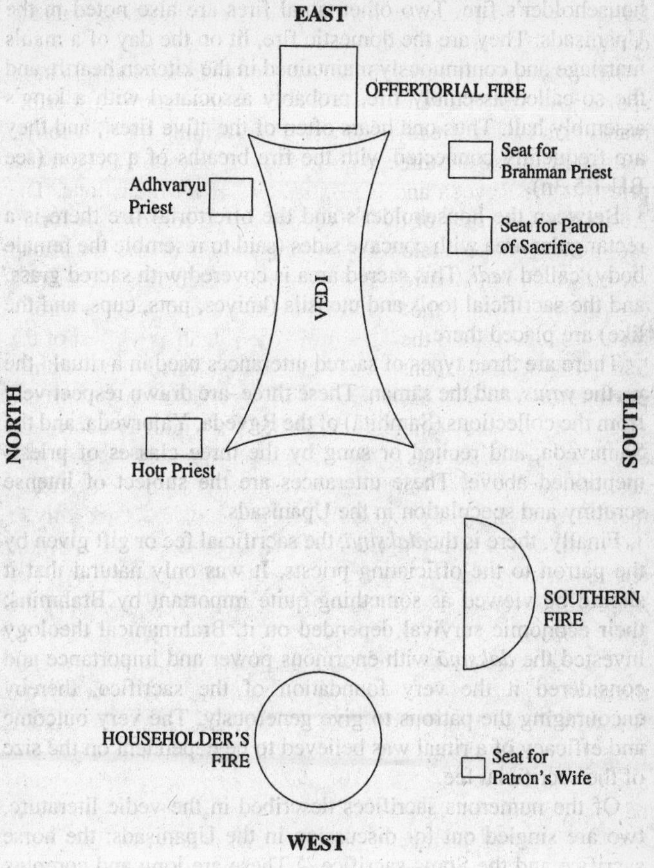

Fig. 3. The Sacrificial Arena

householder's fire. Two other ritual fires are also noted in the Upaniṣads. They are the domestic fire, lit on the day of a man's marriage and continuously maintained in the kitchen hearth, and the so-called assembly fire, probably associated with a king's assembly hall. Thus one hears often of the 'five fires', and they are frequently connected with the fire breaths of a person (see BU 1.5.3n).

Between the householder's and the offertorial fire there is a rectangular area with concave sides (said to resemble the female body) called *vedi*. This sacred area is covered with sacred grass, and the sacrificial tools and utensils (knives, pots, cups, and the like) are placed there.

There are three types of sacred utterances used in a ritual: the *ṛc*, the *yajus*, and the sāman. These three are drawn respectively from the collections (Saṃhitā) of the Ṛgveda, Yajurveda, and the Sāmaveda, and recited or sung by the three classes of priests mentioned above. These utterances are the subject of intense scrutiny and speculation in the Upaniṣads.

Finally, there is the *dakṣiṇā*, the sacrificial fee or gift given by the patron to the officiating priests. It was only natural that it should be viewed as something quite important by Brahmins; their economic survival depended on it. Brahmanical theology invested the *dakṣiṇā* with enormous power and importance and considered it the very foundation of the sacrifice, thereby encouraging the patrons to give generously. The very outcome and efficacy of a ritual was believed to be dependent on the size of the sacrificial fee.

Of the numerous sacrifices described in the vedic literature, two are singled out for discussion in the Upaniṣads: the horse sacrifice and the Soma sacrifice.[25] These are long and complex sacrifices, and I will only delineate here a few major points of each.

The horse sacrifice is performed by a king both to demonstrate his sovereignty and to ritually enhance his dominion. A fine horse with great speed and possessing special bodily marks and

[25] The most convenient place to read about these, as well as the daily fire sacrifice and the building of the fire-altar dealt with in the KaU, is Kane 1962–75, ii. 976–1255. The Soma sacrifice is described in detail in Caland and Henry 1906.

colours is selected and, after an elaborate ritual, set free to roam at will for a whole year. It is guarded by the king's troops. Each day during this year special sacrifices are offered in the presence of the king, and priests recite tales and legends in ten-day cycles. At the end of the year the horse is brought back, killed, and its various parts cooked and offered in sacrifice, a procedure that takes three days.

There are seven types of Soma sacrifices. Chief of these is called Agniṣṭoma (lit. 'Praise of Fire'), and the other Soma sacrifices are modelled after this. The Agniṣṭoma is a rite intended to be performed during the spring and within a single day, although subsidiary rites are spread over several days. The central ceremony is the pressing of the Soma plants, generally by pounding with stones, to obtain the juice. During the day of the pressing, the Soma is pressed three times—in the morning, at noon, and in the evening—and a goat is sacrificed. The juice of the Soma is strained, mixed with milk, and offered to the gods in the fire and drunk by the priests.

There has been much scholarly speculation about the identity of this plant. Its likely home was the hills of the north-western regions, possibly extending into Afghanistan and Iran, since it was known also to the ancient Iranians. Already during the late vedic period, when the centre of Brahmanism had shifted to the Ganges valley, this plant was difficult to obtain; the ritual itself calls for the purchase of the plant, and several substitutes are permitted. Its importance in the ritual is evidenced by the fact that the entire ninth book of the Ṛgveda Saṃhitā consists of Soma hymns. Soma also became a focus of ritual speculation. It was considered the drink of the gods, the drink that made gods immortal and confers immortality on mortals. Soma is contained in the moon, and the drinking of that Soma by the gods explains the waning of the moon. Every month the moon is replenished with Soma and thus waxes. Often, in these documents, Soma is another name for the moon.

Vedic Cosmologies

During the early vedic period the universe was viewed as consisting of three spheres (*loka*): the earth, the sky or firmament, and the space between these two or the intermediate region. The ancient Indians shared this tripartite cosmology with other Indo-European peoples. The phenomena associated with the sky and the intermediate region drew the attention of the early vedic poets in a special way: the rain clouds, lightning, thunder, wind, storm, and rain in the intermediate region, and the sun, moon, stars, and the brilliant vault of heaven in the sky.

This tripartite universe was controlled by personal powers, the gods. For the most part, these gods are associated with their natural counterparts, such as the sun, moon, storm, rivers, and fire. Often the Sanskrit names of the gods are identical to the names of the corresponding cosmic entity; thus, Sūrya is the Sun and Agni is the Fire. Sometimes the names vary, but the connection with the cosmic phenomena is unmistakable; thus Indra is connected with thunder and the releasing of waters, and his weapon is the thunderbolt (BU 3.9.6).

In the early vedic period the gods themselves are distributed among the three spheres: there are the gods of the earth, the gods of the intermediate region, and the gods of the sky. Although this distribution persists, the gods came to be generally located in the sky, the realm of light and immortality. The Sanskrit terms for these three spheres—*bhūḥ, bhuvaḥ, svaḥ*—became sacred sounds, possibly because they contained the totality of the universe (see CU 2.23.2n). Much Upaniṣadic speculation centres on the hidden meaning of these sounds.

In recent studies of vedic cosmology, Witzel (1984) and Brereton (1991) have drawn attention to the importance of the Milky Way and the stars around the Pole Star. Witzel has shown that the expression *svarga loka* (lit. 'bright world', commonly translated as 'heavenly world') refers specifically to the Milky Way. The door to this world is located at the mouth of the two arms extending toward the east from the Milky Way viewed during the winter months in northern India, which explains the importance of the east and the north-east in the ritual and in cosmological speculations. The Milky Way is also the bright ocean of heaven, the celestial waters; it is the source of the rivers that flow from the Himalayan mountains, thus connecting the earthly to the celestial waters.

By the late vedic period, however, we note the emergence of

a new plan of the universe with seven spheres, positing three further regions beyond the sky, called Mahas, Janas, and Tapas, and the furthest world named Satyaloka ('world of truth') or Brahmaloka ('world of Brahman'). Parallel to these seven upper or pleasant worlds, texts from a much later period posit seven descending and unpleasant worlds or hells, but the Upaniṣads show no sign of such a conception.

Another conception of the universe divides it into the world of humans, the world of ancestors or fathers, and the world of gods (BU 1.5.16). Although less tied to observable reality, it is more significant for beliefs regarding the afterlife. The world of humans is, of course, the observable world in which our normal lives are lived. During the early period all humans, or at least those who had lived a ritually correct life, were believed to go to the world of fathers; but the Upaniṣads reveal a new perception of that world according to which only those who are destined to return to and to be reborn in this world follow the path to the world of the fathers, while those destined not to return and to become immortal proceed to the world of the gods (see BU 6.2 and parallels).

This new conception is tied to an emergent world view centred on the doctrine of rebirth. The manner in which the rebirth process was thought to operate is similar to that in which Brahmanical thought viewed the operation of ritual actions. Rites achieve their results by their own autonomous power and according to a ritual law of cause and effect; ritual success does not depend on the will of a god. The moral law that governs the rebirth process operates in a similar manner; those who perform good actions are reborn in good situations, while those who do the opposite proceed to evil births (CU 5.10.7). The correlation between the ritual and ethical spheres apparent in these early texts is made easier by the fact that the same Sanskrit term, *karman* (lit. 'action'), is used for both ritual and moral actions. The ethicization of cosmic processes evident in the Upaniṣads, moreover, remains a constant feature of later Indian cosmologies.

The early view of the mechanism of rebirth and of the escape from the rebirth cycle as depicted in the famous doctrine of five fires (BU 6.2) is tied to the old view of a tripartite and enclosed universe. The firmament, the vault of heaven, is viewed as a solid cover. After they are cremated, humans destined to be reborn go up to the moon in the form of smoke or vapour; from there they return to earth as rain, enter plants, and, when they are eaten by a man, become semen, and finally take on a new life in the womb of a woman. The universe is thus a prison with walls above (firmament) and below (earth). Those who possess the liberating knowledge, however, are able to break this cycle, to escape from this prison. The sun is viewed as a lid that covers the only opening in the vault of heaven, the only door to freedom; the sun permits the liberated individuals to pass through that opening and escape to the immortal condition outside the universe.

Another central concern of the Upaniṣadic thinkers relates to the 'beginnings'; the expression 'in the beginning' (*agre*) is frequent and opens the narrative of creation stories. The creator, the source from which creation emerged, most often is Prajāpati, the principal creator god of the Brāhmaṇas, who is identified with the sacrifice itself (BU 3.9.6). The other two principles located at the 'beginning' with some frequency are Brahman and Ātman, which I will discuss below.

By the time of the later verse Upaniṣads, such as the Śvetāśvatara, new and more theoretical cosmologies had emerged, the most prominent of which is that associated with the Sāṃkhya and Yoga traditions. Since these are some of the oldest documents reflecting Sāṃkhya conceptions of the universe, the precise cosmology underlying them is unclear; that cosmology is certainly different from the classical accounts of Sāṃkhya cosmology contained in scholastic works of later times. Like the latter, however, this early cosmology posits a material source, a primal matter, called *prakṛti* or *pradhāna*. This primal matter, originally unmanifest, contains three qualities or strands (*guṇa*): goodness (*sattva*), energy (*rajas*), and darkness (*tamas*). The visible and manifest universe has proceeded from the original primal matter; the three qualities are distributed in different proportions within the various constituents of the universe. Unlike classical Sāṃkhya, however, this early cosmology posits a single and unique god who rules over the primal matter and regulates the production of the visible universe from it. Besides primal matter and god, there are the individual souls of humans, souls that are trapped within material bodies produced by primal matter. It is through the help of god that these souls can hope to be liberated from the material prison.

Human Physiology and Psychology

Although ritual and cosmological speculations abound in the Upaniṣads, the focus of their enquiry is the human person—the construction of the body, its vital powers and faculties, the cognitive processes, and the essential core of a human being. It is, of course, not surprising that the human being is a central concern of human thought; religious doctrines throughout the world tend to be anthropocentric.

In ancient India, however, the human body was invested with unparalleled cosmological significance and parts of the body were homologized with cosmic phenomena. I have made reference to the ancient cosmogonic hymn found in the Ṛgveda (10.90) and predating the Upaniṣads by several centuries, a hymn that depicts the creation of the universe through the sacrificial dismemberment of the body of a primeval man (*puruṣa*). From the parts of his sacrificed body there emerged not only the *varṇa*s of society, but also the parts of the cosmos: sun from the eye, moon from the mind, wind from the breath, sky from the head, earth from the feet, and so on. I will deal in greater detail with these cosmic connections in the next section; here I want to briefly describe the Upaniṣadic assumptions about human physiology and psychology.

In these documents, the term most frequently used with reference to a living, breathing body is *ātman*, a term liable to misunderstanding and mistranslating, because it can also mean the spiritual self or the inmost core of a human being, besides functioning as a mere reflexive pronoun. The body which is the object of investigation, moreover, is primarily the male body; the female body enters the discussion infrequently and then mostly within the context of male sexual activity. The term *yoni* used in these contexts can mean both the vagina in which the semen is deposited and the womb in which the foetus develops.

The obvious external construction of the human, as well as the animal, body is, of course, known to our authors. The priests butchered sacrificial animals, and this dissection must have provided them with detailed information on the internal organs of animals. This knowledge is displayed, for example, in the opening statement of the BU (1.1.1), which homologizes parts of the horse's body with cosmic realities. The body is distinguished according to vertical and horizontal axes into the left and the right, and into the upper and the lower (the forequarter and the hindquarter, in the case of an animal), each with its own symbolic value. The left, for example, is associated with the female, and the right with the male.

It is, however, the vital powers—powers of movement, evacuation, ejaculation, breathing, and speaking, as well as thinking and the five senses—that are the focus of Upaniṣadic enquiry. The most important of these are breathing, thinking, speech, sight, and hearing. Together, these five are often called 'breaths' (*prāṇa*), 'breath' here carrying the meaning of life and vital force (see BU 1.5.21 for a traditional explanation of why they are called 'breaths'). In dealing with sight and hearing, and to some extent also in the case of the other faculties, these documents clearly distinguish the power or the act of seeing and hearing from the respective external organs, the eyes and the ears. Indeed, they consistently use different Sanskrit terms for the two—*cakṣus* and *śrotra* for sight and hearing, and *akṣan* and *karṇa* for eye and ear, respectively.

Of the vital powers, breathing is the most important. Several Upaniṣads equate breath with life and even with a person's self (*ātman*). The enquiry into the power of breathing led these thinkers to distinguish several types of breath within the body. In general, five breaths are identified; the exact meaning of each is not altogether clear, and the meaning of some appears to have changed over time. In much of this literature, however, the five breaths appear to have the following meanings: breathing out (*prāṇa*), breathing in (*apāna*), the breath that moves up (*udāna*), the breath that traverses (*vyāna*), and the breath that equalizes or links (*samāna*).[26]

26 Breaths, or air circulating in the body, are also an important topic in ancient Indian medicine, the Āyurveda. The terms for the various breaths have been subject to much debate and misunderstanding. It was once thought, for example, that *prāṇa* meant inhalation, and that meaning is found even today in many dictionaries. Bodewitz (1986, 334–6) has shown that *udāna* in some contexts is synonymous with *āpāna* and means inhalation. For a review of the discussion, see Bodewitz 1986; Zysk 1993.

The first, *prāṇa*, is the one most commonly referred to, and it is often used as a generic term for breath, as a term for life, and, in the plural, to refer to the vital powers discussed above. Over time, the word *apāna* comes to mean also the breath that moves down from the navel and is responsible for evacuation and the breaking of wind. *Vyāna* may have meant originally the interval between inhalation and exhalation; thus it is said to be where the out-breath and in-breath meet and it is, therefore, identified with speech, because in speaking one breathes neither in nor out (CU 1.3.3). Later it came to be viewed as the breath responsible for blood circulation. *Samāna*, likewise, came to be located in the belly and to be associated with the digestion of food. The picture that emerges is of a body pervaded by air, which circulates within it along various channels; this vital air is what enlivens the body and makes it perform its many functions. Reference is also made to a 'breath within the mouth' (BU 1.3.7–27) and to a 'central breath' (BU 1.5.21–2), which are viewed as the primary carriers of life.

The inner organ that is the subject of intense scrutiny is the heart. The heart has a cavity at the centre, and is surrounded by the pericardium. Channels or veins run from the heart to the pericardium and to other parts of the body. The cavity of the heart is the seat of the vital powers and the self and plays a central role in the explanations of the three states of awareness—waking, dreaming, and dreamless sleep—as well as of death. In sleep, the cognitive powers distributed throughout the body during the waking hours are gathered together in the cavity of the heart. The space of this cavity is homologized with cosmic space (see CU 3.12.7–9), and in the dream state the person travels about this space seeing and enjoying the same type of things that he experienced while awake. During deep and dreamless sleep, the self slips out of that cardiac space and enters the veins going from the heart to the pericardium; there it remains oblivious to everything (see BU 2.1; 4.3–4). At death the self, together with the vital powers, depart from the heart along a channel and exit through either the crown of the head (TU 1.6) or the eye (BU 4.4.2).

Cosmic Connections

In the preceding survey we noted three areas of concern for the vedic thinkers: the ritual, the cosmic realities, and the human body/person. The ritual sphere includes ritual formulas, prayers, and songs, as well as ritual actions and ceremonies. As we have seen, the vedic thinkers did not make a strict distinction between the gods and cosmic realities; so the cosmic sphere includes both. The central concern of all vedic thinkers, including the authors of the Upaniṣads, is to discover the connections that bind elements of these three spheres to each other. The assumption then is that the universe constitutes a web of relations, that things that appear to stand alone and apart are, in fact, connected to other things. A further assumption is that these real cosmic connections are usually hidden from the view of ordinary people; discovering them constitutes knowledge, knowledge that is secret and is contained in the Upaniṣads. And it is this knowledge of the hidden connections that gives the person with that knowledge power, wealth, and prestige in this world, and heavenly bliss and immortality after death. While in the earlier vedic texts the focus is on the connections between the ritual and cosmic spheres, the concern of the Upaniṣadic thinkers shifts to the human person; the connections sought after are between parts of the human organism and cosmic realities.

In the early vedic literature the term most commonly used for 'connection' is *bandhu*, a term derived from a verb meaning 'to bind', 'to connect'.[27] *Bandhu* commonly means a kin, but when one thing is said to be a *bandhu* of another, the meaning is that the former is connected to or is a counterpart of the latter. The earliest usage of the important term *upaniṣad* indicates that it too carried a similar meaning: *upaniṣad* means 'connection' or 'equivalence'.[28] In addition, the term implies hierarchy; the Upaniṣadic connections are hierarchically arranged, and the quest is to discover the reality that stands at the summit of this

27 For studies of this concept, see Gonda 1965 and Smith 1989.

28 On this meaning of *upaniṣad*, see Renou 1946; and Falk 1986*b*. In the light of these studies, the older view (Deussen 1966 [1906], 13) that the term derives from 'sitting near' a teacher and refers to a group of disciples at the feet of a teacher imbibing esoteric knowledge is clearly untenable.

hierarchically interconnected universe. It is, however, assumed that such connections are always hidden. We see the term used with this meaning in the Upaniṣads themselves, for example, at CU 1.1.10 and 1.13.4. Because of the hidden nature of these connections, the term *upaniṣad* also came to mean a secret, especially secret knowledge or doctrine. It is probably as an extension of this meaning that the term came finally to be used with reference to entire texts containing such secret doctrines, that is, our Upaniṣads.

Another extremely common Upaniṣadic term that refers to the connections and equivalences existing within the universe is 'venerate'. When a text states that someone venerates X as Y, the meaning is that he recognizes the hidden connection or homology between the two (see BU 4.1.2n). Thus, at CU 1.2.10–12, Aṅgiras, Bṛhaspati, and Ayāsya are said to have venerated the High Chant as the breath within the mouth. The text then goes on to reveal the hidden etymologies of the names of those individuals that make them identified with that very breath. The message is clear: anyone who comes to know such a hidden homology becomes himself identified with the things whose homology he has recognized.

An excellent example of such connections is the opening paragraph of the BU where parts of the sacrificial horse's body and even its physical activities (i.e. the ritual sphere) are connected to phenomena in the world (i.e. the cosmic sphere). Elsewhere the ritual sphere is connected to the bodily, and the bodily sphere to the cosmic: the Ṛc is connected to earth, atmosphere, and heaven, and the Sāman to fire, wind, and sun (BU 1.6); the Ṛc, to speech, sight, and hearing, and the Sāman to breath, body, and mind (BU 1.7); and speech, breath, sight, hearing, and mind are connected to fire, wind, sun, quarters (points of the compass), and moon, respectively (BU 1.3.11–16). Some of these connections, such as that between eye and sun, and breath and wind, follow natural associations; others, such as that between mind and moon, are more difficult to fathom at least for the modern reader and may be based on the then current views on the nature of or mythical associations between the mind and the moon.

An important basis for these connections, however, is the phonetic similarity between the Sanskrit words for two things or even the fact that the two terms may have the same number of syllables.[29] One finds with an almost annoying frequency such 'etymological' connections in these documents, especially in the Chāndogya.[30] Thus the connection between the High Chant and the sun (CU 1.3.1) is based on the phonetic similarity between *udgītha* ('High Chant') and *udyan* ('rising'). Some modern scholars have dismissed these as fanciful folk etymologies. These are clearly not 'folk' etymologies; the authors of these documents were learned men, and these documents themselves demonstrate that the science of grammar had already reached a high degree of sophistication. These men clearly knew the philological etymologies of the terms they dealt with; but their quest was not for such common and well-known connections but for deeper and hidden ones, and they found in the sounds of the names a clue to those connections.

This belief that what sounds alike must be alike was founded on the theory that the essence of a thing was expressed in its name and its visible appearance (*nāmarūpa*). The importance given to speech-sounds is evident in the discussions of such special sounds as *bhūḥ*, *bhuvaḥ*, and *svaḥ* (the sounds that correspond to the three worlds), as well as the most basic and powerful sound of all, OṂ. These speech-sounds are both powerful in themselves and provide access to the basic reality of the world, to Brahman. To understand these etymological connections, then, we must enter—which is not the same as to believe in or to accept—the framework of their own world view; dismissing them as fanciful does not further understanding. These phonetic equivalences also highlight the highly oral nature of the vedic texts; they were composed and handed down from generation to generation orally. These texts also came to life within the communities in their oral enactment within ritual recitations, both public and private, as well as in the traditional methods of education.[31]

[29] See e.g. BU 5.5.3–4; 5.14.1–3. Regarding the counting of syllables in ancient Indian texts, see Jamison 1986, esp. p. 165.

[30] These phonetic etymologies occurring in the Upaniṣads have been collected by Singh 1994.

[31] For the essential oral/aural nature of sacred scriptures, see William A. Graham, *Beyond the Written Word: Oral Aspects of Scripture in the History of Religion* (Cambridge: Cambridge University Press, 1987); esp. 65–80, dealing with the Vedas.

Some scholars have argued that these connections amount to the acknowledgement of the identity between disparate realities, while others contend that they merely show resemblance. Whether it is identity or resemblance, those who note these connections also seek to establish a hierarchy of connected things, or, looking at it from a different angle, to discover deeper and deeper realities that serve as the foundation or basis for others (cf. BU 2.9.19–26). Several metaphors are used to indicate this hierarchic connection and dependence of one reality on another, metaphors such as the string on which the world is strung (BU 2.7) and that on which the world is woven back and forth (BU 2.6 and 8). This is possibly the idea that gives some unity to the diverse thoughts of the Upaniṣads, and Brereton (1990, 118) expresses it succinctly: 'each Upanishadic teaching creates an integrative vision, a view of the whole which draws together the separate elements of the world and of human experience and compresses them into a single form. To one who has this larger vision of things, the world is not a set of diverse and disorganized objects and living beings, but rather forms a totality with a distinct shape and character.'

Two significant items within this hierarchically connected and organized universe are called Brahman and Ātman, two concepts that have been pivotal in the development of later Indian philosophies and theologies, two concepts that have been subject to intense scrutiny by modern scholarship. These permit the Upaniṣads to create 'an integrative vision by identifying a single, comprehensive and fundamental principle which shapes the world' (Brereton 1990, 118). It is impossible to analyse them adequately within the confines of this Introduction. Both are viewed in their own way as occupying the summit of the hierarchically arranged and interconnected universe.

Ātman, as I have already pointed out, has many meanings and usages in the Upaniṣadic vocabulary; one such usage refers to the 'Self', the ultimate essence of a human being, even though there is no agreement as to what constitutes that essence. It will, however, be anachronistic to interpret this usage of the term as referring only to some 'spiritual' core of a human being; the image of the physical human body is present even when the Upaniṣads are attempting to isolate that core. Thus in CU

5.12–17 Aśvapati points to the inadequacy of several identifications of the self by stating that the thing so identified is only the head or the bladder or the feet of the self.

Brahman, likewise, has a variety of meanings, and it is impossible to use a single English term to designate all those meanings.[32] Brahman may mean 'a formulation of truth', the Veda, or the ultimate and basic essence of the cosmos. The TU (3.1) provides a basic definition of this term in its latter meaning: 'That from which these beings are born; on which, once born, they live; and into which they pass upon death—seek to perceive that! That is *brahman*!' Brahman thus stands at the summit of the hierarchical scheme, or at the bottom as the ultimate foundation of all things, although it is important to remember that the concept always retains its verbal character as 'the sound expression' of truth or reality. The final *upaniṣad* or equation is between Ātman, the essential I, and Brahman, the ultimate real.

Even though this equation played a significant role in later developments of religion and theology in India and is the cornerstone of one of its major theological traditions, the Advaita Vedānta, it is incorrect to think that the single aim of all the Upaniṣads is to enunciate this simple truth. A close reader of these documents will note the diversity of goals that their authors pursue, chief among which are food, prosperity, power, fame, and a happy afterlife. There are rites to secure greatness, to win a woman's love,[33] to harm the lover of one's wife, to ensure pregnancy, to guard against pregnancy, to assure a safe childbirth—the list can go on. Many scholars ignore these and similar passages in their search for the 'philosophy' or 'the fundamental conception' of the Upaniṣads. But are we justified in doing so? If the compilers of the Upaniṣads thought them significant enough to be included in these collections, who are we to reject them? These passages, I believe, are as important to uncovering the religious history of the period as the passages proclaiming the oneness of Ātman and Brahman.

32 For specific and detailed studies of this term the reader may consult Renou and Silburn 1949; Gonda 1950; and Thieme 1952.

33 Some early translators (e.g. Max Müller) were so offended by these explicit descriptions of sexuality that they either left those passages untranslated or translated them into Latin!

NOTE ON THE TRANSLATION

TEXTS, especially ancient texts—whether they are the Upaniṣads or the Bible—composed in a different language, at a different time, and by people with social and cultural backgrounds and levels of scientific knowledge far different from our own, pose many and diverse problems of understanding and interpretation to their readers and, especially, to their translators.

A comparison with the methods we use to understand another type of data from ancient societies—archaeological discoveries—is instructive. Archaeological findings are only clues, and, just like clues in the investigation of a crime, archaeological clues require the interpretive efforts of the investigator, who alone can unravel the story behind the clues. A long process of *interpretation*, thus, precedes an adequate understanding, a process informed by our knowledge obtained from other sources regarding the culture and society of the people in question and by analogies with other comparable cultures. A similar process of interpretation is also required for an adequate understanding of textual data and must precede any translation. Whether a translator is aware of this or not, a translation is always an interpretation.

In an important way, however, texts are different from archaeological data. Unlike archaeological remains, a text is a living reality; it is its very use and transmission by generations of readers, interpreters, and copyists that have preserved it for our examination. The interpretative history of a text is especially rich when it happens to be a *sacred text*, a text that is perceived by a community or a group of communities as religiously authoritative. Such, indeed, are the group of texts called 'Upaniṣad' translated here.

Unlike archaeological data, therefore, texts, especially sacred texts, come to us already interpreted. Specifically with the Upaniṣads, the interpretative history consists both of formal commentaries and further commentaries on earlier commentaries, and of interpretations implicit in their use as scriptural texts within theological discourses and sectarian debates.

How, then, does a translator's interpretation relate to this history of interpretation? The problem is further complicated by the fact that there is no one native interpretation of the Upaniṣads; across time and sectarian divides, we have a multiplicity of interpretations. If a translation has a theological purpose—if it is produced within a specific sectarian or theological context—a translator may choose one of these interpretations over the others. I have chosen not to do so, even though, like most translators, I have benefited from the insights of commentators. I want in my translation and notes to approximate, as far as our current knowledge permits, the understanding of these documents that their authors had and the meaning they desired to communicate to their contemporary audience.

Like any other historical work, mine is a reconstruction of the past. In this reconstruction, I want to distinguish the interpretative history of the documents, often separated from their composition by a millennium or more, from their original context. Even though there are significant differences in purpose and content between them, one may, nevertheless, profitably compare the Upaniṣads to the Constitution of the United States of America, which also has had an official, and often contradictory, history of interpretation by the Supreme Court. If I am translating the Constitution into Sanskrit, what interpretation should I follow? I would follow none of those interpretations and attempt to reconstruct for the Sanskrit reader the cultural and social context within which the Constitution was drafted. My translation would attempt to present the Constitution to the Sanskrit reader as a window into the world of America in the late eighteenth century, and not as a living document still guiding the destinies of the American people.

Both the Constitution and the Upaniṣads are living documents and play significant roles in the communities within which they are perceived as authoritative. Acts of interpretation of these documents are legitimate activities for lawyers and theologians of the respective communities, and the study of those interpretative histories is an important and legitimate part of historical scholarship; but these are not, I believe, the aim of a translation. My translation is not intended to be a vehicle for propagating religious truths (although, for some, it may perform this function) but for illuminating the distant past of India.

My translation, moreover, is not intended for philologists but for ordinary readers who have little or no access to the original Sanskrit. I have not employed, therefore, the common defensive strategies of philological translations, such as placing within brackets any English word added to draw out the sense of the Sanskrit. I expect my translation to be accurate without being literal, to be readable on its own without reference to the Sanskrit. I have used idiomatic and informal English, especially in translating dialogues and conversations, but avoided vulgarisms, keeping in mind that these are viewed by many as sacred writings.

One notable feature of Sanskrit is its frequent use of pronouns without clear referents; often the referent is not the noun that immediately precedes the pronoun. I have regularly repeated the noun when the use of an English pronoun would be confusing. In dialogues deictic pronouns—that is, pronouns used in conversations while pointing to something—are used often; in translating such oral usages into written prose I have often appended the item pointed to, for example 'this right eye'. The use of these pronouns highlights not only the oral nature of the original dialogues but also the continuing oral transmission of the Upaniṣads.

Phonetic connections between words abound in these documents and play a significant role in Upaniṣadic thought. It is an impossible task to reproduce them in English. I have attempted to alert the reader to the connections hinted at by placing the Sanskrit terms within parentheses. Three terms that cause special difficulty are *prāṇa, ātman,* and *brahman*; they have multiple meanings, but in the original Sanskrit the identity of the term recalls to the reader all the related meanings even when only one is primary within a given context. To alert the English reader to these connections, I have included the Sanskrit term within parentheses.

The internal divisions of these documents and the names given to these units vary. I have called 'Chapter' the largest divisions of each Upaniṣad (except the PU) and have given only numerical designations to the others. The numbers of the smallest units are placed in superscript alongside the text, the symbol § being used in the Notes. Many Upaniṣads have only these two divisions. Some, however, divide the chapters into subsections. The numbers of these subsections appear in large type, covering two lines.

I have based my translation on the excellent edition of Limaye and Vadekar (1958); whenever I have departed from the established text I have noted the reasons. In the case of the KsU, SU, and MuU, however, I have used the critical editions prepared by Frenz (1968–9), Hauschild (1927), and Hertel (1924), respectively.

The following chronological bibliography of translations of the Upaniṣads was published too late to be included in my bibliography: P. Renard, 'Historical Bibliography of Upaniṣads in Translation', *Journal of Indian Philosophy*, 23 (1995): 223–46.

UPANIṢADS

Bṛhadāraṇyaka Upaniṣad

THE Bṛhadāraṇyaka Upaniṣad constitutes the concluding section of the voluminous Śatapatha Brāhmaṇa of the White Yajurveda. Its name, *The Great Āraṇyaka-Upaniṣad*, indicates its character as both an Āraṇyaka and an Upaniṣad. The text has been preserved in two recensions, the Mādhyandina and the Kāṇva; in both the BU forms the final sections of the Śatapatha. The two recensions present basically the same text, although there are differences in some significant readings and in the arrangement of individual sections. This translation follows the Kāṇva recension.

The Upaniṣad consists of three sections: (1) chapters 1–2, called the Madhukāṇḍa (Honey Section), getting its name from the final segment (2.5); (2) chapters 2–3, called the Yājñavalkyakāṇḍa (Yājñavalkya Section), in which this sage plays the central role; and (3) Chapters 5–6, called Khilakāṇḍa (Supplementary Section). In its present form, this Upaniṣad has seen at least three editorial phases. The first consists of individual passages, dialogues, and stories that may have been preserved in the memory of individuals or groups. In the second phase editors must have made three independent collections of them, collections that are preserved as the three sections of the BU. That these sections must have existed as separate texts is indicated by the genealogy of teachers appended to each, as well as by the repetition of the story of Yājñavalkya and his two wives in both the first and the second sections (2.4 and 4.5). It is, of course, likely that these sections underwent further expansion in the third phase when an editor appears to have woven these separate texts into a whole and included them within the Śatapatha Brāhmaṇa. Of the three, the first two sections exhibit greater internal consistency, while the third, which even the native tradition regards as supplementary, consists of disparate and often unconnected fragments. Nevertheless, this section is important especially in showing the diversity of secret recipes—rites, incantations, and esoteric knowledge—that constituted the literature that we have come to call Upaniṣads.

On linguistic and other grounds, there is general agreement that the Bṛhadāraṇyaka, as a whole, is the oldest of the Upaniṣads, even though individual passages in it may be younger than those of others, especially those of the Chāndogya. Together with the latter, the Bṛhadāraṇyaka not only constitutes about two-thirds of the corpus of ancient Upaniṣadic documents but also represents the oldest and the most important part of this literature.

CONTENTS

	5	Debate with Kahola on *brahman*; giving up desires	
	6	Debate with Gārgī : on what is the universe woven?	
	7	Debate with Uddālaka: on what are the worlds strung?	
	8	Debate with Gārgī: on what is the universe woven?	
	9.1–26	Debate with Vidagdha: how many gods are there?	
	9.27–8	Yājñavalkya questions his opponents	
4	1–2	Dialogue between Janaka and Yājñavalkya	
		1.2	Y. rejects Jitvan's view that *brahman* is speech
		1.3	Y. rejects Udaṅka's view that *brahman* is lifebreath
		1.4	Y. rejects Barku's view that *brahman* is sight
		1.5	Y. rejects Gardabhīvipīta's view that *brahman* is hearing
		1.6	Y. rejects Satyakāma's view that *brahman* is the mind
		1.7	Y. rejects Vidagdha's view that *brahman* is the heart
		2.1–4	Y.'s teaching on the self
	3–4	A further dialogue between Janaka and Yājñavalkya	
		3.1–8	Self as one's source of light
		3.9–34	On dreaming and dreamless sleep
		3.35–4.2	On what happens at death
		4.3–6	On the course after death of those who desire
		4.6–25	On the course after death of those who are without desires
	5	Dialogue between Yājñavalkya and his wife Maitreyī	
		5.6–15	Discourse of the self
	6	Lineage of teachers	
5	1	*Brahman* is space	
	2	Prajāpati's instruction to gods and demons	
	3	*Brahman* is the heart	
	4	*Brahman* is the real	
	5	Waters create the real; the real creates the universe	
	6	Person within the heart	
	7	*Brahman* is lightning	
	8	Speech as a cow	
	9	Fire common to all men and the digestive process	
	10	Course of a man after death	
	11	Sickness as austerity	
	12	*Brahman* as food and breath together	
	13	Priests and royalty as breath	
	14	Cosmic correspondences of the Gāyatrī verse	

CHAPTER 1

1 THE head of the sacrificial horse, clearly, is the dawn—its sight is the sun; its breath is the wind; and its gaping mouth is the fire common to all men. The body (*ātman*) of the sacrificial horse is the year—its back is the sky; its abdomen is the intermediate region; its underbelly is the earth; its flanks are the quarters; its ribs are the intermediate quarters; its limbs are the seasons; its joints are the months and fortnights; its feet are the days and nights; its bones are the stars; its flesh is the clouds; its stomach contents are the sand; its intestines are the rivers; its liver and lungs are the hills; its body hairs are the plants and trees; its forequarter is the rising sun; and its hindquarter is the setting sun. When it yawns, lightning flashes; when it shakes itself, it thunders; and when it urinates, it rains. Its neighing is speech itself.

2 The day, clearly, was born afterwards to be the sacrificial cup placed in front of the horse, and its womb is in the eastern sea. The night was born afterwards to be the sacrificial cup placed behind the horse, and its womb is in the western sea. These two came into being to be the sacrificial cups placed in front of and behind the horse. It became a racer and carried the gods. It became a charger and carried the Gandharvas. It became a courser and carried the demons. It became a horse and carried the humans. The sea, indeed, is its counterpart; the sea is its womb.

2 In the beginning there was nothing here at all. Death alone covered this completely, as did hunger; for what is hunger but death? Then death made up his mind: 'Let me equip myself with a body (*ātman*).' So he undertook a liturgical recitation (*arc*), and as he was engaged in liturgical recitation water sprang from him. And he thought: 'While I was engaged in liturgical recitation (*arc*), water (*ka*) sprang up for me.' This is what gave the name to and discloses the true nature of recitation (*arka*). Water undoubtedly springs for him who knows the name and nature of recitation in this way. 2 So, recitation is water.

Then the foam that had gathered on the water solidified and became the earth. Death toiled upon her. When he had become worn out by toil and hot with exertion, his heat—his essence—turned into fire.

3 He divided this body (*ātman*) of his into three—one third became the sun and another the wind. He is also breath divided into three. His head is the eastern quarter, and his two forequarters are the south-east and the north-east. His tail is the west, and his two hindquarters are the south-west and the north-west. His flanks are the south and the north. His back is the sky; his abdomen is the intermediate region; and his chest is this earth. He stands firm in the waters. A man who knows this will stand firm wherever he may go.

4 Then death had this desire: 'Would that a second body (*ātman*) were born for me!' So, by means of his mind, he copulated with speech, death copulated with hunger. Then the semen he emitted became the year. The year simply did not exist before this. He carried him for as long as a year, at the end of which he gave birth to him. As he was born, death opened its mouth to swallow him. He cried out, '*Bhāṇ*!' That is what became speech.

5 Death reflected: 'If I kill him, I will only reduce my supply of food.' So, with that speech and that body (*ātman*) he gave birth to this whole world, to everything that is here—Ṛgvedic verses, Yajurvedic formulas, Sāmavedic chants, metres, sacrifices, people, and animals. He began to eat whatever he gave birth to. 'He eats (*ad*) all'—it is this that gave the name to and discloses the true nature of Aditi. When someone comes to know the name and nature of Aditi in this way, he becomes the eater of this whole world, and the whole world here becomes his food.

6 Then death had this desire: 'Let me make an offering once more, this time with a bigger sacrifice.' So he strenuously toiled and fiercely exerted himself. When he had become worn out by toil and hot with exertion, his splendour—his vigour—departed from him. Now, splendour—vigour—consists of the vital breaths. So, when his vital breaths had departed, his corpse began to bloat. His mind, however, still remained within his corpse.

7 Then he had this desire: 'I wish that this corpse of mine would become fit to be sacrificed so I could get myself a living body (*ātman*)!' Then that corpse became a horse. 'Because it bloated (*aśvat*), it became fit to be sacrificed (*medhya*)'—that is what gave the name to and discloses the true nature of the horse sacrifice

(*aśvamedha*). Only a man who knows the horse sacrifice in this way truly understands it.

Death believed that the horse was not to be confined in any way. At the end of one year, he immolated it as a sacrifice to himself, while he assigned the other animals to the gods. That is why people, when they immolate the horse consecrated to Prajāpati, regard it as an offering to all the gods.

The sun that shines up there, clearly, is a horse sacrifice; the year is its body (*ātman*). The fire that burns down here is the ritual fire; these worlds are its body. Now, there are these two: the horse sacrifice and the ritual fire (*arka*). Yet they constitute in reality a single deity—they are simply death. [Whoever knows this] averts repeated death—death is unable to seize him, death becomes his very body (*ātman*), and he becomes one of these deities.

3 Now, Prajāpati's offspring were of two kinds: gods and demons. Indeed, the gods were the younger of his offspring, while the demons were the older; and they were competing for these worlds. So the gods said to themselves: 'Come, let us overcome the demons during a sacrifice by means of the High Chant.'

2 They then told speech: 'Sing the High Chant for us.' Speech said 'Very well', and sang the High Chant for them. It procured for them by that singing whatever useful there is in speech; it keeps for itself (*ātman*) whatever is pleasant in what it says. The demons thought: 'With this as their Udgātṛ, they are sure to overcome us.' So they rushed at it and riddled it with evil. That evil is the disagreeable things a person says—they are that very evil.

3 Then the gods told breath: 'Sing the High Chant for us.' Breath said, 'Very well,' and sang the High Chant for them. It procured for them by that singing whatever useful there is in breath; it keeps for itself whatever is pleasant in what it smells. The demons thought: 'With this as their Udgātṛ, they are sure to overcome us.' So they rushed at it and riddled it with evil. That evil is the disagreeable things a person smells—they are that very evil.

4 Then the gods told sight: 'Sing the High Chant for us.' Sight said, 'Very well', and sang the High Chant for them. It procured for them by that singing whatever useful there is in sight; it keeps for itself whatever is pleasant in what it sees. The demons thought: 'With this as their Udgātṛ, they are sure to overcome us.' So they

rushed at it and riddled it with evil. That evil is the disagreeable things a person sees—they are that very evil.

5 Then the gods told hearing: 'Sing the High Chant for us.' Hearing said, 'Very well', and sang the High Chant for them. It procured for them by that singing whatever useful there is in hearing; it keeps for itself whatever is pleasant in what it hears. The demons thought: 'With this as their Udgātṛ, they are sure to overcome us.' So they rushed at it and riddled it with evil. That evil is the disagreeable things a person hears—they are that very evil.

6 Then the gods told mind: 'Sing the High Chant for us.' Mind said, 'Very well', and sang the High Chant for them. It procured for them by that singing whatever useful there is in the mind; it keeps for itself whatever is pleasant in what it thinks. The demons thought: 'With this as their Udgātṛ, they are sure to overcome us.' So they rushed at it and riddled it with evil. That evil is the disagreeable things a person thinks—they are that very evil.

In this way they assaulted these deities with evil and riddled them with evil.

7 Then the gods told the breath within the mouth: 'Sing the High Chant for us.' This breath said, 'Very well', and sang the High Chant for them. The demons thought: 'With this as their Udgātṛ, they are sure to overcome us.' So they rushed at it and tried to riddle it with evil. But, like a clod of earth hurled against a rock, they were smashed to bits flying in all directions and perished. As a result, the gods prospered, while the demons came to ruin. When someone knows this, he himself will prosper, while an enemy who hates him will come to ruin.

8 The gods then asked: 'Where has he gone who stood by us like that?'

'Here within the mouth.'

This is Ayāsya, the Āṅgirasa, for it is the essence of the bodily parts.

9 Now, this same deity is called Dur, because death keeps far (*dūra*) from it. And death likewise keeps far from a man who knows this. 10 This same deity drove out from the other deities the evil that is death and chased it to the very ends of the earth. There it threw their evils down. Therefore, one should never visit foreigners or travel to frontier regions lest one run into evil and death.

11 This same deity, after it had driven out from the other deities

the evil that is death, carried them beyond the reach of death.
12 Speech was the first one that it carried. And when speech was
freed from death, it became fire. So, having gone beyond death,
the fire now blazes here. 13 Then it carried breath. And when
breath was freed from death, it became wind. So, having gone
beyond death, the wind now blows here. 14 Then it carried sight.
And when sight was freed from death, it became the sun. So, having gone beyond death, the sun now glows up there. 15 Then it carried hearing. And when hearing was freed from death, it became
the quarters. These quarters have gone beyond death. 16 Then it
carried the mind. And when the mind was freed from death, it
became the moon. So, having gone beyond death, the moon now
shines up there. In the same way, this deity carries beyond the
reach of death anyone who knows this.

17 Then the breath within the mouth procured a supply of food
for itself by singing, for it alone eats whatever food is eaten and
stands firm in this world. 18 But the other deities said to it: 'This
whole world is nothing but food! And you have procured it for
yourself by singing. Give us a share of that food.' It told them,
'Come and gather around me.' They said, 'Very well', and gathered around it on all sides. Therefore, whatever food one eats
through it satisfies also these others. When someone comes to
know this, his people will gather around him in the same way; he
will become their patron, their chief, and their leader; he will
become an eater of food and a sovereign. And if anyone among his
people tries to become a rival of someone who knows this, that
man will be incapable of supporting even his own dependants. On
the other hand, anyone who follows him, as well as anyone who,
while following him, wishes to support his own dependants,
becomes capable of supporting them.

19 This breath is Ayāsya, the Āṅgirasa, for it is the essence of the
bodily parts. Now, the essence of the bodily parts is breath, for it is
very clear—the essence of the bodily parts is breath. Therefore,
any part of the body from which breath departs is sure to wither,
for it is the very essence of the bodily parts.

20 And it is also Bṛhaspati. Bṛhatī, after all, is speech, and it is the
lord (*pati*) of speech. So it is Bṛhaspati. 21 And it is also
Brahmaṇaspati. *Brahman*, after all, is speech, and it is the lord
(*pati*) of speech. So it is Brahmaṇaspati. 22 And it is also the

Sāman. The Sāman, after all, is Speech. 'It is both she (*sā*) and he (*ama*)'—this gave the name to and discloses the true nature of the Sāman. Or maybe it is called Sāman because it is equal in size (*sama*) to a gnat or a mosquito, on the one hand, and to an elephant, to these three worlds, or even to the entire universe, on the other. When anyone comes to know the Sāman in this way, he obtains union with and residence in the same world as the Sāman. 23 And it is also the High Chant (*udgītha*). The 'high' (*ut*) is, after all, breath, for this whole world is held up (*uttabdha*) by breath. And 'chant' (*gītha*) is simply speech. Since it is high (*ut*) and it is chant (*gītha*), it is the High Chant (*udgītha*).

24 This same point was made by Brahmadatta Caikitāneya while he was drinking King Soma: 'May this King make my head shatter apart if Ayāsya Āṅgirasa sang the High Chant by any other means, for by speech and breath alone did he sing it.'

25 When someone knows the wealth of this Sāman, he comes to possess wealth. Now, the Sāman's wealth (*sva*) is the tone (*svara*) itself. For this reason, when someone is about to carry out priestly functions, he hopes for a rich tone in his voice so he can perform his priestly functions with a voice rich in tone. And for the same reason, people always try to find a priest with a rich tone for a sacrifice, that is, one who possesses that wealth. A man undoubtedly comes to possess wealth, when he knows in this way the wealth of the Sāman.

26 When someone knows the gold of this Sāman, he comes to possess gold. Now the Sāman's gold (*suvarṇa*) is the tone (*svara*) itself. A man undoubtedly comes to possess gold, when he knows in this way the gold of the Sāman.

27 When someone knows the basis of this Sāman, he comes to possess a solid basis. Now, the Sāman's basis is speech itself, for, basing itself on speech, the breath sings it. Some, however, take food to be its basis.

28 Next comes the chanting of the purificatory lauds. The Prastotṛ priest sings the Introductory Praise of the Sāman, and, as he is singing the Introductory Praise, the patron of the sacrifice should silently recite:

From the unreal
lead me to the real!

From the darkness
lead me to the light!
From death
lead me to immortality!'

The unreal is death, and the real is immortality—so, when he says, 'From the unreal lead me to the real', what he is really saying is: 'From death lead me to immortality'; in other words, 'Make me immortal.' Darkness is death, and light is immortality—so, when he says, 'From the darkness lead me to the light', what he is really saying is: 'From death lead me to immortality'; in other words, 'Make me immortal.' In the statement, 'From death lead me to immortality', there is nothing obscure.

He may, further, procure a supply of food for himself by singing the remaining lauds. When he is singing them, therefore, he should choose as a reward anything he may desire. An Udgātṛ priest who has this knowledge is able to procure by his singing whatever he desires, either for himself or for the patron of the sacrifice. Now this is true world conquest. When a man knows that Sāman in this way, there is no fear of his being left without a world.

4 In the beginning this world was just a single body (*ātman*) shaped like a man. He looked around and saw nothing but himself. The first thing he said was, 'Here I am!' and from that the name 'I' came into being. Therefore, even today when you call someone, he first says, 'It's I', and then states whatever other name he may have. That first being received the name 'man' (*puruṣa*), because ahead (*pūrva*) of all this he burnt up (*uṣ*) all evils. When someone knows this, he burns up anyone who may try to get ahead of him.

2 That first being became afraid; therefore, one becomes afraid when one is alone. Then he thought to himself: 'Of what should I be afraid, when there is no one but me?' So his fear left him, for what was he going to be afraid of? One is, after all, afraid of another.

3 He found no pleasure at all; so one finds no pleasure when one is alone. He wanted to have a companion. Now he was as large as a man and a woman in close embrace. So he split (*pat*) his body

into two, giving rise to husband (*pati*) and wife (*patnī*). Surely this is why Yājñavalkya used to say: 'The two of us are like two halves of a block.' The space here, therefore, is completely filled by the woman.

He copulated with her, and from their union human beings were born. 4 She then thought to herself: 'After begetting me from his own body (*ātman*), how could he copulate with me? I know—I'll hide myself.' So she became a cow. But he became a bull and copulated with her. From their union cattle were born. Then she became a mare, and he a stallion; she became a female donkey, and he, a male donkey. And again he copulated with her, and from their union one-hoofed animals were born. Then she became a female goat, and he, a male goat; she became a ewe, and he, a ram. And again he copulated with her, and from their union goats and sheep were born. In this way he created every male and female pair that exists, down to the very ants.

5 It then occurred to him: 'I alone am the creation, for I created all this.' From this 'creation' came into being. Anyone who knows this prospers in this creation of his.

6 Then he churned like this and, using his hands, produced fire from his mouth as from a vagina. As a result the inner sides of both these—the hands and the mouth—are without hair, for the inside of the vagina is without hair. 'Sacrifice to this god. Sacrifice to that god'—people do say these things, but in reality each of these gods is his own creation, for he himself is all these gods. From his semen, then, he created all that is moist here, which is really Soma. Food and eater—that is the extent of this whole world. Food is simply Soma, and the eater is fire.

This is *brahman*'s super-creation. It is a super-creation because he created the gods, who are superior to him, and, being a mortal himself, he created the immortals. Anyone who knows this stands within this super-creation of his.

7 At that time this world was without real distinctions; it was distinguished simply in terms of name and visible appearance—'He is so and so by name and has this sort of an appearance.' So even today this world is distinguished simply in terms of name and visible appearance, as when we say, 'He is so and so by name and has this sort of an appearance.'

Penetrating this body up to the very nailtips, he remains there like a razor within a case or a termite within a termite-hill. People do not see him, for he is incomplete as he comes to be called breath when he is breathing, speech when he is speaking, sight when he is seeing, hearing when he is hearing, and mind when he is thinking. These are only the names of his various activities. A man who considers him to be any one of these does not understand him, for he is incomplete within any one of these. One should consider them as simply his self (*ātman*), for in it all these become one. This same self (*ātman*) is the trail to this entire world, for by following it one comes to know this entire world, just as by following their tracks one finds [the cattle]. Whoever knows this finds fame and glory.

8 This innermost thing, this self (*ātman*)—it is dearer than a son, it is dearer than wealth, it is dearer than everything else. If a man claims that something other than his self is dear to him, and someone were to tell him that he will lose what he holds dear, that is liable to happen. So a man should regard only his self as dear to him. When a man regards only his self as dear to him, what he holds dear will never perish.

9 Now, the question is raised: 'Since people think that they will be come the Whole by knowing *brahman*, what did *brahman* know that enabled it to become the Whole?'

10 In the beginning this world was only *brahman*, and it knew only itself (*ātman*), thinking: 'I am *brahman*.' As a result, it became the Whole. Among the gods, likewise, whosoever realized this, only they became the Whole. It was the same also among the seers and among humans. Upon seeing this very point, the seer Vāmadeva proclaimed: 'I was Manu, and I was the sun.' This is true even now. If a man knows 'I am *brahman*' in this way, he becomes this whole world. Not even the gods are able to prevent it, for he becomes their very self (*ātman*). So when a man venerates another deity, thinking, 'He is one, and I am another', he does not understand. As livestock is for men, so is he for the gods. As having a lot of livestock is useful to a man, so each man proves useful to the gods. The loss of even a single head of livestock is painful; how much more if many are lost. The gods, therefore, are not pleased at the prospect of men coming to understand this.

11 In the beginning this world was only *brahman*, only one. Because it was only one, *brahman* had not fully developed. It then created the ruling power, a form superior to and surpassing itself, that is, the ruling powers among the gods—Indra, Varuṇa, Soma, Rudra, Parjanya, Yama, Mṛtyu, and Īśāna. Hence there is nothing higher than the ruling power. Accordingly, at a royal anointing a Brahmin pays homage to a Kṣatriya by prostrating himself. He extends this honour only to the ruling power. Now, the priestly power (*brahman*) is the womb of the ruling power. Therefore, even if a king should rise to the summit of power, it is to the priestly power that he returns in the end as to his own womb. So, one who hurts the latter harms his own womb and becomes so much the worse for harming someone better than him.

12 *Brahman* still did not become fully developed. So it created the Vaiśya class, that is, the types of gods who are listed in groups—Vasus, Rudras, Ādityas, All-gods, and Maruts.

13 It still did not become fully developed. So it created the Śūdra class, that is, Pūṣan. Now, Pūṣan is this very earth, for it nourishes this whole world, it nourishes all that exists.

14 It still did not become fully developed. So it created the Law (*dharma*), a form superior to and surpassing itself. And the Law is here the ruling power standing above the ruling power. Hence there is nothing higher than the Law. Therefore, a weaker man makes demands of a stronger man by appealing to the Law, just as one does by appealing to a king. Now, the Law is nothing but the truth. Therefore, when a man speaks the truth, people say that he speaks the Law; and when a man speaks the Law, people say that he speaks the truth. They are really the same thing.

15 So there came to be the priestly power, the ruling power, the Vaiśya class, and the Śūdra class. Among the gods the priestly power (*brahman*) came into being only in the form of fire, and among humans as a Brahmin; it further became a Kṣatriya in the form of a Kṣatriya, a Vaiśya in the form of a Vaiśya, and a Śūdra in the form of a Śūdra. In the fire, therefore, people seek to find a world for themselves among the gods, and in the Brahmin a world among humans, for *brahman* came into being in these two forms.

If someone were to depart from this world without perceiving his own world, it will be of no use to him as it remains unknown to him, just like the Veda that is not recited or a rite that is left undone. If a man who does not know this performs even a grand and holy rite, it is sure to fade away after his death. It is his self (*ātman*) alone that a man should venerate as his world. And if someone venerates his self alone as his world, that rite of his will never fade away, because from his very self he will produce whatever he desires.

16 Now, this self (*ātman*) is a world for all beings. So, when he makes offerings and sacrifices, he becomes thereby a world for the gods. When he recites the Vedas, he becomes thereby a world for the seers. When he offers libations to his ancestors and seeks to father offspring, he becomes thereby a world for his ancestors. When he provides food and shelter to human beings, he becomes thereby a world for human beings. When he procures fodder and water for livestock, he becomes thereby a world for livestock. When creatures, from wild animals and birds down to the very ants, find shelter in his houses, he becomes thereby a world for them. Just as a man desires the well-being of his own world, so all beings desire the well-being of anyone who knows this. All this is known and has been thoroughly examined.

17 In the beginning this world was only the self (*ātman*), only one. He had this desire: 'I wish I had a wife so I could father offspring. I wish I had wealth so I could perform rites.' That is the full extent of desire; one does not get anything more, even if one desires it. So even today when one is single, one has the desire: 'I wish I had a wife so I could father offspring. I wish I had wealth so I could perform rites.' As long as someone has not obtained either of these, he considers himself to be utterly incomplete. Now, this is his completeness—his mind is himself (*ātman*); his speech is his wife; his breath is his offspring; his sight is his human wealth, for people find wealth with their sight, while his hearing is his divine wealth, for people hear about it with their hearing; and his body (*ātman*) is his rites, for one performs rites with one's body. This is the fivefold sacrifice—the sacrificial animal is fivefold, the human being is fivefold, and this whole world, whatever there is, is fivefold. Anyone who knows this obtains this whole world.

5 Now there are these verses:

> By wisdom and by toil,
> when the father produced
> the seven kinds of food—
> One was common to all here.
> Two he assigned to the gods.
> Three he kept for himself.
> One he gave to the beasts.
>
> All beings depend on it,
> both those that breathe
> and those that do not.
> Why aren't they exhausted,
> when they are eaten every day?
> The man who knows it
> as the inexhaustible—
> he eats food with his face;
> he reaches the gods;
> he lives on invigorating food.

2 'By wisdom and by toil when the father produced the seven kinds of food'—for it is through wisdom and toil that the father produced them. 'One was common to all here'—the food of his that is common to all is what people here eat, and a man who venerates it does not get rid of evil, because it is a mixed food. 'Two he assigned to the gods'—they are the burnt offerings and the non-burnt offerings. That is why people offer burnt and non-burnt offerings to the gods. Others, however, say that they are the new-moon and the full-moon sacrifices. Therefore, one should not offer sacrifices endlessly. 'One he gave to the beasts'—this refers to milk, for in their infancy both animals and men live solely on milk. As soon as a child is born, therefore, they make it lick some ghee or suckle at the breast. So people call a new-born calf a 'non-grass-eater'. 'All beings depend on it, both those that breathe and those that do not'—on milk, indeed, do all beings depend, both those that breathe and those that do not. Now, there are people who claim: 'Anyone who offers oblations of milk for a full year averts repeated death.' One should not believe that, for a man in possession of this knowledge averts repeated death on the very day itself that he offers such an oblation, because he thereby offers the

whole world as a supply of food to the gods. 'Why don't they decrease, when they are eaten every day?'—the inexhaustible is clearly the Person, for he is constantly generating this food. 'The man who knows it as the inexhaustible'—the inexhaustible is clearly the Person, for he generates this food by constant attention and by means of rites. If he stops doing it, the food is sure to be exhausted. 'He eats food with his face'—'face' here means the mouth. 'He reaches the gods; he lives on invigorating food'—this is a eulogy.

3 'Three he kept for himself'—mind, speech, and breath; these he kept for himself (*ātman*). We say: 'I didn't see; my mind was elsewhere. I didn't hear; my mind was elsewhere.' For it is through the mind that one sees and hears. Desire, decision, doubt, faith and lack of faith, steadfastness and lack of steadfastness, shame, reflection, and fear—all these are simply the mind. Therefore, even when someone touches us on the back, we perceive it through the mind. Every sound that exists is simply speech, for the former is fixed up to its limit (on the latter), whereas the latter is not. Out-breath, in-breath, inter-breath, up-breath, link-breath—as forms of breathing, they are all simply breath. These are what constitute this self (*ātman*)—it consists of speech, it consists of mind, and it consists of breath.

4 The three worlds are also these—this world is speech; the middle world is the mind; and the world above is breath.

5 The three Vedas are also these—the Ṛgveda is speech; the Yajurveda is the mind; and the Sāmaveda is breath.

6 The gods, ancestors, and humans are also these—the gods are speech; the ancestors are the mind; and humans are breath.

7 The father, the mother, and the child are also these—the father is the mind; the mother is speech; and the child is breath.

8 What one knows, what one seeks to know, and what one does not know are also these. Whatever someone knows is a form of speech, for speech is what he knows. By becoming that, speech helps him.
9 Whatever someone seeks to know is a form of the mind, for the mind is what he seeks to know. By becoming that, the mind helps
him. 10 Whatever someone does not know is a form of breath, for breath is what he does not know. By becoming that, breath helps him.

11 The earth is the body of speech, and this fire here below is its luminous appearance. So, the extent of the earth and of this fire is the same as the extent of speech.

12 The sky is the body of the mind, and that sun up there is its luminous appearance. So, the extent of the sky and of that sun is the same as the extent of the mind. This pair copulated, and from their union was born breath, which is Indra. And he is without rival, for there has to be another to have a rival. Whoever knows this will have no rival.

13 The waters are the body of breath, and that moon up there is its luminous appearance. So, the extent of the waters and of that moon is the same as the extent of breath.

Now, all these are of equal extent, all are without limit. So those who venerate them as finite win only a limited world, whereas those who venerate them as infinite win a world without limit.

14 Prajāpati is the year, and he is composed of sixteen parts. Fifteen of his parts are the nights, while his sixteenth part is constant. With each passing night he waxes and wanes. With that sixteenth part of his he enters, on the night of the new moon, all beings that sustain life and is born again the next morning. In honour of that divinity, therefore, on that night a man should not take the life of any being that sustains life, not even that of a lizard.

15 A man who knows this is himself the year, and he is Prajāpati composed of sixteen parts. His fifteen parts consist merely of his wealth, while his sixteenth part is his body (*ātman*). Only in his wealth does he wax and wane. His body is the wheel-head, while his wealth is the wheel-plate. So, even though a man may have been plundered of everything he has, if he remains alive with his body (*ātman*) intact, people say: 'He got away with just the wheel-plate!'

16 Now, there are only three worlds: the world of men, the world of ancestors, and the world of gods. One can win this world of men only through a son, and by no other rite, whereas one wins the world of ancestors through rites, and the world of gods through knowledge. The best of these, clearly, is the world of gods, and for this reason they praise knowledge.

17 Next, the rite of transfer. When a man thinks that he is about to die, he tells his son: 'You are the *brahman*! You are the sacrifice! You are the world!' The son replies: 'I am the *brahman*! I am the sacrifice! I am the world!' All the vedic learning that has been

acquired is subsumed under '*brahman*'; all the sacrifices are subsumed under 'sacrifice'; and all the worlds are subsumed under 'world.' That is the full extent of this whole universe—'By becoming the Whole, may he assist me from here.' Therefore, they say that an educated son opens up the world, and for this reason people educate their sons. When a man who knows this departs from this world, he enters his son with these very vital functions (*prāṇa*). And if there is anything he may have done wrong, his son delivers him from all that. That is why he is called 'son'. So it is only through a son that a man finds a secure footing in this world.

Thereupon, these divine and immortal vital functions (*prāṇa*) enter him. 18 From the earth and fire divine speech enters him. Divine speech is that which makes whatever one says happen. 19 From the sky and the sun the divine mind enters him. The divine mind is that which makes a person always happy and never sorrowful. 20 From the waters and the moon the divine breath enters him. The divine breath is that which never falters or fails, whether it is moving or is at rest.

Now, a man who knows this becomes the self (*ātman*) of all beings; he becomes just like this divine breath. All beings are sure to shower a man who knows this with gifts, just as they shower this divine breath with gifts. Whatever grief may afflict these creatures, it remains limited to them. Only what is good goes to him, for it is impossible that anything bad should go to the gods.

21 Next, an examination of the observances. Prajāpati created the vital functions (*prāṇa*). Once they were created, they began to compete with each other. Speech threw out the challenge: 'I'm going to speak!' Sight shot back: 'I'm going to see!' and hearing: 'I'm going to hear!' The other vital functions bragged likewise, each according to its function. Taking the form of weariness, death took hold of them; it captured and shackled them. That is why speech becomes weary, as do sight and hearing. The central breath alone, however, death could not capture. So they sought to know him, thinking: 'He is clearly the best among us; whether he is moving or at rest, he never falters or fails. Come, let us all become forms of him!' So they all became merely forms of him. Therefore, they are called 'breaths' (*prāṇa*) after him. For this

very reason, a family is called after a man in that family who has this knowledge. So, anyone who competes with a man with this knowledge withers away. Yes, he withers away and dies in the end.

That was with respect to the body (*ātman*). 22 What follows is with respect to the divine sphere.

Fire threw out the challenge: 'I'm going to blaze!' The sun shot back: 'I'm going to glow!' and the moon: 'I'm going to shine!' The other deities bragged likewise, each according to its divine function. The wind holds the same position among the deities as the central breath does among the vital functions, for the other deities disappear, but not the wind. The wind is the only deity that does not set.

23 Now there is this verse:

> From which the sun rises,
> And into which it sets;

For it does rise from breath, and into breath it sets.

> The gods made it the Law,
> It's the same today and tomorrow.

What these deities sought to do of old, they continue to do even today. Therefore, a man should undertake a single observance—he should breathe in and breathe out with the thought 'May evil death not capture me.' And if someone undertakes it, let him resolve to pursue it to the end. By doing that he will win union with and the same world as this deity.

6 Clearly, this world is a triple reality: name, visible appearance, and action. Speech is the Uktha among names, because all names arise from it. It is the Sāman among them, because it is the same as all the names. It is *brahman* among them, because it bears all the names.

2 Sight is the Uktha among visible appearances, because all visible appearances arise from it. It is the Sāman among them, because it is the same as all visible appearances. It is *brahman* among them, because it bears all visible appearances.

3 The body (*ātman*) is the Uktha among actions, because all actions arise from it. It is the Sāman among them, because it is the

same as all actions. It is *brahman* among them, because it bears all actions.

While this is a triple reality, yet it is one—it is this self (*ātman*). While the self is one, yet it is this triple reality. Now the immortal here is veiled by the real. Clearly, the immortal is breath, while the real is name and visible appearance; the breath here is veiled by these two.

CHAPTER 2

1 There was once a learned Gārgya named Dṛpta-Bālāki. He said to Ajātaśatru, the king of Kāśi: 'Let me tell you a formulation of truth (*brahman*).' Ajātaśatru replied: 'We'll give you a thousand cows for such a speech! People are sure to rush here, crying, "Here's a Janaka! Here's a Janaka!"'

2 Gārgya then said: 'It is the person up there in the sun that I venerate as *brahman*.' Ajātaśatru replied: 'Don't start a conversation with me about him! I venerate him only as the most eminent of all beings, as their head and king. Anyone who venerates him this way will become the most eminent of all beings, he will become their head and king.'

3 Gārgya then said: 'It is the person up there in the moon that I venerate as *brahman*.' Ajātaśatru replied: 'Don't start a conversation with me about him! I venerate him only as Soma, the great king dressed in white. Anyone who venerates him this way will have Soma pressed for him every day, and his food will never decrease.'

4 Gārgya then said: 'It is the person up there in lightning that I venerate as *brahman*.' Ajātaśatru replied: 'Don't start a conversation with me about him! I venerate him only as the radiant one. Anyone who venerates him this way will become radiant, and he will have radiant children.'

5 Gārgya then said: 'It is the person here in space that I venerate as *brahman*.' Ajātaśatru replied: 'Don't start a conversation with me about him! I venerate him only as the full and non-depleting (*apravṛt*) one. Anyone who venerates him this way will be filled

with children and livestock, and his children will not pass away (*udvṛt*) from this world.'

6 Gārgya then said: 'It is the person here in the wind that I venerate as *brahman*.' Ajātaśatru replied: 'Don't start a conversation with me about him! I venerate him only as Indra Vaikuṇṭha, the invincible weapon. Anyone who venerates him this way will become victorious and invincible, and he will triumph over his adversaries.'

7 Gārgya then said: 'It is the person here in the fire that I venerate as *brahman*.' Ajātaśatru replied: 'Don't start a conversation with me about him! I venerate him only as the irresistible one. Anyone who venerates him this way will become irresistible, and so will his children.'

8 Gārgya then said: 'It is the person here in the waters that I venerate as *brahman*.' Ajātaśatru replied: 'Don't start a conversation with me about him! I venerate him only as a resemblance. Anyone who venerates him this way will obtain only what resembles him and not what does not resemble him; and one who resembles him will be born from him.'

9 Gārgya then said: 'It is the person here in a mirror that I venerate as *brahman*.' Ajātaśatru replied: 'Don't start a conversation with me about him! I venerate him only as the shining one. Anyone who venerates him this way will shine, his children will shine, and he will outshine everyone he meets.'

10 Gārgya then said: 'It is the sound drifting behind a man as he walks that I venerate as *brahman*.' Ajātaśatru replied: 'Don't start a conversation with me about him! I venerate him only as life. Anyone who venerates him this way will live his full life span in this world, and his lifebreath will not leave him before the appointed time.'

11 Gārgya then said: 'It is the person here in the quarters that I venerate as *brahman*.' Ajātaśatru replied: 'Don't start a conversation with me about him! I venerate him only as the inseparable companion. Anyone who venerates him this way will always have a companion, and he will never be cut off from his entourage.'

12 Gārgya then said: 'It is the person here consisting of shadow that I venerate as *brahman*.' Ajātaśatru replied: 'Don't start a conversation with me about him! I venerate him only as death. Anyone who venerates him this way will live a full life in this

world, and death will not approach him before the appointed time.'

13 Gārgya then said: 'It is the person here in the body (*ātman*) that I venerate as *brahman*.' Ajātaśatru replied: 'Don't start a conversation with me about him! I venerate him only as the one possessing a body. Anyone who venerates him this way will come to possess a body, and so will his children.' Thereupon, Gārgya fell silent.

14 'Is that all?' asked Ajātaśatru.

'That's all.'

'It isn't known with just that.'

'Let me come to you as your pupil,' said Gārgya.

15 Ajātaśatru replied: 'Isn't it a reversal of the norm for a Brahmin to become the pupil of a Kṣatriya thinking, "He will tell me the formulation of truth (*brahman*)"? But I'll see to it that you perceive it clearly.' Taking Gārgya by the hand, he got up, and the two went near a sleeping man. He greeted that man in these words: 'O Soma, great king dressed in white!' But he did not get up. Ajātaśatru touched him with his hand and woke him up. Then the man got up.

16 Ajātaśatru asked: 'When this man was asleep here, where was the person consisting of perception? And from where did he return?' Gārgya did not know the answer.

17 Ajātaśatru told him: 'When this man was asleep here, the person consisting of perception, having gathered the cognitive power of these vital functions (*prāṇa*) into his own cognitive power, was resting in the space within the heart. When that person takes hold of them, then the man is said to be asleep. During that time the breath remains in the grasp of that person, as do speech, sight, hearing, and mind. 18 Wherever he may travel in his dream, those regions become his worlds. He may appear to become a great king or an eminent Brahmin, or to visit the highest and the lowest regions. Just as a great king, taking his people with him, may move around in his domain at will, so he, taking the vital functions here with him, moves around his body at will.

19 'When a man is in deep dreamless sleep, on the other hand, and is not aware of anything at all, this is what happens. There are seventy-two thousand veins named Hitā that run from the heart to the pericardium. He slips out of the heart through these veins and

rests within the pericardium. He rests there oblivious to everything, just as a young man, a great king, or an eminent Brahmin remains oblivious to everything at the height of sexual bliss.

20 'As a spider sends forth its thread, and as tiny sparks spring forth from a fire, so indeed do all the vital functions (*prāṇa*), all the worlds, all the gods, and all beings spring from this self (*ātman*). Its hidden name (*upaniṣad*) is: 'The real behind the real,' for the real consists of the vital functions, and the self is the real behind the vital functions.'

2 A man who knows the youngling together with its placement and counterplacement, its post and rope, will undoubtedly hold off the seven enemies who hate him. That youngling, indeed, is one's central breath. Its placement is this; its counterplacement is this; its post is the breath; and its rope is food.

2 These seven who do not decrease stand by him. Rudra attaches himself to him by means of the red streaks in the eye; rain, by means of the tears in the eye; sun, by means of the pupil; fire, by means of the iris; Indra, by means of the white; earth, by means of the lower eyelashes; and sky, by means of the upper eyelashes. When a man knows this, his food will never decrease.

3 In this connection there is this verse:

> There is a cup turned upside down;
> its mouth at the bottom,
> its bottom on top.
> In it is placed dazzling splendour;
> On its rim the seven seers sit,
> as also an eighth—
> speech joined to *brahman*.

'There is a bowl turned upside down, its mouth at the bottom, its bottom on top'—the head here is indeed the 'bowl turned upside down, its mouth at the bottom, its bottom on top'. 'In it is placed dazzling splendour'—'dazzling splendour' is no doubt the vital functions (*prāṇa*); so this statement must refer to the vital functions. 'On its rim the seven seers sit'—the seers are no doubt the vital functions; so this statement must refer to the vital functions. 'As also an eighth—speech joined to *brahman*'—the eighth is speech, and it joins itself to *brahman*.

4 Gotama and Bharadvāja are really these two [ears]—Gotama is this [right] one, and Bharadvāja is this [left] one. Viśvāmitra and Jamadagni are really these two [eyes]—Viśvāmitra is this [right] one, and Jamadagni is this [left] one. Vasiṣṭha and Kaśyapa are really these two [nostrils]—Vasiṣṭha is this [right] one and Kaśyapa is this [left] one. Atri is really speech, for one eats (*atti*) with speech. So Atri is really the same as 'eating' (*atti*). When a man knows this, he becomes the eater of this whole world, and the whole world here becomes his food.

3 There are, indeed, two visible appearances (*rūpa*) of *brahman*—the one has a fixed shape, and the other is without a fixed shape; the one is mortal, and the other is immortal; the one is stationary, and the other is in motion; the one is Sat, and the other is Tyam.

2 The one with a fixed shape consists of everything other than air and the intermediate region; it is mortal and stationary; and it is Sat. That which gives warmth is the essence of the one that has a fixed shape, that is mortal and stationary, and that is Sat—for it is the essence of Sat.

3 The one without a fixed shape, on the other hand, consists of air and the intermediate region; it is immortal and in motion; and it is Tyam. The person within the sun's orb is the essence of the one that is without a fixed shape, that is immortal and in motion, and that is Tyam—for he is the essence of Tyam.

That was with reference to the divine sphere. 4The following is with reference to the body (*ātman*).

The one with a fixed shape is this body itself insofar as it is distinct from breath and the space within the body; it is mortal and stationary; and it is Sat. The eye is the essence of the one that has a fixed shape, that is mortal and stationary, and that is Sat—for it is the essence of Sat.

5 The one without a fixed shape, on the other hand, consists of breath and the space within the body; it is immortal and in motion; and it is Tyam. The person within the right eye is the essence of the one that is without a fixed shape, that is immortal and in motion, and that is Tyam—for he is the essence of Tyam.

6 Now, the visible appearance of this person is like a golden cloth, or white wool, or a red bug, or a flame, or a white lotus, or a

sudden flash of lightning. And when a man knows this, his splendour unfolds like a sudden flash of lightning.

Here, then, is the rule of substitution: 'not ——, not ——', for there is nothing beyond this 'not'. And this is the name—'the real behind the real', for the real consists of the vital functions, and he is the real behind the vital functions.

4 'Maitreyī!' Yājñavalkya once said. 'Look—I am about to depart from this place. So come, let me make a settlement between you and Kātyāyanī.'

2 Maitreyī asked in reply: 'If I were to possess the entire world filled with wealth, sir, would it make me immortal?' 'No,' said Yājñavalkya, 'it will only permit you to live the life of a wealthy person. Through wealth one cannot expect immortality.'

3 'What is the point in getting something that will not make me immortal?' retorted Maitreyī. 'Tell me instead, sir, all that you know.'

4 Yājñavalkya said in reply: 'You have always been very dear to me, and now you speak something very dear to me! Come and sit down. I will explain it to you. But while I am explaining, try to concentrate.' 5 Then he spoke:

'One holds a husband dear, you see, not out of love for the husband; rather, it is out of love for oneself (*ātman*) that one holds a husband dear. One holds a wife dear not out of love for the wife; rather, it is out of love for oneself that one holds a wife dear. One holds children dear not out of love for the children; rather, it is out of love for oneself that one holds children dear. One holds wealth dear not out of love for wealth; rather, it is out of love for oneself that one holds wealth dear. One holds the priestly power dear not out of love for the priestly power; rather, it is out of love for oneself that one holds the priestly power dear. One holds the royal power dear not out of love for the royal power; rather, it is out of love for oneself that one holds the royal power dear. One holds the worlds dear not out of love for the worlds; rather, it is out of love for oneself that one holds the worlds dear. One holds the gods dear not out of love for the gods; rather, it is out of love for oneself that one holds the gods dear. One holds beings dear not out of love for beings; rather, it is out of love for oneself that one holds beings dear. One holds the Whole dear not out of love for the

Whole; rather, it is out of love for oneself that one holds the Whole dear.

'You see, Maitreyī—it is one's self (*ātman*) which one should see and hear, and on which one should reflect and concentrate. For by seeing and hearing one's self, and by reflecting and concentrating on one's self, one gains the knowledge of this whole world.

6 'May the priestly power forsake anyone who considers the priestly power to reside in something other than his self (*ātman*). May the royal power forsake anyone who considers the royal power to reside in something other than his self. May the gods forsake anyone who considers the gods to reside in something other than his self. May beings forsake anyone who considers beings to reside in something other than his self. May the Whole forsake anyone who considers the Whole to reside in something other than his self.

'All these—the priestly power, the royal power, worlds, gods, beings, the Whole—all that is nothing but this self.

7 'It is like this. When a drum is being beaten, you cannot catch the external sounds; you catch them only by getting hold of the drum or the man beating that drum. 8 Or when a conch is being blown, you cannot catch the external sounds; you catch them only by getting hold of the conch or the man blowing that conch. 9 Or when a lute is being played, you cannot catch the external sounds; you catch them only by getting hold of the lute or the man playing that lute.

10 'It is like this. As clouds of smoke billow from a fire lit with damp fuel, so indeed this Immense Being has exhaled all this: Ṛgveda, Yajurveda, Sāmaveda, the Atharva-Āṅgirasa, histories, ancient tales, sciences, hidden teachings (*upaniṣad*), verses, aphorisms, explanations, and glosses—it is that Immense Being who has exhaled all this.

11 'It is like this. As the ocean is the point of convergence of all the waters, so the skin is the point of convergence of all sensations of touch; the nostrils, of all odours; the tongue, of all tastes; sight, of all visible appearances; hearing, of all sounds; the mind, of all thoughts; the heart, of all sciences; the hands, of all activities; the sexual organ, of all pleasures; the anus, of all excretions; the feet, of all travels; and speech, of all the Vedas.

12 'It is like this. When a chunk of salt is thrown in water, it

dissolves into that very water, and it cannot be picked up in any way. Yet, from whichever place one may take a sip, the salt is there! In the same way this Immense Being has no limit or boundary and is a single mass of perception. It arises out of and together with these beings and disappears after them—so I say, after death there is no awareness.'

After Yājñavalkya said this, 13 Maitreyī exclaimed: 'Now, sir, you have totally confused me by saying "after death there is no awareness." He replied:

'Look, I haven't said anything confusing; this body, you see, has the capacity to perceive. 14 For when there is a duality of some kind, then the one can smell the other, the one can see the other, the one can hear the other, the one can greet the other, the one can think of the other, and the one can perceive the other. When, however, the Whole has become one's very self (*ātman*), then who is there for one to smell and by what means? Who is there for one to see and by what means? Who is there for one to hear and by what means? Who is there for one to greet and by what means? Who is there for one to think of and by what means? Who is there for one to perceive and by what means?

'By what means can one perceive him by means of whom one perceives this whole world? Look—by what means can one perceive the perceiver?'

5 This earth is the honey of all beings, and all beings are the honey of this earth. The radiant and immortal person in the earth and, in the case of the body (*ātman*), the radiant and immortal person residing in the physical body—they are both one's self (*ātman*). It is the immortal; it is *brahman*; it is the Whole.

2 These waters are the honey of all beings, and all beings are the honey of these waters. The radiant and immortal person in the waters and, in the case of the body, the radiant and immortal person residing in semen—they are both one's self. It is the immortal; it is *brahman*; it is the Whole.

3 This fire is the honey of all beings, and all beings are the honey of this fire. The radiant and immortal person in the fire and, in the case of the body, the radiant and immortal person residing in speech—they are both one's self. It is the immortal; it is *brahman*; it is the Whole.

[4] This wind is the honey of all beings, and all beings are the honey of this wind. The radiant and immortal person in the wind and, in the case of the body, the radiant and immortal person residing in breath—they are both one's self. It is the immortal; it is *brahman*; it is the Whole.

[5] This sun is the honey of all beings, and all beings are the honey of this sun. The radiant and immortal person in the sun and, in the case of the body, the radiant and immortal person residing in sight—they are both one's self. It is the immortal; it is *brahman*; it is the Whole.

[6] These quarters are the honey of all beings, and all beings are the honey of these quarters. The radiant and immortal person in the quarters and, in the case of the body, the radiant and immortal person residing in hearing—they are both one's self. It is the immortal; it is *brahman*; it is the Whole.

[7] This moon is the honey of all beings, and all beings are the honey of this moon. The radiant and immortal person in the moon and, in the case of the body, the radiant and immortal person residing in the mind—they are both one's self. It is the immortal; it is *brahman*; it is the Whole.

[8] This lightning is the honey of all beings, and all beings are the honey of this lightning. The radiant and immortal person in lightning and, in the case of the body, the radiant and immortal person full of radiance—they are both one's self. It is the immortal; it is *brahman*; it is the Whole.

[9] This thunder is the honey of all beings, and all beings are the honey of this thunder. The radiant and immortal person in thunder and, in the case of the body, the radiant and immortal person connected with sound and tone—they are both one's self. It is the immortal; it is *brahman*; it is the Whole.

[10] This space is the honey of all beings, and all beings are the honey of this space. The radiant and immortal person in space and, in the case of the body, the radiant and immortal person residing in the space within the heart—they are both one's self. It is the immortal; it is *brahman*; it is the Whole.

[11] This Law (*dharma*) is the honey of all beings, and all beings are the honey of this Law. The radiant and immortal person in the Law and, in the case of the body, the radiant and immortal person devoted to the Law—they are both one's self. It is the immortal; it is *brahman*; it is the Whole.

12 This Truth is the honey of all beings, and all beings are the honey of this Truth. The radiant and immortal person in Truth and, in the case of the body, the radiant and immortal person devoted to Truth—they are both one's self. It is the immortal; it is *brahman*; it is the Whole.

13 This humanity is the honey of all beings, and all beings are the honey of this humanity. The radiant and immortal person in humanity and, in the case of the body, the radiant and immortal person existing as a human—they are both one's self. It is the immortal; it is *brahman*; it is the Whole.

14 This self (*ātman*) is the honey of all beings, and all beings are the honey of this self. The radiant and immortal person in the self and the radiant and immortal person connected with the body (*ātman*)—they are both one's self. It is the immortal; it is *brahman*; it is the Whole.

15 This very self (*ātman*) is the lord and king of all beings. As all the spokes are fastened to the hub and the rim of a wheel, so to one's self (*ātman*) are fastened all beings, all the gods, all the worlds, all the breaths, and all these bodies (*ātman*).

16 This is the same honey as Dadhyañc Ātharvaṇa communicated to the Aśvins. Seeing this, the seer declared:

> As thunder discloses the rain, O Heroes,
> I disclose that wonderful skill you displayed for gain;
> When Dadhyañc Ātharvaṇa revealed the honey,
> Through the horse's head to you.

17 This is the same honey as Dadhyañc Ātharvaṇa communicated to the Aśvins. Seeing this, a seer declared:

> You fixed a horse's head, O Aśvins,
> On Dadhyañc Ātharvaṇa;
> True to his word, O mighty ones,
> He revealed to you Tvaṣṭṛ's honey,
> That remains a secret with you.

18 This is the same honey as Dadhyañc Ātharvaṇa communicated to the Aśvins. Seeing this, a seer declared:

> He made a fort with two feet;
> He made a fort with four feet.

He became a bird and entered the fort;
The Person has entered the fort.

This very Person (*puruṣa*) is the fort-dweller (*puriśaya*) in all the forts. There is nothing that is not sheltered by him; there is nothing that is not secured by him.

19 This is the same honey as Dadhyañc Ātharvaṇa communicated to the Aśvins. Seeing this, a seer declared:

Of every form of every being,
the likeness he has assumed;
every form seeks to reveal him.
His steeds are yoked, all ten hundred;
Indra by his wizardry travels in many forms.

He alone is the steeds; he is the ten thousand, the many, the innumerable. This *brahman* is without a before and an after, without an inner and an outer. *Brahman* is this self (*ātman*) here which perceives everything.

That is the teaching.

6 Now the lineage:

Pautimāṣya from Gaupavana; Gaupavana from Pautimāṣya; Pautimāṣya from Gaupavana; Gaupavana from Kauśika; Kauśika from Kauṇḍinya; Kauṇḍinya from Śāṇḍilya; Śāṇḍilya from Kauśika and Gautama; Gautama 2 from Āgniveśya; Āgniveśya from Śāṇḍilya and Ānabhimlāta; Ānabhimlāta from Ānabhimlāta; Ānabhimlāta from Ānabhimlāta; Ānabhimlāta from Gautama; Gautama from Saitava and Prācīnayogya; Saitava and Prācīna-yogya from Pārāśarya; Pārāśarya from Bhāradvāja; Bhāradvāja from Bhāradvāja and Gautama; Gautama from Bhāradvāja; Bhāradvāja from Pārāśarya; Pārāśarya from Vaijavāpāyana; Vaijavāpāyana from Kauśikāyani; Kauśikāyani 3 from Ghṛtakauśika; Ghṛtakauśika from Pārāśaryāyaṇa; Pārāśaryāyaṇa from Pārāśarya; Pārāśarya from Jātūkarṇya; Jātūkarṇya from Āsurāyaṇa and Yāska; Āsurāyaṇa from Traivaṇi; Traivaṇi from Aupajan-dhani; Aupajandhani from Āsuri; Āsuri from Bhāradvāja; Bhāradvāja from Ātreya; Ātreya from Māṇṭi; Māṇṭi from Gautama; Gautama from Gautama; Gautama from Vātsya; Vātsya from Śāṇḍilya; Śāṇḍilya from Kaiśorya Kāpya; Kaiśorya Kāpya from Kumārahārita; Kumārahārita from Gālava;

Gālava from Vidarbhīkauṇḍinya; Vidarbhīkauṇḍinya from Vatsanapād Bābhrava; Vatsanapād Bābhrava from Panthāḥ Saubhara; Panthāḥ Saubhara from Ayāsya Āṅgirasa; Ayāsya Āṅgirasa from Ābhūti Tvaṣṭra; Ābhūti Tvaṣṭra from Viśvarūpa Tvaṣṭra; Viśvarūpa Tvaṣṭra from the two Aśvins; the two Aśvins from Dadhyañc Ātharvaṇa; Dadhyañc Ātharvaṇa from Atharvan Daiva; Atharvan Daiva from Mṛtyu Prādhvaṃsana; Mṛtyu Prādhvaṃsana from Pradhvaṃsana; Pradhvaṃsana from Eka Ṛṣi; Eka Ṛṣi from Vipracitti; Vipracitti from Vyaṣṭi; Vyaṣṭi from Sanāru; Sanāru from Sanātana; Sanātana from Sanaga; Sanaga from Parameṣṭhin; and Parameṣṭhin from Brahman. Brahman is self-existent. Homage to Brahman!

CHAPTER 3

1 Janaka, the king of Videha, once set out to perform a sacrifice at which he intended to give lavish gifts to the officiating priests. Brahmins from the Kuru and Pañcāla regions had flocked there for the occasion, and Janaka of Videha wanted to find out which of those Brahmins was the most learned in the Vedas. So he corralled a thousand cows; to the horns of each cow were tied ten pieces of gold.

2 He then addressed those Brahmins: 'Distinguished Brahmins! Let the most learned man among you drive away these cows.' But no one dared. So Yājñavalkya called to his pupil: 'Sāmaśravas! Son, drive these cows away.' And he drove them away. The Brahmins were furious and murmured: 'How dare he claim to be the most learned?'

Now, Janaka of Videha had a Hotṛ priest named Aśvala. He asked: 'Yājñavalkya, do you really think you are the most learned among us?' Yājñavalkya replied: 'We bow humbly to the most learned man! But we are really after the cows, aren't we?' At this the Hotṛ Aśvala became determined to question him.

3 'Yājñavalkya,' he said, 'tell me—when this whole world is caught in the grip of death, when it is overwhelmed by death, how

can the patron of a sacrifice free himself completely from its grip?' Yājñavalkya replied: 'By means of the Hotṛ priest—that is, by means of the fire, by means of speech. Clearly, the Hotṛ priest of the sacrifice is speech. So this speech—it is this fire here; it is the Hotṛ priest; it is freedom; and it is complete freedom.'

4 'Yājñavalkya,' Aśvala said again, 'tell me—when this whole world is caught in the grip of days and nights, when it is overwhelmed by days and nights, how can the patron of a sacrifice free himself completely from their grip?' Yājñavalkya replied: 'By means of the Adhvaryu priest—that is, by means of sight, by means of the sun. Clearly, the Adhvaryu priest of the sacrifice is sight. So this sight—it is that sun up there; it is the Adhvaryu priest; it is freedom; and it is complete freedom.'

5 'Yājñavalkya,' Aśvala said again, 'tell me—when this whole world is caught in the grip of the fortnights of the waxing and the waning moon, when it is overwhelmed by the fortnights of the waxing and the waning moon, how can the patron of a sacrifice free himself from their grip?' Yājñavalkya replied: 'By means of the Udgātṛ priest—that is, by means of the wind, by means of breath. Clearly, the Udgātṛ priest of the sacrifice is breath. So this breath—it is the wind; it is the Udgātṛ priest; it is freedom; it is complete freedom.'

6 'Yājñavalkya,' Aśvala said again, 'tell me—when this intermediate region provides no support of any kind, how does the patron of a sacrifice climb up to heaven?' Yājñavalkya replied: 'By means of the Brahman priest—that is, by means of the mind, by means of the moon. Clearly, the Brahman priest of the sacrifice is the mind. So this mind—it is that moon up there; it is the Brahman priest; it is freedom; it is the complete freedom.'

These are the types of complete freedom. Next, the equivalents.

7 'Yājñavalkya,' Aśvala said again, 'tell me—today at the sacrifice, how many verses will the Hotṛ priest here use?'

'Three.'

'What are they?'

'The verse recited before the offering and the verse that accompanies the offering. The third is the verse of praise.'

'What does he win through them?'

'Whatever supports life in this world.'

8 'Yājñavalkya,' Aśvala said again, 'tell me—today at the

sacrifice, how many oblations will the Adhvaryu priest here offer in the fire?'

'Three.'

'What are they?'

'The oblations that flare up when they are offered; those that overflow when they are offered; and the ones that lie down when they are offered.'

'What does he win through them?'

'What he wins by offering the oblations that flare up is the world of gods, for, in a way, that world shines. What he wins by offering the oblations that overflow (*ati-nedante*) is the world of ancestors, for, in a way, that world is over above (*ati*). And what he wins by offering the oblations that lie down (*adhi-śerate*) is the world of men, for, in a way, that world is here below (*adha*).

9 'Yājñavalkya,' Aśvala said again, 'tell me—with how many deities will the Brahman priest, seated on the southern side, protect the sacrifice today?' Yājñavalkya replied: 'With one.'

'Who is it?'

'The mind itself, for the mind is without limit and the All-gods are without limit. Limitless also is the world he wins by it.'

10 'Yājñavalkya,' Aśvala said again, 'tell me—today at the sacrifice, how many hymns of praise will the Udgātṛ priest here sing?' Yājñavalkya replied: 'Three.'

'What are they?'

'The hymn recited before the sacrifice and the hymn that accompanies the sacrifice. The hymn of praise is the third.'

'What are they with respect to the body (*ātman*)?'

'The hymn recited before the sacrifice is just the out-breath; the hymn that accompanies the sacrifice is the in-breath; and the hymn of praise is the inter-breath.'

'What does he win through them?'

'He wins the earthly world through the hymn recited before the sacrifice, the intermediate world through the hymn that accompanies the sacrifice, and the heavenly world through the hymn of praise.'

Thereupon, Hotṛ Aśvala fell silent.

2 Then Jāratkārava Ārtabhāga began to question him. 'Yājñavalkya,' he said, 'tell me—how many graspers are

there and how many overgraspers?' Yājñavalkya replied: 'There are eight graspers and eight overgraspers.'

'What are the eight graspers? And what are the eight overgraspers?'

2 'The out-breath is a grasper, which is itself grasped by the in-breath, the overgrasper; for one smells odours by means of the in-breath.

3 'Speech is a grasper, which is itself grasped by word, the overgrasper; for one utters words by means of speech.

4 'The tongue is a grasper, which is itself grasped by flavour, the overgrasper; for one tastes flavours by means of the tongue.

5 'Sight is a grasper, which is itself grasped by visible appearances, the overgrasper; for one sees visible appearances by means of sight.

6 'Hearing is a grasper, which is itself grasped by sound, the overgrasper; for one hears sounds by means of hearing.

7 'The mind is a grasper, which is itself grasped by desire, the overgrasper; for one entertains desires by means of the mind.

8 'The hands are graspers, which are themselves grasped by action, the overgrasper; for one performs actions by means of the hands.

9 'The skin is a grasper, which is itself grasped by touch, the overgrasper; for one senses various types of touch by means of the skin.

'These, then, are the eight graspers and the eight overgraspers.'

10 'Yājñavalkya,' Ārtabhāga said again, 'tell me—since this whole world is food for Death, of which deity is Death the food?' Yājñavalkya replied: 'Death is fire, and it is the food of water. [Whoever knows this] averts repeated death.'

11 'Yājñavalkya,' Ārtabhāga said again, 'tell me—when a man dies, do his breaths depart from him, or do they not?' 'They do not,' replied Yājñavalkya. 'They accumulate within this very body, causing it to swell up and to become bloated. So a dead man lies bloated.'

12 'Yājñavalkya,' Ārtabhāga said again, 'tell me—when a man dies, what is it that does not leave him?' 'His name,' replied Yājñavalkya. 'A name is without limit, and the All-gods are without limit. Limitless also is the world he wins by it.'

13 'Yājñavalkya,' Ārtabhāga said again, 'tell me—when a man

has died, and his speech disappears into fire, his breath into the wind, his sight into the sun, his mind into the moon, his hearing into the quarters, his physical body into the earth, his self (*ātman*) into space, the hair of his body into plants, the hair of his head into trees, and his blood and semen into water—what then happens to that person?' Yājñavalkya replied: 'My friend, we cannot talk about this in public. Take my hand, Ārtabhāga; let's go and discuss this in private.'

So they left and talked about it. And what did they talk about?—they talked about nothing but action. And what did they praise?—they praised nothing but action. Yājñavalkya told him: 'A man turns into something good by good action and into something bad by bad action.'

Thereupon, Jāratkārava Ārtabhāga fell silent.

3 Then Bhujyu Lāhyāyani began to question him. 'Yājñavalkya,' he said, 'once, while we were itinerant students travelling around in the land of the Madras, we visited the home of Patañcala Kāpya. He had a daughter possessed by a Gandharva. We asked him who he was, and the Gandharva said that he was Sudhanvan Āṅgirasa. In the course of asking him about the ends of the worlds, we enquired: "Where in the world are the Pārikṣitas?" I put the same question to you, Yājñavalkya—where are the Pārikṣitas?'

2 Yājñavalkya replied: 'He no doubt told you, "They have gone to the place where those who offer horse sacrifices go."'

'But where do those who offer horse sacrifices go?'

'"The visible world is as wide as the distance the sun's chariot travels in thirty-two days. The earth is twice as wide as the visible world and surrounds it on all sides, while the ocean is twice as wide as the earth and surrounds it on all sides. Now, there is a gap as fine as a razor's edge or a gnat's wing. Taking the form of a bird, Indra handed the Pārikṣitas to the wind. The wind placed them within itself and carried them to the place where those who had offered horse sacrifices were."—What that Gandharva praised in that manner was clearly the wind. Both individual things and the totality of all things, therefore, are just the wind. Whosoever knows this averts repeated death.'

Thereupon, Bhujyu Lāhyāyani fell silent.

4 Then Uṣasta Cākrāyaṇa began to question him. 'Yājñavalkya,' he said, 'explain to me the *brahman* that is plain and not cryptic, the self (*ātman*) that is within all.'

'The self within all is this self of yours.'

'Which one is the self within all, Yājñavalkya?'

'Who breathes out with the out-breath—he is the self of yours that is within all. Who breathes in with the in-breath—he is the self of yours that is within all. Who breathes across with the inter-breath—he is the self of yours that is within all. Who breathes up with the up-breath—he is the self of yours that is within all. The self within all is this self of yours.'

2 Uṣasta Cākrāyaṇa retorted: 'That's a fine explanation! It's like saying "This is a cow and that is a horse!" Come on, give me a real explanation of the *brahman* that is plain and not cryptic, of the self that is within all.'

'The self within all is this self of yours.'

'Which one is the self within all, Yājñavalkya?'

'You can't see the seer who does the seeing; you can't hear the hearer who does the hearing; you can't think of the thinker who does the thinking; and you can't perceive the perceiver who does the perceiving. The self within all is this self of yours. All else besides this is grief!'

Thereupon, Uṣasta Cākrāyaṇa fell silent.

5 Then Kahola Kauṣītakeya began to question him. 'Yājñavalkya,' he said, 'explain to me the *brahman* that is plain and not cryptic, the self that is within all.'

'The self within all is this self of yours.'

'Which one is the self within all, Yājñavalkya?'

'He is the one who is beyond hunger and thirst, sorrow and delusion, old age and death. It is when they come to know this self that Brahmins give up the desire for sons, the desire for wealth, and the desire for worlds, and undertake the mendicant life. The desire for sons, after all, is the same as the desire for wealth, and the desire for wealth is the same as the desire for worlds—both are simply desires. Therefore, a Brahmin should stop being a pundit and try to live like a child. When he has stopped living like a child or a pundit, he becomes a sage. And when he has stopped living like a sage or the way he was before he became a sage, he becomes a

Brahmin. He remains just such a Brahmin, no matter how he may live. All besides this is grief.'

Thereupon, Kahola Kauṣītakeya fell silent.

6 Then Gārgī Vācaknavī began to question him. 'Yājñavalkya,' she said, 'tell me—since this whole world is woven back and forth on water, on what, then, is water woven back and forth?'

'On air, Gārgī.'

'On what, then, is air woven back and forth?'

'On the worlds of the intermediate region, Gārgī.'

'On what, then, are the worlds of the intermediate region woven back and forth?'

'On the worlds of the Gandharvas, Gārgī.'

'On what, then, are the worlds of the Gandharvas woven back and forth?'

'On the worlds of the sun, Gārgī.'

'On what, then, are the worlds of the sun woven back and forth?'

'On the worlds of the moon, Gārgī.'

'On what, then, are the worlds of the moon woven back and forth?'

'On the worlds of the stars, Gārgī.'

'On what, then, are the worlds of the stars woven back and forth?'

'On the worlds of the gods, Gārgī.'

'On what, then, are the worlds of the gods woven back and forth?'

'On the worlds of Indra, Gārgī.'

'On what, then, are the worlds of Indra woven back and forth?'

'On the worlds of Prajāpati, Gārgī.'

'On what, then, are the worlds of Prajāpati woven back and forth?'

'On the worlds of *brahman*, Gārgī.'

'On what, then, are the worlds of *brahman* woven back and forth?'

At this point Yājñavalkya told her: 'Don't ask too many questions, Gārgī, or your head will shatter apart! You are asking too many questions about a deity about whom one should not ask too many questions. So, Gārgī, don't ask too many questions!'

Thereupon, Gārgī Vācaknavī fell silent.

7 Then Uddālaka Āruṇi began to question him. 'Yājñavalkya,' he said, 'once we were living in the land of the Madras learning about the sacrifice in the house of Patañcala Kāpya. He had a wife possessed by a Gandharva. We asked him who he was, and the Gandharva said that he was Kabandha Ātharvaṇa. He then asked Patañcala Kāpya and the students there who were learning about the sacrifice: "Tell me, Kāpya—do you know the string on which this world and the next, as well as all beings, are strung together?" "That, my lord, I do not know," replied Patañcala Kāpya. He then asked Patañcala Kāpya and the students there who were learning about the sacrifice: "Tell me, Kāpya—do you know the inner controller of this world and the next, as well as of all beings, who controls them from within?" "That, my lord, I do not know," replied Patañcala Kāpya. He then told Patañcala Kāpya and the students there who were learning about the sacrifice: "Clearly, Kāpya, if a man knows what that string is and who that inner controller is—he knows *brahman*; he knows the worlds; he knows the gods; he knows the Vedas; he knows the spirits; he knows the self; he knows all."

'And I know it. So, if you drive away the cows meant for the Brahmins, Yājñavalkya, without knowing what that string is and who that inner controller is, your head will shatter apart!'

'Gautama, I do know what that string is and who that inner controller is.'

'Of course, anyone can say, "I know! I know!" Tell us what precisely you know.'

2 Yājñavalkya told him: 'Clearly, Gautama, that string is the wind. It is on the string of wind, Gautama, that this world and the next, as well as all beings, are strung together. That is why people say of a dead man, "His bodily parts have come unstrung", for they are strung together, Gautama, on the string of wind.'

'Quite right, Yājñavalkya. Now tell us who the inner controller is.'

3 'This self (*ātman*) of yours who is present within but is different from the earth, whom the earth does not know, whose body is

the earth, and who controls the earth from within—he is the inner controller, the immortal.

4 'This self of yours who is present within but is different from the waters, whom the waters do not know, whose body is the waters, and who controls the waters from within—he is the inner controller, the immortal.

5 'This self of yours who is present within but is different from the fire, whom the fire does not know, whose body is the fire, and who controls the fire from within—he is the inner controller, the immortal.

6 'This self of yours who is present within but is different from the intermediate region, whom the intermediate region does not know, whose body is the intermediate region, and who controls the intermediate region from within—he is the inner controller, the immortal.

7 'This self of yours who is present within but is different from the wind, whom the wind does not know, whose body is the wind, and who controls the wind from within—he is the inner controller, the immortal.

8 'This self of yours who is present within but is different from the sky, whom the sky does not know, whose body is the sky, and who controls the sky from within—he is the inner controller, the immortal.

9 'This self of yours who is present within but is different from the sun, whom the sun does not know, whose body is the sun, and who controls the sun from within—he is the inner controller, the immortal.

10 'This self of yours who is present within but is different from the quarters, whom the quarters do not know, whose body is the quarters, and who controls the quarters from within—he is the inner controller, the immortal.

11 'This self of yours who is present within but is different from the moon and the stars, whom the moon and the stars do not know, whose body is the moon and the stars, and who controls the moon and the stars from within—he is the inner controller, the immortal.

12 'This self of yours who is present within but is different from space, whom space does not know, whose body is space, and who controls space from within—he is the inner controller, the immortal.

[13] 'This self of yours who is present within but is different from darkness, whom darkness does not know, whose body is darkness, and who controls darkness from within—he is the inner controller, the immortal.

[14] 'This self of yours who is present within but is different from light, whom light does not know, whose body is light, and who controls light from within—he is the inner controller, the immortal.'

That was with respect to the divine sphere. [15] What follows is with respect to beings.

'This self of yours who is present within but is different from all beings, whom all beings do not know, whose body is all beings, and who controls all beings from within—he is the inner controller, the immortal.'

That was with respect to beings. [16] What follows is with respect to the body (*ātman*).

'This self of yours who is present within but is different from the breath, whom the breath does not know, whose body is the breath, and who controls the breath from within—he is the inner controller, the immortal.

[17] 'This self of yours who is present within but is different from speech, whom speech does not know, whose body is speech, and who controls speech from within—he is the inner controller, the immortal.

[18] 'This self of yours who is present within but is different from sight, whom sight does not know, whose body is sight, and who controls sight from within—he is the inner controller, the immortal.

[19] 'This self of yours who is present within but is different from hearing, whom hearing does not know, whose body is hearing, and who controls hearing from within—he is the inner controller, the immortal.

[20] 'This self of yours who is present within but is different from the mind, whom the mind does not know, whose body is the mind, and who controls the mind from within—he is the inner controller, the immortal.

[21] 'This self of yours who is present within but is different from the skin, whom the skin does not know, whose body is the skin, and who controls the skin from within—he is the inner controller, the immortal.

22 'This self of yours who is present within but is different from perception, whom perception does not know, whose body is perception, and who controls perception from within—he is the inner controller, the immortal.

23 'This self of yours who is present within but is different from the semen, whom the semen does not know, whose body is the semen, and who controls the semen from within—he is the inner controller, the immortal.

'He sees, but he can't be seen; he hears, but he can't be heard; he thinks, but he can't be thought of; he perceives, but he can't be perceived. Besides him, there is no one who sees, no one who hears, no one who thinks, and no one who perceives. It is this self of yours who is the inner controller, the immortal. All besides this is grief.'

Thereupon, Uddālaka Āruṇi fell silent.

8 Then (Gārgī) Vācaknavī spoke. 'Distinguished Brahmins!' she said. 'I am going to ask this man two questions. If he can give me the answers to them, none of you will be able to defeat him in a theological debate.'

'Ask, Gārgī.'

2 She said: 'I rise to challenge you, Yājñavalkya, with two questions, much as a fierce warrior of Kāśi or Videha, stringing his unstrung bow and taking two deadly arrows in his hand, would rise to challenge an enemy. Give me the answers to them!'

'Ask, Gārgī.'

3 She said: 'The things above the sky, the things below the earth, and the things between the earth and the sky, as well as all those things people here refer to as past, present, and future—on what, Yājñavalkya, are all these woven back and forth?'

4 He replied: 'The things above the sky, the things below the earth, and the things between the earth and the sky, as well as all those things people here refer to as past, present, and future—on space, Gārgī, are all these woven back and forth.'

5 She responded: 'All honour to you, Yājñavalkya. You really cleared that up for me! Get ready for the second.'

'Ask, Gārgī.'

6 She said: 'The things above the sky, the things below the earth, and the things between the earth and the sky, as well as all those

things people here refer to as past, present, and future—on what, Yājñavalkya, are all these woven back and forth?'

7 He replied: 'The things above the sky, the things below the earth, and the things between the earth and the sky, as well as all those things people here refer to as past, present, and future—on space, Gārgī, are all these woven back and forth.'

'On what, then, is space woven back and forth?'

8 He replied: 'That, Gārgī, is the imperishable, and Brahmins refer to it like this—it is neither coarse nor fine; it is neither short nor long; it has neither blood nor fat; it is without shadow or darkness; it is without air or space; it is without contact; it has no taste or smell; it is without sight or hearing; it is without speech or mind; it is without energy, breath, or mouth; it is beyond measure; it has nothing within it or outside of it; it does not eat anything; and no one eats it.

9 'This is the imperishable, Gārgī, at whose command the sun and the moon stand apart. This is the imperishable, Gārgī, at whose command the earth and the sky stand apart. This is the imperishable, Gārgī, at whose command seconds and hours, days and nights, fortnights and months, seasons and years stand apart. This is the imperishable, Gārgī, at whose command rivers flow from the snowy mountains in their respective directions, some to the east and others to the west. This is the imperishable, Gārgī, at whose command people flatter donors, and gods are dependent on patrons of sacrifices, and forefathers, on ancestral offerings.

10 'Without knowing this imperishable, Gārgī, even if a man were to make offerings, to offer sacrifices, and to perform austerities in this world for many thousands of years, all that would come to naught. Pitiful is the man, Gārgī, who departs from this world without knowing this imperishable. But a man who departs from this world after he has come to know this imperishable—he, Gārgī, is a Brahmin.

11 'This is the imperishable, Gārgī, which sees but can't be seen; which hears but can't be heard; which thinks but can't be thought of; which perceives but can't be perceived. Besides this imperishable, there is no one that sees, no one that hears, no one that thinks, and no one that perceives.

'On this very imperishable, Gārgī, space is woven back and forth.'

12 'Distinguished Brahmins!' said Gārgī. 'You should consider yourself lucky if you escape from this man by merely paying him your respects. None of you will ever defeat him in a theological debate.'

Thereupon, Vācaknavī fell silent.

9 Then Vidagdha Śākalya began to question him. 'Tell me, Yājñavalkya—how many gods are there?' Saying, 'As many as are mentioned in the ritual invocation within the laud to the All-gods', he answered in accordance with this very ritual invocation: 'Three and three hundred, and three and three thousand.'

'Yes, of course,' he said, 'but really, Yājñavalkya, how many gods are there?'

'Thirty-three.'

'Yes, of course,' he said, 'but really, Yājñavalkya, how many gods are there?'

'Six.'

'Yes, of course,' he said, 'but really, Yājñavalkya, how many gods are there?'

'Three.'

'Yes, of course,' he said, 'but really, Yājñavalkya, how many gods are there?'

'Two.'

'Yes, of course,' he said, 'but really, Yājñavalkya, how many gods are there?'

'One and a half.'

'Yes, of course,' he said, 'but really, Yājñavalkya, how many gods are there?'

'One.'

'Yes, of course,' he said, 'but then who are those three and three hundred, and those three and three thousand?'

2 'They are only the powers of the gods,' Yājñavalkya replied. 'There are only thirty-three gods.'

'Who are those thirty-three?'

'The eight Vasus, the eleven Rudras, and the twelve Ādityas—that makes thirty-one. Then there are Indra and Prajāpati, making a total of thirty-three.'

3 'Who are the Vasus?'

'The Vasus are fire, earth, wind, the intermediate region, sun, sky, moon, and stars. They are called Vasus because this whole treasure (*vasu*) is entrusted to them.'

4 'Who are the Rudras?'

'The ten vital functions (*prāṇa*) in a man, with the self (*ātman*) as the eleventh. They make people weep when they depart from this mortal body. They are called Rudras because they make people weep (*rud-*).'

5 'Who are the Ādityas?'

'The Ādityas are the twelve months of the year, for they carry off this whole world as they proceed. They are called Ādityas because they carry off (*ādadānāḥ*) this whole world as they proceed (*yanti*).'

6 'Who is Indra? And who is Prajāpati?'

'Indra is just the thunder, and Prajāpati is the sacrifice.'

'What is thunder?'

'The thunderbolt.'

'What is the sacrifice?'

'The sacrificial animals.'

7 'Who are the six?'

'The six are fire and earth, wind and the intermediate region, sun and sky—for these six are this whole world.'

8 'Who are the three gods?'

'Just these three worlds, for all the gods live in them.'

'Who are the two gods?'

'Food and breath.'

'Who are the one and a half?'

'The purifying wind that is blowing here.
9 Now, some may ask: "But the purifying wind here blows as one only. So how can he be one and a half?" He is one and a half (*adhyardha*) because in him this whole world increases (*adhyardh-*).'

'Who is the one god?'

'Breath. He is called "Brahman" and "Tyad".'

10 'The person whose abode is the earth, whose world is fire, and whose light is the mind—should someone know that person, the final goal of every self (*ātman*), he would be a man who truly knows, Yājñavalkya.'

'I know that person, the final goal of every self, of whom you speak. He is none other than this bodily person. But tell me, Śākalya—who is his god?'

'The immortal,' Śākalya replied.

11 'The person whose abode is passion, whose world is the heart, and whose light is the mind—should someone know that person, the final goal of every self, he would be a man who truly knows, Yājñavalkya.'

'I know that person, the final goal of every self, of whom you speak. He is none other than this person immersed in passion. But tell me, Śākalya —who is his god?'

'Women,' Śākalya replied.

12 'The person whose abode is visible appearances, whose world is sight, and whose light is the mind—should someone know that person, the final goal of every self, he would be a man who truly knows, Yājñavalkya.'

'I know that person, the final goal of every self, of whom you speak. He is none other than that person up there in the sun. But tell me, Śākalya —who is his god?'

'Truth,' Śākalya replied.

13 'The person whose abode is space, whose world is hearing, and whose light is the mind—should someone know that person, the final goal of every self, he would be a man who truly knows, Yājñavalkya.'

'I know that person, the final goal of every self, of whom you speak. He is none other than this person connected with hearing and echo. But tell me, Śākalya —who is his god?'

'The quarters,' Śākalya replied.

14 'The person whose abode is darkness, whose world is the heart, and whose light is the mind—should someone know that person, the final goal of every self, he would be a man who truly knows, Yājñavalkya.'

'I know that person, the final goal of every self, of whom you speak. He is none other than this person consisting of shadow. But tell me, Śākalya —who is his god?'

'Death,' Śākalya replied.

15 'The person whose abode is visible appearances, whose world is sight, and whose light is the mind—should someone know that person, the final goal of every self, he would be a man who truly knows, Yājñavalkya.'

'I know that person, the final goal of every self, of whom you speak. He is none other than this person here in a mirror. But tell me, Śākalya—who is his god?'

'Life,' Śākalya replied.

16 'The person whose abode is the waters, whose world is the heart, and whose light is the mind—should someone know that person, the final goal of every self, he would be a man who truly knows, Yājñavalkya.'

'I know that person, the final goal of every self, of whom you speak. He is none other than this person here in the waters. But tell me, Śākalya —who is his god?'

'Varuṇa,' Śākalya replied.

17 'The person whose abode is semen, whose world is the heart, and whose light is the mind—should someone know that person, the final goal of every self, he would be a man who truly knows, Yājñavalkya.'

'I know that person, the final goal of every self, of whom you speak. He is none other than this person associated with a son. But tell me, Śākalya —who is his god?'

'Prajāpati,' Śākalya replied.

18 At this point Yājñavalkya exclaimed: 'Poor Śākalya! I'm afraid these Brahmins have made you their cat's-paw.'

19 Śākalya said: 'Tell me, Yājñavalkya—what is the formulation of truth (*brahman*) you know that has enabled you here to out-talk these Brahmins of Kuru and Pañcāla?'

'I know the quarters together with their gods and foundations.'

'Since you say that you know the quarters together with their gods and foundations, 20 according to you, who is the god of the eastern quarter?'

'The sun.'

'On what is the sun founded?'

'On sight.'

'On what is sight founded?'

'On visible appearances, for one sees visible appearances with one's sight.'

'On what are visible appearances founded?'

'On the heart, for one recognizes visible appearances with the heart. So visible appearances are founded on the heart.'

'You're absolutely right, Yājñavalkya! 21 According to you, who is the god of the southern quarter?'

'Yama.'

'On what is Yama founded?'

'On the sacrifice.'

'On what is the sacrifice founded?'

'On the sacrificial gift.'

'On what is the sacrificial gift founded?'

'On faith, for a man gives a sacrificial gift only when he has faith. So the sacrificial gift is founded on faith.'

'On what is faith founded?'

'On the heart, for one recognizes faith with the heart. So faith is founded on the heart.'

'You're absolutely right, Yājñavalkya! 22According to you, who is the god of the western quarter?'

'Varuṇa.'

'On what is Varuṇa founded?'

'On water.'

'On what is water founded?'

'On semen.'

'On what is semen founded?'

'On the heart. For that very reason, when someone has a son who is a picture of him, people say: "He's dropped right out of his heart! He's carved from his very heart!" So semen is founded on the heart.'

'You're absolutely right, Yājñavalkya! 23According to you, who is the god of the northern quarter?'

'The moon.'

'On what is the moon founded?'

'On the sacrificial consecration.'

'On what is the sacrificial consecration founded?'

'On truth. For that very reason, they instruct a man consecrated for sacrifice: "Speak the truth." So the sacrificial consecration is founded on truth.'

'On what is truth founded?'

'On the heart, for one recognizes truth with the heart. So truth is founded on the heart.'

'You're absolutely right, Yājñavalkya! 24According to you, who is the god of the zenith, the fixed quarter?'

'Fire.'

'On what is fire founded?'

'On speech.'

'On what is speech founded?'

'On the heart.'

'On what is the heart founded?'

25 At this Yājñavalkya exploded: 'What an imbecile you are to think that it could be founded anywhere other than ourselves! If it were anywhere other than ourselves, dogs would eat it, or birds would tear it up.'

26 'On what are you and your self (*ātman*) founded?'

'On the out-breath.'

'On what is the out-breath founded?'

'On the in-breath.'

'On what is the in-breath founded?'

'On the inter-breath.'

'On what is the inter-breath founded?'

'On the up-breath.'

'On what is the up-breath founded?'

'On the link-breath. About this self (*ātman*), one can only say "not ——, not ——". He is ungraspable, for he cannot be grasped. He is undecaying, for he is not subject to decay. He has nothing sticking to him, for he does not stick to anything. He is not bound; yet he neither trembles in fear nor suffers injury. Now, those are the eight abodes, the eight worlds, the eight gods, and the eight persons. I ask you about that person providing the hidden connection (*upaniṣad*)—the one who carries off these other persons, brings them back, and rises above them? If you will not tell me that, your head will shatter apart.'

Śākalya did not know him, and his head did, indeed, shatter apart. Robbers, moreover, stole his bones, mistaking them for something else.

27 Yājñavalkya then spoke: 'Distinguished Brahmins! If any one of you would like to question me, he may do so; or, if you prefer, all of you may question me together. Or else, if any one of you would like me to, I will question him; or, if you prefer, I will question all of you together.' But those Brahmins did not dare.

28 So he questioned them with these verses:

> Man is like a mighty tree—
>   that's the truth.
> His body hairs are its leaves,
> His skin is its outer bark.
> Blood flows from his skin,

As sap from the bark of a tree.
Blood flows when the skin is pricked,
As sap, when the bark is slit.
His flesh is the sapwood;
His sinews are the fibres—
  that's certain.
His bones are the heartwood;
And his marrow resembles the pith.

A tree when it's cut down,
Grows anew from its root;
From what root does a mortal man grow,
When he is cut down by death?

Do not say, 'From the seed';
For it's produced from him
  while he is still alive;
And like a tree
  sprouting from a seed,
It takes birth at once,
  even before he dies.

A tree, when it's uprooted,
Will not sprout out again;
From what root does a mortal man grow,
When he is cut down by death?

Once he's born,
  he can't be born again.
Who, I ask,
  will beget him again?

Perception, bliss, *brahman*,
The gift of those who give,
The highest good—
  awaits those who know this
  and stand firm.

CHAPTER 4

1 Once when Janaka, the king of Videha, was formally seated, Yājñavalkya came up to him. Janaka asked him:

'Yājñavalkya, why have you come? Are you after cows or subtle disquisitions?' He replied: 'Both, your majesty. 2 Let's hear what they have told you.'

'"*Brahman* is speech." That's what Jitvan Śailini told me,' said Janaka.

'Śailini told you "*Brahman* is speech?" Why, that's like someone telling that he has a father, or a mother, or a teacher! He probably reasoned: "What could a person who cannot speak possibly have?" But did he tell you what its abode and foundation are?'

'He did not tell me that.'

'Then it's a one-legged *brahman*, Your Majesty.'

'Why don't you tell us that yourself, Yājñavalkya?'

'Speech itself is its abode, and space is its foundation. One should venerate it as knowledge.'

'What constitutes knowledge, Yājñavalkya?'

'Speech itself, Your Majesty,' he replied. 'For surely, Your Majesty, it is through speech that we come to know a counterpart. Ṛgveda, Yajurveda, Sāmaveda, the Atharva-Āṅgiras, histories, ancient tales, sciences, hidden teachings (*upaniṣad*), verses, aphorisms, explanations, and glosses; offerings and oblations; food and drink; this world and the next world; and all beings—it is through speech, Your Majesty, that we come to know all these. So clearly, Your Majesty, the highest *brahman* is speech. When a man knows and venerates it as such, speech never abandons him, and all beings flock to him; he becomes a god and joins the company of gods.'

Janaka of Videha exclaimed: 'I'll give you a thousand cows together with bulls and elephants!'

Yājñavalkya replied: 'My father believed that one should never accept a gift before giving instruction. 3Let's hear what else they have told you.'

'"*Brahman* is breath." That's what Udaṅka Śaulbāyana told me,' said Janaka.

'Śaulbāyana told you "*Brahman* is breath?" Why, that's like someone telling that he has a father, or a mother, or a teacher! He probably reasoned: "What could a person who cannot breathe possibly have?" But did he tell you what its abode and foundation are?'

'He did not tell me that.'

'Then it's a one-legged *brahman*, Your Majesty.'

'Why don't you tell us that yourself, Yājñavalkya?'

'Breath itself is its abode, and space is its foundation. One should venerate it as "dear".'

'What constitutes "dear", Yājñavalkya?'

'Breath itself, Your Majesty,' he replied. 'For surely, Your Majesty, it is for the love of one's breath that one officiates at the sacrifice of a man at whose sacrifices one is forbidden to officiate or accepts gifts from a man from whom one is forbidden to accept gifts. And if a man is afraid of getting killed when he travels somewhere, Your Majesty, it is because he loves his breath. So clearly, Your Majesty, the highest *brahman* is breath. When a man knows and venerates it as such, breath never abandons him, and all beings flock to him; he becomes a god and joins the company of gods.'

Janaka of Videha exclaimed: 'I'll give you a thousand cows together with bulls and elephants!'

Yājñavalkya replied: 'My father believed that one should never accept a gift before giving instruction. 4 Let's hear what else they have told you.'

'"*Brahman* is sight." That's what Barku Vārṣṇa told me,' said Janaka.

'Vārṣṇa told you "*Brahman* is sight?" Why, that's like someone telling that he has a father, or a mother, or a teacher! He probably reasoned: "What could a person who cannot see possibly have?" But did he tell you what its abode and foundation are?'

'He did not tell me that.'

'Then it's a one-legged *brahman*, Your Majesty.'

'Why don't you tell us that yourself, Yājñavalkya?'

'Sight itself is its abode, and space is its foundation. One should venerate it as truth.'

'What constitutes truth, Yājñavalkya?'

'Sight itself, Your Majesty,' he replied. 'For surely, Your Majesty, when they ask someone who has seen something with his sight: "Did you see it?" and he replies: "I saw it," it is taken as the truth. So clearly, Your Majesty, the highest *brahman* is sight. When a man knows and venerates it as such, sight never abandons him, and all beings flock to him; he becomes a god and joins the company of gods.'

Janaka of Videha exclaimed: 'I'll give you a thousand cows together with bulls and elephants!'

Yājñavalkya replied: 'My father believed that one should never accept a gift before giving instruction. [5] Let's hear what else they have told you.'

' "*Brahman* is hearing." That's what Gardabhīvipīta Bhāradvāja told me,' said Janaka.

'Bhāradvāja told you "*Brahman* is hearing?" Why, that's like someone telling that he has a father, or a mother, or a teacher! He probably reasoned: "What could a person who cannot hear possibly have?" But did he tell you what its abode and foundation are?'

'He did not tell me that.'

'Then it's a one-legged *brahman*, Your Majesty.'

'Why don't you tell us that yourself, Yājñavalkya?'

'Hearing itself is its abode, and space is its foundation. One should venerate it as limitless.'

'What constitutes the limitless, Yājñavalkya?'

'The quarters themselves, Your Majesty,' he replied. 'Therefore, towards whichever quarter a man may travel, Your Majesty, he will never reach its limit, for the quarters are limitless. And the quarters, Your Majesty, are the same as hearing. So clearly, Your Majesty, the highest *brahman* is hearing. When a man knows and venerates it as such, hearing never abandons him, and all beings flock to him; he becomes a god and joins the company of gods.'

Janaka of Videha exclaimed: 'I'll give you a thousand cows together with bulls and elephants!'

Yājñavalkya replied: 'My father believed that one should never accept a gift before giving instruction. [6] Let's hear what else they have told you,' said Janaka.

' "*Brahman* is the mind." That's what Satyakāma Jābāla told me.'

'Jābāla told you "*Brahman* is the mind?" Why, that's like someone telling that he has a father, or a mother, or a teacher! He probably reasoned: "What could a person who has no mind possibly have?" But did he tell you what its abode and foundation are?'

'He did not tell me that.'

'Then it's a one-legged *brahman*, Your Majesty.'

'Why don't you tell us that yourself, Yājñavalkya?'

'The mind itself is its abode, and space is its foundation. One should venerate it as bliss.'

'What constitutes bliss, Yājñavalkya?'

'The mind itself, Your Majesty,' he replied. 'For surely, Your Majesty, it is with the mind that a man takes a woman to himself and through her fathers a son who resembles him. And that is bliss. So clearly, Your Majesty, the highest *brahman* is the mind. When a man knows and venerates it as such, the mind never abandons him, and all beings flock to him; he becomes a god and joins the company of gods.'

Janaka of Videha exclaimed: 'I'll give you a thousand cows together with bulls and elephants!'

Yājñavalkya replied: 'My father believed that one should never accept a gift before giving instruction. 7 Let's hear what else they have told you.'

'"*Brahman* is the heart." That's what Vidagdha Śākalya told me,' said Janaka.

'Śākalya told you "*Brahman* is the heart?" Why, that's like someone telling that he has a father, or a mother, or a teacher! He probably reasoned: "What could a person who has no heart possibly have?" But did he tell you what its abode and foundation are?'

'He did not tell me that.'

'Then it's a one-legged *brahman*, Your Majesty.'

'Why don't you tell us that yourself, Yājñavalkya?'

'The heart itself is its abode, and space is its foundation. One should venerate it as stability.'

'What constitutes stability, Yājñavalkya?'

'The heart itself, Your Majesty,' he replied. 'For surely, Your Majesty, the heart is the abode of all beings; the heart is the foundation of all beings. For it is on the heart that all the beings are founded. So clearly, Your Majesty, the highest *brahman* is the heart. When a man knows and venerates it as such, the heart never abandons him, and all beings flock to him; he becomes a god and joins the company of gods.'

Janaka of Videha exclaimed: 'I'll give you a thousand cows together with bulls and elephants!'

Yājñavalkya replied: 'My father believed that one should never accept a gift before giving instruction.'

2 Janaka, the king of Videha, got down from his seat, came up to him, and said: 'Homage to you, Yājñavalkya. Please teach me.'

Yājñavalkya replied: 'Just as a king, when he is about to undertake a great expedition, would equip himself with a chariot or a ship, so have you equipped yourself with these hidden teachings (*upaniṣad*). You are so eminent and rich; you have learned the Vedas; and you are versed in the hidden teachings (*upaniṣad*). So can you tell me where you will go when you leave this world?'

'No, sir. I don't know where I'll go.'

'Well, I'll tell you where you will go.'

'Do tell me, sir.'

2 'Clearly, the true name of the person in the right eye is Indha. Even though he is really Indha, people cryptically call him 'Indra', because gods in some ways love the cryptic and despise the plain.
3 What looks like a person in the left eye, on the other hand, is his wife Virāj. Their meeting place is the space within the heart, their food is the red lump in the heart, and their garment is the mesh-like substance within the heart. The path along which they travel is the vein that goes up from the heart. The veins called Hitā that are located in the heart are as fine as a hair split a thousandfold. Along them the sap flows continuously. In some ways, therefore, this person eats food that is more refined than does the bodily self (*ātman*).

4 'The vital functions (*prāṇa*) of this person that are on his front side constitute the eastern quarter; the vital functions on his right side constitute the southern quarter; the vital functions at his back constitute the western quarter; the vital functions on his left side constitute the northern quarter; the vital functions on his upper side constitute the zenith; the vital functions on his bottom side constitute the nadir; and all his vital functions together constitute all the quarters.

'About this self (*ātman*), one can only say "not ——, not ——." He is ungraspable, for he cannot be grasped. He is undecaying, for he is not subject to decay. He has nothing sticking to him, for he does not stick to anything. He is not bound; yet he neither trembles in fear nor suffers injury. Truly, Janaka, you have attained freedom from fear.'

After Yājñavalkya had said this, Janaka of Videha, replied:

'May that freedom be yours too, Yājñavalkya, you who have taught us that freedom from fear. Homage to you! These people of Videha and I myself—here we are at your service!'

3 One day Yājñavalkya paid a visit to Janaka, the king of Videha, thinking to himself, 'I won't tell him.' But once, when the two were engaged in a discussion about the daily fire sacrifice, Yājñavalkya had granted Janaka of Videha a wish. The wish he chose was the freedom to ask any question at will, and Yājñavalkya had granted it to him. So it was the king who now put the question to him first.

2 'Yājñavalkya, what is the source of light for a person here?'

'The sun, Your Majesty, is his source of light,' he replied. 'It is by the light of the sun that a person sits down, goes about, does his work, and returns.'

'Quite right, Yājñavalkya. 3 But when the sun has set, Yājñavalkya, what then is the source of light for a person here?'

'The moon is then his source of light. It is by the light of the moon that a person sits down, goes about, does his work, and returns.'

'Quite right, Yājñavalkya. 4 But when both the sun and the moon have set, Yājñavalkya, what then is the source of light for a person here?'

'A fire is then his source of light. It is by the light of a fire that a person sits down, goes about, does his work, and returns.'

'Quite right, Yājñavalkya. 5 But when both the sun and the moon have set, Yājñavalkya, and the fire has died out, what then is the source of light for a person here?'

'The voice is then his source of light. It is by the light of the voice that a person sits down, goes about, does his work, and returns. Therefore, Your Majesty, when someone cannot make out even his own hand, he goes straightway towards the spot from where he hears a voice.'

'Quite right, Yājñavalkya. 6 But when both the sun and the moon have set, the fire has died out, and the voice is stilled, Yājñavalkya, what then is the source of light for a person here?'

'The self (*ātman*) is then his source of light. It is by the light of the self that a person sits down, goes about, does his work, and returns.'

7 'Which self is that?'

'It is this person—the one that consists of perception among the vital functions (*prāṇa*), the one that is the inner light within the heart. He travels across both worlds, being common to both. Sometimes he reflects, sometimes he flutters, for when he falls asleep he transcends this world, these visible forms of death.
8 When at birth this person takes on a body, he becomes united with bad things, and when at death he leaves it behind, he gets rid of those bad things.

9 'Now, this person has just two places—this world and the other world. And there is a third, the place of dream where the two meet. Standing there in the place where the two meet, he sees both those places—this world and the other world. Now, that place serves as an entryway to the other world, and as he moves through that entryway he sees both the bad things and the joys.

'This is how he dreams. He takes materials from the entire world and, taking them apart on his own and then on his own putting them back together, he dreams with his own radiance, with his own light. In that place this person becomes his own light.
10 In that place there are no carriages, there are no tandems, and there are no roads; but he creates for himself carriages, tandems, and roads. In that place there are no joys, pleasures, or delights; but he creates for himself joys, pleasures, and delights. In that place there are no pools, ponds, or rivers; but he creates for himself pools, ponds, and rivers—for he is a creator.
11 On this subject, there are these verses:

Subduing by sleep the bodily realm,
Remaining awake, he contemplates
the sleeping senses.
Taking the light, he returns to his place—
The golden person!
The single goose!

12 Guarding by breath the lower nest,
The immortal roams outside the nest;
The immortal goes wherever he wants—
The golden person!
The single goose!

13 Travelling in sleep to places high and low,
The god creates many a visible form—
now dallying with women,

now laughing,
now seeing frightful things.

14 All they see is his pleasure ground;
But him no one sees at all.

'So people say that one should not awaken a man who is sound asleep; it is very hard to cure anyone to whom that person has not returned. Now, people also say that this place of his is the same as the place he is in when he is awake, because one sees in a dream the same things one sees when one is awake. Here, in dream, a man becomes his own light.'

'Here, sir, I'll give you a thousand cows! But you'll have to tell me more than that to get yourself released!'

15 'Well, after this person has enjoyed himself and travelled around in that serene realm and seen for himself the good and the bad, he rushes along the same path and through the same opening back again to the realm of dream. Whatever he may have seen in that serene realm does not follow him, because nothing sticks to this person.'

'Quite right, Yājñavalkya. Here, sir, I'll give you a thousand cows! But you'll have to tell me more than that to get yourself released!'

16 'Well, after this person has enjoyed himself and travelled around in that realm of dream and seen for himself the good and the bad, he rushes along the same path and through the same opening back again to the realm where one is awake. Whatever he may have seen in that realm of dream does not follow him, because nothing sticks to this person.'

'Quite right, Yājñavalkya. Here, sir, I'll give you a thousand cows! But you'll have to tell me more than that to get yourself released!'

17 'Well, after this person has enjoyed himself and travelled around in this realm where one is awake and seen for himself the good and the bad, he rushes along the same path and through the same opening back again to the realm of dream.

18 'It is like this. As a large fish moves between both banks, the nearer and the farther, so this person moves between both realms, the realm of dream and the realm where one is awake.

19 'It is like this. As a hawk or an eagle, after flying around in the

sky and getting tired, folds its wings and swoops down into its nest, so this person rushes into that realm where as he sleeps he has no desires and sees no dreams.

20 'Now, he has these veins called Hitā. They are as fine as a hair split a thousandfold and are filled with white, blue, orange, green, and red fluid. Now, when people appear to kill or to vanquish him, when an elephant appears to chase him, or when he appears to fall into a pit, he is only ignorantly imagining dangers that he had seen while he was awake. But when he, appearing to be a god or a king, thinks "I alone am this world! I am all!"—that is his highest world.

21 'Now, this is the aspect of his that is beyond what appears to be good, freed from what is bad, and without fear.

'It is like this. As a man embraced by a woman he loves is oblivious to everything within or without, so this person embraced by the self (*ātman*) consisting of knowledge is oblivious to everything within or without.

'Clearly, this is the aspect of his where all desires are fulfilled, where the self is the only desire, and which is free from desires and far from sorrows.

22 'Here a father is not a father, a mother is not a mother, worlds are not worlds, gods are not gods, and Vedas are not Vedas. Here a thief is not a thief, an abortionist is not an abortionist, an outcaste is not an outcaste, a pariah is not a pariah, a recluse is not a recluse, and an ascetic is not an ascetic. Neither the good nor the bad follow him, for he has now passed beyond all sorrows of the heart.

23 'Now, he does not see anything here; but although he does not see, he is quite capable of seeing, for it is impossible for the seer to lose his capacity to see, for it is indestructible. But there isn't a second reality here that he could see as something distinct and separate from himself.

24 'Nor does he smell anything here; but although he does not smell, he is quite capable of smelling, for it is impossible for the smeller to lose his capacity to smell, for it is indestructible. But there isn't a second reality here that he could smell as something distinct and separate from himself.

25 'Nor does he taste anything here; but although he does not taste, he is quite capable of tasting, for it is impossible for the taster to lose his capacity to taste, for it is indestructible. But there isn't a

second reality here that he could taste as something distinct and separate from himself.

26 'Nor does he speak anything here; but although he does not speak, he is quite capable of speaking, for it is impossible for the speaker to lose his capacity to speak, for it is indestructible. But there isn't a second reality here that he could speak to as something distinct and separate from himself.

27 'Nor does he hear anything here; but although he does not hear, he is quite capable of hearing, for it is impossible for the hearer to lose his capacity to hear, for it is indestructible. But there isn't a second reality here that he could hear as something distinct and separate from himself.

28 'Nor does he think of anything here; but although he does not think, he is quite capable of thinking, for it is impossible for the thinker to lose his capacity to think, for it is indestructible. But there isn't a second reality here about which he could think as something distinct and separate from himself.

29 'Nor does he touch anything here; but although he does not touch, he is quite capable of touching, for it is impossible for the toucher to lose his capacity to touch, for it is indestructible. But there isn't a second reality here that he could touch as something distinct and separate from himself.

30 'Nor does he perceive anything here; but although he does not perceive, he is quite capable of perceiving, for it is impossible for the perceiver to lose his capacity to perceive, for it is indestructible. But there isn't a second reality here that he could perceive as something distinct and separate from himself.

31 'When there is some other thing, then the one can see the other, the one can smell the other, the one can taste the other, the one can speak to the other, the one can hear the other, the one can think of the other, the one can touch the other, and the one can perceive the other.

32 'He becomes the one ocean, he becomes the sole seer! This, Your Majesty, is the world of *brahman*.' So did Yājñavalkya instruct him. 'This is his highest goal! This is his highest attainment! This is his highest world! This is his highest bliss! On just a fraction of this bliss do other creatures live.

33 'Among human beings, when someone is successful and rich, ruling over others and enjoying to the utmost all human

pleasures—that is the highest bliss of human beings. Now, a hundred measures of such human bliss equal a single measure of the bliss enjoyed by the ancestors who have won their world. And a hundred measures of the bliss enjoyed by the ancestors who have won their world equal a single measure of the bliss enjoyed in the world of the Gandharvas. A hundred measures of bliss enjoyed in the world of the Gandharvas equal a single measure of bliss enjoyed by gods-by-rites, that is, those who have become gods by performing rites. A hundred measures of bliss enjoyed by gods-by-rites equal a single measure of bliss enjoyed by gods-by-birth—and, one might add, by those who are learned in the Vedas and who are not crooked or lustful. A hundred measures of bliss enjoyed by gods-by-birth equal a single measure of bliss enjoyed in the world of Prajāpati—and, one might add, by those who are learned in the Vedas and who are not crooked or lustful. A hundred measures of bliss enjoyed in the world of Prajāpati equal a single measure of bliss enjoyed in the world of *brahman*—and, one might add, by those who are learned in the Vedas and who are not crooked or lustful. Now this, undoubtedly, is the highest bliss. This, Your Majesty, is the world of *brahman*.' So said Yājñavalkya.

'Here, sir, I'll give you a thousand cows! But you'll have to tell me more than that to get yourself released!'

At this point Yājñavalkya became alarmed, thinking: 'The king is really sharp! He has flushed me out of every cover.'

34 Yājñavalkya continued: 'After this person has enjoyed himself and travelled around in that realm of dream and seen for himself the good and the bad, he rushes along the same path and through the same opening back again to the realm where one is awake.

35 'It is like this. As a heavily loaded cart goes along creaking, so
this bodily self (*ātman*), saddled with the self (*ātman*) of knowledge, goes along groaning as he is breathing his last.
36 Now a man
grows feeble on account of either old age or sickness.

'It is like this. As a mango or a fig or a berry detaches itself from its stem, so this person frees himself from these bodily parts and rushes along the same path and through the same opening back again to a new life (*prāṇa*).

37 'It is like this. As soldiers, magistrates, equerries, and village

headmen shout, "He's arrived!" and "Here he comes!", as they wait expectantly with food, drink, and lodging for a king who is about to arrive, so all beings shout, "*Brahman* has arrived!" and "Here comes *brahman*!", as they await a man who knows this.

38 'It is like this. As soldiers, magistrates, equerries, and village headmen throng around a king who is about to depart, so at the time of death all the vital functions (*prāṇa*) throng around this self (*ātman*) as he is breathing his last.'

4 'Now, as this self (*ātman*) grows steadily weaker and begins to lose consciousness, these vital functions (*prāṇa*) throng around him. Taking into himself these particles of light, he descends back into the heart. When the person connected with sight turns back, the man loses his ability to perceive visible forms. 2 So people say: "He's sinking; he can't see!"—"He's sinking; he can't smell!"—"He's sinking; he can't taste!"—"He's sinking; he can't speak!"—"He's sinking; he can't hear!"—"He's sinking; he can't think!"—"He's sinking; he can't feel a touch!"—"He's sinking; he can't perceive!" Then the top of his heart lights up, and with that light the self exits through the eye or the head or some other part of the body. As he is departing, his lifebreath (*prāṇa*) departs with him. And as his lifebreath departs, all his vital functions (*prāṇa*) depart with it.

'He then descends into a state of mere awareness and develops into one who is thus endowed with perception. Then learning and rites, as well as memory, take hold of him.

3 'It is like this. As a caterpillar, when it comes to the tip of a blade of grass, reaches out to a new foothold and draws itself onto it, so the self (*ātman*), after it has knocked down this body and rendered it unconscious, reaches out to a new foothold and draws itself onto it.

4 'It is like this. As a weaver, after she has removed the coloured yarn, weaves a different design that is newer and more attractive, so the self, after it has knocked down this body and rendered it unconscious, makes for himself a different figure that is newer and more attractive—the figure of a forefather, or of a Gandharva, or of a god, or of Prajāpati, or of *brahman*, or else the figure of some other being.

5 'Clearly, this self is *brahman*—this self that is made of per-

ception, made of mind, made of sight, made of breath, made of hearing, made of earth, made of water, made of wind, made of space, made of light and the lightless, made of desire and the desireless, made of anger and the angerless, made of the righteous and the unrighteous; this self that is made of everything. Hence there is this saying: "He's made of this. He's made of that." What a man turns out to be depends on how he acts and on how he conducts himself. If his actions are good, he will turn into something good. If his actions are bad, he will turn into something bad. A man turns into something good by good action and into something bad by bad action. And so people say: "A person here consists simply of desire." A man resolves in accordance with his desire, acts in accordance with his resolve, and turns out to be in accordance with his action. 6 On this point there is the following verse:

A man who's attached goes with his action,
  to that very place to which
  his mind and character cling.
Reaching the end of his action,
  of whatever he has done in this world—
From that world he returns
  back to this world,
  back to action.

'That is the course of a man who desires.

'Now, a man who does not desire—who is without desires, who is freed from desires, whose desires are fulfilled, whose only desire is his self—his vital functions (*prāṇa*) do not depart. *Brahman* he is, and to *brahman* he goes. 7 On this point there is the following verse:

When they are all banished,
  those desires lurking in one's heart;
Then a mortal becomes immortal,
  and attains *brahman* in this world.

'It is like this. As a snake's slough, lifeless and discarded, lies on an anthill, so lies this corpse. But this non-corporeal and immortal lifebreath (*prāṇa*) is nothing but *brahman*, nothing but light.'

'Here, sir, I'll give you a thousand cows!' said Janaka, the king of Videha.

8 'On this point there are the following verses:

There is an ancient path
extremely fine and extending far;
It has touched me, I've discovered it!
By it they go up to the heavenly world
released from here,
wise men, knowers of *brahman*.

9 In it are the white and the blue, they say,
the orange, green, and red.
By *brahman* was this path discovered;
By it goes the knower of *brahman*,
the doer of good, the man of light.

10 Into blind darkness they enter,
people who worship ignorance;
And into still blinder darkness,
people who delight in learning.

11 'Joyless' are those regions called,
in blind darkness they are cloaked;
Into them after death they go,
men who are not learned or wise.

12 If a person truly perceives the self,
knowing 'I am he';
What possibly could he want,
Whom possibly could he love,
that he should worry about his body?

13 The self has entered this body, this dense jumble.
If a man finds him,
Recognizes him,
He's the maker of everything—the author of all!
The world is his—he's the world itself!

14 While we are still here, we have come to know it.
If you've not known it, great is your destruction.
Those who have known it—they become immortal.
As for the rest—only suffering awaits them.

15 When a man clearly sees this self as god,
the lord of what was
and of what will be,
He will not seek to hide from him.

16 Beneath which the year revolves
together with its days,
That the gods venerate

as the light of lights,
as life immortal.

17 In which are established
the various groups of five,
together with space;
I take that to be the self—
I who have the knowledge,
I who am immortal,
I take that to be—
the *brahman*,
the immortal.

18 The breathing behind breathing, the sight behind sight,
the hearing behind hearing, the thinking behind thinking—
Those who know this perceive *brahman*,
the first,
the ancient.

19 With the mind alone must one behold it—
there is here nothing diverse at all!
From death to death he goes, who sees
here any kind of diversity.

20 As just singular must one behold it—
immeasurable and immovable.
The self is spotless and beyond space,
unborn, immense, immovable.

21 By knowing that very one a wise Brahmin
should obtain insight for himself.
Let him not ponder over a lot of words;
it just tires the voice!

22 'This immense, unborn self is none other than the one consisting of perception here among the vital functions (*prāṇa*). There, in that space within the heart, he lies—the controller of all, the lord of all, the ruler of all! He does not become more by good actions or in any way less by bad actions. He is the lord of all! He is the ruler of creatures! He is the guardian of creatures! He is the dike separating these worlds so they would not mingle with each other. It is he that Brahmins seek to know by means of vedic recitation, sacrifice, gift-giving, austerity, and fasting. It is he, on knowing whom, a man becomes a sage. It is when they desire him as their world that wandering ascetics undertake the ascetic life of wandering.

'It was when they knew this that men of old did not desire offspring, reasoning: "Ours is this self, and it is our world. What then is the use of offspring for us?" So they gave up the desire for sons, the desire for wealth, and the desire for worlds, and undertook the mendicant life. The desire for sons, after all, is the same as the desire for wealth, and the desire for wealth is the same as the desire for worlds—both are simply desires.

'About this self (*ātman*), one can only say "not ——, not ——". He is ungraspable, for he cannot be grasped. He is undecaying, for he is not subject to decay. He has nothing sticking to him, for he does not stick to anything. He is not bound; yet he neither trembles in fear nor suffers injury.

'These two thoughts do not pass across this self at all: "Therefore, I did something bad"; and "Therefore, I did something good". This self, on the other hand, passes across both those; he is not burnt by anything that he has done or left undone. 23 The same point is made by this Ṛgvedic verse:

> He is a Brahmin's eternal greatness—
> he's not made greater or smaller by action.
> It's his trail that one should get to know;
> And when a man knows him,
> he's no longer stained by bad deeds.

'A man who knows this, therefore, becomes calm, composed, cool, patient, and collected. He sees the self (*ātman*) in just himself (*ātman*) and all things as the self. Evil does not pass across him, and he passes across all evil. He is not burnt by evil; he burns up all evil. He becomes a Brahmin—free from evil, free from stain, free from doubt.

'He is the world of *brahman*, Your Majesty, and I have taken you to him.' So said Yājñavalkya.

'Here, sir, I'll give you the people of Videha together with myself to be your slaves!'

24 Now, this is the immense and unborn self, the eater of food and the giver of wealth. A man who knows this finds wealth. 25 And this is the immense and unborn self, unageing, undying, immortal, free from fear—the *brahman*. *Brahman*, surely, is free from fear, and a man who knows this undoubtedly becomes *brahman* that is free from fear.

5 Now, Yājñavalkya had two wives, Maitreyī and Kātyayanī.
Of the two, Maitreyī was a woman who took part in theological discussions, while Kātyayanī's understanding was limited to
womanly matters. One day, as he was preparing to undertake a different mode of life, 2 Yājñavalkya said: 'Maitreyī , I am about to
go away from this place. So come, let me make a settlement
between you and Kātyayanī.'

3 Maitreyī asked in reply: 'If I were to possess the entire world
filled with wealth, sir, would it, or would it not, make me immortal?' 'No,' said Yājñavalkya, 'it will only permit you to live the life
of a wealthy person. Through wealth one cannot expect immortality.'

4 'What is the point in getting something that will not make me
immortal?' retorted Maitreyī. 'Tell me instead, sir, all that you
know.'

5 Yājñavalkya said in reply: 'You have always been very dear to
me, and now you have made yourself even more so! Come, my
lady, I will explain it to you. But while I am explaining, try to concentrate.' 6 Then he spoke:

'One holds a husband dear, you see, not out of love for the husband; rather, it is out of love for oneself (*ātman*) that one holds a
husband dear. One holds a wife dear not out of love for the wife;
rather, it is out of love for oneself that one holds a wife dear. One
holds children dear not out of love for the children; rather, it is out
of love for oneself that one holds children dear. One holds wealth
dear not out of love for wealth; rather, it is out of love for oneself
that one holds wealth dear. One holds livestock dear not out of
love for livestock; rather, it is out of love for oneself that one holds
livestock dear. One holds the priestly power dear not out of love
for the priestly power; rather, it is out of love for oneself that one
holds the priestly power dear. One holds the royal power dear not
out of love for the royal power; rather, it is out of love for oneself
that one holds the royal power dear. One holds the worlds dear not
out of love for the worlds; rather, it is out of love for oneself that
one holds the worlds dear. One holds the gods dear not out of love
for the gods; rather, it is out of love for oneself that one holds the
gods dear. One holds the Vedas dear not out of love for the Vedas;
rather, it is out of love for oneself that one holds the Vedas dear.
One holds beings dear not out of love for beings; rather, it is out of

love for oneself that one holds beings dear. One holds the Whole dear not out of love for the Whole; rather, it is out of love for oneself that one holds the Whole dear.

'You see, Maitreyī—it is one's self (*ātman*) which one should see and hear, and on which one should reflect and concentrate. For when one has seen and heard one's self, when one has reflected and concentrated on one's self, one knows this whole world.

7 'May the priestly power forsake anyone who considers the priestly power to reside in something other than his self (*ātman*). May the royal power forsake anyone who considers the royal power to reside in something other than his self. May the worlds forsake anyone who considers the worlds to reside in something other than his self. May the gods forsake anyone who considers the gods to reside in something other than his self. May the Vedas forsake anyone who considers the Vedas to reside in something other than his self. May beings forsake anyone who considers beings to reside in something other than his self. May the Whole forsake anyone who considers the Whole to reside in something other than his self.

'All these—the priestly power, the royal power, worlds, gods, beings, the Whole—all that is nothing but this self.

8 'It is like this. When a drum is being beaten, you cannot catch the external sounds; you catch them only by getting hold of the drum or the man beating it. 9 Or when a conch is being blown, you cannot catch the external sounds; you catch them only by getting hold of the conch or the man blowing it. 10 Or when a lute is being played, you cannot catch the external sounds; you catch them only by getting hold of the lute or the man playing it.

11 'It is like this. As clouds of smoke billow from a fire lit with damp fuel, so indeed, my dear, this Immense Being has exhaled all this: Ṛgveda, Yajurveda, Sāmaveda, the Atharva-Āṅgirasa, histories, ancient tales, sciences, hidden teachings (*upaniṣad*), verses, aphorisms, explanations, glosses, sacrifices, oblations, offerings of food and drink, this world, the other world, and all beings—it is that Immense Being who has exhaled all this.

12 'It is like this. As the ocean is the point of convergence of all the waters, so the skin is the point of convergence of all sensations

of touch; the nostrils, of all odours; the tongue, of all tastes; sight, of all visible appearances; hearing, of all sounds; the mind, of all thoughts; the heart, of all sciences; the hands, of all activities; the sexual organ, of all pleasures; the anus, of all excretions; the feet, of all travels; and speech, of all the Vedas.

13 'It is like this. As a mass of salt has no distinctive core and surface; the whole thing is a single mass of flavour—so indeed, my dear, this self has no distinctive core and surface; the whole thing is a single mass of cognition. It arises out of and together with these beings and disappears after them—so I say, after death there is no awareness.'

After Yājñavalkya said this, 14 Maitreyī exclaimed: 'Now, sir, you have utterly confused me! I cannot perceive this at all.' He replied:

'Look—I haven't said anything confusing. This self, you see, is imperishable; it has an indestructible nature. 15 For when there is a duality of some kind, then the one can see the other, the one can smell the other, the one can taste the other, the one can greet the other, the one can hear the other, the one can think of the other, the one can touch the other, and the one can perceive the other. When, however, the Whole has become one's very self (*ātman*), then who is there for one to see and by what means? Who is there for one to smell and by what means? Who is there for one to taste and by what means? Who is there for one to greet and by what means? Who is there for one to hear and by what means? Who is there for one to think of and by what means? Who is there for one to touch and by what means? Who is there for one to perceive and by what means?

'By what means can one perceive him by means of whom one perceives this whole world?

'About this self (*ātman*), one can only say "not ——, not ——". He is ungraspable, for he cannot be grasped. He is undecaying, for he is not subject to decay. He has nothing sticking to him, for he does not stick to anything. He is not bound; yet he neither trembles in fear nor suffers injury.

'Look—by what means can one perceive the perceiver? There, I have given you the instruction, Maitreyī. That's all there is to immortality.'

After saying this, Yājñavalkya went away.

6 Now the lineage:
Pautimāṣya from Gaupavana; Gaupavana from Pautimāṣya; Pautimāṣya from Gaupavana; Gaupavana from Kauśika; Kauśika from Kauṇḍinya; Kauṇḍinya from Śāṇḍilya; Śāṇḍilya from Kauśika and Gautama; Gautama [2] from Āgniveśya; Āgniveśya from Gārgya; Gārgya from Gārgya; Gārgya from Gautama; Gautama from Saitava; Saitava from Pārāśaryāyaṇa; Pārāśaryāyaṇa from Gārgyāyaṇa; Gārgyāyaṇa from Uddālakāyana; Uddālakāyana from Jābālāyana; Jābālāyana from Mādhyandināyana; Mādhyandināyana from Saukarāyaṇa; Saukarāyaṇa from Kāṣāyaṇa; Kāṣāyaṇa from Sāyakāyana; Sāyakāyana from Kauśikāyani; Kauśikāyani [3] from Ghṛtakauśika; Ghṛtakauśika from Pārāśaryāyaṇa; Pārāśaryāyaṇa from Pārāśarya; Pārāśarya from Jātūkarṇya; Jātūkarṇya from Āsurāyaṇa and Yāska; Āsurāyaṇa from Traivaṇi; Traivaṇi from Aupajandhani; Aupajandhani from Āsuri; Āsuri from Bhāradvāja; Bhāradvāja from Ātreya; Ātreya from Māṇṭi; Māṇṭi from Gautama; Gautama from Gautama; Gautama from Vātsya; Vātsya from Śāṇḍilya; Śāṇḍilya from Kaiśorya Kāpya; Kaiśorya Kāpya from Kumārahārita; Kumārahārita from Gālava; Gālava from Vidarbhīkauṇḍinya; Vidarbhīkauṇḍinya from Vatsanapāt Bābhrava; Vatsanapāt Bābhrava from Pathin Saubhara; Pathin Saubhara from Ayāsya Āṅgirasa; Ayāsya Āṅgirasa from Ābhūti Tvāṣṭra; Ābhūti Tvāṣṭra from Viśvarūpa Tvāṣṭra; Viśvarūpa Tvāṣṭra from the two Aśvins; the two Aśvins from Dadhyañc Ātharvaṇa; Dadhyañc Ātharvaṇa from Atharvan Daiva; Atharvan Daiva from Mṛtyu Prādhvaṃsana; Mṛtyu Prādhvaṃsana from Pradhvaṃsana; Pradhvaṃsana from Eka Ṛṣi; Eka Ṛṣi from Vipracitti; Vipracitti from Vyaṣṭi; Vyaṣṭi from Sanāru; Sanāru from Sanātana; Sanātana from Sanaga; Sanaga from Parameṣṭhin; Parameṣṭhin from Brahman. Brahman is self-existent. Homage to Brahman!

CHAPTER 5

1 The world there is full;
The world here is full;

Fullness from fullness proceeds.
After taking fully from the full,
It still remains completely full.

'*Brahman* is space. The primeval one is space. Space is windy.' This was what the son of Kauravyāyaṇī used to say. This is the Veda. Brahmins know it. And by this I know whatever one must know.

2 The three kinds of Prajāpati's children—gods, humans, and demons—once lived with their father Prajāpati as vedic students. After they had completed their studentship, the gods said to him: 'Sir, say something to us.' So he told them the syllable '*Da*', and asked: 'Did you understand?' They replied: 'Yes, we understood. You said to us "Demonstrate restraint (*dāmyata*)!"' 'Yes,' he said, 'you have understood.'

2 Then the humans said to him: 'Sir, say something to us.' So he told them the same syllable '*Da*', and asked: 'Did you understand?' They replied: 'Yes, we understood. You said to us 'Demonstrate bounty (*datta*)!"' 'Yes,' he said, 'you have understood.'

3 Then the demons said to him: 'Sir, say something to us.' So he told them the same syllable '*Da*', and asked: 'Did you understand?' They replied: 'Yes, we understood. You said to us "Demonstrate compassion (*dayadhvam*)!"' 'Yes,' he said, 'you have understood.'

Thunder, that divine voice, repeats the very same syllable: '*Da! Da! Da!*'—Demonstrate restraint! Demonstrate bounty! Demonstrate compassion! One should observe the same triad—restraint, bounty, and compassion.

3 *Hṛdayam*, the heart—it is Prajāpati; it is *brahman*; it is the Whole. This word *hṛ.da.yam* is made up of three syllables. *Hṛ* is one syllable. To a man who knows this his own people, as well as others, bring gifts (*hṛ*-). *Da* is another syllable. To a man who knows this his own people, as well as others, give gifts (*dā*-). *Yam* is the third syllable. A man who knows this goes (*i*-) to heaven.

4 Clearly, that is itself, and that was just this, namely, the real (*satyam*) itself. '*Brahman* is the real (*satyam*)'—a man who

knows this immense and first-born divine being in this manner conquers these worlds. '*Brahman* is the real (*satyam*)'—a man who knows this immense and first-born divine being in this manner, would he ever be conquered himself? For *brahman* is simply the real.

5 In the beginning only the waters were here. Those waters created the real (*satyam*), the real created *brahman*, that is, Prajāpati, and Prajāpati created the gods. The gods venerated only the real (*satyam*), which word is made up of three syllables—*sa, ti,* and *yam. Sa* is one syllable, *ti* is another, and *yam* is the third. The first and the last syllables constitute the real, while the middle syllable is the unreal. So the unreal is trapped on both sides by the real and becomes completely united with the real. The unreal does not injure a man who knows this.

2 Now, the real is the same as that sun up there. The person there within that orb and the person here in the right eye are both based on each other. That one is based on this one through the rays, while this one is based on that one through the vital functions (*prāṇa*). So, when a man is about to die, he sees that orb in all its clarity, and those rays do not confront him.

3 The word *bhūr* ('earth') is the head of the person there within that orb—there is one head, and there is one syllable here. The word *bhuvas* ('intermediate region') is his arms—there are two arms, and there are two syllables here. The word *svar* (= *su.ar*, 'sky') is his feet—there are two feet, and there are two syllables here. His hidden name (*upaniṣad*) is *ahar* ('day'). A man who knows this strikes down (*han-*) and gets rid of (*hā-*) evil.

4 The word *bhūr* ('earth') is the head of the person here in the right eye—there is one head, and there is one syllable here. The word *bhuvas* ('intermediate region') is his arms—there are two arms, and there are two syllables here. The word *svar* ('sky') is his feet—there are two feet, and there are two syllables here. His hidden name (*upaniṣad*) is *aham* ('I'). A man who knows this strikes down (*han-*) and gets rid of (*hā-*) evil.

6 This person here is made of mind and consists of light. Lodged here deep within the heart, he is like a grain of rice or

barley; he is the lord of all, the ruler of all! Over this whole world, over all there is, he rules.

7 '*Brahman* is lightning,' they say. Lightning (*vidyut*) gets its name from cutting (*vidāna*). It cuts off (*vidyati*) from evil a man who knows that *brahman* is lightning. For *brahman* is simply lightning.

8 One should venerate speech as a cow. It has four teats—Svāhā, Vaṣaṭ, Hanta, and Svadhā. The gods live on two of those teats—Svāhā and Vaṣaṭ. Humans live on Hanta, and the ancestors on Svadhā. The bull of this cow is the breath, and her calf is the mind.

9 The fire common to all men is the one within a person, the one through which the food he eats is digested. It is the crackling of that fire that a man hears when he presses his ears shut. When a man is about to die, he no longer hears that noise.

10 Now, a person, on departing from this world, arrives first at the wind. It opens a hole for him there as wide as a cart-wheel. He goes up through that and arrives at the sun. It opens a hole for him there as wide as a large drum. He goes up through that and arrives at the moon. It opens a hole for him there as wide as a small drum. He goes up through that and arrives in a world where there are no extremes of heat or cold. There he lives for years without end.

11 To suffer from a sickness is surely the highest austerity. And a man who knows this wins the highest world. To be taken to the wilderness when one is dead is surely the highest austerity. And a man who knows this wins the highest world. To be placed on the fire when one is dead is surely the highest austerity. And a man who knows this wins the highest world.

12 '*Brahman* is food,' some say. But that is not so, because food spoils in the absence of lifebreath (*prāṇa*). Others say, '*Brahman* is lifebreath.' But that is not so, because lifebreath withers in the absence of food. It is only when these two deities

have come together as one that they reach pre-eminence. It was in this connection that Prātṛda asked his father: 'What good, or even what bad thing, could I do for a person who knows this?' Gesturing with his hand, the father replied: 'Stop, Prātṛda! Who will ever reach pre-eminence by bringing these two together in himself?' He then said to Prātṛda: '*Vi, Ram*.' Now, *vi* is food, for all these beings are contained (*viś-*) in food, and *ram* is the lifebreath, for all these beings rejoice (*ram-*) in the lifebreath. When a man knows this—all beings are contained in him, all beings rejoice in him.

13 *Uktha*. The *uktha* ('Ṛgvedic hymn'), clearly, is breath, for breath raises up (*utthā-*) this whole world. When a man knows this—from him rises (*utthā-*) a son who knows the *uktha*, and he becomes one with and attains the same world as the *uktha*.

2 *Yajus*. The *yajus* ('Yajurvedic formula'), clearly, is breath, for all these beings are joined together (*yuj-*) in breath. When a man knows this—all beings join (*yuj-*) themselves to him to procure supremacy for him, and he becomes one with and attains the same world as the *yajus*.

3 *Sāman*. The *sāman* ('Sāmavedic chant'), clearly, is breath, for all these beings are united (*samyañc*) in breath. When a man knows this—all beings unite themselves to him to procure supremacy for him, and he becomes one with and attains the same world as the *sāman*.

4 *Kṣatra*. The *kṣatra* ('ruling power'), clearly, is breath; for the *kṣatra* is, without question, breath, because breath protects (*trā-*) one from injury (*kṣaṇitu*). When a man knows this—he obtains power (*kṣatra*) that needs no protection (*atra*), and he becomes one with and attains the same world as the *kṣatra*.

14 There are eight syllables in *bhū.mi* ('earth'), *an.ta.ri.kṣa* ('intermediate region'), and *dy.au* (= *di.au*; 'sky'). Now, the first foot of the Gāyatrī verse also consists of eight syllables, so this foot of the Gāyatrī is the same as those. A man who knows this foot of the Gāyatrī in this way wins a territory extending as far as these three worlds.

2 There are eight syllables in *ṛ.caḥ* ('Ṛgvedic verses'), *ya.jūṃ.ṣi* ('Yajurvedic formulas'), and *sā.mā.ni* ('Sāmavedic chants').

Now, the second foot of the Gāyatrī verse also consists of eight syllables; so this foot of the Gāyatrī is the same as those. A man who knows this foot of the Gāyatrī in this way wins a territory extending as far as this triple Veda.

3 There are eight syllables in *prā.ṇa* ('out-breath'), *a.pā.na* ('in-breath'), and *vy.ā.na* (= *vi.ā.na*, 'inter-breath'). Now, the third foot of the Gāyatrī verse also consists of eight syllables; so this foot of the Gāyatrī is the same as those. A man who knows this foot of the Gāyatrī in this way wins a territory extending as far as there are living beings.

Then there is that fourth (*turīya*) vivid foot of the Gāyatrī, which is none other than the sun blazing beyond the sky. The term *turīya* means the same thing as 'fourth' (*caturtha*). 'Vivid foot'—for the sun is in some way visible. 'Beyond the sky'—for the sun blazes far beyond the entire expanse of the sky. A man who knows this foot of the Gāyatrī in this way will likewise blaze with splendour and fame.

4 The Gāyatrī verse is based on that fourth and vivid foot beyond the sky. That foot, in its turn, is based on truth. Now, truth is sight. For, truth is without question sight, and because of that if two people come here now arguing with each other, the one saying 'I saw', and the other saying 'I heard', the one we would trust is the man who says that he saw. Truth, in its turn, is based on strength. Strength, clearly, is breath and is based on breath. Therefore, people say that strength is more powerful than truth. In this way the Gāyatrī is based on what is within the body (*ātman*). So the Gāyatrī protects (*trā-*) one's wealth (*gaya*). Clearly, one's wealth is one's breaths; so it protects the breaths. It got the name 'Gāyatrī' because it protects (*trā-*) one's wealth (*gaya*). And it is the same as the Sāvitrī that one recites. When one recites it on behalf of someone, it protects that person's breaths.

5 Now, there are some who recite this Sāvitrī as an Anuṣṭubh verse, and they argue: 'This way what we recite is speech, because the Anuṣṭubh is speech.' But one should not do so. One should recite the Sāvitrī only as a Gāyatrī verse.

Even if a man who knows this receives a large gift of some sort, it would not equal even a single foot of the Gāyatrī. 6 If someone were to receive a gift of these three worlds filled to capacity, he would have obtained its first foot. If someone were to receive a gift

as extensive as the triple Veda, he would have obtained its second foot. And if someone were to receive a gift extending as far as there are living beings, he would have obtained its third foot. Then there is that fourth vivid foot of the Gāyatrī, which is none other than the sun blazing beyond the sky. And no one can obtain that. From where indeed can one receive a gift as extensive as that?
7 This is the worship of Gāyatrī:

> You are one-footed, Gāyatrī! You are two-footed!
> You are three-footed! You are four-footed!
> You are without feet! For you do not walk!
> Homage to your fourth foot,
> to your vivid foot,
> beyond the sky!

When someone worships in this way, he may direct it against someone he hates, saying: 'May so-and-so not obtain that!' or, 'May the desire of so-and-so not come to pass'—and the desire of the man, against whom he directed his worship, will not come to pass. Or he may say: 'May I obtain that!'

8 In this connection, Janaka, the king of Videha, once said to Buḍila Aśvatarāśvi: 'Hey! Did you not claim to know the Gāyatrī? So how is it that you have turned yourself into an elephant that is dragging loads?' He replied: 'But I did not know its mouth, Your Majesty.' Its mouth is just the fire. So however much one may put into a fire, it burns up all of that. Likewise, however many bad things a man who knows this may do, he eats up all of that and emerges clean and pure, free from ageing and death.

15

> The face of truth is covered
> with a golden dish.
> Open it, O Pūṣan, for me,
> a man faithful to the truth.
> Open it, O Pūṣan, for me to see.
>
> O Pūṣan, sole seer!
> Yama! Sun! Son of Prajāpati!
> Spread out your rays!
> Draw in your light!
> I see your fairest form.
> That person up there,
> I am he!

The never-resting is the wind,
the immortal!
Ashes are this body's lot.
OṂ!
Mind, remember the deed!
Remember!
Mind, remember the deed!
Remember!
O Fire, you know all coverings;
O god, lead us to riches,
along an easy path.
Keep the sin that angers
far away from us;
And the highest song of praise
we shall offer to you!

CHAPTER 6

1 When a man knows the best and the greatest, he becomes the best and the greatest among his own people. The best and the greatest is breath. When a man knows this, he becomes the best and the greatest among his own people and, if he so desires, even among others.

2 When a man knows the most excellent, he becomes the most excellent among his people. The most excellent is speech. When a man knows this, he becomes the most excellent among his own people and, if he so desires, even among others.

3 When a man knows the firm base, he stands firm both on flat land and on rugged terrain. The firm base is sight, for on flat land, as on rugged terrain, one stands firm by means of sight. When a man knows this, he stands firm both on flat land and on rugged terrain.

4 When a man knows the correspondence (*saṃpad*), whatever he desires is fulfilled (*saṃpad-*) for him. Correspondence (*saṃpad*) is hearing, for all these Vedas congregate (*saṃpad-*) in one's hearing. When a man knows this, whatever he desires is fulfilled for him.

5 When a man knows the refuge, he becomes a refuge for his people and a refuge for the common folk. The refuge is the mind. When a man knows this, he becomes a refuge for his people and a refuge for the common folk.

6 When a man knows fecundity, he becomes fecund in offspring and in livestock. Fecundity is the semen. When a man knows this, he becomes fecund in offspring and in livestock.

7 Once these vital functions (*prāṇa*) were arguing about who among them was the greatest. So they went to *brahman* and asked: 'Who is the most excellent of us?' He replied: 'The one, after whose departure you consider the body to be the worst off, is the most excellent among you.'

8 So speech departed. After spending a year away, it came back and asked: 'How did you manage to live without me?' They replied: 'We lived as the dumb would, without speaking with speech, but breathing with the breath, seeing with the eye, hearing with the ear, thinking with the mind, and fathering with semen.' So speech re-entered.

9 Then sight departed. After spending a year away, it came back and asked: 'How did you manage to live without me?' They replied: 'We lived as the blind would, without seeing with the eye, but breathing with the breath, speaking with speech, hearing with the ear, thinking with the mind, and fathering with semen.' So sight re-entered.

10 Then hearing departed. After spending a year away, it came back and asked: 'How did you manage to live without me?' They replied: 'We lived as the deaf would, without hearing with the ear, but breathing with the breath, speaking with speech, seeing with the eye, thinking with the mind, and fathering with semen.' So hearing re-entered.

11 Then the mind departed. After spending a year away, it came back and asked: 'How did you manage to live without me?' They replied: 'We lived as simpletons would, without thinking with the mind, but breathing with the breath, speaking with speech, seeing with the eye, hearing with the ear, and fathering with semen.' So the mind re-entered.

12 Then the semen departed. After spending a year away, it came back and asked: 'How did you manage to live without me?' They replied: 'We lived as the impotent would, without fathering

with semen, but breathing with the breath, speaking with speech, seeing with the eye, hearing with the ear, and thinking with the mind.' So the semen re-entered.

13 Then, as the breath was about to depart, it uprooted those vital functions (*prāṇa*), as a mighty Indus horse would uproot the stakes to which it is tethered. They implored: 'Lord, please do not depart! We will not be able to live without you.' He told them: 'If that's so, offer a tribute to me.' 'We will,' they replied.

14 So speech declared: 'As I am the most excellent, so you will be the most excellent.' Sight declared: 'As I am the firm base, so you will be the firm base.' Hearing declared: 'As I am correspondence, so you will be correspondence.' The mind declared: 'As I am the refuge, so you will be the refuge.' The semen declared: 'As I am fecundity, so you will be fecundity.'

Breath then asked: 'What will be my food and my clothing?'

'Everything that is here is your food, right down to dogs, worms, insects, and flies, and water is your clothing.'

When a man knows in this way that breath (*ana*) is food (*anna*)—nothing he eats becomes an improper food, nothing he accepts becomes an improper food. Therefore, wise and learned people sip some water both when they are preparing to eat and after they have eaten, thinking that they are thus making sure that breath (*ana*) is not left naked (*anagna*).

2 Śvetaketu, the son of Āruṇi, came one day into the assembly of the land of Pañcāla and approached Jaivali Pravāhaṇa while people were waiting upon him. Seeing Śvetaketu, he said: 'Son!' Śvetaketu replied: 'Sir?' Jaivali asked: 'Did your father teach you?' Śvetaketu replied: 'Yes.'

2 'Do you know how people, when they die, go by different paths?'

'No,' he replied.

'Do you know how they return to this world?'

'No,' he replied.

'Do you know how the world beyond is not filled up, even as more and more people continuously go there?'

'No,' he replied.

'Do you know the oblation at whose offering the water, taking on a human voice, rises up and speaks?'

'No,' he replied.

'Do you know the access to the path to the gods or the path to the fathers—that is, what one must do to get on the path to the gods or on the path to the fathers? For have you not heard the seer's words?—

> Two paths mortals have, I've heard:
> the paths to fathers and to gods.
> By these travel all that live
> between the earth and sky.

'I don't know the answer to any of these,' he replied.

3 Then Jaivali invited him to stay. Disregarding the invitation, the boy ran off. He went back to his father and said: 'Well, well! And to think that you once told me I was well educated!'

'What's the matter, my clever boy?'

'That excuse for a prince asked me five questions, and I didn't know the answer to a single one of them.'

'What were they?'

'These,' he said and repeated them briefly.

4 The father replied: 'You know me, son. I have taught you everything I know. Come, let us both go there and live as students.'

'You can go on your own.'

Gautama then came to Pravāhaṇa Jaivali's place. Jaivali gave him a seat and had some water brought for him. Then he presented him with the refreshments due to an honoured guest and said: 'We will grant a wish to the Reverend Gautama.'

5 Gautama said in reply: 'Now that you have promised to grant me a wish, tell me what you told my boy.'

6 'But that, Gautama, is in the category of divine wishes,' responded Jaivali. 'Why don't you make a wish of a human sort?'

7 Gautama replied: 'As you know, I have my share of gold, cows, horses, slave girls, blankets, and clothes. Do not be stingy, your honour, in giving me more than that—in giving me the infinite and the boundless.'

'Then, Gautama, you will have to request it in the correct manner.'

'I come to you, my lord, as a pupil.'

With just these words did the people of old place themselves as pupils under a teacher. And Gautama lived there openly as a pupil. [8] Jaivali then told him:

'This knowledge has never before been in the possession of a Brahmin. Nevertheless, I will disclose it to you, Gautama, lest you or an ancestor of yours cause me harm. Besides, who can refuse a man who speaks like that!

[9] 'A fire—that's what the world up there is, Gautama. Its firewood is the sun; its smoke is the sunbeams; its flame is the day; its embers are the quarters; and its sparks are the intermediate quarters. In that very fire gods offer faith, and from that offering springs King Soma.

[10] 'A fire—that's what a rain cloud is, Gautama. Its firewood is the year; its smoke is the thunderclouds; its flame is lightning; its embers are thunder; and its sparks are hail. In that very fire gods offer King Soma, and from that offering springs rain.

[11] 'A fire—that's what this world down here is, Gautama. Its firewood is the earth; its smoke is the fire; its flame is the night; its embers are the moon; and its sparks are the constellations. In that very fire gods offer rain, and from that offering springs food.

[12] 'A fire—that's what a man is, Gautama. His firewood is the open mouth; his smoke is breath; his flame is speech; his embers are sight; and his sparks are hearing. In that very fire gods offer food, and from that offering springs semen.

[13] 'A fire—that's what a woman is, Gautama. Her firewood is the vulva; her smoke is the pubic hair; her flame is the vagina; when one penetrates her, that is her embers; and her sparks are the climax. In that very fire gods offer semen, and from that offering springs a man.

'He remains alive for as long as he lives, and when he finally dies, [14] they offer him in the fire. Of that fire, the fire is the fire itself; the firewood is the firewood; the smoke is the smoke; the flame is the flame; the embers are the embers; and the sparks are the sparks. In that very fire gods offer man, and from that offering springs a man of brilliant colour.

[15] 'The people who know this, and the people there in the wilderness who venerate truth as faith—they pass into the flame, from the flame into the day, from the day into the fortnight of the waxing moon, from the fortnight of the waxing moon into the six months when the sun moves north, from these months into the

world of the gods, from the world of the gods into the sun, and from the sun into the region of lightning. A person consisting of mind comes to the regions of lightning and leads him to the worlds of *brahman*. These exalted people live in those worlds of *brahman* for the longest time. They do not return.

16 'The people who win heavenly worlds, on the other hand, by offering sacrifices, by giving gifts, and by performing austerities—they pass into the smoke, from the smoke into the night, from the night into the fortnight of the waning moon, from the fortnight of the waning moon into the six months when the sun moves south, from these months into the world of the fathers, and from the world of the fathers into the moon. Reaching the moon they become food. There, the gods feed on them, as they tell King Soma, the moon: 'Increase! Decrease!'. When that ends, they pass into this very sky, from the sky into the wind, from the wind into the rain, and from the rain into the earth. Reaching the earth, they become food. They are again offered in the fire of man and then take birth in the fire of woman. Rising up once again to the heavenly worlds, they circle around in the same way.

'Those who do not know these two paths, however, become worms, insects, or snakes.'

3 'I want to attain greatness'—when a man entertains such a wish, he should do the following. To begin with he should perform the preparatory rites for twelve days. Then, on an auspicious day falling within a fortnight of the waxing moon during the northern movement of the sun, he should collect every type of herb and fruit in a fig-wood dish or a metal bowl. After sweeping around the place of the sacred fire and smearing it with cow dung, he should kindle the fire, spread the sacrificial grass, prepare the ghee according to the usual procedure, make the mixture under a male constellation, and pour an offering of ghee into the fire, saying:

Those stumbling-blocks within you, O Fire,
The gods who frustrate man's desires;
I offer a share to them!
May they be satisfied!
May they satisfy my every desire!
Svāhā!

And she who lies there as a stumbling-block,
thinking, 'I arrange everything!'
You are a true conciliator!
I offer streams of ghee to you!
Svāhā!'

2 He makes an offering of ghee in the fire, saying: 'To the best, svāhā! To the greatest, svāhā!' and pours the remainder into the mixture. [What is meant here is:] 'To the breath, svāhā!'

He makes an offering of ghee in the fire, saying: 'To the most excellent, svāhā!' and pours the remainder into the mixture. [What is meant here is:] 'To speech, svāhā!'

He makes an offering of ghee in the fire, saying: 'To the firm base, svāhā!' and pours the remainder into the mixture. [What is meant here is:] 'To sight, svāhā!'

He makes an offering of ghee in the fire, saying: 'To correspondence, svāhā!' and pours the remainder into the mixture. [What is meant here is:] 'To hearing, svāhā!'

He makes an offering of ghee in the fire, saying: 'To the refuge, svāhā!' and pours the remainder into the mixture. [What is meant here is:] 'To the mind, svāhā!'

He makes an offering of ghee in the fire, saying: 'To fecundity, svāhā!' and pours the remainder into the mixture. [What is meant here is:] 'To semen, svāhā!'

In this way, every time he makes an offering of ghee in the fire he pours the remainder into the mixture.

3 He makes an offering of ghee in the fire, saying: 'To the fire, svāhā!' and pours the remainder into the mixture. He makes an offering of ghee in the fire, saying: 'To Soma, svāhā!' and pours the remainder into the mixture. He makes an offering of ghee in the fire, saying: 'Earth! Svāhā!' and pours the remainder into the mixture. He makes an offering of ghee in the fire, saying: 'Intermediate region! Svāhā!' and pours the remainder into the mixture. He makes an offering of ghee in the fire, saying: 'Sky! Svāhā!' and pours the remainder into the mixture. He makes an offering of ghee in the fire, saying: 'Earth! Intermediate region! Sky! Svāhā!' and pours the remainder into the mixture. He makes an offering of ghee in the fire, saying: 'To priestly power, svāhā!' and pours the remainder into the mixture. He makes an offering of ghee in the fire, saying: 'To royal power, svāhā!' and pours the

remainder into the mixture. He makes an offering of ghee in the fire, saying: 'To what has been, svāhā!' and pours the remainder into the mixture. He makes an offering of ghee in the fire, saying: 'To what will be, svāhā!' and pours the remainder into the mixture. He makes an offering of ghee in the fire, saying: 'To the All, svāhā!' and pours the remainder into the mixture. He makes an offering of ghee in the fire, saying: 'To the Whole, svāhā!' and pours the remainder into the mixture. He makes an offering of ghee in the fire, saying: 'To Prajāpati, svāhā!' and pours the remainder into the mixture.

4 Then he touches the mixture, saying: 'You are the fluttering! You are the glittering! You are the full! You are the steady! You are the only meeting-place! You are the chanted *hiṃ*, and you are the chanting of *hiṃ*. You are the chanted High Chant and you are chanting of the High Chant. You are one priest's call for the gods to hear, and you are the other priest's assent that the gods should hear. You are the flash in the cloud. You are the mighty. You are the lord. You are food. You are the light. You are the end. You are the gatherer.'

5 Then he lifts up the mixture, saying: 'You are power; your power is in me. For he is king, lord, and ruler! May he make me king, lord, and ruler!'

6 Then he sips the mixture, saying:

On that excellent [glory] of Savitṛ
Honey the winds, honey the streams
drip on the righteous man.
Honey-filled may the plants be for us.
Earth! Svāhā!

glory of god [Savitṛ] we reflect
Honey the night, honey the morn,
honey-filled the earthly expanse;
Honey may Father Heaven be to us!
Intermediate region! Svāhā!

that he may stimulate our prayers.
Honey-filled the tree, honey-filled the sun;
filled with honey the cows;
Honey-filled may they be to us!
Sky! Svāhā!

Then he repeats the entire Sāvitrī verse and all the above verses on honey, and says: 'May I indeed become this whole world! Earth! Intermediate region! Sky! Svāhā!' Finally, he sips some water, washes his hands, and lies down behind the fire with his head towards the east. In the morning he worships the sun, saying: 'You are the one lotus among the quarters! May I become the one lotus among men!' Then he returns the way he came and, seated behind the fire, silently recites the lineage.

7 After telling this same thing to his pupil Vājasaneya Yājñavalkya, Uddālaka Āruṇi said: 'Even if one were to pour this mixture on a withered stump, it would sprout new branches and grow new leaves.'

8 After telling this same thing to his pupil Madhuka Paiṅgya, Vājasaneya Yājñavalkya said: 'Even if one were to pour this mixture on a withered stump, it would sprout new branches and grow new leaves.'

9 After telling this same thing to his pupil Cūla Bhāgavitti, Madhuka Paiṅgya said: 'Even if one were to pour this mixture on a withered stump, it would sprout new branches and grow new leaves.'

10 After telling this same thing to his pupil Jānaki Āyasthūṇa, Cūla Bhāgavitti said: 'Even if one were to pour this mixture on a withered stump, it would sprout new branches and grow new leaves.'

11 After telling this same thing to his pupil Satyakāma Jābāla, Jānaki Āyasthūṇa said: 'Even if one were to pour this mixture on a withered stump, it would sprout new branches and grow new leaves.'

12 After telling this same thing to his pupils, Satyakāma Jābāla said: 'Even if one were to pour this mixture on a withered stump, it would sprout new branches and grow new leaves.'

One should not disclose this to anyone who is not a son or a pupil.

13 There are four things made of fig wood: fig-wood spoon, fig-wood cup, fig-wood kindling stick, and the two fig-wood stirring sticks. There are ten types of cultivated grains: rice, barley, sesame, bean, millet, mustard, wheat, lentil, pea, and legume. After grinding these, he pours curd, honey, and ghee on them, and offers an oblation of ghee.

4 Of these beings here, the essence is clearly the earth; of the earth, the waters; of the waters, the plants; of the plants, the flowers; of the flowers, the fruits; of the fruits, man; of man, semen.

2 Prajāpati then thought to himself: 'Now, why don't I prepare a base for that semen?' So he created woman and, after creating her, had intercourse with her. A man, therefore, should have intercourse with a woman. Prajāpati stretched out from himself the elongated stone for pressing Soma and impregnated her with it.

3 Her vulva is the sacrificial ground; her pubic hair is the sacred grass; her labia majora are the Soma-press; and her labia minora are the fire blazing at the centre. A man who engages in sexual intercourse with this knowledge obtains as great a world as a man who performs a Soma sacrifice, and he appropriates to himself the merits of the women with whom he has sex. The women, on the other hand, appropriate to themselves the merits of a man who engages in sexual intercourse with them without this knowledge.

4 Surely it was this knowledge that made Uddālaka Āruṇi exclaim, as also Nāka Maudgalya and Kumārahārita: 'Many are the mortals of Brahmin descent who, engaging in sexual intercourse without this knowledge, depart this world drained of virility and deprived of merit.'

If one discharges semen, whether it is a little or a lot, in sleep or
while awake, 5 one should touch it and also address it with this formula:

> I retrieve this semen that fell on earth today;
> into water or plants though it may have seeped.
> May I regain my virility, my ardour, my passion;
> let the fire and the fire-mounds each return to its place.

As he recites this he should take the semen with his thumb and ring finger and rub it between his breasts or brows.

6 If, moreover, he sees his reflection in water, let him address it thus: 'May vigour, virility, fame, wealth, and merit remain in me!'

Surely, a woman who has changed her clothes at the end of her menstrual period is the most auspicious of women. When she has changed her clothes at the end of her menstrual period, therefore, one should approach that splendid woman and invite her to have
sex. 7 Should she refuse to consent, he should bribe her. If she still

refuses, he should beat her with a stick or with his fists and overpower her, saying: 'I take away the splendour from you with my virility and splendour.' And she is sure to become bereft of splendour. [8] If, on the other hand, she accedes to his wish, he should say: 'I confer splendour on you with my virility and splendour.' And then they are both sure to become full of splendour.

[9] If he wants her to love him, he should slip his penis into her, press his mouth against hers, and stroke her vagina as he softly recites:

> From my body you spring—from every inch!
> Born from my heart, you are my body's pith!
> Make her crazy about me, as if she's been hit
> With a dart carrying a poisoned tip.

[10] If he does not want her to become pregnant, he should slip his penis into her, press his mouth against hers, blow into her mouth and suck back the breath, as he says: 'I take back the semen from you with my virility and semen.' And she is sure to become bereft of semen.

[11] If, on the other hand, he wants her to become pregnant, he should slip his penis into her, press his mouth against hers, suck in the breath first, and then blow it back into her mouth, as he says: 'I deposit the semen in you with my virility and semen.' And she is sure to become pregnant.

[12] In case someone's wife has a lover whom he hates, this is what he should do. He should place some fire in an unbaked pot, spread out a bed of reeds, arranging them in a way that is the reverse of the normal, apply ghee to the tips of those reeds, again in an order that is the reverse of the normal, and offer them in that fire, as he recites:

In my fire you made an offering! So-and-so, I take away your out-breath and your in-breath.

In my fire you made an offering! So-and-so, I take away your sons and livestock.

In my fire you made an offering! So-and-so, I take away your sacrifices and good works.

In my fire you made an offering! So-and-so, I take away your hopes and expectations.

A man cursed by a Brahmin possessing this knowledge is sure to depart from this world bereft of his virility and stripped of his good works. One should, therefore, never try to flirt with the wife of a learned Brahmin who knows this, lest one make an enemy of a man with this knowledge.

13 Now, when a man finds that his wife is having her period, he should make sure that she does not drink from a metal cup or wear fresh clothes for three days. Nor should a low-caste man or woman be allowed to touch her. When the three days are over and she has taken her bath, he should get her to thresh some rice. 14 'I want a son with a fair complexion who will master a single Veda and live out his full life span'—if this is his wish, he should get her to cook that rice with milk, and the two of them should eat it mixed with ghee. The couple thus becomes capable of begetting such a son.

15 'I want a son with a ruddy complexion and tawny eyes who will master two Vedas and live out his full life span'—if this is his wish, he should get her to cook that rice with curd, and the two of them should eat it mixed with ghee. The couple thus becomes capable of begetting such a son.

16 'I want a son with a dark complexion and reddish eyes who will master three Vedas and live out his full life span'—if this is his wish, he should get her to cook that rice in water and the two of them should eat it mixed with ghee. The couple thus becomes capable of begetting such a son.

17 'I want a learned daughter who will live out her full life span'—if this is his wish, he should get her to cook that rice with sesame seeds and the two of them should eat it mixed with ghee. The couple thus becomes capable of begetting such a daughter.

18 'I want a learned and famous son, a captivating orator assisting at councils, who will master all the Vedas and live out his full life span'—if this is his wish, he should get her to cook that rice with meat and the two of them should eat it mixed with ghee. The couple thus becomes capable of begetting such a son. The meat may be that of a young or a fully grown bull.

19 Then, towards morning, following the same ritual procedure as at the cooking of the pot of milk-rice, he should prepare melted butter and offer portions from the pot of milk-rice in the fire, saying: 'To fire, svāhā! To assent, svāhā! To the divine Savitṛ, faithful in procreation, svāhā!' After making these offerings, he takes

the rest out and, after first eating himself, gives some to his partner. After washing his hands, he fills a pot with water and sprinkles her with it three times, saying:

> Get up, Viśvāvasu, and leave this place;
> Find yourself some other luscious girl.
> This wife is here with her husband.

20 Then he embraces her, as he says:

> I am *ama*, you are *sā*—you are *sā*, I am *ama*.
> I am the Sāman chant, you are the Ṛg verse;
> I am the sky, you are the earth.
> Come, let us unite,
> deposit the seed,
> to get a son,
> a male child.

21 Then he spreads apart her thighs, saying: 'Spread apart, earth and sky.' He slips his penis into her, presses his mouth against hers, and strokes her three times in the direction of her hair, as he says:

> May Viṣṇu prepare your womb,
> and Tvaṣṭṛ mould the forms;
> May Prajāpati impregnate you,
> and Dhātṛ lay the foetus in you.
> Lay the foetus, Sinīvāli,
> lay the foetus, you with broad plaits.
> Lay the foetus, you two Aśvins,
> lay the foetus, you two with lotus wreaths.
> 22The golden fire-drills with which
> the Aśvins churned the fire;
> That I invoke as the foetus for you,
> for delivery in the tenth month.
> As fire lies a foetus in the earth,
> and rain in the sky;
> As the wind is the foetus
> of the cardinal points;
> So I place this foetus in you, So-and-so.

23 As she is about to deliver, he sprinkles her with water, saying:

> As from all sides the wind churns a lotus pond,
> so may your foetus stir and

come out with the afterbirth.
This stall with lock and fence is Indra's handiwork—
expel it, Indra,
with the foetus and afterbirth.

24 When a boy is born, he should kindle the fire, place the baby on his lap, mix curd and milk in a metal bowl, and offer spoonfuls of that mixture in the fire, saying:

In this boy may I prosper a thousandfold
and thrive in my own house.
Rich in offspring and livestock,
may disaster never strike his line.
Svāhā!

The breaths in me
I offer in you
with my mind.
Svāhā!

If in this rite I did too much of this,
or too little of that;
May the wise fire, the rectifier of rites,
make ours well done.
Svāhā!

25 He then draws close to the baby's right ear and says three times: 'Speech! Speech!' Next, he feeds the baby a mixture of curd, honey, and ghee with a golden spoon without putting it inside the mouth, as he says: 'The earth I place in you! The intermediate region I place in you! The sky I place in you! Earth, intermediate region, sky—the Whole I place in you!'

26 He then gives a name to the baby, with the words: 'You are the Veda!' It becomes the child's secret name. 27 He then hands him to the mother and gives him her breast, saying:

Your refreshing breast, Sarasvatī, that ever flows,
giving riches, finding treasures, granting gifts;
The breast with which you nourish all you choose,
give it here for him to suck.

28 Then he says to the baby's mother:

You are Ilā, in the family of Mitra and Varuṇa;
you have borne a hero, O heroine.

You've made me the father of a hero;
mother of heroes may you be!

People say of such a son: 'Bravo, you have surpassed your father! Bravo, you have surpassed your grandfather! A man who is born as the son of a Brahmin with this knowledge has surely reached the very pinnacle of prosperity and fame, the pinnacle of eminence in sacred knowledge.'

5 Now the lineage:

The son of Pautimāṣī from the son of Kātyāyanī; the son of Kātyāyanī from the son of Gautamī; the son of Gautamī from the son of Bhāradvājī; the son of Bhāradvājī from the son of Pārāśarī; the son of Pārāśarī from the son of Aupasvastī; the son of Aupasvastī from the son of Pārāśarī; the son of Pārāśarī from the son of Kātyāyanī; the son of Kātyāyanī from the son of Kauśikī; the son of Kauśikī from the son of Ālambī and from the son of Vaiyāghrapadī; the son of Vaiyāghrapadī from the son of Kāṇvī and the son of Kāpī; the son of Kāpī [2] from the son of Ātreyī; the son of Ātreyī from the son of Gautamī; the son of Gautamī from the son of Bhāradvājī; the son of Bhāradvājī from the son of Pārāśarī; the son of Pārāśarī from the son of Vātsī; the son of Vātsī from the son of Pārāśarī; the son of Pārāśarī from the son of Vārkāruṇī; the son of Vārkāruṇī from the son of Vārkāruṇī; the son of Vārkāruṇī from the son of Ārtabhāgī; the son of Ārtabhāgī from the son of Śauṅgī; the son of Śauṅgī from the son of Sāṃkṛtī; the son of Sāṃkṛtī from the son of Ālambāyanī; the son of Ālambāyanī from the son of Ālambī; the son of Ālambī from the son of Jāyantī; the son of Jāyantī from the son of Māṇḍūkāyanī; the son of Māṇḍūkāyanī from the son of Māṇḍūkī; the son of Māṇḍūkī from the son of Śāṇḍilī; the son of Śāṇḍilī from the son of Rāthītarī; the son of Rāthītarī from the son of Bhālukī; the son of Bhālukī from the two sons of Krauñcikī; the two sons of Krauñcikī from the son of Vaidabhṛtī; the son of Vaidabhṛtī from the son of Kārśakeyī; the son of Kārśakeyī from the son of Prācīnayogī; the son of Prācīnayogī from the son of Sāñjīvī; the son of Sāñjīvī from Āsurivāsin, the son of Prāśnī; the son of Prāśnī from Āsurāyaṇa; Āsurāyaṇa from Āsuri; Āsuri [3] from Yājñavalkya; Yājñavalkya from Uddālaka; Uddālaka from Aruṇa; Aruṇa from Upaveśi;

Upaveśi from Kuśri; Kuśri from Vājaśravas; Vājaśravas from Jihvāvat Vādhyoga; Jihvāvat Vādhyoga from Asita Vārṣagaṇa; Asita Vārṣagaṇa from Harita Kaśyapa; Harita Kaśyapa from Śilpa Kaśyapa; Śilpa Kaśyapa from Kaśyapa Naidhruvi; Kaśyapa Naidhruvi from Vāc (speech); Vāc from Ambhiṇī; Ambhiṇī from Āditya (sun).

These white Yajurvedic formulas coming from the sun have been proclaimed by Vājasaneya Yājñavalkya.

4 The lineage up to the son of Sāñjīvī is the same.

The son of Sāñjīvī from Māṇḍūkāyani; Māṇḍūkāyani from Māṇḍavya; Māṇḍavya from Kautsa; Kautsa from Māhitthi; Māhitthi from Vāmakakṣāyaṇa; Vāmakakṣāyaṇa from Śāṇḍilya; Śāṇḍilya from Vātsya; Vātsya from Kuśri; Kuśri from Yajñavacas Rājastambāyana; Yajñavacas Rājastambāyana from Tura Kāvaṣeya; Tura Kāvaṣeya from Prajāpati; Prajāpati from Brahman. Brahman is self-existent. Homage to Brahman!

Chāndogya Upaniṣad

THE Chāndogya (the Upaniṣad of 'the singers of the Sāmaveda', i.e. the Udgātṛ priest) is a section of the Chāndogya Brāhmaṇa belonging to the Tāṇḍya school of the Sāmaveda. Like the Bṛhadāraṇyaka, the Chāndogya is the work of an editor or a series of editors who created an anthology of passages and stories that must have previously existed as separate texts. The unifying theme, if there is one, of the Upaniṣad is the speculation regarding the cosmic and ritual correspondences of the Sāman (the Sāmavedic chant in the Soma sacrifice: see CU 2.2.1 n.) and especially of the High Chant (Udgītha), central element of a Sāman. The preoccupation with these chants is consistent with the fact that the authors were Sāmavedic priests. In a similar fashion, the works of the Ṛgveda speculate on the Uktha (AA 2.3.1, 4), the Ṛgvedic recitation (BU 1.6.1 n.), and the Bṛhadāraṇyaka begins with the parts of a horse, consistent again with the fact that the Adhvaryu, the Yajurvedic priest, is in charge of butchering the sacrificial animal. The fact that the Chāndogya and the Bṛhadāraṇyaka include versions of identical passages and stories indicates that the editors of both have drawn from a common stock of Upaniṣadic lore.

CONTENTS

	13		Correspondences of interjections in Sāmans
2	1		Veneration of Sāman
	2–7		Cosmic and bodily correspondences of the fivefold Sāman
	8		The sevenfold Sāman as speech
	9–10		The sevenfold Sāman as the sun
	11–21		Cosmic and bodily correspondences of the fivefold Sāman
	22		Ways of singing and pronouncing a Sāman
	23.1		Contrast between Law (*dharma*) and *brahman*
	23.2–3		Creation of Vedas and OṂ by Prajāpati
	24		The way to secure the reward of Soma offerings
3	1–11		Sun as honey
		1–5	Honey of sun extracted from all forms of sacred knowledge
		6–10	Different classes of gods subsist on parts of that honey
		11	Sun that does not set
	12		Gāyatrī as the whole universe
	13		Five openings of the heart: their cosmic and bodily correspondences
	14		*Brahman* as one's self within the heart
	15		The universe compared to a chest
	16–17		The sacrifice compared to the life span and activities of a man
	18.1		*Brahman* as mind and space
	18.2–6		Vital functions as the four quarters of *brahman*
4	1–3		Story of Jānaśruti and Raikva: doctrine of wind and breath as gatherers
	4–9		Story of Satyakāma Jābāla: the four quarters of *brahman*
	10–15		Story of Upakosala
		10–14	Correspondences of the three sacred fires
		15	Self as the person in the eye
	16–17		Work of the Brahman priest in rectifying sacrificial errors
5	1–2		Contest among vital functions
		1–2.3	Superiority of breath
		2.4–9	Offerings to vital functions to obtain something great
	3–10		Pravāhaṇa's questions to Śvetaketu and instruction of Uddālaka
		4–9	Doctrine of five fires and transmigration
		10	The two paths of the dead—to gods and to fathers
	11–24		Aśvapati's instruction on the self and *brahman*

		12–17	Rejection of the identity of cosmic entities and the self
		18	Description of the self
		19–24	Offering of food in the five breaths
6	Dialogue between Uddālaka and his son, Śvetaketu		
		1.3–7	Rule of substitution which makes known the unknown
		2	Creation comes from the existent
		3	Three origins of creatures
		4	Three appearances of things: red, white, and black
		5–6	The three parts of food and drink that form various bodily parts
		7	The sixteen parts of man
		8.1–2	The nature of sleep
		8.3–6	The existent as the root of man
		8.7–16.3	The true nature of the self
7	Sanatkumāra instructs Nārada		
		1–15	Progressively greater realities from name to lifebreath
		16–23	The need to perceive activities from thinking to plenitude
		24–6	Correspondence between plenitude and self
8	1–6	The space within the heart as containing all things	
		1	The self free from old age and death
		2	Securing wishes by mere thought
		3	*Brahman* as the real
		4	Self as a dike dividing this world from the world of *brahman*
		5	Praise of the student life
		6	The veins in the heart
	7–12	Prajāpati instructs Indra and Virocaṇa on the true self	
		7–8	Self as physical appearance
		9–10	Self as the person in dream
		11	Self as the person in deep sleep
		12	The true self
	13–15	Glorification of the perfected self	

CHAPTER 1

1 OṂ—one should venerate the High Chant as this syllable, for one begins the High Chant with OṂ. Here is a further explanation of that syllable.

2 The essence of these beings here is the earth; the essence of the earth is the waters; the essence of the waters is plants; the essence of plants is man; the essence of man is speech; the essence of speech is the Ṛg verse; the essence of the Ṛg verse is the Sāman chant; the essence of the Sāman chant is the High Chant. 3 This High Chant is the quintessence of all essences; it is the highest, the ultimate, the eighth.

4 What ultimately is the Ṛg verse? What ultimately is the Sāman chant? What ultimately is the High Chant? These questions have been the subject of critical enquiry.

5 The Ṛg is nothing but speech; the Sāman is breath; and the High Chant is this syllable OṂ. Speech and breath, the Ṛg and the Sāman—each of these sets, clearly, is a pair in coitus.

6 This pair in coitus unites in the syllable OṂ, and when a pair unites in coitus, they satisfy each other's desire. 7 So, when someone knows this and venerates the High Chant as this syllable, he will surely become a man who satisfies desires.

8 Clearly, this syllable signifies assent, for one says 'OṂ' when one assents to something. And assent is nothing but fulfilment. So, when someone knows this and venerates the High Chant as this syllable, he will surely become a man who fulfils desires.

9 It is by means of this syllable that the triple Veda continues—the Adhvaryu priest says 'OṂ' before he issues a call; the Hotṛ says 'OṂ' before he makes an invocation; and the Udgātṛ says 'OṂ' before he sings the High Chant. They do so to honour this very syllable, because of its greatness and because it is the essence.

10 Those who know this and those who do not both perform these rites using this syllable. But knowledge and ignorance are two very different things. Only what is performed with knowledge, with faith, and with an awareness of the hidden connections (*upaniṣad*) becomes truly potent.

Now, then—that was a further explanation of this very syllable.

2 Once, when the gods and the demons, both children of Prajāpati, arrayed themselves against each other, the gods got hold of the High Chant. 'With this we will overpower them', they thought.

2 So they venerated the High Chant as the breath within the nostrils. The demons riddled it with evil. As a result, one smells with it both good and bad odours, for it is riddled with evil.

3 Then they venerated the High Chant as speech. The demons riddled it with evil. As a result, one speaks with it both what is true and what is false, for it is riddled with evil.

4 Then they venerated the High Chant as sight. The demons riddled it with evil. As a result one sees with it both what is good to see and what is not, for it is riddled with evil.

5 Then they venerated the High Chant as hearing. The demons riddled it with evil. As a result, one hears with it both what is good to hear and what is not, for it is riddled with evil.

6 Then they venerated the High Chant as the mind. The demons riddled it with evil. As a result, one envisages with it both what is good to envisage and what is not, for it is riddled with evil.

7 Finally, they venerated the High Chant as just this breath here within the mouth. And when the demons hurled themselves at it, they were smashed to bits like a clod of earth hurled against a target that is a rock. 8 And if anyone contemplates evil against or hurts a person who knows this, he will be smashed to bits like a clod hurled against a target that is a rock. That person is a rock target. 9 One never recognizes with this breath either good or bad odours, for it is free from evil. Therefore, whenever one eats or drinks, one nourishes thereby the other vital functions (*prāṇa*). When, at the end, one fails to find it, one departs; indeed, at the end one leaves the mouth wide open.

10 Aṅgiras venerated the High Chant as that breath. People consider Aṅgiras to be just that, because it is the essence (*rasa*) of the bodily parts (*aṅga*). 11 Bṛhaspati venerated the High Chant as that breath. People consider Bṛhaspati to be just that, because speech is great (*bṛhatī*) and it is the lord (*pati*) of speech. 12 Ayāsya venerated the High Chant as that breath. People consider Ayāsya to be just that, because it proceeds (*ayate*) from the mouth (*āsya*). 13 Then Baka Dālbhya came to know that. He became the Udgātṛ priest of the people of Naimiṣa and secured their desires for them through

his singing. [14] And, indeed, when someone knows this and venerates the High Chant as this syllable, he too will become a man who secures desires through singing.

All that was with respect to the body (*ātman*).

3 What follows is with respect to the divine sphere. One should venerate the High Chant as the sun up there that gives warmth. As it rises (*udyan*), it sings the High Chant (*udgāyati*) for the creatures. As it rises, it dispels darkness and fear. Anyone who knows this is sure to become a man who dispels fear and darkness.

[2] This breath in here and that sun up there are exactly the same. This is warm, and so is that. People call this sound (*svara*), and they call that shine (*svara*) and shining back (*pratyāsvara*). Therefore, one should venerate the High Chant as both this here and that up there.

[3] Now, then, one should venerate the High Chant as just the inter-breath. When one breathes out, it is the out-breath; when one breathes in, it is the in-breath. And the inter-breath is where the out-breath and the in-breath meet. The inter-breath is the same as speech. One speaks, therefore, without breathing out or in. [4] Speech is the same as the Ṛg verse. One recites a Ṛg verse, therefore, without breathing out or in. The Ṛg verse is the same as the Sāman chant. One sings a Sāman chant, therefore, without breathing out or in. The Sāman chant is the same as the High Chant. One sings the High Chant, therefore, without breathing out or in. [5] Even activities other than these, activities that require strength, such as churning a fire, running a race, and stretching a strong bow, are performed without breathing out or in. For this reason, one should venerate the High Chant as just the inter-breath.

[6] Now, then, one should venerate the syllables of the word *udgītha*—High Chant—namely *ud, gī,* and *tha*. The syllable *ud* is simply breath, for people rise up (*ud-sthā*) by means of breath; the syllable *gī* is speech, for speech utterances are called words (*gir*); and the syllable *tha* is food, for this whole world rests (*sthita*) on food. [7] The syllable *ud*, likewise, is the sky, *gī* is the intermediate region, and *tha* is the earth. And again, the syllable *ud* is the sun, *gī* is the wind, and *tha* is the fire. So also, the syllable *ud* is the Sāmaveda, *gī* is the Yajurveda, and *tha* is the Ṛgveda. When someone knows them in this way and venerates these syllables of

the High Chant, namely, *ud*, *gī*, and *tha*—speech will yield for him the milk which is the very milk of speech, and he will come to own and to eat his own food.

8 Now, then, this is how wishes are fulfilled. One should venerate the following as things to turn to. A man should repair to the Sāman chant which he is about to use in a liturgical praise, 9 to the Ṛg verse which supplies the lyrics of that chant, and to the seer who composed that verse. A man should repair to the deity whom he is about to praise with that chant. 10 A man should repair to the metre of the chant which he is about to use in his praise. A man should repair to the arrangement of the chant which he is about to use in his praise. 11 A man should repair to the direction to which he addresses his praise. 12 Turning to himself (*ātman*), finally, he should sing the hymn of praise, focusing his mind completely on his wish. He can certainly expect that the wish he had as he sang the praise will be fulfilled.

4 OṂ—one should venerate the High Chant as this syllable, for one begins the High Chant with OṂ. Here is a further explanation of that syllable.

2 When the gods feared death, what they did was to enter the triple Veda. They covered it with the metres. The fact that the gods covered (*chad*) it with them gave the name to and discloses the true nature of the metres (*chandas*). 3 But death saw the gods there in the Ṛg verses, in the Sāman chants, and in the Yajus formulas, just as one sees a fish in water. When the gods discovered this, they emerged from the Ṛg, Sāman, and Yajus, and entered into the very sound. 4 So, when one finishes a Ṛg verse, or a Sāman chant, or a Yajus formula, one makes the sound OṂ. This syllable—the immortal and the fearless—is that very sound. Upon entering that syllable, the gods became immortal and free from fear.

5 A man who utters this syllable with that knowledge enters this very syllable, the sound that is immortal and free from fear. As the gods became immortal by entering it, so will he.

5 So, then, the High Chant is OṂ, and OṂ is the High Chant. The High Chant is the sun up there, and it is also OṂ, for as it moves it makes the sound OṂ. 2 And this is what Kauṣītaki once told his son: 'I sang the praise of only the sun. Therefore, I have

only you for a child. Turn to its rays, and you will have many children.'

That is with respect to the divine sphere.

3 Now, with respect to the body (*ātman*): it is as the breath here within the mouth that one should venerate as the High Chant, for as it moves it makes the sound OṂ. 4 And this is what Kauṣītaki once told his son: 'I sang the praise of only the breath within the mouth. Therefore, I have only you for a child. Direct your songs of praise at the breaths in their multiplicity with the thought, "I am going to have many children."'

5 So, then, the High Chant is OṂ, and OṂ is the High Chant. That is why the Hotṛ priest from his seat rectifies a High Chant that has been sung improperly.

6 The Ṛg verse is this earth, and the Sāman chant, the fire. The Sāman is thus overlaid on the Ṛg, and, therefore, one sings the Sāman overlaid on the Ṛg. *Sā* is this earth, and *ama*, the fire—and that makes 'Sāma'.

2 The Ṛg verse is the intermediate region, and the Sāman chant, the wind. The Sāman is thus overlaid on the Ṛg, and, therefore, one sings the Sāman overlaid on the Ṛg. *Sā* is the intermediate region, and *ama*, the wind—and that makes 'Sāma'.

3 The Ṛg verse is the sky, and the Sāman chant, the sun. The Sāman is thus overlaid on the Ṛg, and, therefore, one sings the Sāman overlaid on the Ṛg. *Sā* is the sky and *ama*, the sun—and that makes 'Sāma'.

4 The Ṛg verse is the stars, and the Sāman chant, the moon. The Sāman is thus overlaid on the Ṛg, and, therefore, one sings the Sāman overlaid on the Ṛg. *Sā* is the stars and *ama*, the moon—and that makes 'Sāma'.

5 Now, the Ṛg verse is the white lustre of the sun, and the Sāman chant, the dark, the pitch-black. The Sāman is thus overlaid on the
Ṛg, and, therefore, one sings the Sāman overlaid on the Ṛg. 6Now,
sā is the white lustre of the sun and *ama*, the dark, the pitch-black—and that makes 'Sāma'.

Now, the golden person we see within the sun—he has golden hair and a golden beard; he is completely golden, down to the very
tips of his nails. 7 His eyes are like deep blue lotuses. His name is
'Up' (*ud*), for he has risen up (*udita*) above all evils. Anyone who

knows this undoubtedly rises up above all evils. 8 The two songs (*geṣṇa*) of that golden person are the Ṛg and the Sāman. He is therefore the High Chant (*udgītha*), and, because he sings it, also the High Chanter (*udgātṛ*). He rules over the worlds beyond the sun and over the desires of gods.

That was with respect to the divine sphere.

7 Next, with respect to the body (*ātman*)—

The Ṛg verse is speech, and the Sāman chant, the breath. The Sāman is thus overlaid on the Ṛg, and, therefore, one sings the Sāman overlaid on the Ṛg. Sā is speech, and ama, breath—and that makes 'Sāma'.

2 The Ṛg verse is sight, and the Sāman chant, the body (*ātman*). The Sāman is thus overlaid on the Ṛg, and, therefore, one sings the Sāman overlaid on the Ṛg. *Sā* is sight, and *ama,* the body—and that makes 'Sāma'.

3 The Ṛg verse is hearing, and the Sāman chant, the mind. The Sāman is thus overlaid on the Ṛg, and, therefore, one sings the Sāman overlaid on the Ṛg. *Sā* is hearing, and *ama,* the mind—and that makes 'Sāma'.

4 Now, the Ṛg verse is the white lustre of the eye, and the Sāman chant, the dark, the pitch-black. The Sāman is thus overlaid on the Ṛg, and, therefore, one sings the Sāman overlaid on the Ṛg. Now, *sā* is the white lustre of the eye, and *ama*, the dark, the pitch-black—and that makes 'Sāma'.

5 Now, the person one sees within the eye—he, indeed, is the Ṛg verse, he is the Sāman chant, he is the recitation, he is the Yajus formula, he is the formulation of truth (*brahman*).

This person down here has exactly the same appearance as that person up there in the sun, and this person has the same two songs and the same name as he. 6 This person here rules over the worlds below the sun and over the desires of men. So, those who sing as they play the lute—they sing of him and thus obtain wealth. 7 A man who sings the Sāman chants with this knowledge sings of both of them. Through the former he wins the worlds beyond the sun and the desires of gods, 8 while through the latter he wins the worlds below the sun and the desires of men. Therefore, an Udgātṛ priest who possesses this knowledge may truly say: 9 'What desire shall I obtain for you by my singing?' For one who sings the

Sāman chant with this knowledge has, indeed, the power to fulfil desires by singing.

8 There were once three men who had mastered the High Chant—Śilaka Śālāvatya, Caikitāyana Dālbhya, and Pravāhaṇa Jaivali. They said to each other: 'We have clearly mastered the High Chant. So come, let's have a discussion about the High Chant.' 2 They all agreed and sat down. Then Pravāhaṇa Jaivali said to the other two: 'Gentlemen, why don't the two of you talk first? I will listen to the conversation as the two Brahmins talk.'

3 So Śilaka Śālāvatya said to Caikitāyana Dālbhya: 'Come, I'll ask you a question.' 'Go ahead,' he replied.

4 'Where does the Sāman lead to?'

'Sound.'

'Where does sound lead to?'

'Breath.'

'Where does breath lead to?'

'Food.'

'Where does food lead to?'

'Water.'

5 'Where does water lead to?'

'That world up there.'

'Where does that world lead to?'

'One should not take it beyond the heavenly world,' he replied. 'We bring the Sāman to a rest at the heavenly world, for heaven is the place from which the Sāman is sung.'

6 Thereupon, Śilaka Śālāvatya told Caikitāyana Dālbhya: 'It is very clear, Dālbhya, that your Sāman lacks a foundation. And if someone were to say to you now "Your head will shatter apart!" your head is bound to shatter apart.'

7 'All right then, let me learn it from you, sir.'

'Do so,' he replied.

'Where does that world lead to?'

'This world,' he replied.

'Where does this world lead to?'

'One should not take it beyond the world that is the foundation,' he replied. 'We bring the Sāman to a rest at the world that is the foundation, for this foundation is the place from which the Sāman is sung.'

8 Thereupon, Pravāhaṇa Jaivali said: 'It is very clear, Śālāvatya, that your Sāman is limited. And if someone were to say to you now "Your head will shatter apart!" your head is bound to shatter apart.'

'All right then, let me learn it from you, sir.'

'Do so,' he replied.

9 'Where does this world lead to?'

'Space,' he replied. 'Clearly, it is from space that all these beings arise, and into space that they are finally absorbed; for space indeed existed before them and in space they ultimately end. 2 This is the most extensive High Chant; this is without limit. When someone knows it in this way and venerates this most extensive High Chant, that which is most extensive will be his and he will win the most extensive of worlds.'

3 After telling this to Udaraśāṇḍilya, Atidhanvan Śaunaka said: 'So long as they continue to possess the knowledge of this High Chant, your descendants will have the most extensive life in this world, 4 as also a world in the next.' When someone knows and venerates it in this way, he will have the most extensive life in this world, as also a world in the next.

10 Once, when the land of Kuru had been devastated by locusts, there lived in that region one Uṣasti Cākrāyaṇa together with his wife Āṭikī, a pauper living in the village of a rich man. 2 One day he came to beg from the rich man while he was eating some groats. And he told Uṣasti: 'All I have is what I have been served here. I have nothing else.' Uṣasti replied: 3 'Give me some of that.' So he gave him some and said: 'Here is something to drink.'

And Uṣasti replied: 'That would be drinking your leftovers!'

4 'But aren't these also leftovers?'

'Yes,' he replied, 'but if I don't eat them I'll die. Drinking the water, on the other hand, is optional.'

5 After he had eaten himself, Uṣasti took the remainder to his wife. But she had already gathered ample almsfood. So she took what Uṣasti gave her and saved it.

[6] The next morning Uṣasti got up and said: 'If only I had some food, I'd be able to earn a little money. That king over there is getting ready to perform a sacrifice, and he may well choose me to carry out all the priestly functions.' [7] His wife told him: 'But, my lord, we still have the groats.' He ate them and arrived at the sacrifice after it had already started.

[8] There, he sat by the Udgātṛ priests as they were preparing to sing the song of praise in the area designated for it. He then said to the Prastotṛ priest: [9] 'Hey Prastotṛ! If you sing the Introductory Praise without knowing the deity that is linked to it, your head will shatter apart!' [10] He said the same thing to the Udgātṛ priest: 'Hey Udgātṛ! If you sing the High Chant without knowing the deity that is linked to it, your head will shatter apart!' [11] And he said the same thing also to the Pratihartṛ priest: 'Hey Pratihartṛ! If you sing the Response without knowing the deity that is linked to it, your head will shatter apart!' So they stopped singing and sat down in silence.

11 Then the patron of the sacrifice said to him: 'Sir, I'd very much like to know who you are.' And he replied: 'I am Uṣasti Cākrāyaṇa.'

[2] 'It is you, sir, whom I have been searching for to carry out all these priestly functions. I selected these others only when I couldn't find you. [3] But now, sir, you yourself should carry out all the priestly functions for me.'

'All right. But let these same priests, who were authorized at that time, sing the songs of praise. You must, however, give me the same amount of money that you give them.'

'All right,' said the patron of the sacrifice.

[4] At this point the Prastotṛ priest drew close to him and said: 'Sir, you said to me, "Hey Prastotṛ! If you sing the Introductory Praise (*prastāva*) without knowing the deity that is linked to it, your head will shatter apart!" So tell me, who is that deity?'

[5] 'Breath (*prāṇa*),' he replied. 'Clearly, all these beings gather around breath and rise up towards breath. This, then, is the deity linked to the Introductory Praise. If, after I had warned you, you had sung the Introductory Praise without knowing that deity, your head would have shattered apart.'

[6] Then the Udgātṛ priest drew close to him and said: 'Sir, you

said to me, "Hey Udgātṛ! If you sing the High Chant (*udgītha*) without knowing the deity that is linked to it, your head will shatter apart!" So tell me, who is that deity?'

7 'The sun,' he replied. 'Clearly, when the sun is up high (*uccaiḥ*) all these beings sing (*gāyanti*) to it. This, then, is the deity linked to the High Chant. If, after I had warned you, you had sung the High Chant without knowing that deity, your head would have shattered apart.'

8 The Pratihartṛ priest then drew close to him and said: 'Sir, you said to me, "Hey Pratihartṛ! If you sing the Response (*pratihāra*) without knowing the deity that is linked to it, your head will shatter apart!" So tell me, who is that deity?'

9 'Food,' he replied. 'Clearly, it is only by partaking of food (*pratiharamāṇa*) that all these beings live. This, then, is the deity linked to the Response. If, after I had warned you, you had sung the Response without knowing that deity, your head would have shattered apart.'

12 Next comes the High Chant of dogs. One day, while Baka Dālbhya—or it may have been Glāva Maitreya—was on his way to perform his vedic recitation, 2 there appeared before him a white dog. Other dogs gathered around the white one and said to him: 'Please, sir, find some food for us by singing. We are really hungry.' 3 And he told them: 'Come and meet me at this very spot in the morning.' So Baka Dālbhya—or it may have been Glāva Maitreya—kept watch there.

4 Those dogs then filed in, sliding stealthily in just the same way as priests slide stealthily in a file holding on to each other's back to sing the hymn of praise called Bahiṣpavamāna. They sat down together and made the sound '*huṃ*'. 5 They sang: 'OṂ! Let's eat! OṂ! Let's drink! OṂ! May the gods Varuṇa, Prajāpati, and Savitṛ bring here food! Lord of food! Bring here food! Bring! Bring! OṂ!'

13 Now, the interjection '*hā u*' is this world; '*hā i*' is the wind; '*atha*' is the moon; '*iha*' is the body (*ātman*); '*ī*' is fire; 2 '*ū*' is the sun; '*e*' is the invocation; '*au ho i*' is the All-gods; '*hiṃ*' is Prajāpati; '*svara*' ('sound') is breath; '*yā*' is food; and '*virāṭ*' is speech. 3 The thirteenth interjection, that is, the accompanying sound '*huṃ*', is left unexplained.

[4] When a man knows these hidden connections (*upaniṣad*) of the Sāman chants—speech will yield for him the milk which is the very milk of speech, and he will come to own and to eat his own food.

CHAPTER 2

1 To venerate the Sāman chant in its entirety—now, that is a good thing (*sādhu*). So, you see, when something is good (*sādhu*), people say, 'It's valuable (*sāma*),' and when something is not good (*asādhu*), they say, 'It's worthless (*asāma*)'.

[2] And in this regard, when people likewise say, 'He approached him with kind words (*sāman*)', what they intend to say is, 'He approached him with good intention (*sādhu*)'. Similarly, when they say, 'He approached him with unkind words (*asāman*)', what they intend to say is, 'He approached him with ill intention (*asādhu*)'.

[3] And when people likewise say, 'Oh, we've got wealth (*sāman*)!' when they are doing well (*sādhu*), what they intend to say is, 'Oh, we are doing well (*sādhu*)!' Likewise, when they say, 'Oh, we've no wealth (*asāma*)!' when they aren't doing well (*asādhu*), what they intend to say is, 'Oh, we aren't doing well (*asādhu*)!'

[4] When someone knows this and venerates the Sāman chant as good (*sādhu*), he can certainly expect that good things will come his way and fall to his share.

2 In the worlds one should venerate the fivefold Sāman chant. First, in an ascending order, the *Hiṃ*-interjection is the earth; the Introductory Praise is the fire; the High Chant is the intermediate region; the Response is the sun; and the Concluding Chant is the sky.

[2] Next, in the reverse order, the *Hiṃ*-interjection is the sky; the Introductory Praise is the sun; the High Chant is the intermediate region; the Response is the fire; and the Concluding Chant is the earth.

3 When someone knows this and venerates the fivefold Sāman chant in the worlds—the worlds, both in their ascending and in their reverse order, become favourable to him.

3 In rain one should venerate the fivefold Sāman chant. When the wind starts to blow, it is the *Hiṃ*-interjection. When the clouds form, it is the Introductory Praise. When the rain is falling, it is the High Chant. When lightning is striking and thunder is rolling, it is the Response. And when the rain stops, it is the Concluding Chant.

2 When someone knows this and venerates the fivefold Sāman chant in rain—rain falls for him, and he causes rain to fall.

4 In all the waters one should venerate the fivefold Sāman chant. When clouds gather, it is the *Hiṃ*-interjection. When the rain is falling, it is the Introductory Praise. When the easterly rivers flow eastwards, it is the High Chant. When the westerly rivers flow westwards, it is the Response. The ocean is the Concluding Chant.

2 When someone knows this and venerates the fivefold Sāman chant in all the waters—he will never drown in water, and he will have an ample supply of water.

5 In the seasons one should venerate the fivefold Sāman chant. The *Hiṃ*-interjection is the spring; the Introductory Praise is the summer; the High Chant is the rainy season; the Response is the autumn; and the Concluding Chant is the winter.

2 When someone knows this and venerates the fivefold Sāman chant in the seasons—the seasons become favourable to him, and he will enjoy many seasons.

6 In animals one should venerate the fivefold Sāman chant. The *Hiṃ*-interjection is goats; the Introductory Praise is sheep; the High Chant is cows; the Response is horses; and the Concluding Chant is man.

2 When someone knows this and venerates the fivefold Sāman chant in animals—he will obtain animals, and he will become rich in animals.

7 In the vital functions (*prāṇa*) one should venerate the most extensive fivefold Sāman chant. The *Hiṃ*-interjection is breath; the Introductory Praise is speech; the High Chant is sight; the Response is hearing; and the Concluding Chant is the mind.

2 When someone knows this and venerates the fivefold Sāman chant in the vital functions—he will obtain what is most extensive, and he will win the most extensive worlds.

Now, that was the veneration of the fivefold Sāman chant.

8 Next, the veneration of the sevenfold Sāman chant.

In speech one should venerate the sevenfold Sāman chant. Every *huṃ* sound present in speech is the *Hiṃ*-interjection; every *pra* sound is the Introductory Praise (*pra.stāva*); every *ā* sound is the Opening (*ā.di*); 2 every *ud* sound is the High Chant (*ud.gītha*); every *prati* sound is the Response (*prati.hāra*); every *upa* sound is the Finale (*upa.drava*); and every *ni* sound is the Concluding Chant (*ni.dhana*).

3 When a man knows this and venerates the sevenfold Sāman chant in speech—speech will yield for him the milk which is the very milk of speech, and he will come to own and eat his own food.

9 Now, then, one should venerate the sevenfold Sāman chant as the sun up there. The sun is the Sāman chant because it is always the same (*sāma*). It appears the same to everyone, because each one says, 'It faces me! It faces me!'—therefore, the sun is the Sāman chant. 2 One should know that all beings here are linked to it.

Just before sunrise, it is the *Hiṃ*-interjection, and animals are linked to it. Animals, therefore, make the sound *hiṃ*, for they share in the *Hiṃ*-interjection of this Sāman chant.

3 When it has just risen, the sun is the Introductory Praise (*prastāva*), and humans are linked to it. Humans, therefore, are fond of praise (*prastuti*) and acclaim (*praśaṃsā*), for they share in the Introductory Praise of this Sāman chant.

4 At mid-morning, the sun is the Opening (*ādi*), and birds are linked to it. Birds, therefore, fly about in the intermediate region holding themselves up (*ādāya*) without any support, for they share in the Opening of this Sāman chant.

5 Exactly at midday, the sun is the High Chant, and gods are linked to it. Gods, therefore, are the best of Prajāpati's children, for they share in the High Chant of this Sāman chant.

6 When it is past midday but before mid-afternoon, the sun is the Response (*pratihāra*), and embryos are linked to it. Embryos, therefore, are confined (*pratihṛta*) and do not fall out, for they share in the Response of this Sāman chant.

7 When it is past mid-afternoon but before sunset, the sun is the Finale (*upadrava*), and wild animals are linked to it. When they see a man, therefore, wild animals flee (*upadravanti*) into a thicket to hide themselves, for they share in the Finale of this Sāman chant.

8 When it has just set, the sun is the Concluding Chant (*nidhana*), and the ancestors are linked to it. People, therefore, lay their ancestors to rest (*nidadhati*), for they share in the Concluding Chant of this Sāman chant.

In this way, then, one venerates the sevenfold Sāman chant as the sun up there.

10 Now, then, one should venerate the sevenfold Sāman chant according to its own measure and as leading beyond death. *Hiṃ.kā.ra*—the *Hiṃ*-interjection—has three syllables. And *pra.stā.va*—the Introductory Praise—has three syllables. So they are the same.

2 *Ā.di*—the Opening—has two syllables. And *pra.ti.hā.ra*—the Response—has four syllables. Move one syllable from the latter to the former, and then they are the same.

3 *Ud.gī.tha*—the High Chant—has three syllables. And *u.pa.dra.va*—the Finale—has four syllables. With three syllables in each, they are the same. One syllable (*a.kṣa.ra*)—which has three syllables—is left over. So they are the same.

4 *Ni.dha.na*—the Concluding Chant—has three syllables. So it is the same as those.

So there are here altogether twenty-two syllables. 5 With twenty-one of those one reaches the sun; the sun up there is clearly the twenty-first from here. With the twenty-second one conquers what is beyond the sun. That is the vault of the sky, a place free from sorrow.

6 When a man knows this and venerates the sevenfold Sāman

chant according to its own measure and as leading beyond death—he will conquer the sun, and he will even gain a conquest that surpasses the conquest of the sun.

11 The *Hiṃ*-interjection is the mind; the Introductory Praise is speech; the High Chant is sight; the Response is hearing; and the Concluding Chant is breath. This is the Gāyatra Sāman woven upon the vital functions (*prāṇa*).

2 When in this manner a man knows this Gāyatra Sāman woven upon the vital functions—he comes to have full possession of the vital functions; he lives his full life span; he lives a long life; he becomes a big man on account of offspring and livestock; and he becomes a big man on account of his fame. He should be big-minded—that is his basic rule.

12 When one churns the fire-drill, it is the *Hiṃ*-interjection. When the smoke rises, it is the Introductory Praise. When it flares up, it is the High Chant. When the coals form, it is the Response. When the fire dies down, it is the Concluding Chant. When the fire is extinguished, it is the Concluding Chant. This is the Rathantara Sāman woven upon the fire.

2 When in this manner a man knows this Rathantara Sāman woven upon the fire—he becomes an eater of food, radiant with the lustre of sacred knowledge; he lives his full life span; he lives a long life; he becomes a big man on account of offspring and livestock; and he becomes a big man on account of his fame. He should not sip water or spit in the direction of the fire—that is his basic rule.

13 When he calls, it is the *Hiṃ*-interjection. When he asks, it is the Introductory Praise. When he lies down with the woman, it is the High Chant. When he lies upon (*prati*) the woman, it is the Response (*prati.hāra*). When he ejaculates, it is the Concluding Chant. When he withdraws, it is the Concluding Chant. This is the Vāmadevya Sāman woven upon sexual intercourse.

2 When in this manner a man knows this Vāmadevya Sāman woven upon sexual intercourse—he becomes proficient in sexual intercourse and regenerates himself through every sexual inter-

course; he lives his full life span; he lives a long life; he becomes a big man on account of offspring and livestock; and he becomes a big man on account of his fame. He should not hold back from any woman—that is his basic rule.

14 When the sun is rising, it is the *Hiṃ*-interjection. When it has risen, it is the Introductory Praise. Midday is the High Chant. The afternoon is the Response. When it sets, it is the Concluding Chant. This is the Bṛhat Sāman woven upon the sun.

2 When in this manner a man knows this Bṛhat Sāman woven upon the sun—he becomes resplendent and an eater of food; he lives his full life span; he lives a long life; he becomes a big man on account of offspring and livestock; and he becomes a big man on account of his fame. He should not complain against the sun when it scorches—that is his basic rule.

15 When clouds gather, it is the *Hiṃ*-interjection. When the rain-cloud is formed, it is the Introductory Praise. When rain is falling it is the High Chant. When lightning is striking and thunder is rolling, it is the Response. When the rain stops, it is the Concluding Chant. This is the Vairūpa Sāman woven upon the rain.

2 When in this manner a man knows this Vairūpa Sāman woven upon the rain—he keeps in his corral beautiful livestock of various types; he lives his full life span; he lives a long life; he becomes a big man on account of offspring and livestock; and he becomes a big man on account of his fame. He should not complain when it rains—that is his basic rule.

16 The *Hiṃ*-interjection is the spring; the Introductory Praise is the summer; the High Chant is the rainy season; the Response is the autumn; and the Concluding Chant is the winter. This is the Vairāja Sāman woven upon the Seasons.

2 When in this manner a man knows this Vairāja Sāman woven upon the seasons—he becomes resplendent with children, livestock, and the lustre of sacred knowledge; he lives his full life span; he lives a long life; he becomes a big man on account of offspring and livestock; and he becomes a big man on account of his

fame. He should not complain against the seasons—that is his basic rule.

17 The *Hiṃ*-interjection is the earth; the Introductory Praise is the intermediate region; the High Chant is the sky; the Response is the quarters; and the Concluding Chant is the ocean. These are the Śakvarī Sāman chants woven upon the worlds.

2 When in this manner a man knows these Śakvarī Sāman chants woven upon the worlds—he comes to possess the worlds; he lives his full life span; he lives a long life; he becomes a big man on account of offspring and livestock; and he becomes a big man on account of his fame. He should not complain against the worlds—that is his basic rule.

18 The *Hiṃ*-interjection is goats; the Introductory Praise is sheep; the High Chant is cows; the Response is horses; and the Concluding Chant is man. These are the Revatī Sāman chants woven upon animals.

2 When in this manner a man knows these Revatī Sāman chants woven upon animals—he comes to possess animals; he lives his full life span; he lives a long life; he becomes a big man on account of offspring and livestock; and he becomes a big man on account of his fame. He should not complain against animals—that is his basic rule.

19 The *Hiṃ*-interjection is the body hair; the Introductory Praise is the skin; the High Chant is the flesh; the Response is the bones; and the Concluding Chant is the marrow. This is the Yajñāyajñīya Sāman woven upon bodily parts.

2 When in this manner a man knows this Yajñāyajñīya Sāman woven upon the bodily parts—he comes to possess all the bodily parts and does not become defective in any bodily part; he lives his full life span; he lives a long life; he becomes a big man on account of offspring and livestock; and he becomes a big man on account of his fame. He should not eat marrow for a year—that is his basic rule; or else, he should never eat marrow.

20 The *Hiṃ*-interjection is the fire; the Introductory Praise is the wind; the High Chant is the sun; the Response is the

stars; and the Concluding Chant is the moon. This is the Rājana Sāman woven upon the deities.

2 When in this manner a man knows this Rājana Sāman woven upon the deities—he obtains residence in the same world as these deities, and equality and union with them; he lives his full life span; he lives a long life; he becomes a big man on account of offspring and livestock; and he becomes a big man on account of his fame. He should not complain against Brahmins—that is his basic rule.

21 The *Hiṃ*-interjection is the triple Veda; the Introductory Praise is these three worlds; the High Chant is fire, wind, and sun; the Response is the stars, birds, and the glittering specks; and the Concluding Chant is snakes, Gandharvas, and ancestors. This is the Sāman woven upon the Whole.

2 When in this manner a man knows this Sāman woven upon the Whole—he becomes the Whole. 3 In this connection there is this verse:

> There is nothing better, nothing higher,
> than the fivefold set of threes.
> 4 A man who knows that knows the Whole;
> all quarters bring tribute to him.

He should venerate this Sāman with the thought, 'I am the Whole!'—that is his basic rule.

22 'I choose the roaring way of singing the Sāman, the singing that resembles the lowing of an animal'—that is the High Chant of the fire. The indistinct way of singing it is the High Chant of Prajāpati; the distinct way of singing it is the High Chant of Soma; the soft and smooth way of singing it is the High Chant of the wind; the smooth and powerful way of singing it is the High Chant of Indra; the way of singing it that sounds like a heron is the High Chant of Bṛhaspati; and the dissonant way of singing it is the High Chant of Varuṇa. One should employ all these ways of singing, except that of Varuṇa, which alone one should avoid.

2 When a person sings to obtain something, he should do so with the thought, 'Let me obtain immortality for the gods by my singing.' Likewise, he should be careful to keep the following

thoughts in his mind as he sings the songs of praise: 'Let me obtain by my singing food offerings for the ancestors, the fulfilment of wishes for humans, fodder and water for animals, heaven for the patron of the sacrifice, and food for myself (*ātman*).'

3 All the vowels are corporeal forms (*ātman*) of Indra. All the spirants are corporeal forms of Prajāpati. And all the stops are corporeal forms of Death. So, if someone criticizes him for the way he pronounces his vowels, he should tell that man: 'I have taken refuge in Indra, and he will rebut you.' 4 And if someone criticizes him for the way he pronounces his spirants, he should tell that man: 'I have taken refuge in Prajāpati, and he will crush you.' And if someone criticizes him for the way he pronounces his stops, he should tell that man: 'I have taken refuge in Death, and he will burn you up.'

5 One should pronounce all the vowels with resonance and emphasis, thinking, 'Let me give strength to Indra.' One should pronounce all the spirants without swallowing or ejecting them, and with an open passage between the tongue and the place of articulation, thinking, 'Let me surrender myself (*ātman*) to Prajāpati.' One should pronounce all the stops checking slightly and thus separating them from the following sounds so that they are not absorbed into them, thinking, 'Let me save myself from Death.'

23

There are three types of persons whose torso is the Law (*dharma*).

The first is one who pursues sacrifice, vedic recitation, and gift-giving.

The second is one who is devoted solely to austerity.

The third is a celibate student of the Veda living at his teacher's house; that is, a student who settles himself permanently at his teacher's house.

All these gain worlds earned by merit.
A person who is steadfast in *brahman* reaches immortality.

2 Prajāpati incubated the worlds, and, when they had been incubated, the triple Veda sprang from them. He incubated the triple Veda, and, when it had been incubated, these syllables '*bhūr, bhuvaḥ, svar*' sprang from it. 3 He incubated these syllables, and, when they had been incubated, the syllable OṂ

sprang from them. As all the leaves are bored through by a pin, so all words are bored through by OṂ. This whole world is nothing but OṂ.

24 Those who articulate formulations of truth (*brahman*) enquire: 'Since the morning pressing of Soma belongs to the Vasus, the midday pressing to the Rudras, and the third pressing to the Ādityas and the All-gods, 2 what world is then left for the patron of the sacrifice?' If a man does not know the answer to this, how can he carry out a sacrifice? So, only a man who knows it should carry it out.

3 Before the command to recite the morning litany has been issued, the patron sits facing the north behind the householder's fire and sings the Sāman of the Vasus:

4 Open the door to the world!
Let us see you—to win
Sovereignty!

5 Then he puts the offering of ghee in the fire, saying: 'Homage to the fire dwelling on the earth, dwelling in the world! Secure that world for me, for the patron—for that is the patron's world. I will go 6 there after death—I the patron—svāhā! Throw back the bolt!' After saying this, he gets up.

The Vasus present to him the morning pressing.

7 Before the command to undertake the midday pressing has been issued, the patron sits facing the north behind the Āgnīdhrīya fire and sings the Sāman of the Rudras:

8 Open the door to the world!
Let us see you—to win
Broad Sovereignty!

9 Then he puts the offering of ghee in the fire, saying: 'Homage to the wind dwelling in the intermediate world, dwelling in the world! Secure that world for me, for the patron—for that is the patron's world. I will go 10 there after death—I the patron—svāhā! Throw back the bolt!' After saying this, he gets up.

The Rudras present to him the midday pressing.

11 Before the command to undertake the third pressing has been

issued, the patron sits facing the north behind the offertorial fire and sings the Sāman of the Ādityas and of the All-gods:

> 12 Open the door to the world!
> Let us see you—to win
> Full Sovereignty!

That is the Sāman of the Ādityas. 13 Next, the Sāman of the All-gods:

> Open the door to the world!
> Let us see you—to win
> Absolute Sovereignty!

14 Then he pours the offering of ghee in the fire, saying: 'Homage to the Ādityas and the All-gods dwelling in the sky, dwelling in the world! Secure that world for me, for the patron—15 for that is the patron's world. I will go there after death—I the patron—svāhā! Throw back the bolt!' After saying this, he gets up.

16 The Ādityas and the All-gods present to him the third pressing. A man who knows this undoubtedly knows the full measure of the sacrifice.

CHAPTER 3

1 The honey of the gods, clearly, is the sun up there. The cross-bar for it is the sky itself; the hive is the intermediate region; and the larvae are the glittering specks.

2 Its easterly honey cells are simply the easterly rays of the sun—the bees being the Ṛg verses, and the flower, the Ṛgveda—they are the immortal waters.

These very Ṛg verses 3 incubated the Ṛgveda, and, when it had been incubated, its essence sprang from it in the form of lustre, splendour, power, strength, and foodstuff. 4 All that flowed out and made its way to the sun; and that is what constitutes the red appearance of the sun.

2 Its southerly honey cells are simply the southerly rays of the sun—the bees being the Yajus formulas, and the flower, the Yajurveda—they are the immortal waters.

2 These very Yajus formulas incubated the Yajurveda, and, when it had been incubated, its essence sprang from it in the form of lustre, splendour, power, strength, and foodstuff. 3 All that flowed out and made its way to the sun; and that is what constitutes the white appearance of the sun.

3 Its westerly honey cells are simply the westerly rays of the sun—the bees being the Sāman chants, and the flower, the Sāmaveda—they are the immortal waters.

2 These very Sāman chants incubated the Sāmaveda, and, when it had been incubated, its essence sprang from it in the form of lustre, splendour, power, strength, and foodstuff. 3 All that flowed out and made its way to the sun; and that is what constitutes the dark appearance of the sun.

4 Its northerly honey cells are simply the northerly rays of the sun—the bees being the Atharva and Āṅgirasa formulas, and the flower, the Collection of Histories and Ancient Tales—they are the immortal waters.

2 These very Atharva and Āṅgirasa formulas incubated the Collection of Histories and Ancient Tales and, when it had been incubated, its essence sprang from it in the form of lustre, splendour, power, strength, and foodstuff. 3 All that flowed out and made its way to the sun; and that is what constitutes the very dark appearance of the sun.

5 Its upward honey cells are simply the upward rays of the sun—the bees being the secret rules of substitution, and the flower, the formulation of truth (*brahman*)—they are the immortal waters.

2 These very secret rules of substitution incubated the formulation of truth, and, when it had been incubated, its essence sprang from it in the form of lustre, splendour, power, strength, and foodstuff. 3 All that flowed out and made its way to the sun; and that is the flickering of a sort seen in the middle of the sun.

4 These, clearly, are the very essence of the essences, for the

essences are the Vedas, and these are their essence. These are, moreover, the immortal nectar of nectars, for the nectars are the Vedas, and these are their nectar.

6 On the first nectar among these the Vasus subsist with fire as their mouth. The gods, of course, neither eat nor drink. They become sated by just looking at this nectar. 2 Into that same [red] appearance they enter, and from that appearance they emerge.

3 When someone knows this nectar in this way—he becomes one with those very Vasus and, with fire itself as his mouth, becomes sated by just looking at this nectar; he enters into this same appearance and emerges from this appearance; 4 and he will achieve dominion and sovereignty over these very Vasus for as long as the sun shall rise in the east and set in the west.

7 On the second nectar among these the Rudras subsist with Indra as their mouth. The gods, of course, neither eat nor drink. They become sated by just looking at this nectar. 2 Into that same (white) appearance they enter, and from that appearance they emerge.

3 When someone knows this nectar in this way—he truly becomes one with those very Rudras and, with Indra himself as his mouth, becomes sated by just looking at this nectar; he enters into this same appearance and emerges from this appearance; 4 and he will achieve dominion and sovereignty over these very Rudras for as long as the sun shall rise in the south and set in the north, which is twice as long as it will rise in the east and set in the west.

8 On the third nectar among these the Ādityas subsist with Varuṇa as their mouth. The gods, of course, neither eat nor drink. They become sated by just looking at this nectar. 2 Into that same (dark) appearance they enter, and from that appearance they emerge.

3 When someone knows this nectar in this way—he truly becomes one with those very Ādityas and, with Varuṇa himself as his mouth, becomes sated by just looking at this nectar; he enters into this same appearance and emerges from this appearance; 4 and he will achieve dominion and sovereignty over these very Ādityas

for as long as the sun shall rise in the west and set in the east, which is twice as long as it will rise in the south and set in the north.

9 On the fourth nectar among these the Maruts subsist with the moon as their mouth. The gods, of course, neither eat nor drink. They become sated by just looking at this nectar. 2 Into that same (very dark) appearance they enter, and from that appearance they emerge.

3 When someone knows this nectar in this way—he truly becomes one with those very Maruts and, with the moon itself as his mouth, becomes sated by just looking at this nectar; he enters into this same appearance and emerges from this appearance; 4 and he will achieve dominion and sovereignty over these very Maruts for as long as the sun shall rise in the north and set in the south, which is twice as long as it will rise in the west and set in the east.

10 On the fifth nectar among these the Sādhyas subsist with *brahman* as their mouth. The gods, of course, neither eat nor drink. They become sated by just looking at this nectar. 2 They enter into that same (flickering) appearance, and from that appearance they emerge.

3 When someone knows this nectar in this way—he truly becomes one with those very Sādhyas and, with *brahman* itself as his mouth, becomes sated by just looking at this nectar; he enters into this same appearance and emerges from this appearance; 4 and he will achieve dominion and sovereignty over these very Sādhyas for as long as the sun shall rise in the zenith and set in the nadir, which is twice as long as it will rise in the north and set in the south.

11 Thereupon, after rising in the zenith, it will never rise or set. All alone, it will remain in the middle. In this connection, there is this verse:

> 2 There, surely, it has never set,
> nor ever risen.
> By this truth, O gods,
> let me not be stripped
> of the formulation of truth (*brahman*).

3 When someone knows this same hidden teaching (*upaniṣad*)

that is the formulation of truth (*brahman*)—for him the sun neither rises nor sets, for him it is always day.

4 Brahmā taught this very formulation of truth to Prajāpati, Prajāpati to Manu, and Manu to his children. And his father imparted this very formulation of truth to Uddālaka Āruṇi, his eldest son. 5 So, a father should impart this formulation of truth only to his eldest son or to a worthy pupil, 6 and never to anyone else, even if he were to offer him this earth girded by the waters and filled with wealth, because that formulation is far greater than all that!

12 Whatever there is, this entire creation—clearly, all that is the Gāyatrī. And the Gāyatrī is speech, for speech sings (*gāyati*) and protects (*trāyati*) this entire creation.

2 Now, take this Gāyatrī—clearly, it is just the same as this earth here, for this entire creation rests upon the earth and never extends beyond its limits.

3 And take this earth—clearly, it is just the same as this body of a person here, for these vital functions (*prāṇa*) rest within the body and never extend beyond its limits.

4 And take this body of a person here—clearly, it is just the same as this heart here within a person, for these vital functions rest within the heart and never extend beyond its limits.

5 This is the Gāyatrī that consists of four quarters and six types. This is declared in a Ṛg verse:

> 6 Such is his greatness—
> Even greater than that is that person.
> One quarter of him are all creatures,
> Three quarters the immortal in heaven.

7 And take what people call '*brahman*'—clearly, it is nothing but this space here outside a person. And this space here outside a person—8 clearly, it is the same as this space here within a person. 9 And this space here within a person—clearly, it is the same as this space here within the heart; it is full and non-depleting. Anyone who knows this obtains full and non-depleting prosperity.

13 Now, this heart here contains five openings for the deities. As regards its eastern opening—it is the out-

breath, it is sight, it is the sun. And one should venerate it as splendour and as foodstuff. Anyone who knows this becomes full of splendour and an eater of food.

2 As regards its southern opening—it is the inter-breath, it is hearing, it is the moon. And one should venerate it as prosperity and fame. Anyone who knows this becomes prosperous and famous.

3 As regards its western opening—it is the in-breath, it is speech, it is the fire. And one should venerate it as the lustre of sacred knowledge and as foodstuff. Anyone who knows this becomes full of the lustre of sacred knowledge and an eater of food.

4 As regards its northern opening—it is the link-breath, it is the mind, it is the rain. And one should venerate it as renown and beauty. Anyone who knows this becomes renowned and beautiful.

5 As regards its upper opening—it is the up-breath, it is the wind, it is space. And one should venerate it as vigour and might. Anyone who knows this becomes vigorous and mighty.

6 These, indeed, are the five courtiers of *brahman*, the doorkeepers of heaven. When someone knows these five courtiers of *brahman*, these doorkeepers of heaven, in this way—a hero will be born to his family, and he will go to heaven.

7 Now, far above here the light that shines from heaven on the backs of everything, on the backs of all things, in the very highest of the high worlds—it is clearly this very same light here within a man. We see it when, on touching the body, we feel the warmth within it. We hear it when, as we press our ears shut, we hear something like the hum and the noise of a blazing fire. One should venerate this light as something seen and heard. Anyone who knows this will become handsome and famous.

14 *Brahman*, you see, is this whole world. With inner tranquillity, one should venerate it as *jalān*.

Now, then, man is undoubtedly made of resolve. What a man becomes on departing from here after death is in accordance with his resolve in this world. So he should make this resolve:

2–3 'This self (*ātman*) of mine that lies deep within my heart—it is made of mind; the vital functions (*prāṇa*) are its physical form; luminous is its appearance; the real is its intention; space is its essence (*ātman*); it contains all actions, all desires, all smells, and all tastes; it has captured this whole world; it neither speaks nor pays any heed.

'This self (*ātman*) of mine that lies deep within my heart—it is smaller than a grain of rice or barley, smaller than a mustard seed, smaller even than a millet grain or a millet kernel; but it is larger than the earth, larger than the intermediate region, larger than the sky, larger even than all these worlds put together.

4 'This self (*ātman*) of mine that lies deep within my heart—it contains all actions, all desires, all smells, and all tastes; it has captured this whole world; it neither speaks nor pays any heed.

'It is *brahman*. On departing from here after death, I will become that.'

A man who has this resolve is never beset at all with doubts. This is what Śāṇḍilya used to say.

15

This chest does not decay!
Its cavity—the intermediate region
Its bottom—the earth
Its corners—the quarters
Its opening above—the sky
This chest contains wealth.
In it this whole universe rests.

2 Its eastern quarter is called Offering Ladle. Its southern quarter is called Conquering. Its western quarter is called Royal. Its northern quarter is called Prosperous. The offspring of these quarters is the wind. Anyone who knows that, in this way, the offspring of the quarters is the wind will not mourn the loss of a son.

'I am a man who knows that, in this way, the offspring of the quarters is the wind. So may I not have to mourn the loss of a son. 3 Together with so-and-so, so-and-so, so-and-so, I turn to the undecaying chest for protection. Together with so-and-so . . . I turn to the breath for protection. Together with so-and-so . . . I turn to *bhūḥ* for protection. Together with so-and-so . . . I turn to *bhuvaḥ* for protection. Together with so-and-so . . . I turn to *svar* for protection.

4 'The breath is clearly this entire creation, everything there is. So, when I said, "I turn to the breath", it was to this that I thereby turned for protection.

5 'And when I said, "I turn to *bhūḥ* for protection", what I said

thereby was: "I turn to the earth for protection. I turn to the intermediate region for protection. I turn to the sky for protection."

6 'And when I said, "I turn to *bhuvaḥ* for protection", what I said thereby was: "I turn to the fire for protection. I turn to the wind for protection. I turn to the sun for protection."

7 'And when I said, "I turn to *svar* for protection", what I said thereby was: "I turn to the Ṛgveda for protection. I turn to the Yajurveda for protection. I turn to the Sāmaveda for protection."'

16 Now, the sacrifice is a man. His first twenty-four years constitute the morning pressing of Soma. The Gāyatrī metre has twenty-four syllables, and so the morning pressing of Soma is carried out with the Gāyatrī. To this, therefore, are linked the Vasus. The Vasus are the breaths, for they make (*vāsayanti*) this whole world dwell securely. 2 If someone happens to be afflicted with any sickness during this period of life, let him say: 'O Breaths! O Vasus! May this morning offering of mine continue until the midday offering! May I—the sacrifice—not perish amid the breaths, amid the Vasus!' He is sure to recover from it and become healthy again.

3 And his next forty-four years constitute the midday pressing of Soma. The Triṣṭubh metre has forty-four syllables, and so the midday pressing of Soma is carried out with the Triṣṭubh. To this, therefore, are linked the Rudras. The Rudras are the breaths, for they make this whole world weep (*rodayanti*). 4 If someone happens to be afflicted with any sickness during this period of life, let him say: 'O Breaths! O Rudras! May this midday offering of mine continue until the third offering! May I—the sacrifice—not perish amid the breaths, amid the Rudras!' He is sure to recover from it and become healthy again.

5 And finally, his next forty-eight years constitute the third pressing of Soma. The Jagatī metre has forty-eight syllables, and so the third pressing of Soma is carried out with the Jagatī. To this, therefore, are linked the Ādityas. The Ādityas are the breaths, for they take back (*ādadate*) this whole world. 6 If someone happens to be afflicted with any sickness during this period of life, let him say: 'O Breaths! O Ādityas! May this third offering of mine continue until the end of my full life span! May I—the sacrifice—not

perish amid the breaths, amid the Ādityas!' He is sure to recover from it and become healthy again.

7 Surely it was this that Mahidāsa Aitareya knew when he said: 'I am not going to die because of it. So why do you have to afflict me with this?' And he lived to be one hundred and sixteen. Anyone who knows this will also live to be one hundred and sixteen.

17 When a man is hungry, thirsty, and without pleasures—that is his sacrificial consecration; 2 and when he eats, drinks, and enjoys pleasures—by that he performs the preparatory rites; 3 when he laughs, feasts, and has sex—by that he sings the chants and performs the recitations; 4 austerity, generosity, integrity, non-injury, and truthfulness—these are his gifts to the priests.

5 Therefore, they say: 'He will press the Soma! He has pressed the Soma for himself!' That is, indeed, his regeneration. The bath after the sacrifice is simply his death.

6 After Ghora Āṅgirasa had taught the same thing to Kṛṣṇa, the son of Devakī, he continued—he was then altogether free from desires and at the point of death: 'one should turn to these three for protection: "You are the undecaying! You are the imperishable! You are fortified by breath!"' In this connection, there are these two Ṛg verses:

7 Then they see the morning light of the primeval seed,
The light that gleams from beyond the sky.
Far beyond the surrounding darkness,
We see the highest light!
We see the highest shine!
To the god of gods,
To the supreme light,
To the sun,
We have gone!

18 With respect to the bodily sphere (*ātman*), one should venerate: '*Brahman* is the mind', and, with respect to the divine sphere: '*Brahman* is space'. In this way, substitution is carried out in both spheres—both with respect to the bodily sphere and with respect to the divine sphere.

2 Now, *brahman* here is four-legged—with respect to the bodily sphere, speech is one leg, breath is another, sight is the third, and hearing is the fourth; and with respect to the divine sphere, the fire is one leg, the wind is another, the sun is the third, and the quarters are the fourth. In this way, substitution is carried out in both spheres—both with respect to the bodily sphere and with respect to the divine sphere.

3 One of *brahman*'s four legs is speech. With the fire as its light, it gleams and glows. Anyone who knows this gleams and glows with fame, glory, and the lustre of sacred knowledge.

4 Another of *brahman*'s four legs is breath. With the wind as its light, it gleams and glows. Anyone who knows this gleams and glows with fame, glory, and the lustre of sacred knowledge.

5 The third of *brahman*'s four legs is sight. With the sun as its light, it gleams and glows. Anyone who knows this gleams and glows with fame, glory, and the lustre of sacred knowledge.

6 The fourth of *brahman*'s four legs is hearing. With the quarters as its light, it gleams and glows. Anyone who knows this gleams and glows with fame, glory, and the lustre of sacred knowledge.

19 '*Brahman* is the sun'—that is the rule of substitution. Here is a further explanation of it.

In the beginning this world was simply what is non-existing; and what is existing was that. It then developed and formed into an egg. It lay there for a full year and then it hatched, splitting in two, one half becoming silver and the other half gold. 2 The silver half is this earth, while the golden half is the sky. The outer membrane is the mountains; the inner membrane, the clouds and the mist; the veins, the rivers; and the amniotic fluid, the ocean. 3 Now, the hatchling that was born was the sun up there. And as it was being born, cries of joy and loud cheers rose up in celebration, as did all beings and all desires. Therefore, every time the sun rises and every time it returns, cries of joy and loud cheers rise up in celebration, as do all beings and all their hopes.

4 When someone knows this and venerates *brahman* as the sun, he can certainly expect that the pleasing sound of cheering will reach his ears and delight him.

CHAPTER 4

1 There was one Jānaśruti Pautrāyaṇa, a man who was totally devoted to giving and used to give a lot, a man who gave a lot of cooked food. He had hospices built everywhere, thinking: 'People will eat food from me everywhere.'

2 Now, it so happened that some wild geese were flying overhead at night, and one of them said to another: 'Hey, Bright-Eyes! Look out, Bright-Eyes! Look, a light like that of Jānaśruti Pautrāyaṇa has spread out through the sky. Don't touch it, if you don't want to be burnt.'

3 The other replied: 'Come now! Given who he is, why do you speak of him as if he were Raikva, the gatherer?'

'That man—how is he Raikva, the gatherer?'

4 'As the lower throws all go to the one who wins with the highest throw of the dice, so whatever good things people may do, all that goes to him. I say the same of anyone who knows what Raikva knows.'

5 Now, Jānaśruti Pautrāyaṇa overheard this conversation, and, as soon as he got up in the morning, he said to his steward: 'Look, my man! [This is what I heard:]

' "Why do you speak of him as if he were Raikva, the gatherer?" "That man—how is he Raikva, the gatherer?"

6 "As the lower throws all go to the one who wins with the highest throw of the dice, so whatever good things people may do, all that goes to him. I say the same of anyone who knows what Raikva knows." '

7 The steward searched for Raikva and returned, saying: 'I didn't find him.' Jānaśruti told him: 'Look for him, my man, in a place where one would search for a non-Brahmin.'

8 The steward respectfully approached a man under a cart scratching his sores and asked: 'Sir, are you Raikva, the gatherer?' The man replied: 'Yes, I am.' The steward then returned, saying: 'I did find him.'

2 Taking with him six hundred cows, a gold necklace, and a carriage drawn by a she-mule, Jānaśruti Pautrāyaṇa went

back to Raikva and said to him: 2'Raikva, here are six hundred cows, a gold necklace, and a carriage drawn by a she-mule. Please, sir, teach me the deity that you venerate.' 3 But Raikva replied: 'Hey, you! Drive them back to your place, Śūdra! Keep your goods and your cows!'

Then, taking with him a thousand cows, a gold necklace, a carriage drawn by a she-mule, and his daughter, Jānaśruti Pautrāyaṇa went back to him once again 4 and said: 'Raikva, here are a thousand cows, a gold necklace, and a carriage drawn by a she-mule, here is a wife, and here is the village where you live. Sir, please teach me.'

5 Lifting up her face, Raikva said: 'Hey you! Drive them to my place, Śūdra! With just this face you would have swindled me!'

Now, these villages among the Mahāvṛṣa called Raikvaparṇa stand where Jānaśruti lived with Raikva. And this is what Raikva told him.

3 'The gatherer, clearly, is the wind. So, when a fire goes out, it is into the wind that it passes; when the sun sets, it is into the wind that it passes; when the moon sets, it is into the wind that it passes; 2 and when water evaporates, it is into the wind that it passes. For it is the wind that gathers all these.'

That was with respect to the divine sphere. 3 Next, with respect to the body (*ātman*)—

'The gatherer, clearly, is the breath. So, when a man sleeps, it is into the breath that his speech passes; it is also into the breath that sight, hearing, and mind pass. For it is the breath that gathers all these.

4 'These, then, are the two gatherers—the wind among the deities and the breath among the vital functions (*prāṇa*).

5 'Once, while food was being served to Śaunaka Kāpeya and Abhiprātin Kākṣaseni, a vedic student begged for almsfood from them. But they did not give him any. 6 The student then told them:

"One god has swallowed four mighty ones!
Who is he, the guardian of the world?
Mortals do not see him, Kāpeya,
Though, Abhiprātin, he's present everywhere!

You haven't given this food to a man to whom it is due!" 7 Then Śaunaka Kāpeya reflected upon it for a while and gave this reply:

"He's the self (*ātman*) of the gods, the father of creatures!
The wise devourer with golden teeth!
They say his greatness is great,
Who eats what's not food without being eaten!

Thus, O student, do we venerate it. Give this man some alms-food!" 8 So they gave him some.

'The former five and the latter five make a total of ten. And they are the highest throw of the dice. In all the quarters, therefore, ten, the highest throw of the dice, is just food. It is the Virāj metre, the eater of food. Virāj has sunk its teeth into this whole world. When someone knows this—he sinks his teeth into the whole world; he becomes an eater of food.'

4 One day Satyakāma Jābāla said to his mother Jabālā: 'Mother, I want to become a vedic student. So tell me what my lineage is.' 2 She replied: 'Son, I don't know what your lineage is. I was young when I had you. I was a maid then and had a lot of relationships. As such, it is impossible for me to say what your lineage is. But my name is Jabālā, and your name is Satyakāma. So you should simply say that you are Satyakāma Jābāla.'

3 He went to Hāridrumata Gautama then and said: 'Sir, I want to live under you as a vedic student. I come to you, sir, as your student.'

4 Hāridrumata asked him: 'Son, what is your lineage?' And he replied: 'Sir, I don't know what my lineage is. When I asked my mother, she replied: "I was young when I had you. I was a maid then and had a lot of relationships. As such, it is impossible for me to say what your lineage is. But my name is Jabālā, and your name is Satyakāma." So I am Satyakāma Jābāla, sir.'

5 Hāridrumata then told him: 'Who but a Brahmin could speak like that! Fetch some firewood, son. I will perform your initiation. You have not strayed from the truth.' So he initiated the boy and, picking out four hundred of the most skinny and feeble cows, told him: 'Son, look after these.' As he was driving them away, Satyakāma answered back: 'I will not return without a thousand!'

He lived away for a number of years, and when the cows had increased to a thousand this is what happened.

5 The bull called out to him: 'Satyakāma!' He responded: 'Sir?' The bull said: 'Son, we have reached a thousand. Take us back to the teacher's house, 2 and I will tell you one quarter of *brahman*.'

'Please tell me, sir.'

And the bull told him: 'One-sixteenth of it is the eastern quarter; one-sixteenth is the western quarter; one-sixteenth is the southern quarter; and one-sixteenth is the northern quarter. Consisting of these four-sixteenths, this quarter of *brahman* is named Far-flung, my son.

3 'When someone knows this and venerates this quarter of *brahman* consisting of four-sixteenths as Far-flung, he will become far-flung in this world. A man will win far-flung worlds, when he knows this and venerates this quarter of *brahman* consisting of four-sixteenths as Far-flung.'

6 The bull continued: 'The fire will tell you another quarter.' The next morning Satyakāma drove the cows on, and at the spot where they happened to be around sunset he built a fire, corralled the cows, fed the fire with wood, and sat down behind the fire facing the east.

2 The fire then called out to him: 'Satyakāma!' He responded: 'Sir?'

3 'Son, I will tell you a quarter of *brahman*.'

'Please tell me, sir.'

And the fire told him: 'One-sixteenth of it is the earth; one-sixteenth is the intermediate region; one-sixteenth is the sky; and one-sixteenth is the ocean. Consisting of these four-sixteenths, this quarter of *brahman* is named Limitless, my son.

4 'When someone knows this and venerates the quarter of *brahman* consisting of these four-sixteenths as Limitless, there will be no limits for him in this world. A man will win limitless worlds, when he knows this and venerates the quarter of *brahman* consisting of these four-sixteenths as Limitless.'

7 The fire continued: 'A wild goose will tell you another quarter.' The next morning Satyakāma drove the cows on, and at

the spot where they happened to be around sunset he built a fire, corralled the cows, fed the fire with wood, and sat down behind the fire facing the east.

2 A wild goose then flew down and called out to him: 'Satyakāma !' He responded: 'Sir?'

3 'Son, I will tell you a quarter of *brahman*.'

'Please tell me, sir.'

And the wild goose told him: 'One-sixteenth of it is the fire; one-sixteenth is the sun; one-sixteenth is the moon; and one-sixteenth is lightning. Consisting of these four-sixteenths, this quarter of *brahman* is named Radiant, my son.

4 'When someone knows this and venerates the quarter of *brahman* consisting of these four-sixteenths as Radiant, he will become radiant in this world. A man will win radiant worlds, when he knows this and venerates the quarter of *brahman* consisting of these four-sixteenths as Radiant.'

8 The wild goose continued: 'A water-bird will tell you another quarter.' The next morning Satyakāma drove the cows on, and at the spot where they happened to be around sunset he built a fire, corralled the cows, fed the fire with wood, and sat down behind the fire facing the east.

2 A water-bird then flew down and called out to him: 'Satyakāma !' He responded: 'Sir?'

3 'Son, I will tell you a quarter of *brahman*.'

'Please tell me, sir.'

And the water-bird told him: 'One-sixteenth of it is breath; one-sixteenth is sight; one-sixteenth is hearing; and one-sixteenth is the mind. Consisting of these four-sixteenths, this quarter of *brahman* is named Abode-possessing, my son.

4 'When someone knows this and venerates the quarter of *brahman* consisting of these four-sixteenths as Abode-possessing, he will have an abode in this world. A man will win worlds possessing abodes, when he knows this and venerates the quarter of *brahman* consisting of these four-sixteenths as Abode-possessing.'

9 Finally he reached his teacher's house. The teacher called out to him: 'Satyakāma !' He responded: 'Sir?'

2 'Son, you have the glow of a man who knows *brahman*! Tell me—who taught you?'

'Other than human beings,' he acknowledged. 'But, if it pleases you, sir, you should teach it to me yourself, 3 for I have heard from people of your eminence that knowledge leads one most securely to the goal only when it is learnt from a teacher.' So he explained it to him, and, indeed, he did so without leaving anything out.

10 Upakosala Kāmalāyana once lived as a vedic student under Satyakāma Jābāla and tended his fires for twelve years. Now, Satyakāma, although he permitted other students of his to return home, did not permit Upakosala to do so. 2 His wife then told him: 'The student has performed his austerities and faithfully tended the fires. Teach him before the fires beat you to it.' But Satyakāma went on a journey without ever teaching him.

3 Now, Upakosala became so afflicted that he stopped eating. His teacher's wife told him: 'Come on, student, eat. Why have you stopped eating?' He told her: 'The desires that lurk within this man are many and bring various dangers. I am overwhelmed by afflictions, and I will not eat.'

4 The fires then said to each other: 'The student has performed his austerities and faithfully tended us. So come, let us teach him.' And they told him: '*Brahman* is breath. *Brahman* is joy (*ka*). *Brahman* is space (*kha*).'

5 He replied: 'I can understand that *brahman* is breath. But I don't understand how it can be joy or space.'

'Joy is the same as space,' they replied, 'and space is the same as joy.' And they explained to him both breath and space.

11 Thereupon, the householder's fire instructed him: 'Earth, fire, food, and sun—I am the person one sees in the sun; so I am all those.'

2 'When someone knows this and venerates him in this way—he rids himself of bad actions; he provides himself with a world; he lives long and reaches the full span of his life; and the line of his descendants will not die out. We will serve him in this world and the next—when someone knows this and venerates him in this way.'

12 Then the southern fire instructed him: 'The waters, the quarters, the stars, and the moon—I am the person one sees in the moon; so I am all those.'

2 'When someone knows this and venerates him in this way—he rids himself of bad actions; he provides himself with a world; he lives long and reaches the full span of his life; and the line of his descendants will not die out. We will serve him in this world and the next—when someone knows this and venerates him in this way.'

13 Finally, the offertorial fire instructed him: 'Breath, space, sky, and lightning—I am the person one sees in lightning; so I am all those.'

2 'When someone knows this and venerates him in this way—he rids himself of bad actions; he provides himself with a world; he lives long and reaches the full span of his life; and the line of his descendants will not die out. We will serve him in this world and the next—when someone knows this and venerates him in this way.'

14 Then the fires told him: 'Upakosala! Son, now you have this knowledge both of ourselves and of the self (*ātman*). Your teacher, however, will point out the goal to you.'

His teacher finally returned. The teacher called out to him, 'Upakosala!' 2 He responded: 'Sir?'

'Son, your face glows like that of a man who knows *brahman*. Tell me—who taught you?'

'Who could possibly have taught me, sir?'—in so saying, he denies it in a way. And alluding to the fires, he continued: 'These look like this now, but they were different.'

'What did they tell you, son?'

3 'This,' he acknowledged.

'They just told you about the worlds, son. But I will tell you that about which it is said: "When someone knows it bad actions do not stick to him, just as water does not stick to a lotus leaf."'

'Sir, please teach me that.'

And this is what he told him.

15 'The person you see here in the eye—he is the self (*ātman*),' he told him. 'He is the immortal free from fear;

he is *brahman*. So, even if someone pours water or ghee in that eye, it just runs to the two borders.

2 'They call him "Lovely-uniting" (*saṃyadvāma*), for all lovely things (*vāma*) come in concert (*abhisaṃyanti*) to him. All lovely things come in concert also to anyone who knows this.

3 'He is also 'Lovely-leading' (*vāmanī*), for he leads (*nī*) all lovely things (*vāma*). Anyone who knows this also leads all lovely things.

4 'He is also 'Shining' (*bhāmanī*), for he shines in all the worlds. Anyone who knows this also shines in all the worlds.

5 'Now, whether they perform a cremation for such a person or not, people like him pass into the flame, from the flame into the day, from the day into the fortnight of the waxing moon, from the fortnight of the waxing moon into the six months when the sun moves north, from these months into the year, from the year into the sun, from the sun into the moon, and from the moon into the lightning. Then a person who is not human—he leads them to *brahman*. This is the path to the gods, the path to *brahman*. Those who proceed along this path do not return to this human condition.'

16 The wind that purifies—that is the sacrifice. The wind, as it moves, purifies this whole world. Because it purifies this whole world as it moves (*yan*), it is the sacrifice (*yajña*).

Its two tracks are mind and speech. 2 One of those the Brahman priest constructs with his mind, while the Hotṛ, Adhvaryu, and Udgātṛ priests construct the other with their speech.

If it happens that the Brahman priest breaks in and speaks after the start of the morning litany and before its concluding verse, 3 he constructs only one of the tracks, while the other is left out. So his sacrifice founders, just like a one-legged man, when he walks, or a cart, when it moves on just one wheel. And when the sacrifice founders, the patron of that sacrifice also founders. He becomes a pauper after offering the sacrifice.

4 If, on the other hand, the Brahman priest does not break in and speak after the start of the morning litany and before its concluding verse, the priests construct both the tracks, and neither is left out. 5 So his sacrifice becomes steady, just like a man walking with both feet, or a cart moving on both wheels. And when the sacrifice

becomes steady, the patron of the sacrifice also becomes steady. He becomes a rich man after offering the sacrifice.

17 Prajāpati incubated the worlds. And as they were being incubated, he extracted their essences—the fire from the earth, the wind from the intermediate region, and the sun from the sky.

2 He incubated these three deities. And as they were being incubated, he extracted their essences—the Ṛg verses from the fire, the Yajus formulas from the wind, and the Sāman chants from the sun.

3 He incubated this triple Veda. And as they were being incubated, he extracted their essences—the word *bhūḥ* from the Ṛg verses, the word *bhuvaḥ* from the Yajus formulas, and the word *svaḥ* from the Sāman chants.

4 So, if the sacrifice suffers an injury on account of a Ṛg verse, he should make an offering in the householder's fire with the words '*bhūḥ svāhā*!' This way he binds any injury suffered by the Ṛg verses and the sacrifice, using the very essence and power of the Ṛg verses.

5 And if the sacrifice suffers an injury on account of a Yajus formula, he should make an offering in the southern fire with the words '*bhuvaḥ svāhā*!' This way he binds any injury suffered by the Yajus formulas and the sacrifice, using the very essence and power of the Yajus formulas.

6 And if the sacrifice suffers an injury on account of a Sāman chant, he should make an offering in the offertorial fire with the words '*svaḥ svāhā*!' This way he binds any injury suffered by the Sāman chants and the sacrifice, using the very essence and power of the Sāman chants.

7 Just as one binds gold with salt, silver with gold, tin with silver, lead with tin, copper with lead, wood with copper, and leather with wood, 8 so by the power of these worlds and of these deities and of this triple Veda he binds an injury done to a sacrifice. When one who knows this becomes the Brahman priest, that sacrifice is equipped with healing medicine. 9–10 And when one who knows this becomes the Brahman priest, that sacrifice inclines towards the north. There is this verse about the Brahman priest who knows this:

Wherever it turns,
there a human goes.
Alone among the priests,
the Brahman protects,
Like a mare, the men of Kuru.

A Brahman priest who knows this protects the sacrifice, the patron of the sacrifice, and all the priests. Therefore, a man should select as his Brahman priest only someone who knows this, and never someone who is ignorant of this.

CHAPTER 5

1 When a man knows the best and the greatest, he becomes the best and the greatest. The best and the greatest is breath.

2 When a man knows the most excellent, he becomes the most excellent among his people. The most excellent is speech.

3 When a man knows the firm base, he stands firm in this world and the next. The firm base is sight.

4 When a man knows the correspondence (*saṃpad*), his desires, both divine and human, are fulfilled (*saṃpad-*) for him. Correspondence is hearing.

5 When a man knows the refuge, he becomes a refuge for his people. The refuge is the mind.

6 Once the vital functions (*prāṇa*) were arguing about who among them was the greatest, each claiming, 'I am the greatest!' 'I am the greatest!' 7 So these vital functions went to Prajāpati, their father, and asked: 'Sir, who is the greatest among us?' He told them: 'The one, after whose departure the body appears to be in the worst shape, is the greatest among you.'

8 So speech departed. After spending a year away, it returned and asked: 'How did you manage to live without me?' They replied: 'We lived as the dumb would, without speaking, but breathing with the breath, seeing with the eye, hearing with the ear, and reflecting with the mind.' So speech re-entered.

9 Then sight departed. After spending a year away, it returned

and asked: 'How did you manage to live without me?' They replied: 'We lived as the blind would, without seeing, but breathing with the breath, speaking with speech, hearing with the ear, and reflecting with the mind.' So sight re-entered.

10 Then hearing departed. After spending a year away, it returned and asked: 'How did you manage to live without me?' They replied: 'We lived as the deaf would, without hearing, but breathing with the breath, speaking with speech, seeing with the eye, and reflecting with the mind.' So sight re-entered.

11 Then the mind departed. After spending a year away, it returned and asked: 'How did you manage to live without me?' They replied: 'We lived as simpletons would, without reflecting, but breathing with the breath, speaking with speech, seeing with the eye, and hearing with the ear.' So the mind re-entered.

12 Then, as breath was setting off, it so jerked all the other vital functions—in the way a fine horse would jerk all the stakes to which it is tethered—that they all gathered around him and implored: 'Lord, please stay! You are the greatest among us. Do not depart!'

13 Then speech told him: 'As I am the most excellent, so you will be the most excellent.' Sight told him: 'As I am the firm base, so you will be the firm base.' 14 Hearing told him: 'As I am correspondence, so you will be correspondence.' The mind told him: 'As I am the refuge, so you will be the refuge.'

15 Surely, people do not call these 'speeches', or 'sights', or 'hearings', or 'minds'. They call them only 'breaths' (*prāṇa*), for only breath becomes all these.

2 Breath then asked: 'What will be my food?' They replied: 'Everything that is here, right down to dogs and birds.' So this is how breath (*ana*) is actually food (*anna*). Now, its open name is *ana*. For a man who knows this, there is nothing that is not food.

2 Then he asked: 'What will be my clothes?' They replied: 'Water'. Therefore, when people are preparing to eat, they surround that [food] with water both before and after. He is thus used to receiving a garment; he does not remain naked.

3 After telling this to Gośruti Vaiyāghrapadya, Satyakāma

Jābāla said: 'Even if one were to say this to a withered stump, it would sprout new branches and grow new leaves.'

4 Now, if a man is striving to achieve greatness, he should do the following. After undergoing the sacrificial consecration on the night of a new moon day, he should prepare a mixture of every type of herb together with curd and honey on the night of the full moon. He should offer an oblation of ghee in the fire, saying: 'To the best! To the greatest, svāhā!' and pour the remainder into the mixture. 5 He should offer an oblation of ghee in the fire, saying: 'To the most excellent, svāhā!' and pour the remainder into the mixture. He should offer an oblation of ghee in the fire, saying: 'To the firm base, svāhā!' and pour the remainder into the mixture. He should offer an oblation of ghee in the fire, saying: 'To correspondence, svāhā!' and pour the remainder into the mixture. He should offer an oblation of ghee in the fire, saying: 'To the refuge, svāhā!' and pour the remainder into the mixture.

6 He then slides back stealthily and, taking some of the mixture in his cupped hands, recites softly: 'You are power (*ama*), for this whole world is at your side (*amā*). For he is the best and greatest, the king and ruler. May he make me foremost! May he lead me to greatness! May he make me a king and ruler! May I become this whole world!'

7 Then, as he recites this Ṛg verse, he takes a sip of the mixture at each foot of the verse:

> 'We choose that [food] of Savitṛ,'

With that he takes a sip.

> '[that] food of the god [Savitṛ],'

With that he takes a sip.

> 'the greatest, the best creator of all.'

With that he takes a sip.

> 'Bhaga's rich bounty would we create for ourselves.'

With that he drinks the whole of the mixture.

8 He then cleans the goblet or cup and lies down behind the fire on either a skin or the bare ground, remaining silent and unresistant. If he sees a woman, he should know that his rite has been successful. 9 In this connection, there is this verse:

When a man sees a woman in his dreams
During a rite to obtain a wish;
He should recognize its success,
In that dream vision.

3 Śvetaketu, the son of Āruṇi, came one day into the assembly of the land of Pañcāla. Pravāhaṇa Jaivali asked him: 'Son, did your father teach you?' Śvetaketu replied: 'Yes indeed, my lord.'

2 'Do you know where people go from here when they die?'

'No, my lord.'

'Do you know how they return again?'

'No, my lord.'

'Do you know how the two paths—the path to the gods and the path to the fathers—take different turns?'

'No, my lord.'

3 'Do you know how that world up there is not filled up?'

'No, my lord.'

'Do you know how at the fifth offering the water takes on a human voice?'

'No, my lord.'

4 'Did you not say that you had been educated? Without knowing these things how can anyone call himself educated?'

Deeply hurt, Śvetaketu returned to his father's house and told him: 'Without actually teaching me, sir, you told me that you had taught me! 5 That excuse for a prince asked me five questions, and I couldn't answer a single one of them.'

The father said: 'As you report them to me, son, I do not know the answer to even one of them. If I had known them, how could I have not taught them to you?'

6 Gautama then came to the king's place. When he arrived, the king received him with respect. In the morning Gautama went into the assembly hall,.and the king said to him: 'Gautama, sir, choose a gift of human riches.' Gautama responded: 'Keep your human riches, Your Majesty. Tell me exactly what you told my boy.'

The king became worried 7 and ordered him to stay a while longer. Finally he told him: 'As to what you have asked me, Gautama, let me tell you that before you this knowledge had never reached the Brahmins. As a result in all the worlds government has belonged exclusively to royalty.' The king then told him:

4 'A fire—that's what the region up there is, Gautama. Its firewood is the sun; its smoke is the sunbeams; its flame is the day; its embers are the moon; and its sparks are the constellations. 2 In that very fire gods offer faith, and from that offering springs King Soma.

5 'A fire—that's what a rain-cloud is, Gautama. Its firewood is the wind; its smoke is the thunder-cloud; its flame is lightning; its embers are thunder; and its sparks are hail. 2 In that very fire gods offer King Soma, and from that offering springs rain.

6 'A fire—that's what the earth is, Gautama. Its firewood is the year; its smoke is space; its flame is the night; its embers are the quarters; and its sparks are the intermediate quarters. 2 In that very fire gods offer rain, and from that offering springs food.

7 'A fire—that's what a man is, Gautama. His firewood is speech; his smoke is breath; his flame is the tongue; his embers are sight; and his sparks are hearing. 2 In that very fire gods offer food, and from that offering springs semen.

8 'A fire—that's what a woman is, Gautama. Her firewood is the vulva; when she is asked to come close, that is her smoke; her flame is the vagina; when one penetrates her, that is her embers; and her sparks are the climax. 2 In that very fire gods offer semen, and from that offering springs the foetus.

9 'Therefore it is said: "at the fifth offering the waters take on a human voice." Covered by the placenta, the foetus lies inside the womb for nine or ten months or thereabouts and is then born. 2 Once he is born, he lives his allotted life span. When he has departed, when he has reached his appointed time—they take him to the very fire from which he came, from which he sprang.

10 'Now, the people who know this, and the people here in the wilderness who venerate thus: "Austerity is faith"—they pass into the flame, from the flame into the day, from the day into the fortnight of the waxing moon, from the fortnight of the waxing moon into the six months when the sun moves north,

2 from these months into the year, from the year into the sun, from the sun into the moon, and from the moon into lightning. Then a person who is not human—he leads them to *brahman*. This is the path leading to the gods.

3 'The people here in villages, on the other hand, who venerate thus: "Gift-giving is offerings to gods and to priests"—they pass into the smoke, from the smoke into the night, from the night into the fortnight of the waning moon, and from the fortnight of the waning moon into the six months when the sun moves south. These do not reach the year 4 but from these months pass into the world of the fathers, and from the world of the fathers into space, and from space into the moon. This is King Soma, the food of the gods, and the gods eat it. 5 They remain there as long as there is a residue, and then they return by the same path they went—first to space, and from space to the wind. After the wind has formed, it turns into smoke; after the smoke has formed, it turns into a thunder-cloud; 6 after the thunder-cloud has formed, it turns into a rain-cloud; and after a rain-cloud has formed, it rains down. On earth they spring up as rice and barley, plants and trees, sesame and beans, from which it is extremely difficult to get out. When someone eats that food and deposits the semen, from him one comes into being again.

7 'Now, people here whose behaviour is pleasant can expect to enter a pleasant womb, like that of a woman of the Brahmin, the Kṣatriya, or the Vaiśya class. But people of foul behaviour can expect to enter a foul womb, like that of a dog, a pig, or an outcaste woman.

8 'Then there are those proceeding on neither of these two paths—they become the tiny creatures revolving here ceaselessly. "Be born! Die!"—that is a third state.

'As a result, that world up there is not filled up.

'A man should seek to protect himself from that. On this point there is this verse:

> 9 A man who steals gold, drinks liquor,
> and kills a Brahmin;
> A man who fornicates with his teacher's wife—
> these four will fall.
> As also the fifth—he who consorts with them.

10 'A man who knows these five fires in this way, however, is not tainted with evil even if he associates with such people. Anyone who knows this becomes pure and clean and attains a good world.'

11 Prācīnaśāla Aupamanyava, Satyayajña Pauluṣi, Indradyumna Bhāllaveya, Jana Śārkarākṣya, and Buḍila Āśvatarāśvi—these extremely wealthy and immensely learned householders got together once and began a deep examination of these questions: 'What is our self (*ātman*)? What is *brahman*?'

2 And they reached this common conclusion: 'Gentlemen, there is this man Uddālaka Āruṇi. At this very moment he is studying this self here, the one common to all men. Come, let's go and meet him.' So they went to him.

3 Uddālaka, for his part, concluded: 'These extremely wealthy and immensely learned householders are bound to question me, and I will not be able to answer their questions in a complete way. The best thing to do is for me to refer them to someone else.' 4 So he told them: 'Gentlemen, there is this man Aśvapati Kaikeya. At this very moment he is studying this self here, the one common to all men. Come, let's go and meet him.' So they went to him.

5 When they arrived, Aśvapati saw to it that each of them was received with due honour. Getting up in the morning, he said to them:

'In my kingdom there are
no thieves, no misers, no one who drinks;
no one without learning or a sacred fire,
no lecher, much less a whore!

'Gentlemen, as you can see, I am about to perform a sacrifice. And I will give you a gift equal to what I will give each of the officiating priests. So, gentlemen, please stay here a while.'

6 But they told him: 'Surely, when a man is immersed in a particular topic, it is on that topic that he should speak. Currently it is this self here, the one common to all men, that is the focus of your study. So tell us about it.' 7 He replied: 'I'll give my response tomorrow.'

So the next morning they returned to him carrying firewood in their hands. Without even initiating them as students, he said this to them:

12 'Aupamanyava, what do you venerate as the self?'
'The sky, Your Majesty,' he replied.

'What you venerate as the self', Aśvapati told him, 'is this brightly shining self here, the one common to all men. As a result we see in your family Soma being pressed ceaselessly and without a break. 2 You eat food and see what is pleasing. Likewise, when someone knows this self here, the one common to all men, in this way—he eats food and sees what is pleasing, and the lustre of sacred knowledge arises in his family. This, however,' he said, 'is only the head of the self.'

'And if you hadn't come to me,' he continued, 'your head would have shattered apart!'

13 Then he questioned Satyayajña Pauluṣi: 'Prācīnayogya, what do you venerate as the self?'

'The sun, Your Majesty,' he replied.

'What you venerate as the self', Aśvapati told him, 'is this dazzling self here, the one common to all men. As a result we see in your family many a dazzling thing—2 golden armlet, carriage drawn by a she-mule, slave-girl, golden pendant. You eat food and see what is pleasing. Likewise, when someone knows this self here, the one common to all men, in this way—he eats food and sees what is pleasing, and the lustre of sacred knowledge arises in his family. This, however,' he said, 'is only the eye of the self.'

'And if you hadn't come to me,' he continued, 'you would have gone blind!'

14 Then he questioned Indradyumna Bhāllaveya: 'Vaiyāghrapadya, what do you venerate as the self?'

'The wind, Your Majesty,' he replied.

'What you venerate as the self', Aśvapati told him, 'is this self, the one common to all men, which follows diverse paths. As a result tributes come to you from diverse sources, and rows upon rows of chariots fall to your share in diverse ways. 2 You eat food and see what is pleasing. Likewise, when someone knows this self here, the one common to all men, in this way—he eats food and sees what is pleasing, and the lustre of sacred knowledge arises in his family. This, however,' he said, 'is only the breath of the self.'

'And if you hadn't come to me,' he continued, 'your breath would have left you!'

15 Then he questioned Jana: 'Śārkarākṣya, what do you venerate as the self?'

'Space, Your Majesty,' he replied.

'What you venerate as the self', Aśvapati told him, 'is this ample self here, the one common to all men. As a result you have ample children and wealth. 2 You eat food and see what is pleasing. Likewise, when someone knows this self here, the one common to all men, in this way—he eats food and sees what is pleasing, and the lustre of sacred knowledge arises in his family. This, however,' he said, 'is only the trunk of the self.'

'And if you hadn't come to me,' he continued, 'your trunk would have crumbled to pieces!'

16 Then he questioned Buḍila Āśvatarāśvi: 'Vaiyāghrapadya, what do you venerate as the self?'

'The waters, Your Majesty,' he replied.

'What you venerate as the self', Aśvapati told him, 'is this self here, the one common to all men, which is wealth. As a result you are wealthy and prosperous. 2 You eat food and see what is pleasing. Likewise, when someone knows this self here, the one common to all men, in this way—he eats food and sees what is pleasing, and the lustre of sacred knowledge arises in his family. This, however,' he said, 'is only the bladder of the self.'

'And if you hadn't come to me,' he continued, 'your bladder would have burst!'

17 Then he questioned Uddālaka Āruṇi: 'Gautama, what do you venerate as the self?'

'The earth, Your Majesty,' he replied.

'What you venerate as the self', Aśvapati told him, 'is this self here, the one common to all men, which is the firm basis. As a result you have a firm basis in children and livestock. 2 You eat food and see what is pleasing. Likewise, when someone knows this self here, the one common to all men, in this way—he eats food and sees what is pleasing, and the lustre of sacred knowledge arises in his family. This, however,' he said, 'is only the feet of the self.'

'And if you hadn't come to me,' he continued, 'your feet would have withered away!'

18 Then he said to them: 'You who know this self here, the one common to all men, as somehow distinct—you eat food. But when someone venerates this self here, the one common to all men, as measuring the size of a span and as beyond all measure, he eats food within all the worlds, all the beings, and all the selves.

2 'Now, of this self here, the one common to all men—the brightly shining is the head; the dazzling is the eye; what follows diverse paths is the breath; the ample is the trunk; wealth is the bladder; the earth is the feet; the sacrificial enclosure is the stomach; the sacred grass is the body hair; the householder's fire is the heart; the southern fire is the mind; and the offertorial fire is the mouth.

19 'The first morsels of food that one takes, therefore, are to be offered in sacrifice. The first offering he makes, he should offer with the words: "To the out-breath, svāhā!" Thus the out-breath becomes satisfied. 2 And when the out-breath is satisfied, the sight becomes satisfied; when the sight is satisfied, the sun becomes satisfied; when the sun is satisfied, the sky becomes satisfied; when the sky is satisfied, whatever the sky and the sun oversee is satisfied. Once these are satisfied, he himself, possessing children, livestock, a food-supply, fame, and the lustre of sacred knowledge, attains satisfaction.

20 'The second offering he makes, he should offer with the words: "To the inter-breath, svāhā!" Thus the inter-breath becomes satisfied. 2 And when the inter-breath is satisfied, the hearing becomes satisfied; when the hearing is satisfied, the moon becomes satisfied; when the moon is satisfied, the quarters become satisfied; when the quarters are satisfied, whatever the quarters and the moon oversee is satisfied. Once these are satisfied, he himself, possessing children, livestock, a food-supply, fame, and the lustre of sacred knowledge, attains satisfaction.

21 'The third offering he makes, he should offer with the words: "To the in-breath, svāhā!" Thus the in-breath becomes satisfied. 2 And when the in-breath is satisfied, the speech becomes satisfied; when the speech is satisfied, the fire becomes satisfied; when the fire is satisfied, the earth becomes satisfied; when the earth is satisfied, whatever the earth and the fire oversee is satisfied. Once these are satisfied, he himself, possessing children, livestock, a food-supply, fame, and the lustre of sacred knowledge, attains satisfaction.

22 'The fourth offering he makes, he should offer with the words: "To the link-breath, svāhā!" Thus the link-breath becomes satisfied. 2 And when the link-breath is satisfied, the mind becomes satisfied; when the mind is satisfied, the rain becomes satisfied; when the rain is satisfied, the lightning becomes satisfied; when the lightning is satisfied, whatever the lightning and the rain oversee is satisfied. Once these are satisfied, he himself, possessing children, livestock, a food-supply, fame, and the lustre of sacred knowledge, attains satisfaction.

23 'The fifth offering he makes, he should offer with the words: "To the up-breath, svāhā!" Thus the up-breath becomes satisfied. 2 And when the up-breath is satisfied, the wind becomes satisfied; when the wind is satisfied, space becomes satisfied; when space is satisfied, whatever the wind and space oversee is satisfied. Once these are satisfied, he himself, possessing children, livestock, a food-supply, fame, and the lustre of sacred knowledge, attains satisfaction.

24 'If someone were to offer the daily fire sacrifice without knowing this, it would be as if he had removed the burning embers and made his offering on the ashes. 2 If, on the other hand, someone were to offer the daily fire sacrifice with this knowledge, that offering of his is made within all the worlds, all the beings, and all the selves.

3 'When someone offers the daily fire sacrifice with this knowledge, all the bad things in him are burnt up like the tip of a reed stuck into a fire. 4 Therefore, even if a man who has this knowledge were to give his leftovers to an outcaste, thereby he would

have made an offering in that self of his which is common to all men. On this point there is this verse:

As around their mother here
hungry children gather;
So at the fire sacrifice,
do all the beings gather.'

CHAPTER 6

1 There was one Śvetaketu, the son of Āruṇi. One day his father told him: 'Śvetaketu, take up the celibate life of a student, for there is no one in our family, my son, who has not studied and is the kind of Brahmin who is so only because of birth.'

2 So he went away to become a student at the age of 12 and, after learning all the Vedas, returned when he was 24, swell-headed, thinking himself to be learned, and arrogant. 3 His father then said to him: 'Śvetaketu, here you are, my son, swell-headed, thinking yourself to be learned, and arrogant; so you must have surely asked about that rule of substitution by which one hears what has not been heard of before, thinks of what has not been thought of before, and perceives what has not been perceived before?'

4 'How indeed does that rule of substitution work, sir?'

'It is like this, son. By means of just one lump of clay one would perceive everything made of clay—the transformation is a verbal handle, a name—while the reality is just this: "It's clay."

5 'It is like this, son. By means of just one copper trinket one would perceive everything made of copper—the transformation is a verbal handle, a name—while the reality is just this: "It's copper."

6 'It is like this, son. By means of just one nail-cutter one would perceive everything made of iron—the transformation is a verbal handle, a name—while the reality is just this: "It's iron."

'That, son, is how this rule of substitution works.'

7 'Surely, those illustrious men did not know this, for had they known, how could they have not told it to me? So, why don't you, sir, tell me yourself?'

'All right, son,' he replied.

2 'In the beginning, son, this world was simply what is existent—one only, without a second. Now, on this point some do say: "In the beginning this world was simply what is non-existent—one only, without a second. And from what is non-existent was born what is existent."

2 'But, son, how can that possibly be?' he continued. 'How can what is existent be born from what is non-existent? On the contrary, son, in the beginning this world was simply what is existent—one only, without a second.

3 'And it thought to itself: "Let me become many. Let me propagate myself." It emitted heat. The heat thought to itself: "Let me become many. Let me propagate myself." It emitted water. Whenever it is hot, therefore, a man surely perspires; and thus it is from heat that water is produced. 4 The water thought to itself: "Let me become many. Let me propagate myself." It emitted food. Whenever it rains, therefore, food becomes abundant; and thus it is from water that foodstuffs are produced.

3 'There are, as you can see, only three sources from which these creatures here originate: they are born from eggs, from living individuals, or from sprouts.

2 'Then that same deity thought to itself: "Come now, why don't I establish the distinctions of name and appearance by entering these three deities here with this living self (*ātman*), 3 and make each of them threefold." So, that deity established the distinctions of name and appearance by entering these three deities here with this living self (*ātman*), 4 and made each of them threefold.

'Learn from me, my son, how each of these three deities becomes threefold.

4 'The red appearance of a fire is, in fact, the appearance of heat, the white, that of water, and the black, that of food. So vanishes from the fire the character of fire—the transformation is a verbal handle, a name—while the reality is just, "It's the three appearances."

2 'The red appearance of the sun is, in fact, the appearance of heat, the white, that of water, and the black, that of food. So

vanishes from the sun the character of sun—the transformation is a verbal handle, a name—while the reality is just, "It's the three appearances."

3 'The red appearance of the moon is, in fact, the appearance of heat, the white, that of water, and the black, that of food. So vanishes from the moon the character of moon—the transformation is a verbal handle, a name—while the reality is just, "It's the three appearances."

4 'The red appearance of lightning is, in fact, the appearance of heat, the white, that of water, and the black, that of food. So vanishes from lightning the character of lightning—the transformation is a verbal handle, a name—while the reality is just, "It's the three appearances."

5 'It was, indeed, this that they knew, those extremely wealthy and immensely learned householders of old, when they said: "Now no one will be able to spring something upon us that we have not heard of or thought of or understood before." For they derived that knowledge from these three—6 when they noticed anything that was reddish, they knew: "That is the appearance of heat"; when they noticed anything that was whitish, they knew: "That is the appearance of water"; when they noticed anything that was blackish, they knew: "That is the appearance of food"; 7 and when they noticed anything that was somehow indistinct, they knew: "That is a combination of these same three deities".

'Learn from me, son, how, when they enter a man, each of these three deities become threefold.

5 'When one eats food it breaks down into three parts. The densest becomes faeces, the medium becomes flesh, and the finest becomes mind. 2 When one drinks water it breaks down into three parts. The densest becomes urine, the medium becomes blood, and the finest becomes breath. 3 When one eats heat it breaks down into three parts. The densest becomes bones, the medium becomes marrow, and the finest becomes speech. 4 For the mind is made up of food, son; breath, of water; and speech, of heat.'

'Sir, teach me more.'

'Very well, son.'

6 'When one churns curd, its finest part rises to the top and becomes butter. 2 In the same way, son, when one eats food its finest part rises to the top and becomes mind; 3 when one drinks water its finest part rises to the top and becomes breath; 4 and when one eats heat its finest part rises to the top and becomes speech. 5 For the mind is made up of food, son; breath, of water; and speech, of heat.'

'Sir, teach me more.'

'Very well, son.

7 'A man, my son, consists of sixteen parts. Do not eat for fifteen days, but drink water at will. Breath is made of water; so it will not be cut off if one drinks.'

2 Śvetaketu did not eat for fifteen days. Then he came back to his father and said: 'What shall I recite, sir?'

'The Ṛg verses, the Yajus formulas, and the Sāman chants.'

'Sir, I just can't remember them,' he replied. 3 And his father said to him:

'It is like this, son. Out of a huge fire that one has built, if there is left only a single ember the size of a firefly—by means of that the fire thereafter would not burn all that much. Likewise, son, you are left with only one of your sixteen parts; by means of that at present you don't remember the Vedas.

'Eat, and then you will learn from me.'

4 He ate and then came back to his father. And he answered everything that his father asked. 5 And the father said to him:

'It is like this, son. Out of a huge fire that one has built, if there is left only a single ember the size of a firefly and if one were to cover it with straw and set it ablaze—by means of that, the fire thereafter would burn very much. 6 Likewise, son, you were left with only one of your sixteen parts, and when you covered it with food, it was set ablaze—by means of that you now remember the Vedas, for the mind, son, is made up of food; breath, of water; and speech, of heat.'

And he did, indeed, learn it from him.

8 Uddalāka Āruṇi said to his son, Śvetaketu: 'Son, learn from me the nature of sleep. When one says here: "The man is sleeping", son, then he is united with the existent; into him-

self (*sva*) he has entered (*apīta*). Therefore, people say with reference to him: "He is sleeping" (*svapiti*), for then he has entered into himself.

2 'It is like this. Take a bird that is tied with a string. It will fly off in every direction and, when it cannot find a resting-place anywhere else, it will alight back upon the very thing to which it is tied. Similarly, son, the mind flies off in every direction and, when it cannot find a resting-place anywhere else, it alights back upon the breath itself; for the mind, my son, is tied to the breath.

3 'Son, learn from me about hunger and thirst. When one says here: "The man is hungry", then the water drives away with what he has eaten. So, just as one calls someone a "cattle-driver", or a "horse-driver", or a "man-driver", similarly one calls water "hunger"—the "food-driver".

'With regard to this, son, you should recognize this as a bud that has come out. It cannot be without a root, 4 and what could its root be if not food? Likewise, son, with food as the bud, look to water as the root; with water as the bud, look to heat as the root; and with heat as the bud, look to the existent as the root. The existent, my son, is the root of all these creatures—the existent is their resting-place, the existent is their foundation.

5 'When, moreover, one says here: "The man is thirsty", then the heat drives away with what he has drunk. So, just as one calls someone a "cattle-driver", or a "horse-driver", or a "man-driver", similarly one calls heat "thirst"—the "water-driver".

'With regard to this, son, you should recognize this as a bud that has come out. It cannot be without a root, 6 and what could its root be if not water? Likewise, son, with water as the bud, look to heat as the root; and with heat as the bud, look to the existent as the root. The existent, my son, is the root of all these creatures—the existent is their resting-place, the existent is their foundation.

'I have already explained to you, son, how, when they enter a man, each of these three deities become threefold.

'When a man is dying, my son, his speech merges into his mind; his mind, into his breath; his breath, into heat; and heat, into the highest deity.

7 'The finest essence here—that constitutes the self of this whole world; that is the truth; that is the self (*ātman*). And that's how you are, Śvetaketu.'

'Sir, teach me more.'

'Very well, son.

9 'Now, take the bees, son. They prepare the honey by gathering nectar from a variety of trees and by reducing that nectar to a homogeneous whole. 2 In that state the nectar from each different tree is not able to differentiate: "I am the nectar of that tree", and "I am the nectar of this tree". In exactly the same way, son, when all these creatures merge into the existent, they are not aware that: "We are merging into the existent." 3 No matter what they are in this world—whether it is a tiger, a lion, a wolf, a boar, a worm, a moth, a gnat, or a mosquito—they all merge into that.

4 'The finest essence here—that constitutes the self of this whole world; that is the truth; that is the self (*ātman*). And that's how you are, Śvetaketu.'

'Sir, teach me more.'

'Very well, son.

10 'Now, take these rivers, son. The easterly ones flow towards the east, and the westerly ones flow towards the west. From the ocean, they merge into the very ocean; they become just the ocean. In that state they are not aware that: "I am that river", and "I am this river". 2 In exactly the same way, son, when all these creatures reach the existent, they are not aware that: "We are reaching the existent". 3 No matter what they are in this world—whether it is a tiger, a lion, a wolf, a boar, a worm, a moth, a gnat, or a mosquito—they all merge into that.

4 'The finest essence here—that constitutes the self of this whole world; that is the truth; that is the self (*ātman*). And that's how you are, Śvetaketu.'

'Sir, teach me more.'

'Very well, son.

11 'Now, take this huge tree here, son. If someone were to hack it at the bottom, its living sap would flow. Likewise, if someone were to hack it in the middle, its living sap would flow; and if someone were to hack it at the top, its living sap would flow. Pervaded by the living (*jīva*) essence (*ātman*), this tree stands here ceaselessly drinking water and flourishing. 2 When, however, life

(*jīva*) leaves one of its branches, that branch withers away. When it leaves a second branch, that likewise withers away, and when it leaves a third branch, that also withers away. When it leaves the entire tree, the whole tree withers away.

3 'In exactly the same way,' he continued, 'know that this, of course, dies when it is bereft of life (*jīva*); but life itself does not die.

'The finest essence here—that constitutes the self of this whole world; that is the truth; that is the self (*ātman*). And that's how you are, Śvetaketu.'

'Sir, teach me more.'

'Very well, son.

12 'Bring a banyan fruit.'

'Here it is, sir.'

'Cut it up.'

'I've cut it up, sir.'

'What do you see there?'

'These quite tiny seeds, sir.'

'Now, take one of them and cut it up.'

'I've cut one up, sir.'

'What do you see there?'

'Nothing, sir.'

2 Then he told him: 'This finest essence here, son, that you can't even see—look how on account of that finest essence this huge banyan tree stands here.

'Believe, my son: 3 the finest essence here—that constitutes the self of this whole world; that is the truth; that is the self (*ātman*). And that's how you are, Śvetaketu.'

'Sir, teach me more.'

'Very well, son.

13 'Put this chunk of salt in a container of water and come back tomorrow.' The son did as he was told, and the father said to him: 'The chunk of salt you put in the water last evening—bring it here.' He groped for it but could not find it, 2 as it had dissolved completely.

'Now, take a sip from this corner,' said the father. 'How does it taste?'

'Salty.'

'Take a sip from the centre.—How does it taste?'

'Salty.'

'Take a sip from that corner.—How does it taste?'

'Salty.'

'Throw it out and come back later.' He did as he was told and found that the salt was always there. The father told him: 'You, of course, did not see it there, son; yet it was always right there.

3 'The finest essence here—that constitutes the self of this whole world; that is the truth; that is the self (*ātman*). And that's how you are, Śvetaketu.'

'Sir, teach me more.'

'Very well, son.

14 'Take, for example, son, a man who is brought here blindfolded from the land of Gandhāra and then left in a deserted region. As he was brought blindfolded and left there blindfolded, he would drift about there towards the east, or the north, or the south.
2 Now, if someone were to free him from his blindfold and tell him, "Go that way; the land of Gandhāra is in that direction", being a learned and wise man, he would go from village to village asking for directions and finally arrive in the land of Gandhāra. In exactly the same way in this world when a man has a teacher, he knows: "There is a delay for me here only until I am freed; but then I will arrive!"

3 'The finest essence here—that constitutes the self of this whole world; that is the truth; that is the self (*ātman*). And that's how you are, Śvetaketu.'

'Sir, teach me more.'

'Very well, son.

15 'Take, for example, son, a man gravely ill. His relatives gather around him and ask: "Do you recognize me?" "Do you recognize me?" As long as his voice does not merge into his mind; his mind, into his breath; his breath, into heat; and heat, into
the highest deity, he recognizes them.
2 When, however, his voice merges into his mind; his mind, into his breath; his breath, into heat; and heat, into the highest deity, then he no longer recognizes them.

3 'The finest essence here—that constitutes the self of this whole world; that is the truth; that is the self (*ātman*). And that's how you are, Śvetaketu.'

'Sir, teach me more.'

'Very well, son.

16 'Take, for example, son, a manacled man brought here by people shouting: "He's a thief! He has committed a theft! Heat an axe for him!" Now, if he is guilty of the crime, then he turns himself into a lie; uttering a falsehood and covering himself in falsehood, he takes hold of the axe and gets burnt, upon which he is executed. 2 If, on the other hand, he is innocent of the crime, then he turns himself into the truth; uttering the truth and covering himself with the truth, he takes hold of the axe and is not burnt, upon which he is released.

3 'What on that occasion prevents him from being burnt—that constitutes the self of this whole world; that is the truth; that is the self (*ātman*). And that's how you are, Śvetaketu.'

And he did, indeed, learn it from him.

CHAPTER 7

1 'Sir, teach me,' said Nārada as he came up to Sanatkumāra. He replied: 'Come to me with what you know. Then I'll tell you what more there is to know.'

Nārada told him: 2 'I have studied the Ṛgveda, sir, as also the Yajurveda, the Sāmaveda, the Ātharvaṇa as the fourth, the corpus of histories and ancient tales as the fifth Veda among the Vedas, ancestral rites, mathematics, soothsaying, the art of locating treasures, the dialogues, the monologues, the science of gods, the science of the ritual, the science of spirits, the science of government, the science of heavenly bodies, and the science of serpent beings. All that, sir, I have studied.' 3 And he continued: 'Here I am, a man who knows all the vedic formulas but is ignorant of the self. And I have heard it said by your peers that those who know the self pass across sorrow. Here I am, sir, a man full of sorrow. Please, sir, take me across to the other side of sorrow.'

Sanatkumāra said to him: 'Clearly, all that you have studied is nothing but name. [4] The Ṛgveda is name, and so are the Yajurveda, the Sāmaveda, the Ātharvaṇa as the fourth, the corpus of histories and ancient tales as the fifth Veda among the Vedas, ancestral rites, mathematics, soothsaying, the art of locating treasures, the dialogues, the monologues, the science of gods, the science of the ritual, the science of spirits, the science of government, the science of heavenly bodies, and the science of serpent beings. All that is nothing but name. So, venerate the name.

[5] 'If someone venerates *brahman* as name—well, a man obtains complete freedom of movement in every place reached by name, if he venerates *brahman* as name.'

'Sir, is there anything greater than name?'

'Yes, there is something greater than name.'

'Sir, please tell me that.'

2 'Speech is clearly greater than name, for speech makes known the Ṛgveda, as it does the Yajurveda, the Sāmaveda, the Ātharvaṇa as the fourth, the corpus of histories and ancient tales as the fifth Veda among the Vedas, ancestral rites, mathematics, soothsaying, the art of locating treasures, the dialogues, the monologues, the science of gods, the science of the ritual, the science of spirits, the science of government, the science of heavenly bodies, and the science of serpent beings; and sky, earth, wind, space, water, fire, gods, humans, domestic animals, birds, grasses, trees, and wild beasts down to the very worms, moths, and ants; as well as the right (*dharma*) and the wrong (*adharma*), truth and falsehood, good and evil, and the pleasant and the unpleasant. For, if there were no speech, neither the right nor the wrong would be made known, nor even truth or falsehood, good or evil. Speech alone makes all this known. So, venerate speech.

[2] 'If someone venerates *brahman* as speech—well, a man obtains complete freedom of movement in every place reached by speech, if he venerates *brahman* as speech.'

'Sir, is there anything greater than speech?'

'Yes, there is something greater than speech.'

'Sir, please tell me that.'

3 'The mind is clearly greater than speech, for as a closed fist would envelop a couple of myrobalans or jujubes, or a pair of dice, so indeed does the mind envelop both speech and name. When a man makes up his mind: "I should recite the vedic formulas", then he undertakes their recitation; or: "I should perform the rites", then he undertakes their performance; or: "I should try to obtain children and livestock", then he tries to obtain them; or: "I should try to win for myself this world and the next", then he tries to win them. For the self (*ātman*) is the mind, the world is the mind, *brahman* is the mind! So, venerate the mind.'

2 'If someone venerates *brahman* as the mind—well, a man obtains complete freedom of movement in every place reached by the mind, if he venerates *brahman* as the mind.'

'Sir, is there anything greater than the mind?'

'Yes, there is something greater than the mind.'

'Sir, please tell me that.'

4 'Intention is clearly greater than the mind, for it is only after a man has formed an intention that he makes up his mind; after that, he vocalizes his speech—and he vocalizes it to articulate a name. The vedic formulas are contained in the name, and rites, in the vedic formulas.

2 'Now, intention (*saṃkalpa*) is the point of convergence of all these things; intention is their essence (*ātman*); and on intention they are based. The earth and the sky were patterned through an intention; wind and space were patterned through an intention; water and fire were patterned through an intention. According to their intention (*saṃkḷpti*) was patterned (*saṃkalpate*) rain; according to the intention of rain was patterned food; according to the intention of food were patterned the vital breaths (*prāṇa*); according to the intention of the vital breaths were patterned the vedic formulas; according to the intention of the vedic formulas were patterned rites; according to the intention of rites was patterned the world; and according to the intention of the world was patterned the Whole. All that is intention! So, venerate intention.

3 'If someone venerates *brahman* as intention—well, himself remaining constant, firmly based, and steadfast, a man wins the worlds patterned after his intention, worlds that are constant, firmly based, and steadfast; and he obtains complete freedom of

movement in every place reached by intention, if he venerates *brahman* as intention.'

'Sir, is there anything greater than intention?'

'Yes, there is something greater than intention.'

'Sir, please tell me that.'

5 'Thought is clearly greater than intention, for it is only after a man has given some thought that he forms an intention; after that, he makes up his mind; then he vocalizes his speech—and he vocalizes it to articulate a name. The vedic formulas are contained in the name, and rites, in the vedic formulas.

2 'Now, thought is the point of convergence of all these things; thought is their essence (*ātman*); and on thought they are based. Therefore, when a man, although very learned, is thoughtless, people say about him: "He is good for nothing!" no matter what he knows, thinking, "If he was truly learned, he would not be so thoughtless." If, on the other hand, a man of little learning is thoughtful, people are going to listen to him, for thought is the point of convergence of all these; thought is their essence; and on thought they are based. So, venerate thought.

3 'If someone venerates *brahman* as thought—well, himself remaining constant, firmly based, and steadfast, a man wins the worlds that he sets his thought on, worlds that are constant, firmly based, and steadfast; and he obtains complete freedom of movement in every place reached by thought, if he venerates *brahman* as thought.'

'Sir, is there anything greater than thought?'.

'Yes, there is something greater than thought.'

'Sir, please tell me that.'

6 'Deep reflection is clearly greater than thought, for the earth in a sense is reflecting deeply; the intermediate region in a sense is reflecting deeply; the sky in a sense is reflecting deeply; the waters in a sense are reflecting deeply; the hills in a sense are reflecting deeply; and gods and men in a sense are reflecting deeply. Therefore, those who achieve eminence among men in this world have, in some sense, received their share of the fruits of deep reflection. Small-minded men are cantankerous, backbiting, and offensive, whereas those who are noble-minded have, in some

sense, received their share of the fruits of deep reflection. So, venerate deep reflection.

2 'If someone venerates *brahman* as deep reflection—well, a man obtains complete freedom of movement in every place reached by deep reflection, if he venerates *brahman* as deep reflection.'

'Sir, is there anything greater than deep reflection?'

'Yes, there is something greater than deep reflection.'

'Sir, please tell me that.'

7 'Perception is clearly greater than deep reflection, for it is through the faculty of perception that one comes to perceive the Ṛgveda, the Yajurveda, the Sāmaveda, the Ātharvaṇa as the fourth, the corpus of histories and ancient tales as the fifth Veda among the Vedas, ancestral rites, mathematics, soothsaying, the art of locating treasures, the dialogues, the monologues, the science of gods, the science of the ritual, the science of spirits, the science of government, the science of heavenly bodies, and the science of serpent beings; and sky, earth, wind, space, water, fire, gods, humans, domestic animals, birds, grasses, trees, and wild beasts down to the very worms, moths, and ants; as well as the right and the wrong, truth and falsehood, good and evil, the pleasant and the unpleasant, food and drink, this world and the next—it is indeed through the faculty of perception that one perceives these. So, venerate perception.

2 'If someone venerates *brahman* as perception—well, a man wins the worlds possessing perception and knowledge; he obtains complete freedom of movement in every place reached by perception, if he venerates *brahman* as perception.'

'Sir, is there anything greater than perception?'

'Yes, there is something greater than perception.'

'Sir, please tell me that.'

8 'Strength is clearly greater than perception, for one strong man strikes terror into the hearts of even a hundred men of perception. When someone becomes strong, he comes to stand; when he stands, he begins to move about; when he moves about, he comes to be a pupil; when he is a pupil, he comes to be a man who sees, hears, thinks, discerns, performs rites, and perceives. By

strength does the earth persist, by strength also the intermediate region, the sky, the hills, gods, humans, domestic animals, birds, grasses, trees, and wild beasts down to the very worms, moths, and ants. By strength does the world persist. So, venerate strength.

2 'If someone venerates *brahman* as strength—a man obtains complete freedom of movement in every place reached by strength, if he venerates *brahman* as strength.'

'Sir, is there anything greater than strength?'

'Yes, there is something greater than strength.'

'Sir, please tell me that.'

9 'Food is clearly greater than strength. Therefore, if someone were to abstain from eating even for ten days and should continue to live, he nevertheless becomes unable to see, to hear, to think, to discern, to perform rites, or to perceive. Upon returning to food, on the other hand, he becomes a man who is able to see, to hear, to think, to discern, to perform rites, and to perceive. So, venerate food.

2 'If someone venerates *brahman* as food—well, a man wins the worlds possessing food and drink; he obtains complete freedom of movement in every place reached by food, if he venerates *brahman* as food.'

'Sir, is there anything greater than food?'

'Yes, there is something greater than food.'

'Sir, please tell me that.'

10 'Water is clearly greater than food. Therefore, when rain is not plentiful, the vital functions (*prāṇa*) become despondent at the thought, "Food is going to get scarce". When, on the other hand, rain becomes plentiful, the vital functions become joyous at the thought, "There'll be plenty of food". All these are simply specific forms of water—earth, intermediate region, sky, hills, gods, humans, domestic animals, birds, grasses, trees, and wild beasts down to the very worms, moths, and ants; they are simply specific forms of water. So, venerate water.

2 'If someone venerates *brahman* as water (*āp*)—well, a man obtains (*āpnoti*) all his desires and becomes completely satisfied; he obtains complete freedom of movement in every place reached by water, if he venerates *brahman* as water.'

'Sir, is there anything greater than water?'
'Yes, there is something greater than water.'
'Sir, please tell me that.'

11 'Heat is clearly greater than water. So, when that holds back the wind and heats up the space, people say: "It's sizzling! It's a scorcher! It's going to rain." Consequently, after revealing the heat first, there pours down the water. Then, thunder rolls with lightning streaking upward and across the sky. People, therefore, say: "Lightning is flashing! Thunder is rolling! It's going to rain." Consequently, after revealing the heat first, there pours down the water. So, venerate heat.

2 'If someone venerates *brahman* as heat (*tejas*)—well, becoming full of radiance (*tejasvin*), a man wins worlds that are full of radiance, worlds that are bright and free from darkness; he obtains complete freedom of movement in every place reached by heat, if he venerates *brahman* as heat.'

'Sir, is there anything greater than heat?'
'Yes, there is something greater than heat.'
'Sir, please tell me that.'

12 'Space is clearly greater than heat, for both the sun and the moon, as well as lightning, stars, and fire, are found in space. Across space one calls out to someone, across space one hears that call, and across space one answers back. Within space one enjoys pleasure, and throughout space one enjoys pleasure. Within space one is born, and into space one is born. So, venerate space.

2 'If someone venerates *brahman* as space (*ākāśa*)—well, a man wins worlds that are spacious (*ākāśavat*), worlds that are wide open (*prakāśa*), unconfined, and far-flung; he obtains complete freedom of movement in every place reached by space, if he venerates *brahman* as space.'

'Sir, is there anything greater than space?'
'Yes, there is something greater than space.'
'Sir, please tell me that.'

13 'Memory is clearly greater than space. Therefore, if people should assemble who do not remember—even many

such people—they would not be able to hear, consider, or recognize anything. When they do remember, then they would be able to hear, consider, and recognize. Clearly, it is through memory that one recognizes one's children and cattle. So, venerate memory.

2 'If someone venerates *brahman* as memory—well, a man obtains complete freedom of movement in every place reached by memory, if he venerates *brahman* as memory.'

'Sir, is there anything greater than memory?'

'Yes, there is something greater than memory.'

'Sir, please tell me that.'

14 'Hope is clearly greater than memory, for only when it is kindled with hope does memory recite vedic formulas, engage in ritual activities, seek to obtain children and livestock, and aspire to winning this world and the next. So, venerate hope.

2 'If someone venerates *brahman* as hope—well, by mere hope, all his desires are fulfilled and his prayers are answered; he obtains complete freedom of movement in every place reached by hope, if he venerates *brahman* as hope.'

'Sir, is there anything greater than hope?'

'Yes, there is something greater than hope.'

'Sir, please tell me that.'

15 'Lifebreath is clearly greater than hope, for all this is fixed to lifebreath, as spokes are fixed to the hub. Lifebreath proceeds by means of lifebreath; lifebreath gives lifebreath and gives to lifebreath. The father is lifebreath; the mother is lifebreath; a brother is lifebreath; a sister is lifebreath; a teacher is lifebreath; and a Brahmin is lifebreath.

2 'Now, if someone were to talk back somewhat harshly to his father, mother, brother, sister, or teacher, or to a Brahmin, people are sure to rebuke him, saying: "Damn you! You are a patricide! You are a matricide! You are a fratricide! You are a sororicide! You are a teacher-killer! You are a Brahmin-killer!" 3 When their lifebreath has left them, on the other hand, even if someone were to throw them in a pile with a poker and burn them up completely, no one would say to him: "You are a patricide! You are a matricide! You are a fratricide! You are a sororicide! You are a teacher-

killer! You are a Brahmin-killer!"—[4] for only lifebreath becomes all these.

'A man who sees it this way, thinks about it this way and perceives it this way, becomes a man who out-talks. And if people tell him, "You are a man who out-talks", he should readily acknowledge, "Yes, I am a man who out-talks", and not deny it.'

16 'Now, a man out-talks only when he out-talks with truth.'

'Yes, sir, I'm going to be a man who out-talks with truth.'

'Then you should seek to perceive the truth.'

'Sir, I do seek to perceive the truth.'

17 'Now, a man must first perceive before he speaks the truth—when one does not perceive, one does not speak the truth; only when one perceives does one speak the truth. So, it is perception that you should seek to understand.'

'Sir, I do seek to understand perception.'

18 'A man must first think before he perceives—when one does not think, one does not perceive; only when one thinks does one perceive. So, it is thinking that you should seek to perceive.'

'Sir, I do seek to perceive thinking.'

19 'A man must first have faith before he thinks—when one does not have faith, one does not think; only when one has faith does one think. So, it is faith that you should seek to perceive.'

'Sir, I do seek to perceive faith.'

20 'A man must first produce before he has faith—when one does not produce, one does not have faith; only when one produces does one have faith. So, it is production that you should seek to perceive.'

'Sir, I do seek to perceive production.'

21 'A man must first act before he produces—when one does not act, one does not produce; only when one acts does one produce. So, it is action that you should seek to perceive.'

'Sir, I do seek to perceive action.'

22 'A man must first attain well-being before he acts—when one has not attained well-being, one does not act; only when one has attained well-being does one act. So, it is well-being that you should seek to perceive.'

'Sir, I do seek to perceive well-being.'

23 'Now, well-being is nothing but plenitude. There is no prosperity in scarcity. Prosperity is indeed plenitude. So it is plenitude that you should seek to perceive.'

'Sir, I do seek to perceive plenitude.'

24 'Where a man sees, hears, or discerns no other thing—that is plenitude. Where one sees, hears, or discerns some other thing—that is scarcity. Now, plenitude is the immortal, while scarcity constitutes what is mortal.'

'Sir, on what is plenitude based?'

'On one's own greatness. Or, maybe, it is not based on greatness. 2 Cattle and horses, elephants and gold, slaves and wives, farms and houses—these are what people here call greatness. But I don't consider them that way; no, I don't, for they are all based on each other.

25 'Plenitude, indeed, is below; plenitude is above; plenitude is in the west; plenitude is in the east; plenitude is in the south; and plenitude is in the north. Indeed, plenitude extends over this whole world.

'Now, the substitution of the word "I"—"I am, indeed, below; I am above; I am in the west; I am in the east; I am in the south; and I am in the north. Indeed, I extend over this whole world."

2 'Next, the substitution of self—"The self, indeed, is below; the self is above; the self is in the west; the self is in the east; the self is in the south; and the self is in the north. Indeed, the self extends over this whole world?"

'A man who sees it this way, thinks about it this way, and perceives it this way; a man who finds pleasure in the self, who dallies with the self, who mates with the self, and who attains bliss in the self—he becomes completely his own master; he obtains complete freedom of movement in all the worlds. Those who perceive it otherwise, however, are ruled over by others and obtain perishable worlds; they have no freedom of movement in any of the worlds.

26 'When, indeed, a man sees it this way, thinks about it this way, and perceives it this way—lifebreath springs from his self; hope springs from his self; memory springs from his self; space springs from his self; heat springs from his self; water springs from his self; appearance and disappearance spring from his self; food springs from his self; strength springs from his self; perception springs from his self; deep reflection springs from his self; thought springs from his self; intention springs from his self; mind springs from his self; speech springs from his self; name springs from his self; vedic formulas spring from his self; and rites spring from his self. Indeed, this whole world springs from his self.'

2 In this regard there is this verse:

When a man rightly sees,
he sees no death,
no sickness or distress.
When a man rightly sees,
he sees all,
he wins all,
completely.

It is single, it's three- and fivefold.
It's thought to be sevenfold,
nine- or even elevenfold.
One hundred and eleven,
And also twenty thousand.

When one's food is pure, one's being becomes pure; when one's being is pure, one's memory becomes strong; and when one acquires memory, all the knots are cut away. To such a man who has wiped away all stains Lord Sanatkumāra points out the way to cross beyond darkness. It is he whom people refer to as Skanda.

CHAPTER 8

1 'Now, here in this fort of *brahman* there is a small lotus, a dwelling-place, and within it, a small space. In that space there is something—and that's what you should try to discover, that's what you should seek to perceive.'

2 If they ask him: 'Yes, here in this fort of *brahman* there is a small lotus, a dwelling-place, and within it, a small space. But what is there in that space that we should try to discover, that we should seek to perceive?'—he should reply: 3 'As vast as the space here around us is this space within the heart, and within it are contained both the earth and the sky, both fire and wind, both the sun and the moon, both lightning and stars. What belongs here to this space around us, as well as what does not—all that is contained within it.'

4 If they ask him further: 'In this fort of *brahman* is contained the whole world, all beings, and all desires. In that case, when old age overtakes it or when it perishes, what is then left?'—5 he should reply:

'That does not age,
as this body grows old;
That is not killed,
when this body is slain—
That is the real fort of *brahman*,
in it are contained all desires.

'That is the self free from evils—free from old age and death, free from sorrow, free from hunger and thirst; the self whose desires and intentions become real.

'As the subjects of a king here in this world settle down as instructed, and whatever frontier they covet—whatever region, whatever piece of land—they make a living on it; 6 and as here in this world the possession of a territory won by action comes to an end, so in the hereafter a world won by merit comes to an end.

'So, those here in this world who depart without having discovered the self and these real desires do not obtain complete freedom of movement in any of the worlds, whereas those here in this world who depart after discovering the self and these real desires obtain complete freedom of movement in all the worlds.

2 'If such a person desires the world of fathers, by his intention alone fathers rise up. And securing the world of the fathers, he rejoices.

2 'If such a person desires the world of mothers, by his intention alone mothers rise up. And, securing the world of mothers, he rejoices.

3 'If such a person desires the world of brothers, by his intention alone brothers rise up. And, securing the world of brothers, he rejoices.

4 'If such a person desires the world of sisters, by his intention alone sisters rise up. And, securing the world of sisters, he rejoices.

5 'If such a person desires the world of friends, by his intention alone friends rise up. And, securing the world of friends, he rejoices.

6 'If such a person desires the world of perfumes and garlands, by his intention alone perfumes and garlands rise up. And, securing the world of perfumes and garlands, he rejoices.

7 'If such a person desires the world of food and drink, by his intention alone food and drink rise up. And, securing the world of food and drink, he rejoices.

8 'If such a person desires the world of singing and music, by his intention alone singing and music rise up. And, securing the world of singing and music, he rejoices.

9 'If such a person desires the world of women, by his intention alone women rise up. And, securing the world of women, he rejoices.

10 'Whatever may be the object of his desire, anything that he may desire—by his intention alone it rises up. And, securing it, he rejoices.

3 'Now, these real desires are masked by the unreal. Although they are real, they have the unreal for a mask, for when someone close to him departs from this world, he doesn't get to see him here. 2 On the other hand, people who are close to him, whether they are alive or dead, as well as anything else that he desires but does not get—all that he finds by going there, for these real desires of his masked by the unreal are located there.

'Take, for example, a hidden treasure of gold. People who do not know the terrain, even when they pass right over it time and again, would not discover it. In exactly the same way, all these creatures, even though they go there every day, do not discover this world of *brahman*, for they are led astray by the unreal.

3 'Now, this self (*ātman*) is located in the heart. And this is its etymology—"in the heart (*hṛdi*) is this (*ayam*)", and so it is called "heart" (*hṛdayam*). Anyone who knows this goes to the heavenly world every single day.

4 'This deeply serene one who, after he rises up from this body and reaches the highest light, emerges in his own true appearance—that is the self,' he said, 'that is the immortal; that is the one free from fear; that is *brahman*.'

Now, the name of this *brahman* is 'Real' (*satyam*). 5 This word has three syllables: *sa*, *ti*, and *yam*. Of these, *sat* is the immortal, and *ti* is the mortal, while the syllable *yam* is what joins those two together. Because the two are joined together (*yam*) by it, it is called *yam*. Anyone who knows this goes to the heavenly world every single day.

4 Now, this self is a dike, a divider, to keep these worlds from colliding with each other. Days and nights do not pass across this dike, and neither do old age, death, or sorrow, or even good or bad deeds. All evil things turn back from it, for this world of *brahman* is free from evil things.

2 Upon passing across this dike, therefore, a blind man turns out not to be blind, a wounded man turns out not to be wounded, and a sick man turns out not to be sick. Upon passing across this dike, therefore, even the night appears just like day, for, indeed, this world of *brahman* is lit up once and for all.

3 So, only those who find this world of *brahman* (*brahmaloka*) by living the life of a celibate student (*brahmacarya*) come to possess that world, and they obtain complete freedom of movement in all the worlds.

5 Now, what people normally call a sacrifice (*yajña*) is, in reality, the life of a celibate student, for it is by the life of a celibate student that one finds him who (*yaḥ*) is the knower (*jñātā*). And what people normally call an offering (*iṣṭa*) is, in reality, the

life of a celibate student, for it is by seeking (*iṣṭvā*) through the life of a celibate student that one finds the self. 2 Further, what people normally call 'the embarking on a long sacrifice' (*sattrāyaṇa*) is, in reality, the life of a celibate student, for it is by the life of a celibate student that one finds protection (*trāṇa*) for that which is (*sat*), for the self (*ātman*). And what people normally call a vow of silence (*mauna*) is, in reality, the life of a celibate student, for it is through the life of a celibate student that one finds the self and then thinks (*manute*) of it. 3 What people normally call 'the embarking on a fast' (*anāśakāyana*), moreover, is, in reality, the life of a celibate student, for the self one finds by living the life of a celibate student does not perish (*na naśyati*).

And finally, what people normally call 'the embarking to the wilderness' (*araṇyāyana*) is, in reality, the life of a celibate student. Now, Ara and Ṇya are the two seas in the world of *brahman*, that is, in the third heaven from here. In that world are also the lake Airammadīya, the banyan tree Somasavana, the fort Aparājita, and *brahman*'s golden hall Prabhu.

4 So, only those who, by the life of a celibate student, find these two seas, Ara and Ṇya, in the world of *brahman* come to possess that world, and they obtain complete freedom of movement in all the worlds.

6 Now, these veins of the heart consist of the finest essence of orange, white, blue, yellow, and red. The sun up there, likewise, is orange, white, blue, yellow, and red. 2 Just as a long highway traverses both the villages, the one near by and the one far away, so also these rays of the sun traverse both the worlds, the one down here and the one up above. Extending out from the sun up there, they slip into these veins here, and extending out from these veins here, they slip into the sun up there.

3 So, when someone is sound asleep here, totally collected and serene, and sees no dreams, he has then slipped into these veins. No evil thing can touch him, for he is then linked with radiance.

4 Now, when someone here has become extremely infirm, people sit around him and ask: 'Do you recognize me?' 'Do you recognize me?' As long as he has not departed from the body, he would recognize them. 5 But when he is departing from this body, he rises up along those same rays. He goes up with the sound 'OṂ'.

No sooner does he think of it, than he reaches the sun. It is the door to the farther world, open to those who have the knowledge but closed to those who do not. 6In this connection, there is this verse:

> One hundred and one, the veins of the heart.
> One of them runs up to the crown of the head.
> Going up by it, he reaches the immortal.
> The rest, in their ascent, spread out in all directions.

7 'The self (*ātman*) that is free from evils, free from old age and death, free from sorrow, free from hunger and thirst; the self whose desires and intentions are real—that is the self that you should try to discover, that is the self that you should seek to perceive. When someone discovers that self and perceives it, he obtains all the worlds, and all his desires are fulfilled.' So said Prajāpati.

2 Both the gods and the demons became aware of this, and each side talked it over: 'Come, let's discover that self (*ātman*) by discovering which one obtains all the worlds, and all one's desires are fulfilled.' Then Indra set out from among the gods, and Virocana, from among the demons. And going there independently, the two arrived in the presence of Prajāpati carrying firewood in their hands.

3 They lived the life of celibate students for thirty-two years. Then Prajāpati asked them: 'Why have you lived here? What do you want?'

They replied: 'Sir, people report these words of yours: "The self (*ātman*) that is free from evils, free from old age and death, free from sorrow, free from hunger and thirst; the self whose desires and intentions are real—that is the self that you should try to discover, that is the self that you should seek to perceive. When someone discovers that self and perceives it, he obtains all the worlds, and all his desires are fulfilled."'

'So, you have lived here seeking that self.' 4 Prajāpati then told them: 'This person that one sees here in the eye—that is the self (*ātman*); that is the immortal; that is the one free from fear; that is *brahman*.'

'But then, sir, who is the one that's seen here in the water and here in a mirror?'

'It is the same one who is seen in all these surfaces,' replied Prajāpati.

8 'Look at yourselves (*ātman*) in a pan of water. And let me know if there is anything you do not perceive about yourselves.' So they looked into a pan of water. Prajāpati asked them: 'What do you see?'

And they replied: 'Sir, we see here our entire body (*ātman*), a perfect likeness down to the very hairs of the body, down to the finger nails.'

2 Prajāpati told them then: 'Adorn yourself beautifully, dress well, and spruce yourself up, and then look into a pan of water.' So they adorned themselves beautifully, dressed well, and spruced themselves up, and then looked into a pan of water. Prajāpati asked them: 'What do you see?'

3 And they replied: 'Sir, as the two of us here are beautifully adorned, well dressed, and all spruced up, in exactly the same way are these, sir, beautifully adorned, well dressed, and all spruced up.'

'That is the self (*ātman*); that is the immortal; that is the one free from fear; that is *brahman*,' Prajāpati told them. And the two of them left with contented hearts.

4 Seeing the two depart, Prajāpati observed: 'There they go, without learning about the self (*ātman*), without discovering the self! The side that will hold to this correspondence (*upaniṣad*), whether it is the gods or the demons, is bound to be vanquished.'

Now, Virocana, his heart totally content, went back to the demons and announced to them this correspondence (*upaniṣad*): 'It is the body (*ātman*) that one should extol in this world. It is the body that one should care for. When someone extols the body alone in this world, when he cares only for the body, he wins both this world and the next.' 5 Therefore, even today people here say of a man who gives no gifts, has no faith, and offers no sacrifices: "What a demonic fellow!" This is, indeed, the correspondence (*upaniṣad*) that demons hold to; they perform the funerary rites for the body of a dead person with offerings of food, garments, and ornaments, for they believe that in this way they will win the next world.

9 Indra, on the other hand, even before he had reached the gods, saw this danger: 'If this is the self—then, just as it becomes

beautifully adorned when this body is beautifully adorned, well dressed when this body is well dressed, and spruced up when this body is spruced up, in exactly the same way it is bound to become blind when this body becomes blind, lame when this body becomes lame, and crippled when this body becomes crippled. Upon the death of the body, indeed, it too is bound to die. I see nothing worthwhile in this.'

2 So he returned again carrying firewood in his hands. Prajāpati said to him: 'Maghavan, didn't you leave together with Virocana with contented hearts? So, why have you come back? What do you want?'

He replied: 'If this is the self—then, sir, just as it becomes beautifully adorned when this body is beautifully adorned, well dressed when this body is well dressed, and spruced up when this body is spruced up, in exactly the same way it is bound to become blind when this body becomes blind, lame when this body becomes lame, and crippled when this body becomes crippled. Upon the death of the body, indeed, it too is bound to die. I see nothing worthwhile in this.'

3 Prajāpati told him: 'It is exactly as you say, Maghavan. But I will explain it to you further. Stay here for another thirty-two years.'

So he lived there for another thirty-two years, after which Prajāpati spoke to him:

10 'The one who goes happily about in a dream—that is the self; that is the immortal; that is the one free from fear; that is *brahman*.'

Indra then left, his heart content. But even before he had reached the gods, he saw this danger: 'It is true that this self does not become blind when this body becomes blind, or lame when the body becomes lame. This self is clearly unaffected by the faults of the body—2 it is not killed when this body is slain or rendered lame when this body becomes lame. Nevertheless, people do in a way kill it and chase after it; it does in a way experience unpleasant things; and in a way it even cries. I see nothing worthwhile in this.'

3 So he returned again carrying firewood in his hands. Prajāpati said to him: 'Maghavan, didn't you leave with a contented heart? So, why have you come back? What do you want?'

He replied: 'It is true, sir, that this self does not become blind when this body becomes blind, or lame when the body becomes lame. This self is clearly unaffected by the faults of this body—[4] it is not killed when this body is slain or rendered lame when this body becomes lame. Nevertheless, people do in a way kill it and chase after it; it does in a way experience unpleasant things; and in a way it even cries. I see nothing worthwhile in this.'

Prajāpati told him: 'It is exactly as you say, Maghavan. But I will explain it to you further. Stay here for another thirty-two years.'

So he lived there for another thirty-two years, after which Prajāpati spoke to him:

11 'When one is fast asleep, totally collected and serene, and sees no dreams—that is the self; that is the immortal; that is the one free from fear; that is *brahman*.'

Indra then left, his heart content. But even before he had reached the gods, he saw this danger: 'But this self as just explained, you see, does not perceive itself fully as, "I am this"; it does not even know any of these beings here. It has become completely annihilated. I see nothing worthwhile in this.'

2 So he returned again carrying firewood in his hands. Prajāpati said to him: 'Maghavan, didn't you leave with a contented heart? So, why have you come back? What do you want?'

He replied: 'But, sir, this self as just explained, you see, does not perceive itself fully as, "I am this", nor even does it know any of these beings here. It has become completely annihilated. I see nothing worthwhile in this.'

3 Prajāpati told him: 'It is exactly as you say, Maghavan. But I will explain it to you further, but only under the following condition—stay here for another five years.'

So he lived there for another five years. Altogether, that makes one hundred and one years. That is why people say: 'For one hundred and one years did Maghavan live as a celibate student with Prajāpati.'

Prajāpati then spoke to him:

12 'This body, Maghavan, is mortal; it is in the grip of death. So, it is the abode of this immortal and non-bodily self.

One who has a body is in the grip of joy and sorrow, and there is no freedom from joy and sorrow for one who has a body. Joy and sorrow, however, do not affect one who has no body.

2 'The wind is without a body, and so are the rain-cloud, lightning, and thunder. These are without bodies. Now, as these, after they rise up from the space up above and reach the highest light, emerge in their own true appearance, 3 in the very same way, this deeply serene one, after he rises up from this body and reaches the highest light, emerges in his own true appearance. He is the highest person. He roams about there, laughing, playing, and enjoying himself with women, carriages, or relatives, without remembering the appendage that is this body. The lifebreath is yoked to this body, as a draught animal to a cart.

4 'Now, when this sight here gazes into space, that is the seeing person, the faculty of sight enables one to see. The one who is aware: "Let me smell this"—that is the self; the faculty of smell enables him to smell. The one who is aware: "Let me say this"—that is the self; the faculty of speech enables him to speak. The one who is aware: "Let me listen to this"—that is the self; the faculty of hearing enables him to hear. 5 The one who is aware: "Let me think about this"—that is the self; the mind is his divine faculty of sight. This very self rejoices as it perceives with his mind, with that divine sight, these objects of desire found in the world of *brahman*.

6 'It is this self that the gods venerate, as a result of which they have obtained all the worlds and have had all their desires fulfilled. Likewise, when someone discovers this self and comes to perceive it, he will obtain all the worlds and have all his desires fulfilled.'

That was what Prajāpati said.

13 From the dark I go into the multicoloured, and from the multicoloured into the dark. Shaking off evil, like a horse its hair, and freeing myself, like the moon from Rāhu's jaws, I, the perfected self (*ātman*), cast off the body, the imperfect, and attain the world of *brahman*.

14 Now, what is called space is that which brings forth name and visible appearance. That within which they are

located—that is *brahman*; that is the immortal; that is the self (*ātman*).

I go into Prajāpati's assembly hall and dwelling! I am the glory of the Brahmins, the glory of the Kṣatriyas, the glory of the Vaiśyas! I have attained glory! I am the glory of glories! Let me not go to the grey and toothless state, to the toothless, grey, and slobbery state!

15 All this Brahmā told to Prajāpati; Prajāpati to Manu; and Manu to his children.

From the teacher's house—where he learned the Veda in the prescribed manner during his free time after his daily tasks for the teacher—he returns, and then, in his own house, he does his daily vedic recitation in a clean place, rears virtuous children, draws in all his sense organs into himself, and refrains from killing any creature except for a worthy person—someone who lives this way all his life attains the world of *brahman*, and he does not return again.

Taittirīya Upaniṣad

THE Taittirīya Upaniṣad constitutes chapters 7, 8, and 9 of the Taittirīya Āraṇyaka, which is itself a supplement added to the Taittirīya Brāhmaṇa of the Black Yajurveda. The three chapters of this Upaniṣad are named 'Chapter on Instruction' (*śikṣāvallī*), 'Chapter on Bliss' (*ānandavallī*), and 'Chapter of Bhṛgu' (*bhṛguvallī*). In the Taittirīya Āraṇyaka, these three chapters are followed by the final tenth chapter that comprises the Mahānārāyaṇa Upaniṣad, not translated in this collection.

CONTENTS

CHAPTER 1

1 OṂ

May Mitra be kind to us!
May Varuṇa, may Aryaman!
May Indra Bṛhaspati!
And Viṣṇu of long strides!
Homage to *brahman*!
Homage to you, Wind!
You alone are the visible *brahman*!
I will proclaim you,
And you alone as the visible *brahman*!
I will proclaim you as the right!
I will proclaim you as the true!
May it help me.
May it help the teacher.
Yes, may it help me.
And may it help the teacher.

OṂ

Peace! Peace! Peace!

2 OṂ! We will now explain phonetics—phoneme, accent, quantity, strength, articulation, and connection. That describes the field of phonetics.

3 May both of us attain fame!
May both of us obtain the lustre of sacred knowledge!

Next, we will explain the hidden connection (*upaniṣad*) of combination with reference to five topics—the worlds, the lights, knowledge, progeny, and the body (*ātman*). They call these the 'large-scale combinations'.

With reference to the worlds—the preceding word is the earth, the following word is the sky, their union is space, [2] and their link is the wind. So it is with reference to the worlds.

With reference to the lights—the preceding word is the fire, the following word is the sun, their union is the waters, and their link is lightning. So it is with reference to the lights.

With reference to knowledge—the preceding word is the teacher,
3 the following word is the pupil, their union is knowledge, and their link is instruction. So it is with reference to knowledge.

With reference to the progeny—the preceding word is the mother, the following word is the father, their union is the child, and their link is procreation. So it is with reference to progeny.

4 With reference to the body (*ātman*)—the preceding word is the lower jaw, the following word is the upper jaw, their union is speech, and their link is the tongue. So it is with reference to the body.

These are the large-scale combinations. When someone knows these large-scale combinations (*saṃdhā*) as explained here—he will possess (*saṃ-dhā-*) offspring, livestock, the lustre of sacred knowledge, a food-supply, and the heavenly world.

4 The dazzling bull among vedic hymns,
Sprung from the immortal,
Sprung from vedic hymns—
That is Indra!
May he deliver me with wisdom!

In my memory, O God, may the immortal be fixed!
My body, may it be untrammelled!
My tongue, may it say the sweetest things!
My ears, may they hear the wealth of sacred lore!

You are *brahman*'s chest,
Covered with wisdom.
Guard what I have heard.

She brings, she extends, 2 quickly she produces,
For herself and always for me—
clothes and cows,
food and drink.
So, bring Prosperity, bring her to me,
rich in sheep and kine.
Svāhā!

Students, may they come to me! Svāhā!
Students, may they flock to me! Svāhā!
Students, may they rush to me! Svāhā!
Students, may they be controlled! Svāhā!
Students, may they be tranquil! Svāhā!

3 May I be famous among men! Svāhā!

More affluent than the very rich! Svāhā!
May I, O Bhaga, enter you! Svāhā!
May you, O Bhaga, enter me! Svāhā!
In you, O Bhaga, branched a thousandfold,
In you I shall be cleansed! Svāhā!

As waters flow down the slope;
And the months with the passing of the days;
So, O Creator, from everywhere,
May students come to me! Svāhā!
You are a neighbour!
Shine on me!
Come to me!

5 *Bhūr*, *bhuvas*, and *suvar*: these are the three Calls. Māhācamasya, however, has taught a fourth such utterance, namely *mahas*. This last is *brahman*—it is the body (*ātman*), while the other deities are the limbs.

This world down here is *bhūr*, the intermediate region is *bhuvas*, that world up there is *suvar*, 2 and the sun is *mahas*, for all the worlds are made joyous (*mah-*) by the sun. The fire is *bhūr*, the wind is *bhuvas*, the sun is *suvar*, and the moon is *mahas*, for all the lights are made joyous by the moon. The Ṛg verses are *bhūr*, the Sāman chants are *bhuvas*, the Yajus formulaś are *suvar*, 3 and *brahman* (= OṂ) is *mahas*, for all the Vedas are made joyous by *brahman*. The out-breath is *bhūr*, the in-breath is *bhuvas*, the inter-breath is *suvar*, and food is *mahas*, for all the breaths are made joyous by food.

So these four are divided in four ways, making four sets of four Calls. Anyone who knows them knows *brahman*, and all the gods offer tribute to him.

6 In this space here within the heart lies the immortal and golden person consisting of the mind. And this thing that hangs like a nipple between the two palates, it is Indra's passage. Bursting through the two halves of the skull at the point where the hairs part, he establishes himself in the fire by making the call *bhūr*, in the wind by making the call *bhuvas*, 2 in the sun by making the call *suvar*, and in *brahman* by making the call *mahas*. He obtains sovereignty and becomes the lord of the mind, the lord of speech, the lord of sight, the lord of hearing, and the lord of

perception. And thereafter, this is what he becomes—the *brahman* whose body is space, whose self is truth, whose pleasure ground is the lifebreath, and whose joy is the mind; the *brahman* who is completely tranquil and immortal. Prācīnayogya, venerate it in this manner.

7

Earth	Intermediate Region	Sky	Quarters	Intermediate Quarters
Fire	Wind	Sun	Moon	Stars
Waters	Plants	Trees	Space	Body (*ātman*)

That was with respect to beings. Now with respect to the body:

Out-breath	Inter-breath	In-breath	Up-breath	Link-breath
Sight	Hearing	Mind	Speech	Touch
Skin	Flesh	Sinew	Bones	Marrow

After making this analysis, a seer proclaimed: 'Clearly, this whole world is fivefold. By means of the fivefold one surely secures the fivefold.'

8 *Brahman* is OṂ. This whole world is OṂ. When one says OṂ, it indicates compliance. Thus, when they are instructed, 'O! Make him listen!', they do make him listen. They say OṂ before singing the Sāman chants; they say OṂ ŚOṂ before they recite the hymns of praise; the Adhvaryu priest says OṂ before giving his response; the Brahman priest says OṂ before singing the introductory praise. One says OṂ in giving one's permission to conduct the fire sacrifice. When a Brahmin is about to recite the Veda publicly, he first says 'OṂ', and then, 'May I grasp the Veda (*brahman*).' And he does, indeed, grasp the Veda.

9 The right, yes; but also the private and public recitation of the Veda. The truth, yes; but also the private and public recitation of the Veda. Austerity, yes; but also the private and public recitation of the Veda. Self-control, yes; but also the private and public recitation of the Veda. Tranquillity, yes; but also the private and public recitation of the Veda. The fires, yes; but also the private and public recitation of the Veda. The fire sacrifice, yes; but also the private and public recitation of the Veda. Guests, yes; but also the private and public recitation of the Veda. Humaneness,

yes; but also the private and public recitation of the Veda. Children, yes; but also the private and public recitation of the Veda. Procreation, yes; but also the private and public recitation of the Veda. Progeny, yes; but also the private and public recitation of the Veda.

'Just the truth'—that was the view of Rāthītara, the Truthful.

'Just austerity'—that was the view of Pauruśiṣṭi, the Ever-Austere.

'Nothing but the private and public recitation of the Veda'—that was the view of Maudgalya the Painless; for that is austerity, that indeed is austerity.

10 I am the shaker of the tree!
My fame is like a mountain peak!
immaculate up on high,
immortal wealth of victory,
I am a treasure shining bright!
Undecaying, immortal, and wise!

This was the vedic recitation of Triśaṅku.

11 After the completion of vedic study, the teacher admonishes his resident pupil: 'Speak the truth. Follow the Law. Do not neglect your private recitation of the Veda. After you have given a valuable gift to the teacher, do not cut off your family line.

'Do not neglect the truth. Do not neglect the Law. Do not neglect your health. Do not neglect your wealth. Do not neglect your private and public recitation of the Veda. 2 Do not neglect the rites to gods and ancestors.

'Treat your mother like a god. Treat your father like a god. Treat your teacher like a god. Treat your guests like gods.

'You should perform only those rites that are irreproachable, and never other types of rites. You should hold in high esteem only those good practices you have observed in me, 3 and never other types of practices. You should greet with honour any Brahmin who is superior to us by offering him a seat.

'You should give with faith, and never without faith. You should give with dignity. You should give with modesty. You should give with trepidation. You should give with comprehension.

'Now, if you ever have a doubt regarding a rite or a practice—
4 should there be experienced, qualified, and gentle Brahmins devoted to the Law who are able to make a judgement in that matter, you should observe how they act in that regard and behave likewise. Similarly, with regard to practices subject to criticism—should there be experienced, qualified, and gentle Brahmins devoted to the Law who are able to make a judgement in that matter, you should observe how they act in these matters and behave likewise.

'This is the rule of substitution. This is the teaching. This is the hidden teaching (*upaniṣad*) of the Veda. This is the admonition. You should worship in this way. You should, indeed, worship this in this way.

12

May Mitra be kind to us!
May Varuṇa, may Aryaman!
May Indra Bṛhaspati!
May Viṣṇu of long strides!

Homage to *brahman*!
Homage to you, Wind!
You alone are the visible *brahman*!

I have proclaimed you,
And you alone as the visible *brahman*!
I have proclaimed you as the right!
I have proclaimed you as the true!
It has helped me.
It has helped the teacher.
Yes, it has helped me.
And it has helped the teacher.

OṂ
Peace! Peace! Peace!

CHAPTER 2

1 A man who knows *brahman* obtains the highest there is. On this we have the following verse:

Truth and knowledge,
Th'infinite and *brahman*—
A man who knows them as
hidden in the deepest cavity,
hidden in the highest heaven;
Attains all his desires,
together with the wise *brahman*.

From this very self (*ātman*) did space come into being; from space, air; from air, fire; from fire, the waters; from the waters, the earth; from the earth, plants; from plants, food; and from food, man. Now, a man here is formed from the essence of food. This here is his head; this is his right side; this is his left side; this is his torso (*ātman*); and this is his bottom on which he rests. On this too we have the following verse:

2 From food, surely, are they born;
all creatures that live on earth.
On food alone, once born, they live;
and into food in the end they pass.
For food is the foremost of beings,
so it's called 'all herbs'.

All the food they'll secure for themselves,
when they worship *brahman* as food;
For food is the foremost of beings,
so it's called 'all herbs'.

From food beings come into being;
By food, once born, they grow.
'It is eaten and it eats beings.'
Therefore it is called 'food'.

Different from and lying within this man formed from the essence of food is the self (*ātman*) consisting of lifebreath, which suffuses that man completely. Now, he has the appearance of a man; so, corresponding to his manlike appearance, the self consisting of lifebreath assumes a manlike appearance. Of this self, the head is simply the out-breath; the right side is the inter-breath; the left side is the in-breath; the torso (*ātman*) is space; and the bottom on which it rests is the earth. On this too we have the following verse:

3 Lifebreath—gods breathe along with it
as do men and beasts.
For lifebreath is the life of beings,
so it's called 'all life'.

A full life they'll surely live, when they
worship *brahman* as lifebreath.
For lifebreath is the life of beings,
so it's called 'all life'.

Of that, this here is the embodied self (*ātman*); this belongs to the former.

Different from and lying within this self consisting of breath is the self (*ātman*) consisting of mind, which suffuses this other self completely. Now, he has the appearance of a man; so, corresponding to its manlike appearance, the self consisting of mind assumes a manlike appearance. Of this self, the head is simply the Yajus formulas; the right side is the Ṛg verses; the left side is the Sāman chants; the torso (*ātman*) is rules of substitution; and the bottom on which it rests is the Atharva-Āṅgirases. On this too we have the following verse:

4 Before they reach it, words turn back,
together with the mind;
One who knows that bliss of *brahman*,
he is never afraid.

Of that, this here is the embodied self (*ātman*); this belongs to the former.

Different from and lying within this self consisting of mind is the self (*ātman*) consisting of perception, which suffuses this other self completely. Now, he has the appearance of a man; so, corresponding to its manlike appearance, the self consisting of perception assumes a manlike appearance. Of this self, the head is simply faith; the right side is the truth; the left side is the real; the torso (*ātman*) is the performance; and the bottom on which it rests is the celebration. On this too we have the following verse:

5 It's perception that conducts the sacrifice.
It's perception that performs the rites.
It's perception that all the gods
Venerate as the foremost *brahman*.

'*Brahman* is perception'—
he who knows this,
and neglects this not,
Leaving the evils behind in his body
He attains all his wishes.

Of that, this here is the embodied self (*ātman*); this belongs to the former.

Different from and lying within this self consisting of perception is the self (*ātman*) consisting of bliss, which suffuses this other self completely. Now, he has the appearance of a man; so, corresponding to its manlike appearance, the self consisting of bliss assumes a manlike appearance. Of this self, the head is simply the pleasure; the right side is the delight; the left side is the thrill; the torso (*ātman*) is the bliss; and the bottom on which it rests is the *brahman*. On this too we have the following verse:

6 If a man thinks '*Brahman* is the non-existent',
he becomes himself non-existent!
If a man thinks '*Brahman* is the existent',
people then know him to be existent.

Of that, this here is the embodied self (*ātman*); this belongs to the former.

Now, the following questions arise from the foregoing:

Does any man who knows this not
attain that world when he dies?
Or does any man who knows this
attain that world when he dies?

He had this desire: 'Let me multiply myself. Let me produce offspring.' So he heated himself up. When he had heated himself up, he emitted this whole world, everything that is here. After emitting it, he entered that very world. And after entering it, he became in turn *Sat* and *Tyat*, the distinct and the indistinct, the resting and the never resting, the perceived and the non-perceived, the real (*satya*) and the unreal (*anṛta*). He became the real, everything that is here; that is why people call all this *Sat*. On this too we have the following verse:

7 In the beginning this world was the non-existent,
and from it arose the existent.
By itself it made a body (*ātman*) for itself;
therefore it is called 'well-made'.

And precisely because it is well-made, it is the essence, for only when one has grasped that essence does one attain bliss. Now, who would breathe in, who would breathe out, if that essence were not there in space as bliss, for it is that essence that causes bliss. For when a man finds within that invisible, incorporeal (*anātmya*), indistinct, and supportless essence, the fearless state on which to rest, then he becomes free from fear. When, on the other hand, a man creates a hollow or a fissure within it, then he experiences fear. Now, this is the fear experienced by a man who thinks that he knows. On this too we have the following verse:

8 The fear of it makes the wind blow.
The fear of it makes the sun rise.
The fear of it makes them run—
fire and moon,
and death, the fifth.

Next follows an analysis of bliss.

Take a young man—a good young man who is learned, very quick, solidly built, and extremely strong. And assume that he owns this whole earth filled with wealth. That would constitute a single measure of human bliss.

A single measure of bliss that human Gandharvas enjoy—and also a man versed in the Vedas and free from desires—is a hundred times greater than human bliss.

A single measure of bliss that divine Gandharvas enjoy—and also a man versed in the Vedas and free from desires—is a hundred times greater than the bliss of human Gandharvas.

A single measure of bliss that the forefathers who live in their world for a long time enjoy—and also a man versed in the Vedas and free from desires—is a hundred times greater than the bliss of divine Gandharvas.

A single measure of bliss that those who are gods by birth enjoy—and also a man versed in the Vedas and free from desires—is a hundred times greater than the bliss of the forefathers who live in their world for a long time.

A single measure of bliss that those who have become gods by performing rites enjoy—and also a man versed in the Vedas and free from desires—is a hundred times greater than the bliss of those who are gods by birth.

A single measure of bliss that the gods enjoy—and also a man versed in the Vedas and free from desires—is a hundred times greater than the bliss of those who have become gods by performing rites.

A single measure of bliss that Indra enjoys—and also a man versed in the Vedas and free from desires—is a hundred times greater than the bliss of the gods.

A single measure of bliss that Bṛhaspati enjoys—and also a man versed in the Vedas and free from desires—is a hundred times greater than the bliss of Indra.

A single measure of bliss that Prajāpati enjoys—and also a man versed in the Vedas and free from desires—is a hundred times greater than the bliss of Bṛhaspati.

A single measure of bliss that *brahman* enjoys—and also a man versed in the Vedas and free from desires—is a hundred times greater than the bliss of Prajāpati.

He who is here in a man and he who is there in the sun—they are one and the same. After a man who knows this departs from this world—he first reaches the self (*ātman*) that consists of food, then the self that consists of lifebreath, then the self that consists of mind, then the self that consists of perception, and finally the self that consists of bliss. On this too we have the following verse:

9 Before they reach it, words turn back,
together with the mind;
One who knows that bliss of *brahman*,
he is never afraid.

He does not agonize, thinking: 'Why didn't I do the right thing? Why did I do the wrong thing?' A man who knows this frees himself (*ātman*) from these two thoughts. From these two thoughts, indeed, a man who knows this frees himself. That is the hidden teaching (*upaniṣad*).

CHAPTER 3

1 Bhṛgu, the son of Varuṇa, once went up to his father Varuṇa and said: 'Sir, teach me *brahman*.' And Varuṇa told him this: 'Food, lifebreath, sight, hearing, mind, speech.' He further said: 'That from which these beings are born; on which, once born, they live; and into which they pass upon death—seek to perceive that! That is *brahman*!'

So Bhṛgu practised austerities. After he had practised austerities, [2] he perceived: '*Brahman* is food—for, clearly, it is from food that these beings are born; on food, once born, do they live; and into food do they pass upon death.'

After he had perceived this, he went up to his father Varuṇa once again and said: 'Sir, teach me *brahman*.' Varuṇa told him: 'Seek to perceive *brahman* by means of austerity. *Brahman* is austerity.'

So Bhṛgu practised austerities. After he had practised austerities, [3] he perceived: '*Brahman* is the lifebreath—for, clearly, it is from the lifebreath that these beings are born; through the lifebreath, once born, do they live; and into the lifebreath do they pass upon death.'

After he had perceived this, he went up to his father Varuṇa once again and said: 'Sir, teach me *brahman*.' Varuṇa told him: 'Seek to perceive *brahman* by means of austerity. *Brahman* is austerity.'

So Bhṛgu practised austerities. After he had practised austerities, [4] he perceived: '*Brahman* is the mind—for, clearly, it is from the mind that these beings are born; through the mind, once born, do they live; and into the mind do they pass upon death.'

After he had perceived this, he went up to his father Varuṇa once again and said: 'Sir, teach me *brahman*.' Varuṇa told him: 'Seek to perceive *brahman* by means of austerity. *Brahman* is austerity.'

So Bhṛgu practised austerities. After he had practised austerities, [5] he perceived: '*Brahman* is perception—for, clearly, it is from perception that these beings are born; through perception, once born, do they live; and into perception do they pass upon death.'

After he had perceived this, he went up to his father Varuṇa once again and said: 'Sir, teach me *brahman*.' Varuṇa told him: 'Seek to perceive *brahman* by means of austerity. *Brahman* is austerity.'

So Bhṛgu practised austerities. After he had practised austerities, [6] he perceived: '*Brahman* is bliss—for, clearly, it is from bliss that these beings are born; through bliss, once born, do they live; and into bliss do they pass upon death.'

This is the doctrine of Bhṛgu, the son of Varuṇa. It is firmly established in the highest firmament. When someone comes to know this—he will become firmly established; he will become a man who has food, who eats food; he will become a big man on account of his offspring, livestock, and the lustre of sacred knowledge; he will become a big man on account of his fame.

7 One should not belittle food—that is the rule. The lifebreath is food, and the body is the food-eater. The body is based on the lifebreath, and the lifebreath, on the body. Thus, this food is based on food. When someone knows this food that is based on food—he will become firmly established; he will become a man who has food, who eats food; he will become a big man on account of his offspring, livestock, and the lustre of sacred knowledge; he will become a big man on account of his fame.

8 One should not reject food—that is the rule. Water is food, and fire is the food-eater. Fire is based on water, and water, on fire. Thus, this food is based on food. When someone knows this food that is based on food—he will become firmly established; he will become a man who has food, who eats food; he will become a big man on account of his offspring, livestock, and the luster of sacred knowledge; he will become a big man on account of his fame.

9 One should prepare a lot of food—that is the rule. The earth is food, and space is the food-eater. Space is based on the earth, and the earth, on space. Thus, this food is based on food. When someone knows this food that is based on food—he will become firmly established; he will become a man who has food, who eats food; he will become a big man on account of his

offspring, livestock, and the lustre of sacred knowledge; he will become a big man on account of his fame.

10 One should never turn anyone away from one's home—that is the rule. Therefore, he should procure a lot of food by every means at his disposal. And people will say of him: 'Food is readily available to him.' When he makes the food ready during the first portion, food becomes readily available to him during the first portion. When he makes the food ready during the middle portion, food becomes readily available to him during the middle portion. When he makes the food ready during the final portion, food becomes readily available to him during the final portion. [2] And so it is for anyone who knows this.

In speech, as rest; in the out-breath and the in-breath, as activity and rest; in the hands, as action; in the feet, as movement; in the anus, as evacuation—these are its human appellations. Now, its divine appellations—in the rain, [3] as contentment; in lightning, as power; in livestock, as fame; in the stars, as light; in the generative organ, as reproduction, immortality, and bliss; in space, as totality.

Let him venerate it as the foundation, and he will have a foundation. Let him venerate it as might, and he will become mighty. Let him venerate it as mind, and he will have a quick mind. [4] Let him venerate it as bowing in homage, and his desires will bow to his will. Let him venerate it as *brahman*, and he will possess *brahman*. Let him venerate it as 'dying around *brahman*', and his rivals filled with hate will die around him, and so will his detestable foes.

He who is here in a man and he who is up there in the sun—they are one and the same. [5] After a man who knows this departs from this world—he first reaches the self (*ātman*) that consists of food, then the self that consists of lifebreath, then the self that consists of mind, then the self that consists of perception, and finally the self that consists of bliss; and, eating whatever he likes and assuming whatever appearance he likes, he continues to travel across these worlds and to sing this Sāman chant:

Hā u! Hā u! Hā u!
[6] I am food! I am food! I am food!
I eat food! I eat food! I eat food!
I set the rhythm! I set the rhythm! I set the rhythm!

I am the first-born of truth,
born before the gods,
in the navel of the immortal.

The one who gives me
will indeed eat me.

I am food!
I eat him who eats the food!
I have conquered the whole universe!
I am like the light in the firmament!

[And so will] anyone who knows this. That is the hidden teaching (*upaniṣad*).

Aitareya Upaniṣad

THE Aitareya Upaniṣad consists of chapters 4–6 of the second book of the Aitareya Araṇyaka, which has altogether five books. The Araṇyaka itself is part of the Aitareya Brāhmaṇa belonging to the Aitareya school of the Ṛgveda. The distinction between the Upaniṣad proper and the rest of the Araṇyaka is somewhat artificial, there being little difference in the topics covered. Indeed, the third book explicitly calls itself Saṃhitā Upaniṣad, and the second book contains speculations on the Ṛgvedic recitation, Uktha, a subject treated in several Upaniṣads. The native tradition itself considers the Araṇyaka to contain three Upaniṣads: the first consists of chapters 1–3 of book 2; the second is our Upaniṣad; and the third consists of book 3 (see Keith 1909, 39–40).

CONTENTS

CHAPTER 1

1 IN the beginning this world was the self (*ātman*), one alone, and there was no other being at all that blinked an eye. He thought to himself: 'Let me create the worlds.'

2 So he created these worlds—the flood, the glittering specks, the mortal, and the waters. Now, the flood is up there beyond the sky, and its foundation is the sky. The glittering specks are the intermediate world. The mortal is the earth, and what is underneath are the waters.

3 He further thought to himself: 'Now that these worlds are in place, I had better create their keepers.' From those very waters he drew out and gave a definite shape to a man. 4 He incubated that man. From that man so incubated—

—a mouth was hatched like an egg; from the mouth sprang speech, and from speech, fire.

—a pair of nostrils was hatched; from the nostrils sprang breath, and from breath, the wind.

—a pair of eyes was hatched; from the eyes sprang sight, and from sight, the sun.

—a pair of ears was hatched; from the ears sprang hearing, and from hearing, the quarters.

—a skin was hatched; from the skin sprang the body hairs, and from the body hairs, plants and trees.

—a heart was hatched; from the heart sprang the mind, and from the mind, the moon.

—a navel was hatched; from the navel sprang the in-breath, and from the in-breath, death.

—a penis was hatched; from the penis sprang semen, and from semen, the waters.

2 Once these deities were created, they fell into this vast ocean here. It afflicted him with hunger and thirst. Those deities then said to him: 'Find us a dwelling in which we can establish ourselves and eat food.' 2 So he brought a cow up to them, but they said: 'That's totally inadequate for us.' Then he brought a horse up to them, but they said: 'That's totally inadequate for us.'

3 Finally he brought a man up to them, and they exclaimed: 'Now,
this is well made!' for man is indeed well made.
Then he told them: 'Enter, each into your respective dwelling.'
4 So, the fire became speech and entered the mouth; the wind
became breath and entered the nostrils; the sun became sight and
entered the eyes; the quarters became hearing and entered the ears;
the plants and trees became body hairs and entered the skin; the
moon became mind and entered the heart; death became the in-
breath and entered the navel; the waters became semen and
entered the penis.
5 Thereupon, hunger and thirst told him: 'Find one for us also.'
He told them: 'I give you a share in what belongs to these very
deities, and I make you sharers with them.' As a consequence, to
whatever deity one may make an offering, hunger and thirst share
it with that deity.

3 He then thought to himself: 'Now that these worlds and their
keepers are in place, I had better create food for them.' 2 So he
incubated the waters. When the waters were incubated, there
emerged from them something solid. And the solid thing that
emerged was food.
3 No sooner was it created than it sought to escape. He tried to
capture it with speech. But he was unable to capture it with speech,
for had he captured it with speech, one would satisfy one's appetite
by simply mentioning food.
4 He tried to capture it with the out-breath. But he was unable to
capture it with the out-breath, for had he captured it with the out-
breath, one would satisfy one's appetite by simply breathing upon
food.
5 He tried to capture it with sight. But he was unable to capture
it with sight, for had he captured it with sight, one would satisfy
one's appetite by simply looking at food.
6 He tried to capture it with hearing. But he was unable to capture it with hearing, for had he captured it with hearing, one would
satisfy one's appetite by simply hearing about food.
7 He tried to capture it with the skin. But he was unable to capture it with the skin, for had he captured it with the skin, one would
satisfy one's appetite by simply touching food.
8 He tried to capture it with the mind. But he was unable to

capture it with the mind, for had he captured it with the mind, one would satisfy one's appetite by simply thinking about food.

9 He tried to capture it with the penis. But he was unable to capture it with the penis, for had he captured it with the penis, one would satisfy one's appetite by simply ejaculating food.

10 Finally, he tried to capture it with the in-breath, and then he managed to consume it. So, the wind is the one that captures food, for the wind (*vāyu*) is the food-finder (*annāyu*).

11 Then he thought to himself: 'How can this possibly carry on without me?' And he thought: 'Through which of these shall I enter?' He thought: 'If speaking is done through speech; if breathing out is done through the out-breath; if seeing is done through sight; if hearing is done through hearing; if touching is done through the skin; if thinking is done through the mind; if breathing in is done through the in-breath; and if ejaculating is done through the penis—then who am I?'

12 So he split open the head at the point where the hairs part and entered through that gate. This gate (*dvār*) has the name 'Split' (*vidṛti*), and that is the heaven of pleasure (*nānanda*). He has three dwellings, three levels of sleep—this is one dwelling, this is another, and this is the third.

13 After he was born, he contemplated the creatures with the thought: 'Will anyone declare there to be another here?' But he saw only that man, the *brahman*, the utmost, and he said, 'This (*idam*) I have seen (*adarśam*)!' 14 Therefore, he is called 'Idandra'. Now, his name is Idandra; but even though he is Idandra, people cryptically call him Indra, because the gods somehow love the cryptic.

CHAPTER 2

At the outset, this embryo comes into being within a man as semen. That is the radiance gathered from all the bodily parts; so he bears himself (*ātman*) in himself (*ātman*). And when a man deposits the semen in a woman, he gives birth to it. That is his first birth.

[2] It becomes one with the woman's body (*ātman*), as if it were a part of her own body. As a result, it does not harm her. And she nourishes this self (*ātman*) of his that has entered her. [3] As she nourishes him, so he should nourish her. The woman carries him as the embryo. At the beginning, he takes care of the child even before its birth. When he takes care of the child even before its birth, he is thereby taking care of himself (*ātman*) for the continuance of these worlds, for it is in this way that these worlds continue. That is his second birth.

[4] And he—this self (*ātman*) of his—is appointed to carry out holy rites, while his other self, after it has done all it has to do, becomes old and dies. As soon as he departs from this world, he is born again. That is his third birth.

[5] This very point has been made by a seer:

> I knew all the births of these gods,
> While I was still within the womb.
> A hundred iron forts encaged me,
> Then the falcon—swiftly I flew away.

Vāmadeva spoke this way while he was still lying here within the womb. [6] Knowing this, he went up after the dissolution of this body and, having obtained all his desires in the heavenly world up there, became immortal.

CHAPTER 3

'Who is this self (*ātman*)?'—that is how we venerate.

[2] Which of these is the self? Is it that by which one sees? Or hears? Or smells odours? Or utters speech? Or distinguishes between what is tasty and what is not? Is it the heart and the mind? Is it awareness? Perception? Discernment? Cognition? Wisdom? Insight? Steadfastness? Thought? Reflection? Drive? Memory? Intention? Purpose? Will? Love? Desire? But these are various designations of cognition.

[3] It is *brahman*; it is Indra; it is Prajāpati; it is all the gods. It is these five immense beings—earth, wind, space, the waters, and the lights; it is these beings, as well as those that are some sort of

mixture of trivial beings, living beings of various sorts—those born from eggs, from wombs, from sweat, and from sprouts. It is horses, cattle, men, and elephants. It is everything that has life—those that move, those that fly, and those that are stationary.

Knowledge is the eye of all that, and on knowledge it is founded. Knowledge is the eye of the world, and knowledge, the foundation. *Brahman* is knowing.

4 It is with this self consisting of knowledge that he went up from this world and, having obtained all his desire in the heavenly world up there, became immortal.

Kauṣītaki Upaniṣad

THE Kauṣītaki Upaniṣad consists of books 3–6 of the Kauṣītaki (also called Śāṅkhāyana) Āraṇyaka, which itself is part of the Kauṣītaki Brāhmaṇa of the Ṛgveda. Both the Brāhmaṇa and the Āraṇyaka of the Śāṅkhāyana school are texts that in many ways correspond to the parallel texts of its sister school, the Aitareya, although the latter texts are somewhat earlier than those of the Śāṅkhāyana (for a comparison of the documents of these two schools of the Ṛgveda, see Keith 1909, 26–39). The transmission of the KsU has been less faithful than that of many other ancient Upaniṣads; Frenz's (1968–9) edition and translation have shown that the sequence of passages in the vulgate edition is probably incorrect. I have followed the sequence and the numbering established by Frenz. I have not adopted completely his reconstituted text, which places within parenthesis dubious passages and makes several additions. Although plausible in themselves, I feel that a translation such as this should by and large follow the text established by the native tradition.

CONTENTS

13 Gaining pre-eminence by knowing the superiority of breath over other vital functions
14 Rite of transfer to the son when a father is about to die

3 Indra's instruction to Pratardana
1 On understanding Indra
2 Indra as breath, the self consisting of intelligence
3–4 The superiority of breath over other vital functions
Breath as intelligence
What happens at death?
5–7 Superiority of intelligence over other faculties
8 Intelligence as the self beyond all diversity

4 Dialogue between Ajātaśatru and Bālāki on *brahman*
2–18 Ajātaśatru rejects different identifications of *brahman*
19 Instruction of Bālāki by Ajātaśatru: explanation of sleep
20 Breath as the self consisting of intelligence

CHAPTER 1

1 ONCE, when Citra Gāṅgāyani was preparing to perform a sacrifice, he chose Āruṇi as the officiating priest. But Āruṇi sent his son, Śvetaketu, instead, telling him: 'Go and officiate at his sacrifice.'

After Śvetaketu had taken his seat, Citra questioned him: 'Son of Gautama, is there a closed door in the world in which you will place me, or does it have another road? I fear that you will place me in a false world.' Śvetaketu replied: 'I don't know it, but I'll ask my teacher.'

So he went back to his father and asked him: 'Here are the questions he asked me. How should I answer him?' The father told him: 'Even I do not know the answer to them. Within the very sacrificial arena let us, after we have performed our vedic recitation, receive what outsiders may give us. Come, let us both go.'

Then, carrying firewood in his hands, Āruṇi went up to Citra Gāṅgāyani and said: 'Let me come to you as your pupil.' And Citra said to him: 'Gautama, you have proved yourself worthy of the formulation of truth (*brahman*), since you have not succumbed to pride. Come, I'll see to it that you perceive it clearly.'

2 Citra continued: 'When people depart from this world, it is to the moon that they all go. By means of their lifebreaths the moon swells up in the fortnight of waxing, and through the fortnight of waning it propels them to new birth. Now, the moon is the door to the heavenly world. It allows those who answer its question to pass. As to those who do not answer its question, after they have become rain, it rains them down here on earth, where they are born again in these various conditions—as a worm, an insect, a fish, a bird, a lion, a boar, a rhinoceros, a tiger, a man, or some other creature—each in accordance with his actions and his knowledge.'

When someone approaches it, the moon asks: 'Who are you?' And he should reply:

> The semen, O Seasons, is gathered,
> from the radiant one,

from the one with fifteen parts,
from the one who is born,
from the one linked to the fathers.
Then you sent me into a man, the agent;
and, through that man as the agent,
you poured me into a mother.
Here I am born, given birth to as an addition,
as the thirteenth, the added month,
by a father of twelve parts.
I recognize it.
I understand it.
So lead me, O Seasons, to immortality.

By that truth, by that austerity—
I am the season!
I am the offspring of the season!
Who am I?
I am you!

The moon lets him pass.

3 He then gets on the path leading to the gods and reaches first the world of fire, then the world of wind, then the world of Varuṇa, then the world of Indra, then the world of Prajāpati, and finally the world of *brahman*.

Now, in this world are located the lake Āra, the watchmen Muhūrta, the river Vijarā, the tree Ilya, the plaza Sālajya, the palace Aparājita, the doorkeepers Indra and Prajāpati, the hall Vibhu, the throne Vicakṣaṇa, and the couch Amitaujas.

4 *a* He first arrives at the lake Āra. He crosses it with his mind, but those who go into it without a complete knowledge drown in it. Then he arrives near the watchmen Muhūrta, but they flee from him. Then he arrives at the river Vijarā, which he crosses with just his mind. There he shakes off his good and bad deeds, which fall upon his relatives—the good deeds upon the ones he likes and the bad deeds upon the ones he dislikes. It is like this—as a man driving a chariot would look down and observe the two wheels of his chariot, so he looks down and observes the days and nights, the good and bad deeds, and all the pairs of opposites. Freed from his good and bad deeds, this man, who has the knowledge of *brahman*, goes on to *brahman*.

4 *b* The beloved Mānasī and her twin Cākṣuṣī have picked flowers and bring them here—so also the two Jagatī, Ambā and Ambālī, and other celestial nymphs such as Ambikā. *Brahman* tells them: 'Run to him with my glory! He has already arrived at the river Vijarā! He will never grow old!' Five hundred celestial nymphs go out to meet him—one hundred carrying garlands, one hundred carrying lotions, one hundred carrying cosmetic powders, one hundred carrying clothes, and one hundred carrying fruits. And they adorn him with the ornaments of *brahman*. Then, decked with the ornaments of *brahman*, this man, who has the knowledge of *brahman*, goes on to *brahman*.

5 He then arrives at the tree Ilya, and the fragrance of *brahman* permeates him. Then he arrives at the plaza Sālajya, and the flavour of *brahman* permeates him. Then he arrives at the palace Aparājita, and the radiance of *brahman* permeates him. Then he arrives near the doorkeepers, Indra and Prajāpati, and they flee from him. Then he arrives at the hall Vibhu, and the glory of *brahman* permeates him.

Then he arrives at the throne Vicakṣaṇa. Its two front legs are the Sāman chants Bṛhat and Rathantara; its two back legs are the Sāman chants Śyaita and Naudhasa; its two lengthwise supports are the Sāman chants Vairūpa and Vairāja; and its two side supports are the Sāman chants Śākvara and Raivata. The throne itself is wisdom, for wisdom enables a man to be discerning.

Then he arrives at the couch Amitaujas. It is lifebreath. Its two front legs are the past and the present; its two back legs are prosperity and nourishment; its two lengthwise supports are the Sāman chants Bṛhat and Rathantara; its two head supports are the Sāman chants Bhadra and Yajñāyajñīya; the strings stretching lengthwise are the Ṛg verses and the Sāman chants; those stretching crosswise are the Yajus formulas; the coverlet is the Soma stalks; the second cover is the High Chant; and the pillow is prosperity.

On that couch sits *brahman*. A man who knows this mounts it, first with his foot. *Brahman* then asks him: 'Who are you?' He should reply—

6 'I am the season! I am the offspring of the season. I was born from the womb of space as the semen for the wife, as the

radiance of the year, as the self (*ātman*) of every being! You are the self of every being. I am who you are.'

Brahman then asks him: 'Who am I?'

And he should reply: 'The real.'

'What is the real (*satyam*)?'

'Sat is whatever is other than the gods and the lifebreaths (*prāṇa*), while Tyam consists of the gods and the lifebreaths. All of that is comprehended by this word "real" (*satyam*). That is the full extent of this whole world. And you are this whole world.'

That is what he then said to *brahman*. This very point has been made in this verse:

7 Yajus is the belly, Sāman, the head;
The Ṛg is the body of this great seer;
He is imperishable,
He consists of *brahman*.
'He is *brahman*'—
So should he be known.

Brahman then asks him: 'By what means do you grasp my masculine names?'

He should reply: 'With my breath.'

'And my neuter names?'

'With my mind.'

'And my feminine names?'

'With my speech.'

'And my odours?'

'With my sense of smell.'

'And my visible appearances?'

'With my sight.'

'And my sounds?'

'With my hearing.'

'And my tasting of food?'

'With my tongue.'

'And my actions?'

'With my hands.'

'And my pleasure and pain?'

'With my body.'

'And my bliss, delight, and procreation?'

'With my sexual organ.'

'And my movements?'

'With my feet.'

'And my thoughts, objects of perception, and desires?'

'With my intellect.'

Brahman then tells him: 'I see that you have truly attained my world. It is yours, so-and-so!' Whatever victory and success belongs to *brahman*—the same victory he wins, the same success he attains, when a man comes to know this.

CHAPTER 2

1 '*Brahman* is breath'—that is what Kauṣītaki used to say. Now, of this breath that is *brahman*—the messenger is the mind; the guard is sight; the crier is hearing; and the maid is speech.

And, indeed, anyone who knows that the mind is the messenger of this breath that is *brahman* comes to possess a messenger; anyone who knows that sight is its guard comes to possess a guard; anyone who knows that hearing is its crier comes to possess a crier; and anyone who knows that speech is its maid comes to possess a maid.

And to this very breath that is *brahman* all these deities bring offerings without its having to ask. All beings, likewise, bring offerings to a man who knows this without his ever having to ask. 'He should not ask'—that is his secret instruction (*upaniṣad*).

It is like this. Take a man who begs in a village and receives nothing. He would sit down, vowing: 'I'll never eat anything given from here.' Thereupon, the very same people who may have previously spurned him offer him invitations.

For one who does not ask, this becomes the rule—the very people who give food invite him, saying: 'We'll give you.'

2 '*Brahman* is breath'—that is what Paiṅgya used to say. Now, of this breath that is *brahman*—the sight is confined behind speech; the hearing is confined behind sight; the mind is confined behind hearing; and the breath is confined behind the mind.

To this very breath that is *brahman*, indeed, all these deities bring offerings without its having to ask. All beings, likewise, bring offerings to a man who knows this without his ever having to ask. 'He should not ask'—that is his secret instruction (*upaniṣad*).

It is like this. Take a man who begs in a village and receives nothing. He would sit down, vowing: 'I'll never eat anything given from here.' Thereupon, the very same people who may have previously spurned him offer him invitations.

For one who does not ask, this becomes the rule—the very people who give food invite him, saying: 'We'll give you.'

3 Next, the capture of 'an identical object of value'. When a person sets his heart on 'an identical object of value' [as someone else], this is what he should do. Either on the full moon or on the new moon, or under an auspicious constellation during the bright half of the month, he should put firewood into his sacred fire, sweep around it, spread sacred grass around it, and sprinkle water around it. Then, bending his right knee, he offers the following oblations of ghee with a spoon:

The deity named Speech is a captor. May he capture this for me from so-and-so.
To that deity, svāhā!
The deity named Smell is a captor. May he capture this for me from so-and-so.
To that deity, svāhā!
The deity named Sight is a captor. May he capture this for me from so-and-so.
To that deity, svāhā!
The deity named Hearing is a captor. May he capture this for me from so-and-so.
To that deity, svāhā!
The deity named Mind is a captor. May he capture this for me from so-and-so.
To that deity, svāhā!
The deity named Intelligence is a captor. May he capture this for me from so-and-so.
To that deity, svāhā!

Then, after he smells the fragrance of the smoke and rubs his body with the ghee, he should go out silently and either make his objective known in person or dispatch a messenger. And so, indeed, he will take possession of it.

4 Next, divinely secured love. If someone desires to be the favourite of a particular man or woman, or of a group of men or women, he should make the same offerings of ghee in the very same manner on one of the auspicious days given above:

> So-and-so, I offer your speech in me, svāhā!
> So-and-so, I offer your smelling in me, svāhā!
> So-and-so, I offer your sight in me, svāhā!
> So-and-so, I offer your hearing in me, svāhā!
> So-and-so, I offer your mind in me, svāhā!
> So-and-so, I offer your intelligence in me, svāhā!

Then, after he smells the fragrance of the smoke and rubs his body with ghee, he should go out silently and either seek to come into bodily contact with the person(s) in question or simply stand upwind engaged in conversation with the individual(s) in question. He will, indeed, become their favourite! They will, indeed, love him!

5 Next, the control of Pratardana, which is also called 'the daily fire sacrifice offered internally'. Clearly, a man is unable to breathe while he is speaking. So, during that time he offers his breath in his speech. A man is, likewise, unable to speak while he is breathing. So, during that time he offers his speech in his breath.

One offers these two endless and deathless offerings without interruption, whether one is awake or asleep. All other offerings, on the other hand, are limited, for they consist of ritual activities. It is because they knew this that people in ancient times refrained from offering the daily fire sacrifice.

6 '*Brahman* is the Uktha'—that is what Śuṣkabhṛṅgāra used to say. One should venerate it as the Ṛg; then, for the sake of his pre-eminent prosperity, all beings will recite praises (*abhi-arc*) for him. One should venerate it as the Yajus; then, for the sake of his pre-eminent prosperity, all beings will unite (*yuj*) with him. One should venerate it as the Sāman; then, for the sake of his pre-eminent prosperity, all beings will bow down (*sam-nam*) to him.

One should venerate it as prosperity; one should venerate it as glory; and one should venerate it as radiance. Then, just as the Uktha is the most prosperous, the most glorious, and the most splendid among the Recitations of Praise, in exactly the same way someone who knows this becomes the most prosperous, the most glorious, and the most splendid of all beings.

Now, this self of the sacrifice, this self consisting of rites—the Adhvaryu priest puts it together and weaves upon it the self consisting of the Yajus formulas; upon the self consisting of the Yajus formulas the Hotṛ priest weaves the self consisting of the Ṛg verses; and upon the self consisting of the Ṛg verses the Udgātṛ priest weaves the self consisting of the Sāman chants. Such is the self of the triple Veda—and this becomes, therefore, the self of Indra, [the self of him] who knows this.

7 Next, there are three modes of veneration of Sarvajit Kauṣītaki. Now, this is how Sarvajit Kauṣītaki used to venerate the rising sun. Wearing the upper garment in the sacrificial position, he would fetch some water, pour it into the water pot three times, and say: 'You are the one who gathers! Gather my sin!' He used to worship the midday sun in exactly the same way, saying: 'You are the one who gathers up! Gather up my sin!' And he used to worship the setting sun in exactly the same way, saying: 'You are the one who gathers completely! Gather my sin completely!' And the sun did gather completely whatever sin he had committed by day or night.

Likewise, when a man knows this and worships the sun in exactly the same way, the sun gathers completely whatever sin he may commit by day or night.

8 *a* Every month, moreover, on the night of the new moon one should worship the moon as it becomes visible in the west using the very same procedure. Or else one may throw two green blades of grass towards it, saying:

> My heart, the fine kindling stick,
> is placed within the moon—
> this, I do reckon, I know.
> So may I not have to weep
> for my children's misfortune!

His children, indeed, will not die before him.

8 *b* Now, when a man is preparing to engage in sexual intercourse with his wife, he should touch her heart, saying:

Your heart, O lady so good to lie on,
rests within Prajāpati.
Therefore, O queen of immortality,
may you not encounter
your children's misfortune!

Her children, indeed, will not die before her.

8 *c* Now, the preceding is for a man who has a son. As for one who does not have a son, on the other hand, he should first recite silently these three Ṛg verses:

Swell up, O Soma!
May virility
gather in you from all sides!
Be there
at the gathering of power!
May juices and powers,
May virile energies,
gather in you, who crush the enemies;
As you swell, O Soma, to immortality,
you capture in the sky the highest glory.
That tiny drop,
the Ādityas make to swell;
That imperishable drop,
the imperishable ones drink;
With that drop,
may king Varuṇa and Bṛhaspati,
the guardian gods of the world,
make us swell!

He then says: 'Do not swell yourself up by means of our lifebreath, our children, or our livestock. Swell yourself up instead by means of the lifebreath, children, and livestock of the man who hates us and whom we hate.' Then he turns a full circle towards his right, saying: 'I turn the way of Indra! I turn the way of the sun!'

9 On the night of the full moon, furthermore, one should worship the moon as it becomes visible in the east using the very same procedure, saying:

'You are King Soma, the radiant! You are Prajāpati, with five mouths!

'The Brahmin is one mouth of yours; with that mouth you eat the kings. Make me a food-eater with that mouth.

'The king is one mouth of yours; with that mouth you eat the Vaiśyas. Make me a food-eater with that mouth.

'The falcon is one mouth of yours; with that mouth you eat the birds. Make me a food-eater with that mouth.

'The fire is one mouth of yours; with that mouth you eat this world. Make me a food-eater with that mouth.

'There is a fifth mouth in you; with that mouth you eat all beings. Make me a food-eater with that mouth.

'Do not waste away by means of our lifebreath, our children, or our livestock. Waste away instead by means of the life, children, and livestock of the man who hates us and whom we hate.' Then he turns a full circle towards his right, saying: 'I turn the way of the deities! I turn the way of the sun!'

10 Now, when a man returns from a journey, he should sniff his son's head, saying:

From my body you spring—from every inch!
From my heart you are born!
You're my self, son, you have rescued me!
May you live a hundred years!

With that he confers the name on him.

Be a rock! Be an axe!
Be indestructible gold!
You are the radiance called son!
May you live a hundred years!

With that he pronounces his son's name and then embraces him, saying: 'As Prajāpati embraced his children for their safety, so I embrace you, so-and-so!' Then he recites this silently in his son's right ear:

O Indra! O Maghavan! O Ṛjīṣin!
Grant him ample wealth,
bestowing all treasures.

O Indra, you with fine cheeks!
Grant him a hundred years to live,
and countless heroic sons.

And in his left ear:

Grant him, O Indra,
the finest treasures and quickness of mind
good fortune and increase of wealth,
bodily safety and sweetness of speech,
fine weather every day of his life.

Then he sniffs his son's head three times, saying:

Be not cut off! Do not weaken!
O my son, live a life,
a hundred years long!
With your name,
I kiss your head,
So-and-so!

Then he makes the sound '*huṃ*' over his son's head, saying: 'With the same "*huṃ*" sound the cows make as they low, I make the "*huṃ*" sound upon your head.'

11 Next, the 'dying around of the deities'. The *brahman* shines forth here when the fire is burning; but when the fire stops burning it dies, and its radiance goes to the sun, and its lifebreath to the wind. The *brahman* shines forth here when the sun is shining; but when the sun stops shining it dies, and its radiance goes to the moon, and its lifebreath to the wind. The *brahman* shines forth here when the moon is shining; but when the moon stops shining it dies, and its radiance goes to the lightning, and its lifebreath, to the wind. The *brahman* shines forth here when the lightning is flashing; but when the lightning stops flashing, it dies, and its radiance goes to the quarters, and its lifebreath to the wind. Now, when they have entered into the wind, when they have crept into the wind, all these deities do not lose their self-identity, but emerge from it once again.

That was with respect to the deities. Next, with respect to the body (*ātman*):

12 The *brahman* shines forth here when one is speaking with one's speech; but when one stops speaking it dies, and its radiance goes to one's sight, and its lifebreath to one's breath. The *brahman* shines forth here when one is seeing with one's sight; but when one stops seeing it dies, and its radiance goes to one's hearing, and its lifebreath to one's breath. The *brahman* shines forth here when one is hearing with one's hearing; but when one stops hearing it dies, and its radiance goes to one's mind, and its lifebreath to one's breath. The *brahman* shines forth here when one is thinking with one's mind; but when one stops thinking it dies, and its radiance goes to one's breath, and its lifebreath to one's breath. Now, when they have entered the breath, when they have crept into the breath, all these deities do not lose their self-identity, but emerge from it once again.

And, therefore, when someone knows this, even if both the mountain ranges, the southern and the northern, were to rush at him determined to level him, they would not succeed in levelling him. On the contrary, the people who hate him and the people he himself hates will die around him.

13 Next, gaining pre-eminence. Once these deities, each arguing for its own pre-eminence, departed from this body. When that happened, the body lay there like a log, without breathing, and withered.

Then speech entered the body, but, although it spoke with its speech, it still remained there lying prostrate.

After that, sight entered the body, but, although it spoke with its speech and saw with its sight, it still remained there lying prostrate.

After that, hearing entered the body, but, although it spoke with its speech, saw with its sight, and heard with its hearing, it still remained there lying prostrate.

After that, the mind entered the body, but, although it spoke with its speech, saw with its sight, heard with its hearing, and thought with its mind, it still remained there lying prostrate.

Finally, the breath entered the body, and straightway it got up.

After all these deities had recognized the pre-eminence of breath and united themselves with that very breath, which is the self consisting of intelligence, they all departed together from this body, and, entering the wind and with space as their self (*ātman*), went to heaven.

In exactly the same way, a person who knows this, after he has recognized the preeminence of breath and united himself with that very breath, which is the self consisting of intelligence, departs from this body accompanied by all these, and, entering the wind and with space as their self, goes to heaven. He goes to where these gods are. And because the gods are immortal, upon reaching there a man who knows this becomes immortal.

14 Next, the father–son ceremony, which is also called the rite of transfer. A father, when he is close to death, calls his son. After the house has been strewn with fresh grass, the fire has been kindled, and a pot of water has been set down along with a cup, the father lies down covered in a fresh garment. The son comes and lies on top of him, touching the various organs of the father with his own corresponding organs. Alternatively, the father may execute the transfer with the son sitting and facing him. The father then makes the transfer to the son:

'I will place my speech in you,' says the father. 'I place your speech in me,' responds the son.

'I will place my breath in you,' says the father. 'I place your breath in me,' responds the son.

'I will place my sight in you,' says the father. 'I place your sight in me,' responds the son.

'I will place my hearing in you,' says the father. 'I place your hearing in me,' responds the son.

'I will place my tasting of food in you,' says the father. 'I place your tasting of food in me,' responds the son.

'I will place my actions in you,' says the father. 'I place your actions in me,' responds the son.

'I will place my pleasures and pains in you,' says the father. 'I place your pleasures and pains in me,' responds the son.

'I will place my bliss, delight, and procreation in you,' says the father. 'I place your bliss, delight, and procreation in me,' responds the son.

'I will place my movements in you,' says the father. 'I place your movements in me,' responds the son.

'I will place my mind in you,' says the father. 'I place your mind in me,' responds the son.

'I will place my intelligence in you,' says the father. 'I place your intelligence in me,' responds the son.

If he finds it difficult to talk, the father should say very briefly: 'I will place my vital functions (*prāṇa*) in you.' And the son should respond: 'I place your vital functions in me.'

Then, as the son, turning around towards his right, goes away toward the east, his father calls out to him: 'May glory, the lustre of sacred knowledge, and fame attend you!' The son, for his part, looks over his left shoulder, hiding his face with his hand or covering it with the hem of his garment, and responds: 'May you gain heavenly worlds and realize your desires!'

If the father recovers his health, he should either live under the authority of his son or live as a wandering ascetic. But if he happens to die, they should perform the appropriate final rites for him.

CHAPTER 3

1 Once Pratardana, the son of Divodāsa, arrived at the favourite residence of Indra as a result of war and valour. And Indra said to him: 'Choose a present, Pratardana.' But Pratardana replied: 'Why don't you yourself choose something for me that you consider most beneficial to a human being?' Indra retorted: 'Surely, a superior does not choose for someone who is inferior to him. You had better choose yourself.' And Pratardana replied: 'Well then, I'll do without the present.' Indra, however, did not deviate from the truth, for Indra is the truth. And he told Pratardana:

'Perceive just me. What I consider to be most beneficial to a human being is that he should perceive me. I killed the three-headed son of Tvaṣṭṛ, as well as the Arunmukhas. I handed over the Yatis to the hyenas. Breaking numerous agreements, I smashed the Prāhlādīyas in the sky, the Paulomas in the intermediate region, and the Kālakāñjas on the earth. And I did not lose even a hair of my body in the process.

'When a man perceives me, nothing that he does—whether it is stealing, or performing an abortion, or killing his own father or mother—will ever make him lose a single hair of his body. And when he has committed a sin, his face does not lose its colour.'

2 And Indra continued: 'I am breath (*prāṇa*), the self (*ātman*) consisting of intelligence. So venerate me as life and immortality. Breath is life. And life is breath, for as long as breath remains in this body, so does life; and hence it is through breath that one attains immortality in this world, and through intelligence, true intentions. Anyone who venerates me as life and immortality gets to live his full life span in this world and wins an immortal and imperishable state in the heavenly world.'

'But there are some people who say that the vital functions (*prāṇa*) come together into a unified whole. For, no one is able to bring himself to perceive separately a name with his speech, a visual appearance with his sight, a sound with his hearing, or a thought with his mind. When the vital functions have become a unified whole, however, they make him perceive all these one by one—as speech speaks, all the vital functions speak along with it; as sight sees, all the vital functions see along with it; as hearing hears, all the vital functions hear along with it; as the mind thinks, all the vital functions think along with it; and as the breath breathes, all the vital functions breathe along with it.'

'That's exactly so,' said Indra. 'But there does exist among the vital functions one that is pre-eminent.'

3 'A man continues to live after his speech leaves him, for we see people who are dumb. A man continues to live after his sight leaves him, for we see people who are blind. A man continues to live after his hearing leaves him, for we see people who are deaf. A man continues to live after his mind leaves him, for we see people who are imbeciles. And a man continues to live after his arms are cut off and after his legs are cut off, for we see such people.

'But only the breath, you see, is the self consisting of intelligence. When it grasps this body, it enables the body to get up (*utthā*), and for this reason one should venerate it as the Uktha. This is how one comes to possess the Whole in one's breath.

'Now, breath is intelligence, and intelligence is breath—one comes to see this, one comes to perceive this, in the following way. When a man is fast asleep and sees no dreams at all, then these become unified within this very breath—his speech then merges into it together with all the names; his sight merges into it together with all the visible appearances; his hearing merges into it together with all the sounds; and his mind merges into it together with all the thoughts. And when he awakens these fly off—as from a blazing fire sparks fly off in every direction, so from this self the vital functions (*prāṇa*) fly off to their respective stations, and from the vital functions, the gods, and from the gods, the worlds.

'When this very breath that is the self consisting of intelligence grasps this body, it enables the body to get up (*utthā*), and for this reason one should venerate it as the Uktha. This is how one comes to possess the Whole in one's breath.

'Breath is intelligence, and intelligence is breath—one finds the proof of this, one comes to perceive this, in the following way. When a man is sick and about to die, he becomes extremely weak and finally loses consciousness. People then say: "Has his breath, perhaps, already left him?" At this point, he ceases to hear, he ceases to see, he ceases to speak with his speech, and he ceases to think. Then these become unified within this very breath—his speech merges into it together with all the names; his sight merges into it together with all the visible appearances; his hearing merges into it together with all the sounds; and his mind merges into it together with all the thoughts. And when the breath finally departs from this body, it is together with all these that it departs.

4 'Speech releases from this breath all the names, and through speech one grasps all the names. The sense of smell releases from it all the odours, and through the sense of smell one grasps all the odours. Sight releases from it all the visible appearances, and through sight one grasps all the visible appearances. Hearing releases from it all the sounds, and through hearing one grasps all the sounds. The mind releases from it all the thoughts, and through the mind one grasps all the thoughts. This is how one comes to possess the Whole in one's breath. Breath is intelligence, and intelligence is breath, for they both live in this body together, and together they depart from it.

Next, we will explain how, [drawn] from this intelligence, all beings become one.

5 'Speech is one part drawn from it, and name is the particle of being that corresponds externally to speech. The sense of smell is one part drawn from it, and odour is the particle of being that corresponds externally to the sense of smell. Sight is one part drawn from it, and visible appearance is the particle of being that corresponds externally to sight. Hearing is one part drawn from it, and sound is the particle of being that corresponds externally to hearing. The tongue is one part drawn from it, and the taste of food is the particle of being that corresponds externally to the tongue. The hands are one part drawn from it, and action is the particle of being that corresponds externally to the hands. The body is one part drawn from it, and pleasure and pain constitute the particle of being that corresponds externally to the body. The sexual organ is one part drawn from it, and bliss, delight, and procreation constitute the particle of being that corresponds externally to the sexual organ. The feet are one part drawn from it, and movements constitute the particle of being that corresponds externally to the feet. Intelligence is one part drawn from it, and thoughts, objects of perception, and desires constitute the particle of being that corresponds externally to the intelligence.

6 'When someone mounts speech by means of intelligence, he grasps all names through his speech. When someone mounts the sense of smell by means of intelligence, he grasps all odours through his sense of smell. When someone mounts sight by means of intelligence, he grasps all visible appearances through his sight. When someone mounts hearing by means of intelligence, he grasps all sounds through his hearing. When someone mounts the tongue by means of intelligence, he grasps all tastes of food through his tongue. When someone mounts the hands by means of intelligence, he grasps all actions through his hands. When someone mounts the body by means of intelligence, he grasps pleasures and pains through his body. When someone mounts the sexual organ by means of intelligence, he grasps bliss, delight, and procreation through his sexual organ. When someone mounts the feet by means of intelligence, he grasps all movements through his

feet. When someone mounts thinking by means of intelligence, he grasps thoughts, objects of perception, and desires through his intelligence.

7 'For without intelligence, speech would not make someone perceive any name. So, one says: "My mind was elsewhere. I did not perceive that name." For without intelligence, the sense of smell would not make someone perceive any odour. So, one says: "My mind was elsewhere. I did not perceive that odour." For without intelligence, sight would not make someone perceive any visible appearance. So, one says: "My mind was elsewhere. I did not perceive that visible appearance." For without intelligence, hearing would not make someone perceive any sound. So, one says: "My mind was elsewhere. I did not perceive that sound." For without intelligence, the tongue would not make someone perceive the taste of any food. So, one says: "My mind was elsewhere. I did not perceive the taste of that food." For without intelligence, the hands would not make someone perceive any action. So, one says: "My mind was elsewhere. I did not perceive that action." For without intelligence, the body would not make someone perceive any pleasure or pain. So, one says: "My mind was elsewhere. I did not perceive that pleasure or that pain." For without intelligence, the sexual organ would not make someone perceive any bliss, delight, or procreation. So, one says: "My mind was elsewhere. I did not perceive that bliss, delight, or procreation." For without intelligence, the feet would not make someone perceive any movement. So, one says: "My mind was elsewhere. I did not perceive that movement." For without intelligence, no thinking could take place, and one would not perceive any object of perception.

8 'It is not the speech that a man should seek to apprehend; rather, he should get to know the one who speaks it. It is not the odour that a man should seek to apprehend; rather, he should get to know the one who smells it. It is not the visible appearance that a man should seek to apprehend; rather, he should get to know the one who sees it. It is not the sound that a man should seek to apprehend; rather, he should get to know the one who hears it. It is not the taste of food that a man should seek to apprehend; rather, he should get to know the one who apprehends the taste of food. It

is not the action that a man should seek to apprehend; rather, he should get to know the one who performs it. It is not the pleasure and pain that a man should seek to apprehend; rather, he should get to know the one who apprehends pleasure and pain. It is not the bliss, delight, or procreation that a man should seek to apprehend; rather, he should get to know the one who apprehends bliss, delight, or procreation. It is not the movement that a man should seek to apprehend; rather, he should get to know the one who moves. It is not the mind that a man should seek to apprehend; rather, he should know the one who thinks.

'These, then, are the particles of being; there are just ten of them. They exist in correlation to intelligence, just as the ten particles of intelligence exist in correlation to the external elements. For, if the particles of being did not exist, there would be no particles of intelligence, and, inversely, if the particles of intelligence did not exist, there would be no particles of being, because from either of them independently no image would be produced.

'Nevertheless, there is no diversity in all this. As in a chariot the rim is fastened to the spokes and the spokes to the hub, in just the same way these particles of being are fastened to the particles of intelligence, and the particles of intelligence are fastened to breath. This very breath is the self consisting of intelligence; it is bliss, unageing, and immortal. It does not become more by good actions or in any way less by bad actions, for it is the one that makes those people perform good actions whom it wants to lead up from these worlds and makes those people perform bad actions whom it wants to push down from these worlds. He is the ruler of the world. He is the sovereign of the world. He is the lord of the world. One should realize: "He is my self (*ātman*)."'

CHAPTER 4

1 Now, Gārgya Bālāki was a learned and widely travelled man, who had lived in the land of Uśinara, in the land of Satvan and Matsya, in the land of Kuru and Pañcāla, and in the land of Kāśi and Videha. Once he visited Ajātaśatru, the king of Kāśi, and said

to him: 'Let me tell you a formulation of truth (*brahman*).' Ajātaśatru replied: 'We'll give you a thousand cows! At a speech such as that, people are sure to rush here, shouting: "Here's a Janaka! Here's a Janaka!"'

2 The great in the sun; the food in the moon; the radiance in lightning; the sound in thunder; Indra Vaikuṇṭha in the wind; the full in space; the irresistible in the fire; the truth in the waters—that was with respect to the divine sphere. Next, with respect to the body (*ātman*)—resemblance in a mirror; companion in a shadow; life in an echo; death in a sound; Yama in a dream; Prajāpati in the body; [the essence] of speech in the right eye; [the essence] of truth in the left eye.

3 Bālāki then said: 'It is that person in the sun that I venerate.' Ajātaśatru replied: 'Don't engage me in a conversation about him! I venerate him only as the most eminent of all beings, as their head. Anyone who venerates him in this way will become the most eminent of all beings, he will become their head.'

4 Bālāki then said: 'It is that person in the moon that I venerate.' Ajātaśatru replied: 'Don't engage me in a conversation about him! I venerate him only as Soma, the great king dressed in white, the essence (*ātman*) of food. Anyone who venerates him in this way will become the essence of food.'

5 Bālāki then said: 'It is that person in lightning that I venerate.' Ajātaśatru replied: 'Don't engage me in a conversation about him! I venerate him only as the essence (*ātman*) of radiance. Anyone who venerates him in this way will become the essence of radiance.'

6 Bālāki then said: 'It is that person in thunder that I venerate.' Ajātaśatru replied: 'Don't engage me in a conversation about him! I venerate him only as the essence (*ātman*) of sound. Anyone who venerates him in this way will become the essence of sound.'

7 Bālāki then said: 'It is that person in the wind that I venerate.' Ajātaśatru replied: 'Don't engage me in a conversation about

him! I venerate him only as Indra Vaikuṇṭha, the invincible weapon. Anyone who venerates him in this way will become victorious and invincible, and he will triumph over his adversaries.'

8 Bālāki then said: 'It is that person in space that I venerate.' Ajātaśatru replied: 'Don't engage me in a conversation about him! I venerate him only as the full and non-depleting *brahman*. Anyone who venerates him in this way will become filled with children and livestock, with fame and the lustre of sacred knowledge, and with the heavenly world; he will live his full life span.'

9 Bālāki then said: 'It is that person in the fire that I venerate.' Ajātaśatru replied: 'Don't engage me in a conversation about him! I venerate him only as the irresistible one. Anyone who venerates him in this way will become irresistible among those who are outsiders.'

10 Bālāki then said: 'It is that person in the waters that I venerate.' Ajātaśatru replied: 'Don't engage me in a conversation about him! I venerate him only as the essence (*ātman*) of truth. Anyone who venerates him in this way will become the essence of truth.'

That was with respect to the divine sphere. Next, with respect to the body (*ātman*):

11 Bālāki then said: 'It is that person in a mirror that I venerate.' Ajātaśatru replied: 'Don't engage me in a conversation about him! I venerate him only as a resemblance. When anyone venerates him in this way, only children who resemble him will be born to him, and none who does not resemble him.'

12 Bālāki then said: 'It is that person in a shadow that I venerate.' Ajātaśatru replied: 'Don't engage me in a conversation about him! I venerate him only as the inseparable companion. Anyone who venerates him in this way will find a companion; he will be a man who has a companion.'

13 Bālāki then said: 'It is that person in an echo that I venerate.' Ajātaśatru replied: 'Don't engage me in a conversation about him! I venerate him only as life. Anyone who venerates him in this way will not become unconscious before his appointed time.'

14 Bālāki then said: 'It is that person in a sound that I venerate.' Ajātaśatru replied: 'Don't engage me in a conversation about him! I venerate him only as death. Anyone who venerates him in this way will not die before his appointed time.'

15 Bālāki then said: 'It is that person who, as one sleeps, roams about in dreams that I venerate.' Ajātaśatru replied: 'Don't engage me in a conversation about him! I venerate him only as King Yama. When anyone venerates him in this way, this whole world submits itself to his supremacy.'

16 Bālāki then said: 'It is that person in the body that I venerate.' Ajātaśatru replied: 'Don't engage me in a conversation about him! I venerate him only as Prajāpati. Anyone who venerates him in this way propagates himself through children and livestock, fame and the lustre of sacred knowledge, and the heavenly world; he will live his full life span.'

17 Bālāki then said: 'It is that person in the right eye that I venerate.' Ajātaśatru replied: 'Don't engage me in a conversation about him! I venerate him only as the essence (*ātman*) of speech, as the essence of fire, as the essence of light. Anyone who venerates him in this way will become the essence of all these.'

18 Bālāki then said: 'It is that person in the left eye that I venerate.' Ajātaśatru replied: 'Don't engage me in a conversation about him! I venerate him only as the essence (*ātman*) of truth, as the essence of lightning, as the essence of radiance. Anyone who venerates him in this way will become the essence of all these.'

19 Thereupon, Bālāki fell silent. 'Is that all, Bālāki?' asked Ajātaśatru. 'That's all,' replied Bālāki. Ajātaśatru then

said to him: 'In vain have you engaged me in a conversation with you by saying: "Let me tell you a formulation of truth (*brahman*)." It is the one who is the maker of the persons you have talked about, Bālāki, whose handiwork they are, that one should seek to know.'

Bālāki then went up to him carrying firewood in his hands and said: 'Let me come to you as your pupil.' But Ajātaśatru said to him: 'I consider it a total reversal of the norm for a Brahmin to become a pupil of a Kṣatriya. But come, I'll see to it that you perceive it clearly.' Taking Bālāki by the hand, he went out, and the two went near a sleeping man. Ajātaśatru greeted the man in these words: 'O Soma, great king dressed in white!' But he remained lying down. Then he prodded him with a stick. And immediately the man got up.

Ajātaśatru then asked: 'Bālāki, where was this person lying down just now? Where was he just now? And from where did he come just now?' Bālāki did not know any of this. So, Ajātaśatru told him: 'Now, as to the questions regarding where this person was lying down just now, and where he was just now, and where he came from just now—there are in a person veins called Hitā that extend from the heart to the pericardium. They are as fine as a hair split a thousandfold. They contain the finest fluids of orange, white, black, yellow, and red. When a person is asleep and sees no dreams, he remains within these veins.

20 'Then these become unified within this very breath—his speech then merges into it together with all the names; his sight merges into it together with all the visible appearances; his hearing merges into it together with all the sounds; and his mind merges into it together with all the thoughts. And when he awakens these scatter—as from a blazing fire sparks fly off in every direction, so from this self (*ātman*) the vital functions (*prāṇa*) fly off to their respective stations, and from the vital functions, the gods, and from the gods, the worlds.

'This very breath, which is the self (*ātman*) consisting of intelligence, penetrates this bodily self up to the very hairs of the body, up to the very nails. Just as a razor within a case or a termite within a termite-hill, so this self consisting of intelligence penetrates this bodily self up to the very hairs of the body, up to the very nails.

To this self (*ātman*) cling these other selves (*ātman*), as to a chieftain, his own people. It is like this—just as a chieftain makes use of his own people, and his own people make themselves useful to a chieftain, so this self consisting of intelligence makes use of these other selves, and these other selves make themselves useful to this self.

'For as long as Indra did not understand this self, the demons were prevailing over him. But when he came to know it, he smashed the demons, conquered them, and secured the supremacy, sovereignty, and lordship over all the gods. A man who knows this, likewise, wipes off all evils and secures the supremacy, sovereignty, and lordship over all beings—yes he does, when a man knows this.'

Kena Upaniṣad

THE Kena Upaniṣad, also called the Talavakāra Upaniṣad, belongs to the Talavakāra or the Jaiminīya branch of the Sāmaveda. It appears as part of the Jaiminīya Upaniṣad-Brāhmaṇa (4.18–21). At some point in time, it began to circulate as an independent Upaniṣad and came to be called by its first word, *kena* ('by whom'), a custom also seen in the case of the Īśā Upaniṣad. The KeU falls roughly into two parts. The first, consisting of the first two sections, is in verse, except for a brief gloss at the beginning of section 2, and presents *brahman* as essentially unknowable and inexpressible. The second, consisting of the final two sections, is in prose and shows how the gods and their powers have proceeded from *brahman*, here identified as the creator of all.

CONTENTS

CHAPTER 1

By whom impelled, by whom compelled,
does the mind soar forth?
By whom enjoined does the breath,
march on as the first?
By whom is this speech impelled,
with which people speak?
And who is the god that joins
the sight and hearing?

2 That which is the hearing behind hearing,
the thinking behind thinking,
the speech behind speech,
the sight behind sight—
It is also the breathing behind breathing—
Freed completely from these,
the wise become immortal,
when they depart from this world.

3 Sight does not reach there;
neither does thinking or speech.
We don't know, we can't perceive,
how one would point it out.

It is far different from what's known.
And it is farther than the unknown—
so have we heard from men of old,
who have explained it all to us.

4 Which one cannot express by speech,
by which speech itself is expressed—
Learn that that alone is *brahman*,
and not what they here venerate.

5 Which one cannot grasp with one's mind,
by which, they say, the mind itself is grasped—
Learn that that alone is *brahman*,
and not what they here venerate.

6 Which one cannot see with one's sight,
by which one sees the sight itself—
Learn that that alone is *brahman*,
and not what they here venerate.

7 Which one cannot hear with one's hearing,
by which hearing itself is heard—
Learn that that alone is *brahman*,
and not what they here venerate.

8 Which one cannot breathe through breathing,
by which breathing itself is drawn forth—
Learn that that alone is *brahman*,
and not what they here venerate.

CHAPTER 2

'If you think "I know it well"—perhaps you do know ever so little the visible appearance of *brahman*; there is that part of it you know and there is the part which is among the gods. And so I think what you must do is to reflect on it, on that unknown part of it:

2 I do not think
that I know it well;
But I know not
that I do not know.
Who of us knows that,
he does know that;
But he knows not,
that he does not know.

3 It's envisioned by one who envisions it not;
but one who envisions it knows it not.
And those who perceive it perceive it not;
but it's perceived by those who perceive it not.

4 When one awakens to know it,
one envisions it, for then
one gains the immortal state.
One gains power by one's self (*ātman*),
And by knowledge, the immortal state.

5 If in this world a man comes to know it,
to him belongs the real.
If in this world a man does not know it,
great is his destruction.
Discerning it among each and every being,

the wise become immortal,
when they depart from this world.'

CHAPTER 3

Brahman won the victory for the gods. Although it was won by *brahman*, the gods were jubilant at the victory, telling themselves: 'Ours alone is this victory! Ours alone is this greatness!'

2 *Brahman* read their minds and made itself visible to them. But they did not recognize it, as they wondered 'What is this strange apparition?'

3 So they told Fire, 'Jātavedas, find out what this strange apparition is.' He said, 'Very well', 4 and scurried to it. It asked him: 'Who are you?' And he replied: 'I? Why, I am Fire! I am Jātavedas!'

5 'I see! And what sort of power do you have?'

'I can burn up this whole world, yes, everything on earth!'

6 So it placed a blade of grass in front of him and said, 'Burn this.' He went at it at full speed but could not burn it.

He returned forthwith and said: 'I wasn't able to find out what this strange apparition is.' 7 Then they told Wind, 'Wind, find out what this strange apparition is.' He said, 'Very well,' 8 and scurried to it. It asked him: 'Who are you?' And he replied: 'I? Why, I am Wind! I am Mātariśvan!'

9 'I see! And what sort of power do you have?'

'I can carry away this whole world, yes, everything on earth!'

10 So it placed a blade of grass in front of him and said, 'Carry this away.' He went at it at full speed but could not carry it away.

He returned forthwith and said: 'I wasn't able to find out what this strange apparition is.' 11 Then they told Indra, 'Maghavan, find out what this strange apparition is.' He said, 'Very well,' 8and scurried to it. But it vanished from his sight.

12 Then, at that very spot in the sky, he came across a woman of great beauty, Umā, the daughter of Himavat. He asked her: 'What was that strange apparition?'

CHAPTER 4

'*Brahman*,' she replied. 'You are jubilant here at the victory won by *brahman*.' Then Indra immediately realized that it was *brahman*.

2 That is why these gods, namely Fire, Wind, and Indra, somehow surpass the other gods, for they came into close contact with it.

3 And that is why Indra somehow surpasses the other gods, for he both came into close contact with it and was the first to recognize it as *brahman*.

4 Here is its rule of substitution: the cry 'Ah!' when lightning has flashed, the cry 'Ah!' when it made them blink—such it is with respect to the divine sphere. 5 And with respect to the body (*ātman*)—when something here comes to the mind somehow and through it the imagination suddenly recollects something.

6 Now, its name is *tadvana*, and it should be venerated as *tadvana*. When someone knows it as such, all beings long for him.

7 [STUDENT:] 'Sir, teach me the hidden connection (*upaniṣad*).'

[TEACHER:] 'You have been taught the hidden connection (*upaniṣad*)—indeed, we have taught you the hidden connection (*upaniṣad*) relating to *brahman* itself. 8 Of this hidden connection (*upaniṣad*)—austerity, self-control, and rites are the foundation, the Vedas are all the limbs, and truth is the abode.'

9 When someone comes to know this hidden connection (*upaniṣad*) in this way, he undoubtedly wipes out evil and becomes firmly established in the heavenly world that is endless and invincible.

Kaṭha Upaniṣad

THE Kaṭha (also called Kāṭhaka) Upaniṣad belongs at least formally to the Kāṭhaka school of the Black Yajurveda. It is clear, however, that this Upaniṣad is a late work and did not form an integral part of the Brāhmaṇa of that school. Its relationship to that school, however, is established by the episode of Naciketas and Death (see KaU 1.1–4 n). This episode (together with other sections dealing with the establishment of various ritual fires), in all likelihood, was originally part of the Kāṭhaka Brāhmaṇa, although it is now found in the Taittirīya Brāhmaṇa (3.11.8.1–6) and not in the Kāṭhaka.

In some manuscripts the KaU is divided into two sections, the first comprising the first three chapters (*vallī*), and the second, the last three. The text as we have it clearly does not form a coherent and unified whole. The first two chapters, containing the dialogue between Naciketas and Yama, provide the old context of the Upaniṣad, which seeks to provide an Upaniṣadic twist to the three wishes of Naciketas. The last chapters, especially sections 4–6 with the repetitive refrain 'So, indeed, is that', are probably an appendix superimposed on that examination of the three wishes. The KaU is a challenging text for any translator. It contains several difficult and unique terms whose meanings are far from clear; its thought is often convoluted and its expressions curt and elliptic; and it has been subject to textual corruptions.

CONTENTS

CHAPTER 1

UŚAN, the son of Vājaśravas, once gave away all his possessions. He had a son named Naciketas. 2 Young as he was, faith took hold of him while the cows presented as sacrificial gifts were being led away, and he reflected:

3 'They've drunk all their water, eaten all their fodder,
They have been milked dry, they are totally barren—
"Joyless" are those worlds called,
to which a man goes
who gives them as gifts.'

4 So he asked his father: 'Father, to whom will you give me?' He repeated it for a second time, and again for a third time. His father yelled at him: 'I'll give you to Death!'

5 [NACIKETAS *reflects*.] I go as the very first of many.
I go as the middlemost of many.
What's it that Yama must do,
That he will do with me today?

6 [A VOICE.] Look ahead! See how they have gone,
those who have gone before us!
Look back! So will they go,
those who will come after us.
A mortal man ripens like grain,
And like grain he is born again.

7 A Brahmin guest enters a house
as the fire in all men.
Bring water, O Vaivasvata,
that is how they appease him.

8 Hopes and expectations, fellowship and goodwill,
Children and livestock, rites and gifts—
all these a Brahmin wrests from the foolish man,
in whose house he resides without any food.

[DEATH.] 9 Three nights, O Brahmin, you stayed in my house,
a guest worthy of homage, without any food;
Three wishes, therefore, deign to make in return.
So homage to you, O Brahmin!
And may I fare well!

[NACIKETAS] 10 That with his temper cooled, his anger subdued,
Gautama, O Death, be to me well-disposed.

That he greet me with joy, when by you I'm dismissed—
this is the first of my three wishes.

[DEATH.] 11 He'll be affable in the future, just as before;
Auddālaka Āruṇi, I have dismissed you.
He'll have restful nights, his anger subdued,
seeing you released from the jaws of Death.

[NACIKETAS.] 12 In the world of heaven there is no fear;
there one has no fear of old age or you.
Transcending both these—both hunger and thirst,
beyond all sorrows, one rejoices in heaven.

13 You, O Death, are studying,
the fire-altar that leads to heaven;
Explain that to me, a man who has faith;
People who are in heaven enjoy th'immortal state—
It is this I choose with my second wish.

[DEATH.] 14 I shall explain to you—
and heed this teaching of mine,
O Naciketas, you who understand—
the fire-altar that leads to heaven,
to the attainment of an endless world,
and is its very foundation.
Know that it lies hidden,
In the cave of the heart.

[NARRATOR.] 15 He described to him that fire-altar—
the beginning of the world—
What type the bricks, how many; and how they are to be laid.
And he repeated it exactly as described.
Delighted at him, then, Death said to him again;
16 Well-pleased, the large-hearted one said to him:

[DEATH.] Here I grant you another wish today.
This fire-altar will bear your very name.
Take also this glittering disk of gold.

17 This is a three-Nāciketa man—
Uniting with the three, performing the triple rite,
he crosses over birth and death.
Perceiving the *brahman* that is being born,
as the god who is to be adored,
recognizing this disk of gold to be that,
he attains unending peace.

18 This is a three-Nāciketa man—
Knowing these three, and, with that knowledge,

Piling the altar of Naciketas,
he shoves aside the fetters of death before him,
passes beyond sorrow,
and rejoices in heaven.

19 This, Naciketas, is your fire that leads to heaven,
which you chose with your second wish.
People will proclaim this your very own fire.
Choose your third wish, O Naciketas.

[NACIKETAS.] 20 There is this doubt about a man who is dead.
'He exists,' say some; others, 'He exists not.'
I want to know this, so please teach me.
This is the third of my three wishes.

[DEATH.] 21 As to this even the gods of old had doubts,
for it's hard to understand, it's a subtle doctrine.
Make, Naciketas, another wish.
Do not press me! Release me from this.

[NACIKETAS.] 22 As to this, we're told, even the gods had doubts;
and you say, O Death, it's hard to understand.
But another like you I can't find to explain it;
and there's no other wish that is equal to it.

[DEATH.] 23 Choose sons and grandsons who'd live a hundred years!
Plenty of livestock and elephants, horses and gold!
Choose as your domain a wide expanse of earth!
And you yourself live as many autumns as you wish!

24 And if you would think this is an equal wish—
You may choose wealth together with a long life;
Achieve prominence, Naciketas, in this wide world;
And I will make you enjoy your desires at will.

25 You may ask freely for all those desires,
hard to obtain in this mortal world;
Look at these lovely girls, with chariots and lutes,
girls of this sort are unobtainable by men—
I'll give them to you; you'll have them wait on you;
but about death don't ask me, Naciketas.

[NACIKETAS.] 26 Since the passing days of a mortal, O Death,
sap here the energy of all the senses;
And even a full life is but a trifle;
so keep your horses, your songs and dances!

27 With wealth you cannot make a man content;
Will we get to keep wealth, when we have seen you?

And we get to live only as long as you will allow!
So, this alone is the wish that I'd like to choose.

28 What mortal man with insight,
who has met those that do not die or grow old,
himself growing old in this wretched and lowly place,
looking at its beauties, its pleasures and joys,
would delight in a long life?

29 The point on which they have great doubts—
what happens at that great transit—
tell me that, O Death!
This is my wish, probing the mystery deep.
Naciketas wishes for nothing
other than that.

CHAPTER 2

[DEATH.] 1 The good is one thing, the gratifying is quite another;
their goals are different, both bind a man.
Good things await him who picks the good;
by choosing the gratifying, one misses one's goal.

2 Both the good and the gratifying
present themselves to a man;
The wise assess them, note their difference;
and choose the good over the gratifying;
But the fool chooses the gratifying
rather than what is beneficial.

3 You have looked at and rejected, Naciketas,
things people desire, lovely and lovely to look at;
This disk of gold, where many a man founders,
you have not accepted as a thing of wealth.

4 Far apart and widely different are these two:
ignorance and what's known as knowledge.
I take Naciketas as one yearning for knowledge;
the many desires do not confound you.

5 Wallowing in ignorance, but calling themselves wise,
thinking themselves learned, the fools go around,
staggering about like a group of blind men,
led by a man who is himself blind.

6 This transit lies hidden from a careless fool,
who is deluded by the delusion of wealth.
Thinking 'This is the world; there is no other',
he falls into my power again and again.

7 Many do not get to hear of that transit;
and even when they hear,
many don't comprehend it.
Rare is the man who teaches it,
lucky is the man who grasps it;
Rare is the man who knows it,
lucky is the man who's taught it.

8 Though one may think a lot, it is difficult to grasp,
when it is taught by an inferior man.
Yet one cannot gain access to it,
unless someone else teaches it.
For it is smaller than the size of an atom,
a thing beyond the realm of reason.

9 One can't grasp this notion by argumentation;
Yet it's easy to grasp when taught by another.
You're truly steadfast, dear boy,
you have grasped it!
Would that we have, Naciketas,
one like you to question us!

10 What you call a treasure, I know to be transient;
for by fleeting things one cannot gain the perennial.
Therefore I have built the fire-altar of Naciketas,
and by fleeting things I have gained the eternal.

11 Satisfying desires is the foundation of the world;
Uninterrupted rites bring ultimate security;
Great and widespread praise is the foundation—
These you have seen, wise Naciketas,
And having seen, firmly rejected.

12 The primeval one who is hard to perceive,
wrapped in mystery, hidden in the cave,
residing within th'impenetrable depth—
Regarding him as god, an insight
gained by inner contemplation,
both sorrow and joy the wise abandon.

13 When a mortal has heard it, understood it;
when he has drawn it out,
and grasped this subtle point of doctrine;

He rejoices, for he has found
something in which he could rejoice.
To him I consider my house
to be open Naciketas.

[NACIKETAS?] 14 Tell me what you see as—
Different from the right doctrine and from the wrong;
Different from what's done here and what's left undone;
Different from what has been and what's yet to be.'

[DEATH?] 15 The word that all the Vedas disclose;
The word that all austerities proclaim;
Seeking which people live student lives;
That word now I will tell you in brief—
It is OṂ!

16 For this alone is the syllable that's *brahman*!
For this alone is the syllable that's supreme!
When, indeed, one knows this syllable,
he obtains his every wish.

17 This is the support that's best!
This is the support supreme!
And when one knows this support,
he rejoices in *brahman*'s world.

[DEATH] 18 The wise one—
he is not born, he does not die;
he has not come from anywhere;
he has not become anyone.
He is unborn and eternal, primeval and everlasting.
And he is not killed, when the body is killed.

[The dialogue between Naciketas and Death ends here.]

19 If the killer thinks that he kills;
If the killed thinks that he is killed;
Both of them fail to understand.
He neither kills, nor is he killed.

20 Finer than the finest, larger than the largest,
is the self (*ātman*) that lies here hidden
in the heart of a living being.
Without desires and free from sorrow,
a man perceives by the creator's grace
the grandeur of the self.

21 Sitting down, he roams afar.
Lying down, he goes everywhere.

The god ceaselessly exulting—
Who, besides me, is able to know?

22 When he perceives this immense, all-pervading self,
as bodiless within bodies,
as stable within unstable beings—
A wise man ceases to grieve.

23 This self cannot be grasped,
by teachings or by intelligence,
or even by great learning.
Only the man he chooses can grasp him,
whose body this self chooses as his own.

24 Not a man who has not quit his evil ways;
Nor a man who is not calm or composed;
Nor even a man who is without a tranquil mind;
Could ever secure it by his mere wit.

25 For whom the Brahmin and the Kṣatriya
are both like a dish of boiled rice;
and death is like the sprinkled sauce;
Who truly knows where he is?

CHAPTER 3

Knowers of *brahman*, men with five fires,
and with the three fire-altars of Naciketas,
They call these two 'Shadow' and 'Light',
the two who have entered—
the one into the cave of the heart,
the other into the highest region beyond,
both drinking the truth
in the world of rites rightly performed.

2 May we master the fire-altar of Naciketas,
a dike
for those who have sacrificed;
the imperishable, the highest *brahman*,
the farther shore
for those who wish to cross the danger.

3 Know the self as a rider in a chariot,
and the body, as simply the chariot.

Know the intellect as the charioteer,
and the mind, as simply the reins.

4 The senses, they say, are the horses,
and sense objects are the paths around them;
He who is linked to the body (*ātman*), senses, and mind,
the wise proclaim as the one who enjoys.

5 When a man lacks understanding,
and his mind is never controlled;
His senses do not obey him,
as bad horses, a charioteer.

6 But when a man has understanding,
and his mind is ever controlled;
His senses do obey him,
as good horses, a charioteer.

7 When a man lacks understanding,
is unmindful and always impure;
He does not reach that final step,
but gets on the round of rebirth.

8 But when a man has understanding,
is mindful and always pure;
He does reach that final step,
from which he is not reborn again.

9 When a man's mind is his reins,
intellect, his charioteer;
He reaches the end of the road,
that highest step of Viṣṇu.

10 Higher than the senses are their objects;
Higher than sense objects is the mind;
Higher than the mind is the intellect;
Higher than the intellect is the immense self;

11 Higher than the immense self is the unmanifest;
Higher than the unmanifest is the person;
Higher than the person there's nothing at all.
That is the goal, that's the highest state.

12 Hidden in all the beings,
this self is not visibly displayed.
Yet, people of keen vision see him,
with eminent and sharp minds.

13 A wise man should curb his speech and mind,
control them within th'intelligent self;

He should control intelligence within the immense self,
and the latter, within the tranquil self.

14 Arise! Awake! Pay attention,
when you've obtained your wishes!
A razor's sharp edge is hard to cross—
that, poets say, is the difficulty of the path.

15 It has no sound or touch,
no appearance, taste, or smell;
It is without beginning or end,
undecaying and eternal;
When a man perceives it,
fixed and beyond the immense,
He is freed from the jaws of death.

16 The wise man who hears or tells
the tale of Naciketas,
an ancient tale told by Death,
will rejoice in *brahman*'s world.

17 If a man, pure and devout, proclaims this great secret
in a gathering of Brahmins,
or during a meal for the dead,
it will lead him to eternal life!

CHAPTER 4

The Self-existent One pierced the apertures outward,
therefore, one looks out, and not into oneself.
A certain wise man in search of immortality,
turned his sight inward and saw the self within.

2 Fools pursue outward desires,
and enter the trap of death spread wide.
But the wise know what constitutes th'immortal,
and in unstable things here do not seek the stable.

3 Appearance and taste, smell and sounds,
touches and sexual acts—
That by which one experiences these,
by the same one understands—
what then is here left behind?

So, indeed, is that!

4 That by which one perceives both
the states of sleep and of being awake;
Knowing that it's th'immense, all-pervading self,
a wise man does not grieve.

5 When a man perceives close at hand
this living, honey-eating self,
The lord of what was and what will be—
it does not seek to hide from him.

So, indeed, is that!

6 He who was born before heat,
who before the waters was born,
who has seen through living beings—
Entering the cave of the heart,
[one sees] him abiding there.

So, indeed, is that!

7 She who comes into being with breath,
Aditi, who embodies divinity,
who was born through living beings—
Entering the cave of the heart,
[one sees] her abiding there.

So, indeed, is that!

8 Jātavedas is hidden within the two fire-drills,
fostered, as a fetus by women with child;
With offering should men as they awake,
worship the fire each and every day.

So, indeed, is that!

9 From which the sun rises,
and into which it sets;
In it are fixed all the gods;
beyond it no one can ever pass.

So, indeed, is that!

10 Whatever is down here, the same is over there;
and what is over there is replicated down here.
From death to death he goes, who sees
here any kind of diversity.

So, indeed, is that!

[11] With your mind alone you must understand it—
there is here no diversity at all!
From death to death he goes, who sees
here any kind of diversity.

So, indeed, is that!

[12] A person the size of a thumb
resides within the body (*ātman*);
The lord of what was and what will be—
from him he does not hide himself.

So, indeed, is that!

[13] The person the size of a thumb
is like a fire free of smoke;
The lord of what was and what will be;
the same today and tomorrow.

So, indeed, is that!

[14] As the rain that falls on rugged terrain,
runs hither and thither along the mountain slopes;
So a man who regards the laws as distinct,
runs hither and thither after those very laws.

[15] As pure water poured into pure water
becomes the very same;
So does the self of a discerning sage
become, O Gautama.

CHAPTER 5

The unborn one, free of crooked thoughts,
has a fort with eleven gates;
One who attends to it will not grieve,
but, freed from it, he will be set free.

So, indeed, is that!

[2] The goose seated in the light, the Vasu seated in the sky;
The Hotṛ seated at the altar, the guest seated in the house;

Seated in men, seated in the wide expanse,
Seated in the truth, seated in heaven;
Born from water, born from cows,
Born from the truth, born from rocks;
The great truth!

3 The out-breath he conducts upward,
the in-breath he drives backward;
All the gods worship him,
the Dwarf seated in the middle.

4 When this embodied self dwelling in the body
comes unglued and is freed from the body—
what then is here left behind?

So, indeed, is that!

5 Not by the out-breath, not by the in-breath;
does any mortal live;
By another do people live, on which those two depend.

6 Come, I'll tell you this secret and eternal
formulation of truth (brahman);
And what happens to the self (*ātman*), Gautama,
when it encounters death.

7 Some enter a womb by which
an embodied self obtains a body,
Others pass into a stationary thing—
according to what they have done,
according to what they have learned.

8 This person, creating every desire,
who lies awake within those who sleep;
That alone is the Pure! That is *brahman*!
That alone is called the Immortal!
On it all the worlds rest;
beyond it no one can ever pass.

So, indeed, is that!

9 As the single fire, entering living beings,
adapts its appearance to match that of each;
So the single self within every being,
adapts its appearance to match that of each,
yet remains quite distinct.

10 As the single wind, entering living beings,
adapts its appearance to match that of each;
So the single self within every being,
adapts its appearance to match that of each,
yet remains quite distinct.

11 As the sun, the eye of the whole world,
is not stained by visual faults external to it;
So the single self within every being,
is not stained by the suffering of the world,
being quite distinct from it.

12 The one controller, the self within every being,
who makes manifold his single appearance;
The wise who perceive him as abiding within themselves,
they alone, not others, enjoy eternal happiness.

13 The changeless, among the changing,
the intelligent, among intelligent beings,
the one, who despenses desires among the many;
The wise who perceive him within themselves;
they alone, not others, enjoy unending bliss.

14 'This is that'—so they think, although
the highest bliss can't be described.
But how should I perceive it?
Does it shine?
Or does it radiate?

15 There the sun does not shine,
nor the moon and stars;
There lightning does not shine,
of this common fire need we speak!
Him alone, as he shines, do all things reflect;
this whole world radiates with his light.

CHAPTER 6

Its roots above, its branches below,
this is the eternal banyan tree.
That alone is the Bright! That is *brahman*!
That alone is called the Immortal!
On it all the worlds rest;
beyond it no one can ever pass.

So, indeed, is that!

2 All that is here, whatever that lives,
having arisen, moves within the breath;
Great is the fear, the bolt is raised up;
those who know it become immortal.

3 The fear of it makes the fire burn;
The fear of it makes the sun shine;
The fear of it makes them run—
Indra and Wind,
and Death, the fifth.

4 If one were able to realize it here,
before his body dissolves;
It will serve him to obtain a body
within the created worlds.

5 As in a mirror, so in the body (*ātman*);
As in a dream, so in the fathers' world;
As in water a thing becomes somewhat visible,
so in the Gandharva world;
Somewhat as in shadows and light,
so in *brahman*'s world.

6 The separate nature of the senses;
Their rise and fall as they come
Separately into being—
when a wise man knows this,
he does not grieve.

7 Higher than the senses is the mind;
Higher than the mind is the essence;
Higher than the essence is the immense self;
Higher than the immense is the unmanifest.

8 Higher than the unmanifest is the person,
pervading all and without any marks.
Knowing him, a man is freed,
and attains immortality.

9 His appearance is beyond the range of sight;
no one can see him with his sight;
With the heart, with insight, with thought,
has he been contemplated—
Those who know this become immortal.

10 When the five perceptions are stilled,
together with the mind,
And not even reason bestirs itself;
they call it the highest state.

11 When senses are firmly reined in,
that is Yoga, so people think.
From distractions a man is then free,
for Yoga is the coming-into-being,
as well as the ceasing-to-be.

12 Not by speech, not by the mind,
not by sight can he be grasped.
How else can that be perceived,
other than by saying 'He is!'

13 In just two ways can he be perceived:
by saying that 'He is',
by affirming he's the real.
To one who perceives him as 'He is',
it becomes clear that he is real.

14 When they are all banished,
those desires lurking in one's heart;
Then a mortal becomes immortal,
and attains *brahman* in this world.

15 When the knots are all cut,
that bind one's heart on earth;
Then a mortal becomes immortal—
For such is the teaching.

16 One hundred and one, the veins of the heart.
One of them runs up to the crown of the head.
Going up by it, he reaches the immortal.
The rest, in their ascent, spread out in all directions.

17 A person the size of a thumb in the body (*ātman*),
always resides within the hearts of men;
One should draw him out of the body with determination,
like a reed from the grass sheath;
One should know him
as immortal and bright.
One should know him
as immortal and bright.

18 Then, after Naciketas received this body of knowledge,
and the entire set of yogic rules taught by Death,
He attained *brahman*; he became free from aging and death;
so will others who know this teaching about the self.

Īśā Upaniṣad

THE Īśā Upaniṣad (also called 'Īśāvasya Upaniṣad') forms the fortieth chapter of the Vājasaneyi Saṃhitā of the White Yajurveda. Just as the Kena Upaniṣad, the IU gets its name from its first word, *īśā* ('by the Lord'). It is the only Upaniṣad that forms an integral part of a vedic Saṃhitā, and is, therefore, also known as the 'Saṃhitā Upaniṣad'. As a text of the White Yajurveda, the IU shows many similarities in thought and expressions with the BU. Nevertheless, the doctrines and ideas of the IU show that this document belongs broadly to the time and milieu that produced other similar texts with a strong theistic and devotional tendency, such as the SU, MU, and, to a somewhat lesser extent, the KaU. The IU is placed first in all the indigenous collections of Upaniṣads.

THIS whole world is to be dwelt in by the Lord,
whatever living being there is in the world.
So you should eat what has been abandoned;
and do not covet anyone's wealth.

2 Just performing works in this world,
you should desire to live your hundred years.
Thus, and not otherwise, in fact,
does work not smear off on you.

3 'Demonic' are those worlds called,
in blind darkness they are cloaked;
Into them after death they go,
all those people who kill the self.

4 Although not moving, the one is swifter than the mind;
the gods cannot catch it, as it speeds on in front.
Standing, it outpaces others who run;
within it Mātariśvan places the waters.

5 It moves—yet it does not move
It's far away—yet it is near at hand!
It is within this whole world—yet
it's also outside this whole world.

6 When a man sees all beings
within his very self,
and his self within all beings,
It will not seek to hide from him.

7 When in the self of a discerning man,
his very self has become all beings,
What bewilderment, what sorrow can there be,
regarding that self of him who sees this oneness.

8 He has reached the seed—without body or wound,
without sinews, not riddled by evil.
Self-existent and all-encompassing,
the wise sage has dispensed objects
through endless years.

9 Into blind darkness they enter,
people who worship ignorance;
And into still blinder darkness,
people who delight in learning.

10 It's far different from knowledge, they say,
Different also from ignorance, we're told—
so have we heard from wise men,
who have explained it to us.

11 Knowledge and ignorance—
a man who knows them both together,
Passes beyond death by ignorance,
and by knowledge attains immortality.

12 Into blind darkness they enter,
people who worship non-becoming;
And into still blinder darkness,
people who delight in becoming.

13 It's far different from coming-into-being, they say,
Different also from not coming-into-being, we're told—
so have we heard from wise men,
who have explained it all to us.

14 The becoming and the destruction—
a man who knows them both together;
Passes beyond death by the destruction,
and by the becoming attains immortality.

15 The face of truth is covered
with a golden dish.
Open it, O Pūṣan, for me,
a man faithful to the truth.
Open it, O Pūṣan, for me to see.

16 O Pūṣan, sole seer!
Yama! Sun! Son of Prajāpati!
Spread out your rays!
Draw in your light!
I see your fairest form.
That person up there,
I am he!

17 The never-resting is the wind,
the immortal!
Ashes are this body's lot.
OṂ!
Mind, remember the deed!
Remember!
Mind, remember the deed!
Remember!

18 O Fire, you know all coverings;
O god, lead us to riches,
  along an easy path.
Keep the sin that angers,
  far away from us;
And the highest song of praise,
  we shall offer to you!

Śvetāśvatara Upaniṣad

THE Śvetāśvatara Upaniṣad, traditionally ascribed to the Black Yajurveda, is a somewhat late text composed under the influence of both the Sāṃkhya-Yoga tradition and the emerging theistic tendencies. Its thought and vocabulary are close to those of the other famous theistic document, the Bhagavad Gītā. Just like the latter text, the SU appears somewhat chaotic in its presentation because it seeks to integrate numerous and divergent cosmologies and theologies into its religious doctrine. Further, the numerous citations from older vedic texts indicate that the author is attempting to support his doctrines with vedic proof-texts, often presented with new interpretations. It is clear, however, that a major aim of the author is to establish that the God who creates and from whom one expects salvation is *one*. This point is driven home by the repeated use of the term *eka*, 'one' or 'alone'. This Upaniṣad is named after the teacher of its doctrine, one Śvetāśvatara (lit. 'man with a white mule').

This translation follows the critical edition of the SU established by Hauschild (1927), taking into account some of the textual emendations suggested by Rau (1964). Departing from my normal practice, I have chosen to translate the SU in prose, even though the text itself is in verse. The technical nature of much of the text and its complex philosophical arguments make it difficult to render it into verse while keeping it accurate and readable.

CHAPTER 1

PEOPLE who make enquiries about *brahman* say:

What is the cause of *brahman*? Why were we born? By what do we live? On what are we established? Governed by whom, O you who know *brahman*, do we live in pleasure and in pain, each in our respective situation?

2 Should we regard it as time, as inherent nature, as necessity, as chance, as the elements, as the source of birth, or as the Person? Or is it a combination of these? But that can't be, because there is the self (*ātman*). Even the self is not in control, because it is itself subject to pleasure and pain.

3 Those who follow the discipline of meditation have seen God, the self, and the power, all hidden by their own qualities. One alone is he who governs all those causes, from 'time' to 'self.'

4–5 We study it—

as a wheel that is one-rimmed and threefold, with sixteen tips, fifty spokes, twenty counter-spokes, and six sets of eight, whose single rope is of many forms; that divides itself into three different paths; and whose delusion regarding the one springs from two causes.

as a river whose waters are the five sense organs; whose fierce crocodiles are the five sources of birth; whose waves are the five breaths; whose primal source is the five types of perception; which has five whirlpools; whose rapid current is the five types of sorrow; which divides itself in fifty ways; and which has five sections.

6 Within this vast wheel of *brahman*, on which all subsist and which abides in all, a goose keeps moving around. When he perceives himself (*ātman*) as distinct from the impeller, delighted by that knowledge he goes from there to immortality.

7 This highest *brahman*, however, has been extolled thus: There is a triad in it—oneself, the foundation, and the imperishable. When those who know *brahman* have come to know the distinction

between them, they become absorbed in and totally intent on *brahman* and are freed from the womb.

8 This whole world is the perishable and the imperishable, the manifest and the unmanifest joined together—and the Lord bears it, while the self (*ātman*), who is not the Lord, remains bound, because he is the enjoyer. When he comes to know God, he is freed from all fetters.

9 There are two unborn males—the one knows and the other is ignorant; the one is Lord and the other is not the Lord. There is just one unborn female, who is joined to the enjoyer and the objects of enjoyment. And then there is the self (*ātman*), limitless and displaying every form, not engaged in any activity. When someone finds these three, he finds this *brahman*.

10 The primal source is perishable, while Hara is immortal and imperishable. The one God rules over both the perishable and the self (*ātman*). By meditating on him, by striving towards him, and, further, in the end by becoming the same reality as him, all illusion disappears.

11 When one has known God, all the fetters fall off; by the eradication of the blemishes, birth and death come to an end; by meditating on him, one obtains, at the dissolution of the body, a third—sovereignty over all; and in the absolute one's desires are fulfilled.

12 This can be known, for it abides always within one's body (*ātman*). Higher than that there is nothing to be known. When the enjoyer discerns the object of enjoyment and the impeller—everything has been taught. That is the threefold *brahman*.

13 When a fire is contained within its womb, one cannot see its visible form and yet its essential character is not extinguished; one can grasp the fire once again from its womb by means of tinder. In just the same way, one can grasp both within the body by means of the syllable OṂ.

14 When one makes one's own body the bottom slab and the syllable OṂ the upper drill, by twirling it constantly through meditation one would see God, just as one would the hidden thing.

15–16 Like oil in sesame seeds and butter in curds, like water in the river-bed and fire in the fire-drills, so, when one seeks it with truth and austerity, one grasps that self (*ātman*) in the body (*ātman*)—that all-pervading self, which is contained [in the body], like butter in milk.

That is *brahman*, the highest object of the teachings on hidden connections (*upaniṣad*), an object rooted in austerity and the knowledge of the self.

CHAPTER 2

Yoking first his mind, and extending then his thoughts, Savitṛ, having recognized the fire as the light, brought it here from the earth.

2 With minds yoked, we [make the offering] under the stimulus of the god Savitṛ for the strength to go to heaven.

3 Yoking the gods, as they go to heaven with their mind and to the firmament with their thought, may Savitṛ stimulate them to create the lofty light.

4 They yoke their minds, they yoke their thoughts, those inspired poets of the lofty poet. That one alone who knows the patterns has apportioned the offerings. Resounding is the praise of the god Savitṛ.

5 I yoke with adorations the ancient formulation (*brahman*) of you two. The praises spread wide, like the suns on their course. All the sons of the immortal hear them, when they have reached the heavenly abodes.

6 Where the fire is churned, where the wind wafts, where the Soma juice flows over—there the mind is born.

7 By means of Savitṛ and his stimulus let a man take delight in that ancient formulation (*brahman*). Make there a source of birth for yourself. And the gifts you have given, not even an iota [would fall] from you [to someone else's lot].

8 When he keeps his body straight, with the three sections erect, and draws the senses together with the mind into his heart, a wise man shall cross all the frightful rivers with the boat consisting of that formulation (*brahman*).

9 Compressing his breaths in here and curbing his movements, a man should exhale through one nostril when his breath is exhausted. A wise man should keep his mind vigilantly under control, just as he would that wagon yoked to unruly horses.

10 Level and clean; free of gravel, fire, and sand; near noiseless running waters and the like; pleasing to the mind but not offensive to the eye; provided with a cave or a nook sheltered from the wind—in such a spot should one engage in yogic practice.

11 Mist, smoke, sun, wind, fire, fireflies, lightning, crystal, moon—these are the apparitions that, within yogic practice, precede and pave the way to the full manifestation in *brahman*.

12 When earth, water, fire, air, and ether have arisen together, and the body made up of these five becomes equipped with the attribute of yoga, that man, obtaining a body tempered by the fire of yoga, will no longer experience sickness, old age, or suffering.

13 Lightness, health, the absence of greed, a bright complexion, a pleasant voice, a sweet smell, and very little faeces and urine—that, they say, is the first working of yogic practice.

14 Just as a disk smeared with clay, once it is cleaned well, shines brightly, so also an embodied person, once he has perceived the true nature of the self, becomes solitary, his goal attained, and free from sorrow.

15 When, by means of the true nature of the self, which resembles a lamp, a man practising yogic restraint sees here the true nature of *brahman*, he is freed from all fetters, because he has known God, unborn, unchanging, and unsullied by all objects.

16 This God does pervade all quarters. He was born the first, yet he remains within the womb. He it is, who was born; he, who will be born. His face everywhere, he stands turning west towards men.

17 He who abides as God in the fire; who abides in the waters; who has entered every being; who abides in the plants; who abides in the trees—to that God adoration! Adoration!

CHAPTER 3

Who alone, wielding the net, reigns by his sovereign powers, reigns over all worlds by his sovereign powers; who also alone is present at their rise and birth—those who know this become immortal.

2 There is only one Rudra; he has not tolerated a second who would reign over these worlds by his sovereign powers. After drawing in all beings, he stands as the protector at the end of time turning west towards men.

3 Eyes everywhere and face everywhere, arms everywhere and feet everywhere, he forges with his two hands, he forges with the wings, producing the heaven and earth, the one God.

4 Who, as the source and origin of the gods and the ruler over them all, as the god Rudra, and as the great seer, in the beginning created Hiraṇyagarbha—may he furnish us with lucid intelligence.

5 That form of yours, O Rudra, which is benign and not terrifying, which is not sinister-looking—with that most auspicious form of yours, O Mountain-dweller, look upon us.

6 The arrow, O Mountain-dweller, that you hold in your hand to shoot—make it benign, O Mountain-protector; hurt not man or beast.

7 Who is higher than that, higher than *brahman*, the immense one hidden in all beings, in each according to its kind, and who alone encompasses the whole universe—when people know him as the Lord, they become immortal.

8 I know that immense Person, having the colour of the sun and beyond darkness. Only when a man knows him does he pass beyond death; there is no other path for getting there.

9 This whole world is filled by that Person, beyond whom there is nothing; beneath whom there is nothing; smaller than whom there is nothing; larger than whom there is nothing; and who stands like a tree planted firmly in heaven.

10 What is higher than that is without visible appearance and free from affliction. Those who know it become immortal; as for the rest, only suffering awaits them.

11 Who is the face, head, and neck of all, who resides deep in the heart of all beings, and who pervades everything—he is the Blessed One. Therefore, the Benign One is present everywhere.

12 The Person, clearly, is the immense Lord. He is the one who sets in motion the real. The Imperishable One rules over the light, this totally flawless attainment.

13 The Person the size of a thumb abiding within the body (*ātman*) always resides within the hearts of people. With the heart, with insight, with thought has he been contemplated. Those who know this become immortal.

14 The Person had a thousand heads, a thousand eyes, and a thousand feet. Having encompassed the earth on all sides, he extended ten fingers' breadth beyond it.

15 This whole world is just the Person, whatever there was and whatever there will be. Even over immortality he rules, when he rises above [the world] through food.

16 With hands and feet everywhere, with eyes, heads, and faces everywhere, and with ears everywhere, that remains encompassing everything in the world—

17 That, which appears to possess the powers of all the senses but is devoid of every sense, which is the lord, the ruler of the whole world, the vast refuge of the whole world.

18 Within the fort with nine gates, the embodied one flutters to the outside like a goose; it is the master of the whole world, of both the immobile and the mobile.

19 He moves swiftly, but he has no feet; he grasps, but he has no hands; he sees, but he has no eyes; he hears, but he has no ears. He knows what is there to know, but there is no one who knows him. They call him the first and immense Person.

20 Finer than the finest, larger than the largest, is the self that lies here hidden in the heart of a living being. A man who, by the creator's grace, sees that desireless one as the majesty and as the Lord will be free from sorrow.

21 I know that unageing and ancient one as the self in all beings, as present in all because of his pervasiveness; the one, about whom

those who enquire after *brahman* proclaim—he always brings about the cessation of birth.

CHAPTER 4

Who alone, himself without colour, wielding his power creates variously countless colours, and in whom the universe comes together at the beginning and dissolves in the end—may he furnish us with lucid intelligence.

2 The fire is simply that; the sun is that; the wind is that; and the moon is also that! The bright one is simply that; *brahman* is that; the waters are that; and Prajāpati is that!

3 You are a woman; you are a man; you are a boy or also a girl. As an old man, you totter along with a walking-stick. As you are born, you turn your face in every direction.

4 You are the dark blue bird, the green one with red eyes, the raincloud, the seasons, and the oceans. You live as one without a beginning because of your pervasiveness, you, from whom all beings have been born.

5 One unborn male [billy-goat], burning with passion, covers one unborn female [nanny-goat] coloured red, white, and black, and giving birth to numerous offspring with the same colours as hers, while another unborn male leaves her after he has finished enjoying her pleasures.

6 Two birds, who are companions and friends, nestle on the very same tree. One of them eats a tasty fig; the other, not eating, looks on.

7 Stuck on the very same tree, one person grieves, deluded by her who is not the Lord. But when he sees the other, the contented Lord—and the Lord's majesty—his grief disappears.

8 The syllable amidst the Ṛg, the syllable upon which all the gods are seated in the highest heaven—when a man does not know it, what will he do with a Ṛg. Seated here together are people who do know it!

9 Metres, sacrifices, rites, religious observances, the past, the future, and what the Vedas proclaim—from that the illusionist creates this whole world, and in it the other remains confined by the illusory power.

10 One should recognize the illusory power as primal matter, and the illusionist, as the great Lord. This whole living world is thus pervaded by things that are parts of him.

11 Who alone presides over womb after womb; in whom this whole world comes together and dissolves—when someone recognizes that Lord who fulfils wishes as the God who is to be adored, he attains this unending peace.

12 Who, as the source and origin of the gods and the ruler over them all, as the god Rudra, and as the great seer, looked on as Hiraṇyagarbha was being born—may he furnish us with lucid intelligence.

13 Who is the Supreme Lord of the gods; on whom the worlds rest; who rules over the bipeds and the quadrupeds here—to what god shall we offer oblations?

14 Who is finer than the finest, in the midst of disorder; who is the creator of the universe displaying various forms; who, alone, encompasses the universe—when someone recognizes him as the Benign One, he attains unending peace.

15 It is he who protects the world at the right time, the lord of the universe hidden in all beings. When someone thus knows him, after whom seers and gods strive, he severs the fetters of death.

16 When someone knows the one who is extremely fine, like the spume on top of the ghee, as the Benign One hidden in all beings; when someone recognizes him, who alone encompasses the universe, as God—he is freed from all fetters.

17 That God, the maker of all, the immense self (*ātman*), is always residing in the hearts of people. With the heart, with insight, with thought has he been contemplated. Those who know this become immortal.

18 When there was darkness, then there was neither day nor night, neither the existent nor the non-existent—the Benign One alone

was there. He was the imperishable, he was 'the excellent [glory] of Savitṛ', and from him has come forth the ancient wisdom.

19 No one will catch hold of him from above, from across, or in the middle. There is no likeness of him, whose name is Immense Glory.

20 His appearance is beyond the range of sight; no one can see him with his sight. Those who know him thus with their hearts—him, who abides in their hearts—and with insight become immortal.

21 'He is the Unborn One!'—so some man, filled with awe, takes refuge with Rudra—'Protect me always with that kindly face of yours!'

22 'Do not hurt us in our offspring or descendants, in our life, in our cattle or horses. Do not slay in anger, O Rudra, our valiant men. Oblations in hand, we invite you to your seat.'

CHAPTER 5

Two things, knowledge and ignorance, are set down in the imperishable and infinite fort of *brahman*, where they lie hidden. Now, ignorance is the perishable and knowledge is the immortal. But the one who rules over both knowledge and ignorance is another—

2 who alone presides over womb after womb, and thus over all visible forms and all the sources of birth; who in the beginning carried this Kapila born of the seer together with his body of knowledge and would look on him as he was being born.

3 Spreading out one net after another in diverse ways within this world, this God gathers them in. After creating it once again, the Lord likewise tears it down. The immense self (*ātman*) exercises his sovereignty over the whole world.

4 As the draught-ox shines, lighting up all the quarters, above, below, and across, so this God, blessed and adorable, alone rules over wombs and inherent natures.

5 Who, as the womb of all, not only ripens by his inherent nature, but also would bring all those in need of ripening to full

development, and who would apportion all the qualities—he alone rules over this whole universe.

6 It is hidden in the secret Upaniṣads of the Veda. Recognize it, O Brahmins, as the womb of *brahman*. The gods of old and the seers who knew it became of one essence with it and so came to be immortal.

7 The one who, in association with the qualities, performs fruitful actions also enjoys the fruits of that very act. Displaying every form, endowed with the three qualities, and along three paths he roams about as the lord of vital breaths together with his own actions.

8 He is as large as a thumb and equal in appearance to the sun when he is equipped with the faculties of imagination and self-consciousness. But one sees also another no larger than the tip of an awl who is equipped only with the quality of intelligence and the quality of the body (*ātman*).

9 When the tip of a hair is split into a hundred parts, and one of those parts further into a hundred parts—the individual soul (*jīva*), on the one hand, is the size of one such part, and, on the other, it partakes of infinity.

10 It is neither a woman nor a man, nor even a hermaphrodite; it is ruled over by whichever body it obtains.

11 The birth and growth of the body (*ātman*) takes place through the offerings of intention, touch, and sight, and by means of food, drink, and impregnation; whereas the embodied self assumes successively in different situations the physical appearances that correspond to its actions.

12 The embodied self assumes numerous physical appearances, both large and small, in accordance with its qualities. One sees also another cause of their union in accordance with the qualities of the actions and the body (*ātman*).

13 Who is without beginning or end, in the midst of disorder; who is the creator of the universe displaying various forms; who, alone, encompasses the universe—when someone recognizes him as God, he is freed from all fetters.

14 Who is to be grasped with one's heart, who is called 'Without-a-Lord', who brings about existence and non-existence, who is the

Benign One, and who produces both the creation and its constituent parts—those who know him as God have cast aside their bodies.

CHAPTER 6

Some wise men say it is inherent nature, while others say it is time—all totally deluded. It is rather the greatness of God present in the world by means of which this wheel of *brahman* goes around.

2 Who always encompasses this whole world—the knower, the architect of time, the one without qualities, and the all-knowing one—it is at his command that the work of creation, to be conceived of as earth, water, fire, air, and space, unfolds itself.

3 After completing that work and drawing it back again; after joining himself with the realities one after another—with one, with two, with three, or with eight, as well as with time and with the subtle qualities of the body (*ātman*);

4 and after undertaking the works endowed with the qualities; *he* who would apportion all the modes of existence—when they are no more, the work he has produced is destroyed—*he* carries on, when the work is dissolved, as someone other than those realities.

5–6 One sees him as the beginning, as the basis and cause of the joining, as beyond the three times, and also as without parts. He, from whom the unfolding of the world has come forth, is higher than and different from the time-confined forms of the tree.

After we have first venerated that adorable God displaying every form, the source of all beings, as residing within one's heart, and then recognized him as the one who bestows righteousness and removes evil, as the Lord of prosperity, as abiding within ourselves (*ātman*), as the Immortal residing in all beings—

7 we will find this highest Great-Lord among lords, the highest God among gods, the highest master among masters, the God beyond the highest as the adorable Lord of the universe.

8 One cannot find in him either an obligation to act or an organ with which to act; neither can one see anyone equal to him, let alone someone who surpasses him. One hears about his highest and truly diverse power, which is part of his very nature and is the working of his knowledge and strength.

9 There is no one in the world who is his master, nor anyone who rules over him. He has no distinguishing mark. He is the cause, the Overlord over the overlords of the sense organs, and he has neither parent nor overlord.

10 The one God who covers himself with things issuing from the primal source, from his own inherent nature, as a spider, with the threads—may he procure us dissolution in *brahman*.

11 The one God hidden in all beings, pervading the universe, the inner self of all beings, the overseer of the work, dwelling in all beings, the witness, the spectator, alone, devoid of qualities,

12 the one controller of the many who are inactive, who makes the single seed manifold—the wise who perceive him as abiding within themselves (*ātman*), they alone, not others, enjoy eternal happiness.

13 The changeless, among the changing, the intelligent, among intelligent beings, the one, who dispenses desires among the many—when a man knows that cause, which is to be comprehended through the application of Sāṃkhya, as God, he is freed from all fetters.

14 There the sun does not shine, nor the moon and stars; there lightning does not shine, of this common fire need we speak! Him alone, as he shines, do all things reflect; this whole world radiates with his light.

15 He is the one goose in the middle of this universe. He himself resides as fire within the ocean. Only when a man knows him does he pass beyond death; there is no other path for getting there.

16 He is the creator of all; the knower of all; his own source of birth; the knower; the architect of time; the one without qualities; the one with all knowledge; the Lord of both the primal source and of individual souls; the ruler over the qualities; and the cause of liberation from remaining within, and bondage to the rebirth cycle.

17 He who is one with him, immortal, abiding as the Lord, the knower, present everywhere, and the protector of this universe—he rules this living world eternally. There is no other cause to becoming the Lord.

18 Who at first created the *brahman* and delivered to him the Vedas; who manifests himself by his own intelligence—in that God do I, desirous of liberation, seek refuge—

19 in him, who, like a fire whose fuel is spent, is without parts, inactive, tranquil, unblemished, spotless, and the highest dike to immortality.

20 Only when people will be able to roll up the sky like a piece of leather will suffering come to an end, without first knowing God.

21 By the power of his austerities and by the grace of God, the wise Śvetāśvatara first came to know *brahman* and then proclaimed it to those who had passed beyond their order of life as the highest means of purification that bring delight to the company of seers.

22 This supreme secret was proclaimed during a former age in the Vedānta. One should never disclose it to a person who is not of a tranquil disposition, or who is not one's son or pupil.

23 Only in a man who has the deepest love for God, and who shows the same love towards his teacher as towards God, do these points declared by the Noble One shine forth.

Muṇḍaka Upaniṣad

THE Muṇḍaka Upaniṣad does not form part of a larger vedic text, although tradition ascribes it to the Atharvaveda. This ascription, however, should not be taken too seriously, because most later Upaniṣads that did not form part of any other vedic collection were, almost by default, ascribed to the Atharva Veda.

The title 'Muṇḍaka' has been the subject of some discussion. It literally means 'shaven' or 'shaven-headed'. On the basis of this title, some have suggested that the MuU was composed by and/or intended for shaven-headed ascetics. They have interpreted the 'head-vow' (*śirovrata*) mentioned at the conclusion of the Upaniṣad as a reference to the shaving of the head and as another indication that the text was meant for ascetics. Although such an interpretation is plausible, especially in light of the MuU's anti-ritual attitude and its use of the terms *yati*, probably in the sense of ascetic (MuU 3.1.5; 3.2.6), and *saṃnyāsa*, in the sense of ascetic renunciation (MuU 3.2.6), I do not think it is certain. The text also uses the term *muṇḍaka* for 'chapter', clearly an unusual term.

More than any other Upaniṣad, the MuU engages in a direct and frontal attack against both vedic ritualism and the vedic texts that embody the ritual tradition. It establishes a clear distinction between a lower class of religious texts, the old vedic texts and ancillary literature, and a higher class consisting of texts that teach the imperishable *brahman* and contain the knowledge passed down in a tradition reaching back to *Brahman* (here as God) himself. It is this higher knowledge that MuU refers to as 'Vedānta' (3.2.6), one of the earliest recorded use of this significant term.

This translation is based on the critical edition of the MuU by Hertel (1924), an edition that is somewhat different from the vulgate upon which is based the commentary traditionally ascribed to Śaṃkara.

CONTENTS

CHAPTER 1

1 BRAHMĀ arose as the first among gods,
as the creator of all,
as the guardian of the world.
To Atharvan, his firstborn son, he disclosed
the knowledge of *brahman*,
of all knowledge the root.

2 The knowledge of *brahman*,
which Brahmā taught him—
both the higher and the lower—
Atharvan of old disclosed to Aṅgir,
Aṅgir, to Bhāradvāja Satyavāha,
Bhāradvāja, to Aṅgiras.

3 Śaunaka, a wealthy householder, once went up to Aṅgiras in the prescribed manner and asked: 'What is it, my lord, by knowing which a man comes to know this whole world?' 4 This is what Aṅgiras told him.

Two types of knowledge a man should learn—those who know *brahman* tell us—the higher and the lower. 5 The lower of the two consists of the Ṛgveda, the Yajurveda, the Sāmaveda, the Atharvaveda, phonetics, the ritual science, grammar, etymology, metrics, and astronomy; whereas the higher is that by which one grasps the imperishable.

6 What cannot be seen, what cannot be grasped,
without colour, without sight or hearing,
without hands or feet;
What is eternal and all-pervading,
extremely minute, present everywhere—
That is the immutable,
which the wise fully perceive.

7 As a spider spins out threads, then draws them into itself;
As plants sprout out from the earth;
As head and body hair grows from a living man;
So from the imperishable all things here spring.

[Ritualists argue:]

8 Through heat *brahman* is built up;
thereby food is produced.

From food comes breath,
mind, truth, and worlds,
and immortality in rites.

9 He is omniscient, he knows all;
knowledge is his austerity.
From him is born this *brahman*,
as also name, appearance, and food.

2

Here is the truth:

The rites that the wise poets
saw in the vedic formulas,
stretched in many ways
across the three Vedas—
Perform them always,
you who long for the truth;
That's your path to the world of those
who correctly perform the rites.

2 When the flame flickers after the fire is lit,
let him then make his offerings,
between the two pourings of ghee.

3 A man's daily fire sacrifice that remains
without the new-moon, the full-moon,
and the four-month sacrifice;
and without offerings to guests;
That is performed without an offering to all the gods,
or without following the rules;
Will rob him of his worlds, up to the very seventh.

4 The Black, the Terrible, the Swift-as-the-mind,
The Blood-red, the Smoke-coloured, the Sparkling,
And the glittering Goddess—
These are the seven flickering tongues of flame.

5 When a man moves within these,
as they are shining bright,
receiving oblations offered at the proper time;
Then, as sunbeams, these carry him
to where the king of gods resides,
the only place to reside.

6 'Come! Come!' say the oblations shining bright,
As they carry their offerer on the sun's rays of light,

They praise him, telling him flattering things:
'This is yours, this *brahman*'s world,
Built by good deeds and rites well done.'

[The Author replies:]

7 Surely, they are floating unanchored,
these eighteen forms of the sacrifice,
the rites within which are called inferior.
The fools who hail that as the best,
return once more to old age and death.

8 Wallowing in ignorance, but calling themselves wise,
thinking they are learned, the fools go around,
hurting themselves badly, like a group of blind men,
led by a man who is himself blind.

9 Wallowing in ignorance time and again,
the fools imagine, 'We have reached our aim!'
Because of their passion, they do not understand,
these people who are given to rites.
Therefore, they fall, wretched and forlorn,
when their heavenly stay comes to a close.

10 Deeming sacrifices and gifts as the best,
the imbeciles know nothing better.
When they have enjoyed their good work,
atop the firmament,
They return again to this abject world.

11 But those in the wilderness, calm and wise,
who live a life of penance and faith,
as they beg their food;
Through the sun's door they go, spotless,
to where that immortal Person is,
that immutable self.

12 When he perceives the worlds as built with rites,
A Brahmin should acquire a sense of disgust—
'What's made
can't make
what is unmade!'
To understand it he must go, firewood in hand,
to a teacher well versed in the Vedas,
and focused on *brahman*.

13 To that student of tranquil mind and calm disposition,
who had come to him in the right manner,

that learned man faithfully imparted,
The knowledge of *brahman*,
by which he understood that Person—
the true, the imperishable.

CHAPTER 2

1 Here is the truth:

As from a well-stoked fire sparks fly by the thousands,
all looking just like it,
So from the imperishable issue diverse things,
and into it, my friend, they return.

2 That Person, indeed, is divine,
he has no visible form;
He is both within and without,
unborn, without breath or mind;
He is radiant, and farther than
the farthest imperishable.

3 From him issue breath and mind,
and all the organs,
wind, fire, water, and space,
And the earth that bears everything.

4 His head is the fire, his eyes the sun and moon;
His ears are the quarters; his speech the Vedas disclosed;
His breath is the wind, his heart the universe;
and with his feet he is, indeed,
the inmost self of every being.

5 From him comes the fire whose firewood is the sun;
From the moon comes rain; plants grow upon earth;
And in the woman the man spills his seed—
From the Person have issued many creatures.

6 Ṛg verses, Sāman chants, Yajus formulas,
As well as sacrificial consecrations:
from him do they spring;
All sacrifices, rites, sacrificial gifts:
from him do they spring;
The year, the sacrificer, and the worlds—

Worlds where the sun and the moon shine—
from him do they spring.

7 Gods, celestial beings, humans, beasts, and birds:
from him in diverse ways they spring;
In-breath and out-breath, barley and rice,
penance, faith, and truth,
the chaste life and the rules of rites:
from him do they spring.

8 The seven breaths, the seven flames,
the seven oblations, the seven pieces of wood:
from him do they spring.
These seven worlds in which the breaths move
as they lay hidden, seven by seven, within the cave:
from him do they spring.

9 From him spring all oceans and hills;
From him flow rivers of all types;
From him spring all plants and the sap by which
he abides in things as their inmost self.

10 All this is simply that Person—
rites, penance, prayer (*brahman*), the highest immortal.
One who knows this, my friend, hidden within the cave,
cuts the knot of ignorance in this world.

2

Though manifest, it is lodged in the cave,
this vast abode named 'Aged'.
In it are placed this whole world;
In it are based what moves or breathes—
what moves or breathes, what blinks the eye,
what's most desirable, beyond perception,
what people desire most.

2 What is smaller than the smallest and intensely bright,
in which rest these worlds and those who live therein—
It is the imperishable *brahman*;
It is breath, it is the immortal.
It is what we must strike, my friend.
Strike it!

3 Take, my friend, this bow,
this great weapon of *upaniṣad*;
Place veneration on it
as the whetted arrow;
Stretch it with the thought fixed on the nature of that;

That very imperishable is the target, my friend.
Strike it!

4 The bow is OṂ, the arrow's the self,
The target is *brahman*, they say.
One must strike that undistracted.
He will then be lodged in that.
Like the arrow, in the target.

5 That alone is the self, you must understand,
On which are woven the earth,
intermediate region, and sky,
the mind, together with all breaths.
Put away other words, for this
is the dike to the immortal.

6 Where the veins come together like spokes,
in it is that one, taking birth in many ways.
'It is OṂ'—meditate thus on this self;
Good luck to you, as you cross
beyond the darkness!

7a Who knows all, who observes all,
to whom belongs all greatness on earth—
He is this self in the divine fort of *brahman*,
having a secure footing in the sky.

7b Consisting of thought, controller of body and breaths;
he has a secure footing in food,
after having settled in the heart.
By perceiving him the wise see
what becomes visible as the immortal
in the form of bliss.

8 When one sees him—
both the high and the low;
The knot of one's heart is cut,
all doubts are dispelled;
and his works come to an end.

9 In that high golden container is *brahman*,
stainless and partless,
the brilliant light of lights!
This is what they know,
those who know the self.

10 There the sun does not shine,
nor the moon and the stars;

There lightning does not shine,
of the common fire need we speak!
Him alone, as he shines, do all things reflect;
this whole world radiates with his light.

11 *Brahman* alone here extends to the east;
brahman, to the west;
it alone, to the south, to the north,
it alone extends above and below;
It is *brahman* alone that extends
over this whole universe,
up to its widest extent.

CHAPTER 3

1 Two birds, companions and friends,
nestle on the very same tree.
One of them eats a tasty fig;
the other, not eating, looks on.

2 Stuck on the very same tree,
one person grieves, deluded
by her who is not the Lord;
But when he sees the other,
the contented Lord—and his majesty—
his grief disappears.

3 When the seer sees that Person,
the golden-coloured, the creator, the Lord,
as the womb of *brahman*;
Then, shaking off the good and the bad,
the wise man becomes spotless,
and attains the highest identity.

4 It is breath that is visible in all beings—
Be a man who perceives, who knows this,
and thereby a man who out-talks;
a man who dallies with the self,
who finds pleasure in the self,
and thus an active man.
He is *brahman*!
and of those who know *brahman*,
He is the best!

5 By truth can this self be grasped—
by austerity, by right knowledge,
and by a perpetually chaste life.
It lies within the body, brilliant and full of light,
which ascetics perceive,
when their faults are wiped out.

6 The real alone he wins, never the unreal.
Along the real runs the path to the gods,
On which the seers proceed, their desires fulfilled,
To where that highest treasure of the real is found.

7 It is large, heavenly, of inconceivable form;
yet it appears more minute than the minute.
It is farther than the farthest,
yet it is here at hand;
It is right here within those who see,
hidden within the cave of their heart.

8 Not by sight, not by speech, nor by any other sense;
nor by austerities or rites is he grasped.
Rather the partless one is seen by a man, as he meditates,
when his being has become pure,
through the lucidity of knowledge.

9 By thought is this subtle self to be known,
into which breath has entered in five ways;
By the senses is laced th'entire thought of people,
in which, when it is pure, this self becomes disclosed.

10 Whatever world a man, whose being is purified,
ponders with his mind,
and whatever desires he covets;
that very world, those very desires, he wins.
A man who desires prosperity, therefore,
should worship one who knows the self.

2 He knows this highest abode of *brahman*,
placed in which shines everything bright.
The wise men, free from desires,
who worship the Person,
go beyond what is here bright.

2 One who hankers after desires in his thoughts,
is born here and there through his actions.
But when one's desires are fulfilled,
and one's self is made perfect,
all his desires disappear in this very world.

3 This self cannot be grasped,
by teachings or by intelligence,
or even by great learning.
Only the man he chooses can grasp him,
whose body this self chooses as his own.

4 This self cannot be grasped,
by a weak man or through carelessness,
or even by austerity without the marks.
But when a wise man strives by these means,
this self enters his *brahman*-abode.

5 The seers, sated with knowledge,
when they have attained him,
become free from passion and tranquil,
and their selves are made perfect.
The wise, their selves controlled,
when they attain him altogether,
he who is present in All,
they enter into that very All.

6 The ascetics who have firmly determined their goal
through a full knowledge of the Vedānta,
have their being purified
by the discipline of renunciation.
In the worlds of *brahman*, at the time of the final end,
having become fully immortal,
they will all be fully liberated.

7 The fifteen parts have retired to their foundations;
And all the senses, to the respective divinities;
Works and the self consisting of knowledge—
all unite in the highest immutable.

8 As the rivers flow on and enter into the ocean
giving up their names and appearances;
So the knower, freed from name and appearance,
reaches the heavenly Person, beyond the very highest.

9 When a man comes to know that highest *brahman*, he himself becomes that very *brahman*. A man without the knowledge of *brahman* will not be born in his family. He passes beyond sorrow, he passes beyond evil. Freed from the knots of his heart, he will become immortal. 10 This point has been made in the Ṛgvedic verse:

Who are versed in the Vedas and perform rites,
Who are grounded in *brahman*,
Who offer for themselves, with faith in the lone seer,
  to these alone let a man teach
  this knowledge of *brahman*,
So long as they have duly performed the head-vow.

11 Here is the truth that the seer Aṅgiras proclaimed of old. A man who has not performed the head-vow may not learn it.

Homage to the highest seers!
Homage to the highest seers!

Praśna Upaniṣad

THE Praśna Upaniṣad consists of the sage Pippalāda's answer to six questions posed by six learned Brahmins. The title of the Upaniṣad, *Praśna* ('question'), is derived from these questions; and each of its six chapters is also called a *praśna* or 'question'. This setting appears to be borrowed from the similar format in SB 10.6.1 and CU 5.11. Although the questions are diverse, they all focus on the centrality of breath within the cosmology and soteriology of the text.

The Praśna is traditionally ascribed to the Atharvaveda, and the name of the teacher of PU, Pippalāda, connects it to the Paippalāda branch of the Atharvaveda. The PU, nevertheless, has not come down to us as part of a larger Atharvavedic Brāhmaṇa. Just like the earlier verse Upaniṣads, the PU was composed, in all likelihood, as an independent text, possibly with a loose connection to the Atharvavedic tradition. Atharvavedic ascriptions are somewhat suspect because tradition considers almost all late Upaniṣads, beginning with the Muṇḍaka, as belonging to the Atharvaveda.

CONTENTS

QUESTION 1

SUKEŚA Bhāradvāja, Śaibya Satyakāma, Sauryāyaṇī Gārgya, Kausalya Āśvalāyana, Bhārgava Vaidarbhi, and Kabandhī Kātyānana—now these were men devoted to *brahman*, grounded in *brahman*, and in search of the highest *brahman*. They went to the Venerable Pippalāda carrying firewood in their hands, thinking: 'Surely, he will teach us all that.'

2 The seer told them: 'Live here for another year practising austerity, chastity, and faith. Ask all the questions you want, and, if I know, I will answer them all.'

3 Then Kabandhī Kātyānana came up to him and asked: 'Lord, from where do these creatures come?'

4 He told Kabandhī: 'The Lord of Creatures [Prajāpati], naturally, has a yearning for creatures. So he heated himself through exertion. When he had heated himself through exertion, he produced a couple—substance and lifebreath—thinking, "These two will turn out creatures for me in many different ways."

5 'Lifebreath is clearly the sun, while the moon is simply substance. And this whole world—both what has form and what is without form—is substance. Substance, therefore, is a form.

6 'Now, when the sun, as it rises, enters the eastern quarter, it thereby gathers the eastern lifebreaths in its rays. Likewise, when it illuminates the southern, the western, and the northern quarters, when it illuminates the nadir, the zenith, and the intermediate directions, when it illumines the whole world, it thereby gathers
all the lifebreaths in its rays. 7Here rises the fire common to all as
the dazzling lifebreath and fire! The same thing has been expressed in a Ṛgvedic verse:

8 Golden, dazzling, fiery;
the light, the highest course,
the one, the glowing—
Here rises the sun with a thousand rays,
moving in a hundred ways,
the lifebreath of created beings.

9 'Prajāpati is the year. It has two courses, the southern and the

northern. Now, those who venerate thus: "The best action is offerings to gods and priests!" win only the lunar world. They are the ones who return again. Therefore, the seers here who yearn for children proceed along the southern course. This course of the fathers, clearly, is substance.

10 'Those who seek the self by means of austerity, chastity, faith, and knowledge, on the other hand, proceed by the northern course and win the sun. Clearly, it is the abode of lifebreaths; it is the immortal, free from fear; it is the highest course; from it they do not return; and so, it is the final stoppage. On this there is this verse:

> 11 Some call him—
> a father with five feet and twelve parts,
> who dwells on the far side of the sky,
> at the very source.
> But others here call him—
> the radiant one on the near side,
> hitched to the one with seven wheels
> and six spokes.

12 'Prajāpati is the month. Substance is its dark fortnight, and lifebreath is its bright fortnight. Therefore, people here who are seers perform sacrifices during the bright fortnight, while others do so during the other fortnight.

13 'Prajāpati is the day and night, of which lifebreath is the day and substance is the night. So those who make love during the day spill their lifebreath, whereas making love during the night is the same as observing chastity.

14 'Prajāpati is food. From it comes semen; from semen are produced these creatures. 15 So, those who undertake the vow of Prajāpati produce a couple.

> To them belong the world of *brahman*,
> who practise chastity and austerity,
> in whom truth is well established.
> 16 To them belongs that stainless world of *brahman*
> in whom there is no crookedness,
> no falsehood or deceit.'

QUESTION 2

Then Bhārgava Vaidarbhi asked him: 'Lord, just how many deities are there who support a creature? Which of them, thus, become manifest? And which is the most excellent of them?'

2 He told Bhārgava: 'Space is such a deity, and so are wind, fire, waters, earth, speech, mind, sight, and hearing. As they become manifest, they say: "We are the ones who shore up this reed and support it."

3 'Lifebreath, the most excellent of them, told them: "Don't delude yourself! It is I who, dividing myself into five parts, shore up this reed and support it." But they didn't believe him. 4 So, out of pride, he started to set off. As he was setting off, then, all the others set off, and as he was settling down, they all settled down. Just as all the bees set off when the queen bee sets off, and settle down when she settles down, so did speech, mind, sight, and hearing. Delighted, then, they praised the lifebreath:

5 This burns as fire—this as sun;
This as rain and Maghavan, this as wind;
This as earth and the divine substance;
As real and not-real;
And what is immortal.

6 Ṛg verses, Yajus formulas, and Sāman chants;
The sacrifice, the Brahmin and Kṣatriya ranks—
Everything is fixed on lifebreath,
As spokes on the hub.

7 You are Prajāpati, you move in the womb;
it is also you who are born.
To you, Lifebreath, creatures bring tribute;
with the senses (*prāṇa*) you dwell.

8 You are the best bearer of offerings to the gods.
You are the first oblation to the fathers.
You are the truth that the seers practised,
the Atharvans and the Aṅgirases.

9 O Lifebreath—
by your radiance you are Indra!
as the guardian you are Rudra!
as the sun you move in mid-space;
you are the lord of lights!

10 O Lifebreath—
when you send down the rains,
these creatures of yours stand in joy,
thinking, "There'll be
as much food as we want!"

11 O Lifebreath—
you are the Vrātya, you are the lone seer,
you are the eater of all, the lord of the household!
we are the ones who give you food;
you are our father, Mātariśvan!

12 Your form that abides in speech,
Your form in hearing and in sight,
Your form extended within the mind,
Make them all propitious!
Do not depart from us!

13 In the power of lifebreath is this whole world,
As also what exists in the third heaven.
Protect us, as a mother, her sons.
Grant us prosperity and wisdom.'

QUESTION 3

Then Kausalya Āśvalāyana asked him: 'Lord, from what does this lifebreath arise? How does it enter this body? How does it divide itself and settle down? By what path does it set off? How is it designated outside the body (*ātman*) and how within the body?'

2 He told Kausalya: 'You ask too many questions! But since you are a very eminent Brahmin, I will answer you.

3 'The lifebreath here arises from the self (*ātman*).

As this shadow here, upon a man,
So this mind is stretched upon lifebreath;
And it enters by a path created by the mind.

4 'As only a sovereign king appoints administrators, telling them, "You govern these villages, and you govern these other villages," in just the same way the lifebreath here assigns the other breaths to their respective places. 5 The in-breath settles in the anus and the sexual organ, while the lifebreath itself settles in sight and

hearing through the mouth and nostrils. The link-breath (*samāna*), on the other hand, settles in the mid-region, for it makes the food that has been offered alike (*sama*). And from it arise these seven flames here.

6 'The self (*ātman*) resides within the very heart. There are 101 veins here in the body. Each of them branch into 100 more, and each of these branches into 72,000 more. Along these veins travels the link-breath. 7 Now, the up-breath rises up along one of these and conducts a person to a good world if he has done good deeds, to a bad world if he has done bad deeds, and to the world of men if he has done both.

8 'Now, the sun rises as the external lifebreath, for this conforms to the lifebreath residing within sight. The deity in the earth—that deity is there on account of the in-breath of a person. The space that is in between is the link-breath, and the wind is the inter-breath.

9–10 'The up-breath is fire. Therefore, when one's fire is extinguished, one returns again to the lifebreath with the faculties uniting in the mind and with whatever thought one then has. United with heat, then, the lifebreath, together with the self, leads him to the world that accords with his conception.

11 'When a man knows this and thus understands the lifebreath, his line of progeny will not be cut off, and he will become immortal. On this there is this verse:

12 The origin, entrance, position,
the fivefold expansion of lifebreath;
how it relates to what's in the body—
A man who knows this becomes immortal.'

QUESTION 4

Then Sauryāyaṇī Gārgya asked him: 'Lord, which are the ones that go to sleep within a person here? Which are the ones that keep awake in him? Which of these deities sees dreams? Who experiences this bliss? And which is the one in which all these are established?'

[2] He told Sauryāyaṇī: ‘As, when the sun is setting, all the rays of light gather together within that glowing orb and shoot out again every time it rises, so, Gārgya, all of them gather together within the highest deity—the mind. As a result, a person in that condition does not hear, does not see, does not smell, does not taste, does not feel, does not speak, does not grasp, does not experience sexual pleasure, does not excrete, and does not move about. About him people say: “He is asleep.”

[3] ‘It is the fires that are the breaths which keep awake in this fort. Clearly, the householder’s fire is this in-breath here, and the southern fire is the inter-breath. Because of its being taken out (*praṇayana*)—since it is taken out of the householder’s fire—the offertorial fire is the out-breath (*prāṇa*). [4] The link-breath (*samāna*) gets its name from the fact that it makes these two offerings alike (*sama*)—the exhalation and the inhalation. The patron of the sacrifice, clearly, is the mind. The very fruit of the sacrifice is the up-breath, and every day it conducts the patron of the sacrifice to *brahman*.

[5] ‘There, in sleep, this deity experiences his greatness. He sees again whatever he has seen before; he hears again the very things he has heard before; and he experiences over again what he has experienced before in various places and in remote regions. Being himself the whole world, he sees the whole world—things he has seen and things he has not seen, things he has heard and things he has not heard, things he has experienced and things he has not experienced, the real and the unreal.

[6] ‘When, however, he is overpowered by heat, this deity does not see any dreams here. Then, in this body there arises this bliss.

[7] ‘As birds rest on the tree where they nest, so, my friend, all these rest on the highest self (*ātman*)—[8] earth and the elements of earth; waters and the elements of water; fire and the elements of fire; wind and the elements of wind; space and the elements of space; sight and visible objects; hearing and aural objects; smell and olfactory objects; taste and gustatory objects; touch and tactile objects; speech and the objects of speech; hands and the objects that can be grasped; sexual organ and objects that can be enjoyed; anus and what can be excreted; feet and objects across which one can travel; mind and the objects of the mind; intellect and the objects of the intellect; the perception of ego and the objects

falling under that perception; reason and the objects of reason; light and the objects that can be illuminated; lifebreath and what it can support.

9 'This intelligent self, namely the Person—who is really the one who sees, feels, hears, smells, tastes, thinks, understands, and acts—rests on the highest, that is, the imperishable self, 10 and attains the highest, the imperishable.

'Whoever perceives that shining imperishable devoid of shadow, body, or blood—whoever so perceives, my friend—knowing the whole, he becomes the whole world. On this there is this verse:

> 11 That on which rest the breaths and beings,
> and, with all the deities, the intelligent self;
> Whoever knows that, my friend, as the imperishable;
> He, knowing the whole world,
> has entered the whole world indeed.'

QUESTION 5

Then Śaibya Satyakāma asked him: 'Lord, if some man were to meditate on the syllable OṂ [= AUṂ] until his death, what is the world that he would win through that meditation?'

2 He told Śaibya: 'Satyakāma, the syllable OṂ is clearly both the higher and the lower *brahman*. Either of these two, therefore, can be attained through this same medium by a man who knows it.

3 'If a man meditates on its first phoneme [A], he gets his knowledge just from that; so he comes back to earth very quickly and is led to the human world by the Ṛg verses. There, possessing a natural propensity for austerity, chastity, and faith, he enjoys greatness.

4 'If, on the other hand, a man becomes mentally absorbed in the first two phonemes [AU], he reaches the intermediate region and is led up to the lunar world by the Yajus formulas. After enjoying sovereign power in the lunar world, he returns.

5 'A man who meditates on that highest person by means of this very syllable OṂ with all three of its phonemes [AUṂ], on the contrary, enters into the effulgence in the sun. He becomes released from evil, just like a snake from his slough. He is led to the world

of *brahman* by the Sāman chants and beholds the fort-dwelling person far beyond this entire mass of living beings. On this there are these two verses:

6 The three phonemes lead to the deathless,
when they are combined,
joined to one another,
and not disjointed.
When they are rightly combined
in performances external, internal, or in between,
a man who knows does not tremble.

7 With Ṛg verses, this world;
With Yajus formulas, the mid-regions;
With Sāman chants, the place
which poets proclaim.
By OṂ alone as the support
Does a man who knows it attain
that which is serene,
beyond old age and death,
free from fear, the supreme.'

QUESTION 6

Then Sukeśa Bhāradvāja asked him: 'Hiraṇyanābha, a prince of Kosala, once came to me, Lord, and asked this question: "Do you know the person consisting of sixteen parts?" I told the prince: "I don't know him. If I had known him, how could I have not told you. Up to his very roots, surely, a man withers when he tells a lie. That's why I can't tell you a lie." He got on to his chariot silently and went away. So I ask you: Who is that person?'

2 He told Sukeśa: 'Right here within the body, my friend, is that person in whom the sixteen parts come into being.

3 'That person thought to himself: "Who is the one that when he sets off, I will set off and when he settles down, I will settle down?" 4 He then created the lifebreath, and from the lifebreath, faith, space, wind, fire, water, earth, senses, mind, and food; from food, strength, austerity, vedic formulas, rites, and worlds; and in the worlds, name.

5 'Now, take these rivers. They flow towards the ocean and, upon reaching it, merge into the ocean and lose their name and visible appearance; one simply calls it the ocean. In just the same way, these sixteen parts of the person who is the perceiver proceed towards the person and, upon reaching him, merge into that person, losing their names and visible appearances; one simply calls it the person. He then becomes partless and immortal. On this there is this verse:

> 6 In whom the parts are fixed,
> as spokes on a hub—
> You should know that person, who is to be known,
> so that death may not disturb you.'

7 Pippalāda then said to all of them: 'That is everything I know about this highest *brahman*, higher than which there is nothing.' 8 They praised him, saying: 'You are, indeed, our father, for you have taken us to the farthest shore beyond ignorance.'

Homage to the supreme seers! Homage to the supreme seers!

Māṇḍūkya Upaniṣad

THE Māṇḍūkya Upaniṣad is traditionally assigned to the Atharvaveda, even though several teachers called Māṇḍūkeya are listed in the literature of the Ṛgveda (e.g. AA 3.1). This small document deals with the sacred syllable OṂ and identifies it with the whole world, with Brahman, and with the self (*ātman*). The three constituent phonemes of the syllable OṂ are further identified with the three states of the self—the waking, the dreaming, and deep sleep. The historical importance of the MaU is dependent on the famous gloss, *Kārikā* (also called *Āgamaśāstra*), by Gauḍapāda, who is traditionally identified as the teacher of the teacher of Śaṃkara, the great exponent of monistic philosophy (Advaita Vedānta).

OṂ—this whole world is that syllable! Here is a further explanation of it. The past, the present, and the future—all that is simply
OṂ; and whatever else that is beyond the three times, that also is
simply OṂ—2 for this *brahman* is the Whole. *Brahman* is this self
(*ātman*); that [*brahman*] is this self (*ātman*) consisting of four
quarters.
3 The first quarter is Vaiśvānara—the Universal One—situated
in the waking state, perceiving what is outside, possessing seven
limbs and nineteen mouths, and enjoying gross things.
4 The second quarter is Taijasa—the Brilliant One—situated in
the state of dream, perceiving what is inside, possessing seven
limbs and nineteen mouths, and enjoying refined things.
5 The third quarter is Prājña—the Intelligent One—situated in
the state of deep sleep—deep sleep is when a sleeping man entertains no desires or sees no dreams—; become one, and thus being
a single mass of perception; consisting of bliss, and thus enjoying
bliss; and having thought as his mouth. 6 He is the Lord of all; he is
the knower of all; he is the inner controller; he is the womb of all—
for he is the origin and the dissolution of beings.
7 They consider the fourth quarter as perceiving neither what is
inside nor what is outside, nor even both together; not as a mass of
perception, neither as perceiving nor as not perceiving; as unseen;
as beyond the reach of ordinary transaction; as ungraspable; as
without distinguishing marks; as unthinkable; as indescribable; as
one whose essence is the perception of itself alone; as the cessation of the visible world; as tranquil; as auspicious; as without a
second. That is the self (*ātman*), and it is that which should be perceived.
8 With respect to syllables, OṂ is this very self (*ātman*); whereas with respect to the constituent phonemes of a syllable, it is as
follows. The constituent phonemes are the quarters, and the quarters are the constituent phonemes, namely, 'a', 'u', and 'm'.
9 The first constituent phoneme—'a'—is Vaiśvānara situated in
the waking state, so designated either because of obtaining (*āpti*)
or because of being first (*ādimattva*). Anyone who knows this is
sure to obtain all his desires and to become the first.
10 The second constituent phoneme—'u'—is Taijasa situated in
the state of dream, so designated either because of heightening
(*utkarṣa*) or because of being intermediate (*ubhayatva*). Anyone

who knows this is sure to heighten the continuity of knowledge and to become common; and a man without the knowledge of *brahman* will not be born in his lineage.

[11] The third constituent phoneme—'m'—is Prājña situated in the state of deep sleep, so designated either because of construction (*miti*) or because of destruction (*apīti*). Anyone who knows this is sure to construct this whole world and to become also its destruction.

[12] The fourth, on the other hand, is without constituent phonemes; beyond the reach of ordinary transaction; the cessation of the visible world; auspicious; and unique.

Accordingly, the very self (*ātman*) is OṂ. Anyone who knows this enters the self (*ātman*) by himself (*ātman*).

NOTES

The numbers which cue the notes refer to the internal divisions of the text as described in the Note on the Translation (p. lix)

Bṛhadāraṇyaka Upaniṣad

CHAPTER 1

1.1 *Sacrificial horse*: regarding the horse sacrifice, see Int., p. xliv. Here the bodily parts and activities of the sacrificial horse are equated with the diverse elements and phenomena of the universe (Int., p. liii). To understand some of the homologies, we must visualize the horse as standing facing the east (the same is true at BU 1.2.3). The head of the horse is here clearly distinguished from the body, and two sets of cosmic realities are related to elements of the head and the body, respectively.

fire common to all men: this fire (*vaiśvānara*) is somewhat ill-defined. It often refers to the sun, but also to the digestive fire in the body (BU 5.9) and to a specific ritual fire. Speculations regarding the identity of this fire (cf. SB 10.6.1) are found in the Brāhmaṇas, and those speculations dovetail into the search for the identity of *brahman* and the self in the Upaniṣads (cf. CU 5.11).

body: on the uses of the important term *ātman*, see Int., p. lv. The term frequently, as in this passage, refers to the physical body, here distinguished from the head, or to a living body as distinct from a corpse (BU 1.2.7). Throughout these Upaniṣads the two closely related meanings of 'body' and 'self' (as the essential core of a human being) are present whenever the term *ātman* is used, even though the one or the other meaning may occupy the foreground within a particular context (see CU 5.18.2n.).

1.2 *sacrificial cup*: the reference is to two special cups used for the Soma drink. Here these cups are identified with the day and the night.

demons: see BU 1.3.1n.

counterpart: on the technical meaning of this term (cf. BU 4.1.2), see Int., p. lii.

2 This section deals simultaneously with cosmogony and with the establishment of the horse sacrifice.

2.1 *In the beginning . . . in this way*: this is a passage full of word play and phonetic equivalences (see Int., p. liii). The Sanskrit verb *arc-* may mean 'to recite liturgical texts' or 'to shine', and it is related to the term *arka*, whose meanings include liturgical recitation, radiance, and lightning; it is also a technical term for a special sacred fire used in the horse sacrifice. The term *ka* has several meanings, most importantly water and pleasure. All these meanings of the terms appear to be implied in this long and intricate word play establishing connections among various things. Knowledge of these connections is facilitated by the perceived etymological relations between the words. The Sanskrit abstract nouns used to indicate these relationships imply both how a word originated and the true nature of the thing denoted by that word. I regularly use the somewhat awkward and long expression 'gave the name to and discloses the true nature of' to convey the pregnant meaning of the simple Sanskrit abstract nouns in these contexts.

death: as we see in the next section, the creative work of death, here personified as a deity, has both a ritual and a sexual dimension. Both involve toil (*tapas*) and exertion (*śrama*), two activities connected both with the ritual endeavours of the priests and the creative activities of the gods: see Kaelber 1989; Olivelle 1993, 9–11

water sprang from him: the water created by death is the cosmic waters, identified in the next section with the waters of the ocean whose foam created the dry land.

2.3 *He divided this body*: the body that death received was fire. Of the three parts, one remained as fire, while the other two became the sun and the wind.

the south-east and the north-east: the Sanskrit reads *asau cāsau ca* ('that and that') used here deictically to refer to the intermediate quarters, south-east, north-east, etc. Such expressions are common in these texts and testify to their oral character (see BU 1.4.6 n. and 'Note on the Translation').

2.4 *So, by means of . . . with hunger*: I follow the Mādhyandina reading *aśanāyāṃ* in preference to the Kāṇva *aśanāyā*. According to the latter reading, the translation would be: '. . . mind, death, that is, hunger, copulated with speech.'

bhāṇ: this term has a double meaning in Sanskrit. It is both the cry of a baby and a verbal root meaning 'to speak'.

2.5 *this whole world*: see BU 1.4.9–10 n.

eater of this whole world: food is a central theme in these documents. The metaphor of eater and food is used frequently to indicate the power of one over another. The rich and powerful are often compared to the eater, and the poor and weak to the food: see Rau 1957, 34–5; Geib 1976; Smith 1990. A good example of this metaphor is KsU 2.9. Eating the whole world, thus, means total dominion over the world.

2.7 *not to be confined in any way*: at a horse sacrifice, the sacrificial horse is let loose to wander at will for a year, during which time the king has to guard it without confining it. I follow the emendation suggested by Maue: *tam anavarudhyam ivāmanyata* (see Brereton 1982, 449).

repeated death: the meaning of this concept is not altogether clear, but the implication is that a person subject to this type of death would die a second or third time after his natural death on earth. This idea is important because it probably influenced the development of the pivotal doctrines of later religion: rebirth and *karma*. This concept does not exist in the early vedic texts, and its use is limited almost exclusively to the Upaniṣads. For a discussion of this concept in vedic texts and the possible location of its origin, see Witzel 1989, 201–2. In this sentence, the usual 'whoever knows this' is probably implied (see BU 3.2.7; 3.3.2).

3.1 *gods and demons*: in vedic mythology the gods (*deva*) were viewed as the natural adversaries of the demons (*asura*). The term demon is somewhat misleading, because both these classes are divine beings, here said to be the children of the same creator god/father, humans being the third class of his children (BU 5.2.1; CU 1.2.1). Ancient Iranian evidence from the Avesta show that *ahura* (= *asura*) was a term applied to high gods. In India, however, the *asuras* became demoted to a lower level and came to be viewed as demoniac and evil, even though the ancient meaning survives as when the epithet *asura* is applied to gods such as Varuṇa and Mitra. Gods were able to prevail over the demons because of their superior knowledge of the ritual techniques.

High Chant [udgītha]: the central part of a five-part hymn (*stotra*) sung during a Soma sacrifice (see CU 1.1.8–9n; 2.2.1n). In the Upaniṣads, the High Chant is often identified with the mystic syllable OṂ with which the High Chant opens (cf. CU 1.1.1 f.). The importance of this chant in the ritual and the Upaniṣadic ritual speculation is evidenced by the frequency of its use in the Upaniṣads, especially the CU.

3.2–6 *speech*: the reference here, and in parallel passages elsewhere in the Upaniṣads, is not to the external organs such as the eye or the ear but to the faculties of speech, sight, hearing, and thought, and to the power of breathing that gives vitality to all the faculties (Int., p. l). These vital functions are here and elsewhere personified and are often referred to as 'deities' (*deva*): see BU 1.3.9n. Discussions of the superiority of breath over the other vital functions are frequent: BU 1.5.21; 6.1.1–14; CU 5.1.6–5.2.2; KsU 2.13; 3.3; PU 2.1–4.

Udgātṛ: see Int., p. xlii.

3.8 *Ayāsya*: this etymological play derives the term for the breath within the mouth (*ayāsya*) from *ayam* ('here') *āsye* ('within the mouth'); the term is further seen as related to a well-known seer Ayāsya Āṅgirasa, the latter term being derived from: 'of the bodily parts' (*aṅga*) 'the essence' (*rasa*). Thus breath is seen as what gives life and vitality to the various parts of the body. In the parallel passage at BU 1.3.19, a part of the body from which breath departs is said to wither.

3.9 *this same deity*: i.e., the breath within the mouth. The term *devatā* (and also *deva*: lit. 'god' or 'deity') is used in these texts with a broad range of meanings that may appear confusing to the English reader with a restricted notion of divinity. Often, as in this and the following passages (§§ 10–18), the term refers to various vital functions of the body. In other instances, the term is used with reference to cosmic realities, such as the sun, moon, and fire. In a similar way, the phrase 'the divine sphere' (*adhidaivam*) refers to these cosmic entities, as opposed to what pertains to the human body (*adhyātman*): see BU 1.5.22.

3.17 *supply of food*: I translate the somewhat unclear compound *annādya* as 'supply of food' or 'foodstuff'. The first term, *anna*, means food; the second term may be either *adya* or *ādya* (Rau 1957, 34), and may mean 'fit to be eaten' or simply 'food'. What the compounding of these terms specifically means is unclear. Sometimes the compound appears to be synonymous with the simple *anna* ('food'). I think, however, that the expression has the meanings of 'the food that is under one's control' (that is, food that one can consume independently, as opposed to food that one must receive from others) and 'foodstuff' (that is, anything that may be used as food). See Willman-Grabowska 1928, 2: 47–50; she concludes that the compound may mean an abundance of food.

3.19 *Ayāsya*: see BU 1.3.8n.; cf. CU 6.11.

3.20 *Bṛhatī*: a type of metre with 36 syllables in a stanza of four lines with 8, 8, 12, and 8 syllables, respectively. The term can also mean large or great.

3.21 *Brahman*: the term here means a sacred utterance, especially the ritual formulas contained in the Vedas. In this sense, the term is often used as a synonym of Veda. The transition, however, from this and similar meanings, to 'formulation of truth' (see BU 2.1.1 n.) and finally to the abstract meaning of the source of reality or the absolute reality is made easily and imperceptibly; often several of these meanings appear to operate at the same time.

3.22–3 *And it is . . . it is the High Chant*: see CU 1.6.1–8 for a parallel text.

Sāman: a liturgical text that is sung, as opposed to others, such as Ṛg and Yajus, that are recited. The Sāmans are contained in the Sāmaveda. See Int., p. xliv.

held up: the prefix *ut* in Sanskrit can indicate several related senses, including up, high, and loud. This allows it to be connected with *uttabdha* ('held up').

3.24 *King Soma*: Soma, the drink that was at the heart of the vedic ritual (Int., p. xlv), was divinized early in vedic mythology. He is often identified with the moon and 'king' is frequently attached to his name. See Macdonell 1898, 104–15.

make my head shatter apart: this expression has been subject to much discussion. The Sanskrit verb *vi-pat-* can have the meaning 'fly off in many directions' or 'burst asunder'. The expression, as Insler (1989–90) has pointed out, may have been used metaphorically at first to mean something like our colloquial use 'blow your mind', or 'go nuts'. Thus, when one enquires too much about things better left alone, one may say 'you will go crazy if you continue to think about it' (see this usage in BU 3.6.1). The metaphor may have been turned into a threat and a curse with fatal consequences later on, and the myth of the shattering of Śākalya's head (see BU 3.9.26) may have been the basis of this transformation.

3.24–6 *wealth, gold... tone*: the connection between 'wealth' (*sva*) and 'tone' (*svara*) is established by their phonetic similarity in Sanskrit. In a similar way, 'gold' (*suvarṇa*) is related to tone.

voice, speech: throughout this passage, the translation uses 'speech' and 'voice' to translate the same Sanskrit word *vāc*, a word that captures both meanings.

3.28 *purificatory lauds* [pavamāna or bahiṣpavamāna]: a set of ritual formulas sung at a Soma sacrifice (see CU 1.12.4 n.; 2.2.1 n.). The entire ritual is too complex to be described here. For a description (which may be too technical for the ordinary reader), see Kane 1962–75, ii, 1166–70.

3.28 *Prastoṭr*: one of the Sāmavedic priests, the chief among whom is the Udgāṭr. See Int., p. xlii.

Introductory Praise: the first of the five parts into which a Sāman is divided. For a detailed description, see CU 2.2.1 n.

world conquest: the possession of a world or a living space (*loka*) is one of the main objectives of the vedic religious practice. Proper rituals, ritual knowledge, and a son are all said to assure a person of such a world after death. For extended meanings of this term, see BU 1.4.16. For a detailed discussion, see Gonda 1966.

4.5 *From this 'creation' came into being*: the term 'creation' probably refers both to the physical creation and to the term 'creation' (BU 1.2.1 n), highlighting the close association in vedic thought between an object and its name (see also BU 1.4.1). The same close connection is found in the frequently used expression 'name and visible appearance' (*nāmarūpa*) to indicate a distinct physical reality (e.g. BU 1.4.7). This account of creation shows how both things and their names originated.

4.6 *churned like this*: this is a good example of the oral nature of these texts. The reciter would have demonstrated, by churning with his palms and blowing with his mouth, exactly what 'like this' meant. The reference is to how a fire is produced by using a fire-drill, which consists of a bottom slab with a centre depression on which a long stick is twirled either with the hands or using a string wrapped around it. The resultant friction ignited the tinder placed on the slab. The blowing with the mouth would make the fire blaze. The depression on the slab is often compared to a vagina, and the churning stick to a penis. The entire production of fire by this method has highly sexual connotations, as suggested by the rest of this passage dealing with semen. The fire that chars the depression in the slab makes it smooth and without fibrous material (hair), just like the insides of a vagina; the text also points out the original reason why the mouth and palms lost their hair. Here too the oral nature is evident, because the text only says: 'the inner sides of both these are without hair'; the reciter would then be pointing to his palms and mouth. See Note on the Translation, p. lix.

Food and eater: see BU 1.2.5 n.

gods superior to brahman: see BU 1.4.11.

4.7 *name and visible appearance*: see BU 1.4.5 n. The term *rūpa* has been traditionally translated as 'form'. I believe that this is misleading, especially if we give 'form' a philosophical, or even Aristotelian, connotation. Bodewitz (1985) has shown that *viśvarūpa* (lit. 'omniform'), a term used especially with reference to the sun (see e.g. CU 5.13.1) and gold, actually means having many shining colours, and therefore, glittering or dazzling: 'Evidence for the interpretation of the *-rūpa* compounds as referring to color and outward impression ('glitter') rather than to form has been adduced from the oldest Vedic literature' (Bodewitz 1985, 16). The term *rūpa* may refer to more than mere colour (for example also to shape), but it clearly indicates the way something appears to our sight (see BU 1.6.2).

termite: the meaning of the term *viśvaṃbhara* (also at KsU 4.20), here translated as termite, is unclear. Suggested meanings include fire, insect, and scorpion: see Hume's note to BU 1.4.7 and Frenz's (1968–9) translation of KsU 4.20. The term may refer not specifically to termites, but to ants and anthills in general.

4.8 *it is dearer*: on the self as the most dear thing, see BU 2.4.5; 4.5.6.

4.9–10 *the Whole*: the exact sense of the term *sarva*, here translated as 'the Whole', has been much debated. As Gonda 1955*a* has shown, the term in its earliest usage did not mean 'everything' but carried the sense of completeness, wholeness, and health. It is, thus, opposed to what is partial, broken, sick, or hurt. In the Upaniṣads the term is used to indicate not all things in the universe but a higher-level totality that encompasses the universe. Gonda (1955a, 64) observes that the phrase *sarvaṃ khalv idaṃ brahma* at CU 3.14.1 does not mean ' "*Brahman* is everything here", but "*Brahman* is the complete here, this whole (one)", or: "*Brahman* is what is the whole, complete here, is what is entire, perfect, with no part lacking, what is safe and well etc., i.e. Completeness, Totality, the All seen as the Whole." ' Unless the context dictates otherwise, I translate *sarvam* throughout as 'the Whole', and the phrase *idaṃ sarvam* as 'this whole world'. To the English reader the term 'whole' should evoke the senses of totality and completeness (all there is), as well as perfection, soundness, and wholesomeness.

4.11 *In the beginning . . . better than him*: *brahman*, the source of the universe, is here connected with both the priestly power and the Brahmin class (see BU 1.4.15), while the ruling power and the Kṣatriya class are connected with the gods. Thus the Brahmin becomes the source or womb (*yoni*) of the Kṣatriya, even as the Kṣatriya surpasses the Brahmin in power. On a Brahmin prostrating himself before a Kṣatriya, see Rau 1957, 70. Note that here and in the following paragraphs the terms for the power or state of a Brahmin, Kṣatriya, etc. (*brahma, kṣatra*) can at the same time refer to actual people of these social classes (*brāhmaṇa, kṣatriya*).

4.11 *worse* (pāpīyān), *better* (śreyān): these terms should be understood within the context of the class distinctions existent within ancient Indian society. The 'worse' are people who are poor and powerless, while the 'better' are the rich and the powerful. The two terms frequently refer specifically to the economic standing of a person, as at CU 4.16.3. For a discussion of these terms, see Rau 1957, 32–4.

4.12 *Vasus . . . Maruts*: on these divine groups, see BU 3.9.2–5; CU 3.16.1 n, 5 n.

4.15 *find a world*: see BU 1.3.28 n.

after his death: the Sanskrit term *antataḥ* may also mean 'in the end'. I do not think, however, that the reference here is to the exhaustion of merit in a heavenly world which, within the context of the rebirth theory, causes a man to be reborn again in this world.

produce whatever he desires: see CU 8.2

4.16 *he makes offerings and sacrifices*: the words for making offerings and sacrifices (*juhoti* and *yajate*) are technical terms. The first refers to the pouring of ghee (*homa*) into the offertorial fire while saying *svāhā*, while the second is the oblation of various sacrificial materials while saying *vaṣaṭ*. Together they appear to comprehend all forms of sacrificial acts. Becoming a world here may be a reference to the doctrine of debts: Olivelle 1993, 46–53.

4.17 *the full extent of desire*: see BU 3.5.1; 4.4.22.

fivefold: five was a sacred number. The sacrifice is frequently said to be fivefold, and a variety of reasons are given for this, for example, the five types of vegetable offerings (TS 6.5.11.4). Further, the year consists of the five seasons, the four common ones plus the rainy season. Here the fivefoldness of reality is reduced to the five components of a human being. A man's completeness is to be found within himself, and not in a wife, son, or ritual. See Olivelle 1993, 54.

5.1 *Why aren't they exhausted*: the reference is to the seven kinds of food.

The man who knows it: i.e. food. This is a difficult passage and the translation is uncertain. The sense appears to be that a man who knows food to be inexhaustible and the reason for its being inexhaustible (i.e. the Person) assures himself of an inexhaustible supply of food.

5.2 *one should not offer sacrifices endlessly*: the meaning of *iṣṭiyājuka*, which I have translated 'offer sacrifices endlessly', is unclear. Others take *iṣṭi* as 'wish', and translate: 'one should not sacrifice to obtain a wish.' But the context favours interpreting *iṣṭi* as sacrifice. Perhaps the meaning is that the new and full moon sacrifices are sufficient, and one should not sacrifice all the time. A similar view is expressed later with reference to the offering of milk during a whole year, the author asserting that one needs to do that just once.

All beings depend . . . that do not: the statement that those who breathe, as well as those that do not, live on milk is unclear. Perhaps those that do not breathe may be foetuses, who live on the mother's blood (= milk), or plants that live on milky sap.

repeated death: see BU 1.2.7 n.

Person: I regularly translate the Sanskrit term *puruṣa* as 'Person', unless the term refers clearly to a male human being. The term literally means 'man', but in this literature it has cosmological and cosmogonic dimensions and often refers to the creator. See Int., p. xxvii.

5.3 *Every sound . . . the latter is not*: the phrase 'for the former is fixed up to its limit [i.e. on speech], whereas the latter is not [fixed on anything]' is extremely obscure and elliptic. As Brereton (1988, 6) has shown, the meaning probably is that 'all sound has a distinct beginning, an end and an identifiable form; therefore, it is limited and structured. Speech, on the other hand, is not always articulated; and therefore it does not always have a limit, a fixed place, or a determined arrangement. All sound is the "speech" of a being or an object . . . but not all speech is heard, and therefore not all speech is sound.'

Out-breath . . . link-breath: on the five types of breath, see Int., p. li.

5.4 *the middle world*: the atmosphere, the region where birds fly and the clouds move.

the world above: the sky or heaven, where the sun, moon, and celestial bodies move.

5.7 *the father . . . is breath*: the order (speech, mind, breath) is here broken. Perhaps, as Limaye and Vadekar (1958, 193) note, we should read 'mother, father, and child', in which case the normal order would be restored.

5.12 *This pair*: the identity of the pair that copulated is unclear. They could be speech and mind (so Deussen 1897), or sun and fire (so Müller 1879–84 and Hume 1931), or sky and earth. Since the sky and sun are identified with the mind, and the earth and fire with speech, in some sense the pair may consist of these two sets of three.

5.14 *Prajāpati is the year*: the year is identified with totality and immortality, and, therefore, with the creator god Prajāpati. It is here taken as consisting of lunar months, and Prajāpati is thus identified with the moon. The moon's fifteen digits are inconstant, as they disappear one by one each night. The sixteenth is the constant part, which never disappears; it is by means of it that the moon reappears after the night of the new moon.

any being that sustains life: as Wezler (1992, 406–7) has shown, the term *prāṇabhṛt* in all likelihood refers not to all living beings (i.e. those who have breath) but to the animals that support human life, that is, animals that are eaten by humans.

5.15 *wheel-plate*: the meaning of *pradhi* here is uncertain. It is generally translated as 'rim, felly', and the grammatical subject of the final saying *pradhināgāt* ('He went with the rim') is generally taken to be a man who lost his wealth. To make any sense of this, then, one has to add (following the commentator Śaṃkara, but I believe unjustifiably) the word 'lost', and translate the saying as: 'He has come off with the loss of a felly!' (Hume 1931). I think the subject of the saying is not the man who lost the wealth but the robber who plundered it. Thus, if the robbed man is still alive, his friends might breathe a sigh of relief and say, 'Thank God! The robber got away with just the wheel-plate, [i.e. the external things that can be replaced], but at least you [i.e. the hub] are all right.' This is probably the meaning of this pithy saying. The term *pradhi*, moreover, probably means not the rim but the section from the hub (wheel-head) to the rim of a wheel, that is, the wheel-plate, and the wheel in question was probably solid rather than made with spokes. The solid wheel-plate, moreover, was made of several sections, and it is possible that *pradhi* refers to these sections, especially to the half-moon shaped sections at each end (see examples in Sparreboom 1985). Another interpretation is offered by Joel Brereton (personal communication). If the wheel consisted of many pieces called *pradhi*, then the meaning could be that the person robbed escaped with just one such piece. This makes sense within the context of a race; even if the entire chariot is destroyed, a man may win the race if he just attaches a piece of the wheel to the horse or bull and crosses the finishing-line (see, for example, the story of Mudgala in RV 10.102). The expression would then be metaphorical, as our 'on a wing and a prayer'. For the metaphor of the wheel, see BU 2.5.15; CU 7.15.1; KsU 3.8; MU 2.2.6; PU 2.6; 6.6; SU 1.4.

5.17 *rite of transfer*: for a detailed study of this rite performed when a person is about to die, and on old age in general, see Sprockhoff

1979; see also Olivelle 1993, 123–6. A version of this rite is given in KsU 2.14.

By becoming the Whole . . . from here: this is probably the wish of the father; it is, however, unclear whether it is spoken out loud or expresses merely his thought. On the term 'Whole', see BU 1.4.9–10 n.

son: a common etymology of *putra* ('son') derives it from two words *put* (the name of a hell) and *trā-* ('to rescue'). Thus, a son is 'son' because he rescues the father from the Put hell, or, as in this passage, he rescues the father from his sins: see Sprockhoff 1979, 388–9; Olivelle 1993, 46.

vital functions: the term *prāṇa* (lit. 'breath') is used frequently in the Upaniṣads to refer to all or some of the vital functions, including the five senses, the mind, other mental faculties, and the various breaths (see BU 3.9.26). The reason for this is made clear in BU 1.5.21. Here the vital functions are the three mentioned as the three types of food that Prajāpati reserved for himself, that is, mind, speech, and breath (BU 1.5.3).

5.21 *compete with each other*: on the relative superiority of the vital functions, see BU 1.3.2–6 n. The central breath here appears to be the same as the divine breath at BU 1.5.20; see also BU 2.2.1.

5.22 *divine sphere*: on the use of *deva* ('divine') with reference to cosmic entities, see BU 1.3.9 n.

The other deities disappear: the reference is probably to the fact the sun and the moon set, and a fire is extinguished.

5.23 *From which . . . and tomorrow*: see AV 10.8.16; KaU 4.9. The term 'law' (*dharma*) here refers to ritual and moral rules: see KaU 4.14 n.

6.1 *visible appearance* [rūpa]: see BU 1.4.7 n.

Uktha, brahman, Sāman: Uktha is the technical term for Ṛgvedic verses that are recited during a sacrifice (cf. BU 1.3.22–3 n). The term *brahman* (cf. BU 1.3.21 n.) in this passage refers, in all likelihood, to the Yajus formulas. The basis for the triple identification here is again the phonetic similarity of the terms—*uktha* and *uttiṣṭhati* ('arises'); *sāman* and *sama* ('same'); *brahman* and *bibharti* ('bears'). On the cosmic identification of the three types of vedic formulas, see CU 1.6.

6.3 *body*: the term *ātman* here may have a connotation wider than 'body', but is still not the abstract universal 'Self' of later philosophy. The term here possibly refers to the concrete individuality of a person that is the basis of all actions, an individuality that includes, but may not be limited to, the bodily existence of the person.

6.3 *veiled*: on the veiling of the immortal, see CU 8.3.1–3.

the real: here opposed to the immortal, is the manifest world: see BU 2.3.1; 5.5.1.

CHAPTER 2

1.1 *Dṛpta-Bālāki*: this expression can also mean 'the proud Bālāki', and the context appear to show that he was indeed proud. It is unclear whether *dṛpta* is part of his name or merely an epithet; in Sanskrit folk tales, the meaning of a name often indicates the character of the person. For a variant of this story, see KsU 4.1.

Here's a Janaka: the fame of Janaka, an ancient king of Videha, evidently was already widespread when this story about Ajātaśatru was put together.

formulation of truth; the term *brahman* here straddles the meanings of 'formulation of truth' (Thieme 1952, 117 f.; Int., p. lvi) and 'the ultimate reality': see also CU 1.7.5. As Thieme (1952, 119, n 3) has pointed out, the grammar of the sentence makes '*brahman*' the direct object of 'tell', and makes it unlikely that the sentence would mean 'Let me tell you *about brahman*.' In some places, such as CU 3.5.1–2, *brahman* appears to be a body of texts, parallel to other vedic collections.

1.2 *venerate*: see BU 4.1.1 n.

I venerate . . . and king: there is an *iti*, the Sanskrit marker for the end of a quotation, after this sentence. Thus, the last sentence here and in the following paragraphs (§§ 3–13) may be an editorial comment rather than a part of the quote ascribed to Ajātaśatru (so Max Müller 1879–84 and Deussen 1897). I think it more likely to be part of the quote.

1.4 *radiant*: the Sanskrit *tejasvin*, like the English 'brilliant', carries here the literal meaning of 'shining' and 'radiant' (lightning), as well as the extended meanings of 'distinguished' and 'having great talent' (children).

1.5 *non-depleting*: the term *apravartin* is generally translated as 'inactive', or 'quiescent'; but *pra-vṛt-* can refer to a vessel that is overturned or spilled and is thus opposed to a vessel that is full (Brereton, personal communication). Space is thus full and always remains full. See also CU 3.12.9.

1.6 *Vaikuṇṭha*: the meaning of this term, which later becomes an epithet associated with Viṣṇu, is unclear. Renou (1948, 63) suggests the meaning 'not blunted', i.e. always sharp. I take the term *senā* to mean a weapon rather than an army, the reference, as with Vaikuṇṭha, being to Indra's weapon.

1.8 *resemblance*: the reference here is to the reflection that one sees in water (see CU 8.8).

1.17 *the space within the heart*: see BU 2.3.3; 4.2.3; 4.4.22; CU 8.1.1–3; TU 1.6.1; MuU 2.2.6.

1.19 *the veins of the heart*: see BU 4.2.3; 4.3.20; KsU 4.19.

He slips out of the heart : the reference, in all likelihood, is to the person consisting of perception mentioned in § 17.

height of sexual bliss: I take *atighnīm ānandasya* as referring not just to 'the summit of bliss' but to the apparent loss of awareness resulting from orgasmic bliss. Otherwise the comparison makes little sense, since the point the author wishes to make is that in deep sleep a person enjoys bliss but is not conscious of anything.

1.20 *As a spider . . . from a fire*: for these images, see MuU 1.1.7; 2.1.1; SU 6.10.

Its hidden name: the phrase 'The real behind the real' is called here '*upaniṣad*', which I have translated as 'hidden name' following BU 2.3.6, where the same phrase is called the 'name'. Renou (1946, 57) takes *upaniṣad* here to have the primitive meaning of 'connection'.

The real behind the real [satyasya satyam]: for this and related formulations, see Ortel 1937 (especially p. 28). Such expressions appear to refer to the essential core of something, here the 'truly real' or the quintessence of what is normally perceived as the real. In other expressions, such as 'the sight of sight' or 'the hearing of hearing' (cf. BU 4.4.18; SU 1.2; Ortel 1937, 27), the meaning appears to include the power or the entity that is behind the external act of seeing or hearing, i.e. that without which hearing would not take place. In this sense food is said to be the 'breath of breath' in TA 3.7.3.

2 This entire section is obscure and full of riddles. Brereton (1991) has attempted with some success to make sense of it, but much still remains unclear. The central point Brereton makes is that throughout this passage the riddles and their explanations refer simultaneously to the human body and the celestial bodies, especially the sun and the seven stars of the Big Dipper. I am indebted to him for the following explanations.

2.1 *youngling*: the term *śiśu* can refer to a child or the young of an animal (here, possibly a horse), as well as to the fire and the sun.

2.1 *placement* [ādhāna] *counterplacement* [pratyādhāna]: these terms are obscure. The former can mean a bridle, but is more commonly used with reference to the placing of the sacrificial fire. The latter (a hapax) must mean something that stands counter to or opposite the former. Brereton thinks that the two terms at the cosmic level may refer to the two places of fire, on earth as fire and in the sky as the sun. The explanatory portion identifies the youngling as the central breath, which is located at the navel (BU 1.5.21–2). The placement and counterplacement of that breath are indicated with the repetition of the deictic pronoun *idam* ('this' or 'here'), common in these oral compositions. Many translators, following the commentator Śaṃkara, take the two to mean the head and the body. Brereton thinks that they may refer to the upper and lower halves of the body, on the one hand, and to the earth and sky, on the other.

2.3 *There is a cup . . . joined to brahman*: this verse is adapted from AV 19.49.8. The cup is probably the sky that appears as a bowl or, more specifically, the northern sky where Ursa Major and the Pole Star—stars that never set—are visible. 'Dazzling splendour' may be a reference to the sun. On the meaning of *viśvarūpa* as dazzling, see BU 1.4.7 n. The seven seers are the seven stars of Ursa Major; their names are given in § 4. The reference to speech in the last line, which is different from the AV reading, as well as the appended commentary, overlays the image of the head upon that of the sky, inviting the reader to see the connections between the two.

2.4 *Gotama and Bharadvāja . . . with speech*: vedic mythology considered the seven stars of Ursa Major as these seven seers; for a detailed account of them see Mitchiner 1982. Here these seers/stars are identified with the seven organs located in the head. The Sanskrit, once again, uses deictic pronouns to refer to these organs. In an oral exposition, the teacher would have pointed with his hand to the respective organs as he said 'this'. The organs given within brackets follow the explanation of the commentator Śaṃkara; one can, however, never be sure of these identifications (see Brereton, 1991, 2–7).

speech: the Sanskrit term *vāc* refers to both the function and the organ of speech, and the passage from the first (in § 3) to the second (in § 4) is often imperceptible. Here, speech with which one eats is, of course, the tongue or the entire mouth.

eater, food: on this metaphor, see BU 1.2.5 n.

3.1 *Sat, Tyam*: these are the component phonemes of the term *satyam* ('the real'), which is viewed as signifying the totality of the real.

The two phonemes refer to the two aspects of this totality, but what each refers to is unclear. Following KsU 1.6, I take Sat (lit. 'the existent') to refer to the visible and mortal world, and Tyam to the invisible and the immortal. Other passages analyse this word differently, making Sat the immortal component: see CU 8.3.4–5; this interpretation is followed by Jamison (1986, 167) and Brereton (see ibid., n. 5). For a study of *satyam*, see van Buitenen 1968.

3.2 *That which gives warmth*: i.e. the sun.

3.4 *this body itself*: the original has just the deictic pronoun *idam* ('this'), which here probably refers to the whole body. The space within the body may be the same as the space within the heart that is the subject of much speculation in the Upaniṣads: see BU 2.1.17 n.

3.5 *The person within the right eye*: for parallels, see BU 5.5.2; CU 1.7.5; 4.15.1; 8.7.5.

3.6 *red bug*: the exact zoological species referred to by the term *indragopa* ('red bug' taking bug in its colloquial American sense of a tiny creature) is unclear. Lienhard (1978) has shown that the earlier translations as firefly and cochineal are inaccurate, and that the term refers to a tiny velvety red mite (*Trombidiiae*) that appears in large numbers in India early in the rainy season and is totally harmless.

rule of substitution: I take *ādeśa* here as a technical term in the grammatical tradition for the rule of substitution, that is, one form of a word that stands as a substitute for another (see Thieme 1968*b*). It is a general maxim that the substitute behaves like the original (*sthānin*). Such rules within the Upaniṣadic tradition are said to be 'secret' (e.g. in CU 3.5.1), thus approximating the meaning of *upaniṣad*. In the present context, when the self is described in words other than itself, one has to insert the negative particle *na* ('not'). The phrase *neti neti*, commonly translated as 'not thus, not thus', has been the subject of much discussion both within the indigenous exegetical traditions and among modern scholars. I think the *iti* here has been over interpreted; it is merely a device to refer to the preceding word, i.e. 'the word *na*'. This is clearly brought out in the other places where the same expression is used, and where it is followed by the use of 'not' in a series of phrases. The point, however, is that in referring to the self all statement must carry the negative particle *na*. See BU 3.9.26; 4.2.4; 4.4.22; 4.5.15. For 'substitution', see also CU 3.18.1 n.

the real behind the real: see BU 2.1.20 n. For other enigmatic phrases with reference to the ultimate, see CU 3.14.1 n.

4 For another version of this story with a longer introduction, see BU 4.5. Both versions have been studied in detail by Hanfeld 1976, 71–115. It appears that the BU 4.5 version is later for a variety of reasons, including the fact that it interprets Yājñavalkya's departure specifically as ascetic renunciation (see BU 4.5.1 n.).

4.1 *Maitreyī, Katyāyanī* : the two wives of Yājñavalkya.

I am about to depart: the reason for Yājñavalkya's departure is not stated, but, following the interpretation of the version in BU 4.5.1 (see note to this), it is traditionally assumed that he was leaving home to assume an ascetic form of life. In this version, however, the setting is probably the imminent death of Yājñavalkya, which would necessitate the partitioning of his estate (Sprockhoff 1981, 68–76). It is recognized in ancient Indian law that a father can divide his property among his sons while he is still alive. On the issue relating to the partitioning of ancestral property, see Kane 1962–75, iii. 563–72.

settlement: here probably refers to a division of property between the two wives, or at least making some provision for their livelihood.

4.5 *One holds a husband dear*: there is a nice transition here from the common meaning of 'dear' in § 4 to its more sophisticated meaning in § 5, which enquires into the underlying reason why various people and positions are dear to a man. For the same theme, see BU 1.4.8.

love for oneself: I think the text uses *ātman* as a reflexive pronoun 'oneself' or 'himself' in the first part, and gradually shifts to a more philosophical sense of the term as 'self' towards the end of § 5 and in §§ 6 and 14.

children: the term *putra* is literally 'son', but here in the plural I think it has a broader meaning of children irrespective of their gender.

priestly power, royal power: the terms *brahma* and *kṣatra* indicate the power or essence of the derivative terms *brāhmaṇa* and *kṣatriya*. Brereton ('Yājñavalkya's Curse', 9) thinks *brahma* here 'refers to the ability to formulate the truth' (see BU 2.1.1 n.).

4.6 *May the priestly power forsake*: following Brereton ('Yājñavalkya's Curse'), I take the verb *parādāt* as an injunctive verb expressing a wish, here amounting to a curse. Others take it as an aorist and translate: 'The Brahmin's position has forsaken anyone.'

4.7–9 *It is like this . . . that lute*: for a similar statement, see KsU 3.8.

4.10 *Ṛgveda . . . glosses*: regarding this list of traditional vedic learning, see Horsch 1966, 5–45; Faddegon 1926; CU 7.1.2 n. In these lists the terms Ṛgveda, Yajurveda, and Sāmaveda refer only to the three vedic 'collections' (*saṃhitā*). Atharva-Aṅgiras probably refers to the texts that are sometime named simply Atharvan (CU 7.1.2) and later came to be called the Atharvaveda. The 'sciences' here probably refer to the various bodies of traditional lore relating to such things as snakes and stars. The difference between 'explanation' (*anuvyākhyāna*) and 'gloss' (*vyākhyāna*) is uncertain, although both refer to exegetical elaborations of a root text.

4.11 *point of convergence* [ekāyana]: see CU 7.1.2 n.; 7.4–5.

4.12 *When a chunk . . . no awareness*: this simile, especially the final statement about the nature, the rise, and the disappearance of the Immense Being, must have caused some problems already to the editor of the version at BU 4.5.13 for him to amend the reading. It has caused problems also to modern scholars, especially with regard to how the Immense Being could arise out of 'these beings' and be destroyed (which is the literal meaning of *vinaśyati*) with them. I have followed Hanfeld's (1976, 79–81 n. 6) explanation. The meaning is that the Immense Being, here identified with the self, comes into view in this world through the medium of the vital functions (which I take to be the meaning of 'these beings') and disappears with them at death. A detailed explanation of how this happens is given at BU 4.3.19–38; 4.4.1–2. In fact, the simile in this version, with the piece of salt which is visible at one time and invisible at another, is more to the point than the one given at BU 4.5.13.

4.13 *Look . . . to perceive*: I follow Thieme (1968*a*) in translating the somewhat elliptic final phrase and in taking the deictic *idaṃ* ('this') to mean 'this body'. This fits with what follows, because duality is based on the body, which houses the vital functions. Others take the phrase to mean that 'this', i.e. what Yājñavalkya had just stated, is capable of being understood.

4.14 *For when . . . perceive the perceiver*: for similar statements, see BU 3.4.2; 4.3.31; 4.5.15. For the reason why the self does not perceive either after death or in deep sleep, see BU 4.3.23–31 n.

5.1 *in the case of the body*: it is awkward, I understand, to translate *ātman* as both body and self within the same paragraph (see also §§ 14–15; Int., p. xlix). But I think there is a similar shift in emphasis from the body to the self in the original. Unfortunately, in English we cannot use the same word to express both meanings and are forced to make these uncomfortable and awkward selections. The parenthetical insertion of the Sanskrit term is meant to help the English reader see the subtlety of the shift in the original. On the doctrine of honey, see also CU 3.1–11.

5.15 *As all the spokes . . . wheel*: on the image of the wheel, see BU 1.5. 15n.

5.16 *As thunder . . . to you*: RV 1.116.12. Briefly, the story behind this passage is as follows. Dadhyañc knew the place where the honey was located but had been forbidden by Indra from revealing it. The Aśvins resorted to the strategy of replacing Dadhyañc's head with that of a horse. Dadhyañc then taught it to the Aśvins, and, when Indra carried out his threat, the Aśvins restored Dadhyañc's original head. See Macdonell 1898, 141–2. The heroes to whom the verse is addressed are the Aśvins, and their wonderful skill is related to the substitution of the horse's head. In this and the following paragraphs, the author identifies the honey-doctrine given earlier with the mythical teaching imparted by Dadhyañc to the Aśvins (see the genealogy of teachers at BU 2.6).

5.17 *You fixed . . . with you*: RV 1.117.22.

5.18 *fort*: a metaphor for the body, and especially for the cavity in the heart. See KaU 5.1 (fort with eleven gates); MuU 2.2.7*a*; SU 1.6; 3.18. Here again we have phonetic equivalences: *puruṣa* ('Person', sometime the soul) is so called because he dwells (*śaya*) in the fort (*pura*). The two-footed are humans, and the four–footed are animals. A bird, more often a goose, is a common symbol for the soul and the sun (see Vogel 1962).

5.19 *Of every form . . . in many forms*: RV 6.47.18.

CHAPTER 3

1.1 *Videha, Kuru, Pañcāla*: for the geography of these regions, see Fig. 2 and the List of Names. The Brahmins of the Kuru-Pañcāla region were viewed as the most eminent, and it is likely that many of the Brāhmaṇa texts were composed in that region (see Witzel 1987). The underlying message of this text is that Yājñavalkya had the courage to challenge, the cunning to outwit, and the intelligence to outsmart these eminent Brahmins. If the BU was composed in a region to the east of Kuru-Pañcāla, the heart of old Brahmin culture, then we can detect in this debate elements of a regional rivalry (see Int., p. xxxix).

to the horns . . . gold: on the use of gold to decorate the ears and horns of domestic animals, see Rau 1973, 49.

1.2–6 *Hotṛ, Adhvaryu, Udgātṛ, Brahman*: they are the four chief officiants at a sacrifice. See the Int., p. xlii.

1.6 *intermediate region provides no support of any kind*: see CU 2.9.4.

equivalents [saṃpad]: the reference is probably to things that correspond because they are numerically equivalent.

1.7 *The verse recited before . . . verse of praise*: the Sanskrit words for these three types of verses, *puronuvākyā, yājyā,* and *śasyā,* are the technical terms for three kinds of ritual formulas recited before, during, and after an oblation, respectively.

Whatever supports life: see BU 1.5.14 n.

1.8 *The oblations that . . . down when they are offered*: these three types of oblations are ghee (blazing up), milk (boiling over), and cakes (lying down in the fire). The connection between the way the offerings behave when they are offered in the fire and the world the offerer wins thereby is largely based on phonetic equivalences.

1.9 *All-gods*: here probably refers to an unspecified number of gods, or to the innumerable gods in general. Thus it relates to the limitless world the offerer wins. In later mythology All-gods (*viśvedeva*) is a distinct class of gods.

2.1 *grasper* [graha], *overgrasper* [atigraha]: these terms have a *double entendre* here. Within the ritual, *graha* refers to a cup used to draw out Soma and *atigraha* refers to the offering of extra cupfuls of Soma. Within the context of the body, *graha* is a sense organ and *atigraha* is the sense object grasped by it. The passage attempts to show how the grasper itself is grasped by what it grasps, i.e. the sense object (see KaU 3.10).

2.2 *The out-breath . . . means of the in-breath*: this sentence is somewhat unclear. We should have expected here a statement about the nose rather than the out-breath. The Mādhyandina recension appears to have attempted to emend the text by substituting 'odours' for the first 'in-breath' and 'out-breath' for the second 'in-breath'. The translation would then be: 'The out-breath is a grasper, which is itself grasped by the odour, the overgrasper; for one smells odours by means of the out-breath.' Here 'out-breath' (*prāṇa*) may refer to the nose.

2.10 *food for Death*: see BU 1.2.5.

repeated death: see BU 1.2.7 n. In this sentence, the usual 'whoever knows this' (see BU 1.2.7; 3.3.2), although omitted, is probably implied.

2.13 *physical body, self*: a distinction is made here between *śarīra* ('physical body' or 'corpse') and *ātman*. The exact meaning of the latter is unclear, but it must be related to the physical elements and the organic powers of the human being, since all the other items fall within those categories. The *ātman* here may thus refer to the vital aspects of the body, as opposed to the corporeal. A similar distinction between a corpse and a living body is made at BU 1.2.7.

3 For a variant of this story, see BU 3.7.

3.1 *Madras*: see Fig. 2 and the List of Names.

3.2 *there is a gap*: the narrow gap through which the Pārikṣitas (see the List of Names) escaped exists at the place where the ocean meets the sky at the horizon. We need to visualize the universe as two inverted bowls, the earth and the sky, which meet at the horizon.

4.1 *plain and not cryptic*: see BU 4.2.2.

Which one is the self within all: this question, repeated at 3.4.2 and 3.5.1, implies that there are many aspects of the human personality that are viewed as 'self' (see CU 8.7–12). Uṣasta wants Yājñavalkya to specify which of these constitutes the self within all.

4.2 *That's a fine explanation*: for a similar dissatisfaction and a sarcastic reply, see BU 3.8.5.

You can't see the seer: regarding the impossibility of perceiving the perceiver, see BU 2.4.14; 3.7.23.

5.1 *both are simply desires*: what 'both' refers to is unclear, since there are altogether three desires listed. The commentator Śaṃkara explains that, even though there are three listed, they fall under the two rubrics of means and end, sons and wealth being means for obtaining a good world.

He remains just . . . he may live: the syntax of this sentence is very unclear. Taking the phrase ending *kena syāt* as a question ('How would he become a Brahmin?': Deussen, 1879–84, Hume 1931, Senart 1934) creates a translation that is at best a tautology. I take *kena syāt yena syāt* as a variant form of *yena kena syāt*. The point the author wants to make is that when a person has reached the condition of a Brahmin (here redefined as the highest spiritual state; see also BU 3.8.11), he may live any way he pleases without affecting that state. See the parallel passage at BU 4.4.22.

6 For another version of Gārgī's questioning, see BU 3.8.

6.1 *woven back and forth*: the terms *ota* and *prota* are undoubtedly technical terms borrowed from weaving. They have been traditionally translated as warp and woof. The problem with that translation is that then the third item—that *on which* the weaving takes place and which is the basis of all the questions—makes little sense, since the warp and the woof are not woven on anything but by themselves form the cloth. We have then to think of the third either as the loom or as a place where the loom is fixed. Rau (1970, 17) has shown that these terms (derived from *ā ve-*, which is an equivalent of *apa ve-*, and *pra ve-*) refer to the back-and-forth movement of the shuttle in the process of weaving. Similar meanings of the prefixes *apa* and *pra* are found in the common terms *apāna* ('breathing in') and *prāṇa* ('breathing out'). So both *ota* and *prota* refer to the weaving of the woof or weft, the former referring to the movement of the shuttle towards the weaver and the latter to its movement away from the weaver. Then the third item upon which the weaving takes place is clear: it is the warp.

your head will shatter apart: see BU 1.3.24n.

7 Another version of this story is found at BU 3.3.

7.1 *He knows the spirits* [bhūtavid]: this expression may also mean that he knows the beings, but I think the expression has a meaning similar to *bhūtavidyā* ('demonology') listed at CU 7.1.2 (see note to this).

7.2 *His bodily parts have come unstrung*: the bodily parts of a dead man fall apart because the string that kept them together, namely, breath (here equated with its macrocosmic counterpart wind), has been cut off. The image appears to be that of a string of beads; the beads fall off when the string is broken.

7.23 *He sees . . . no one who perceives*: see BU 3.4.2; 3.8.11; 4.3.23–30.

8 Gārgī questioned Yājñavalkya in a similar way at BU 3.6.

8.3 *woven back and forth*: see BU 3.6.1 n.

8.5 *All honour . . . up for me*: I think that Gārgī's response is dripping with sarcasm. She is not satisfied at all with the first answer and is telling Yājñavalkya, in effect, to get serious! This, I believe, is the reason why her second question is a repetition of the first. For a similar dissatisfaction at Yājñavalkya's first attempt at an answer, see BU 3.4.2.

8.8 *imperishable*: the Sanskrit term *akṣara* means both 'imperishable' and 'syllable', especially the sacred syllable OM: see CU 1.1.1. The passage from the one to the other meaning is easy, and often both meanings may be implied. See Van Buitenen 1955, 1959.

8.9 *stand apart*: the meaning is that these entities remain in their assigned positions without coming together or colliding with each other. The orderly functioning of the universe is here ascribed to the power of the Imperishable Being.

8.9 *snowy mountains*: the Himalayas, from which originate most of the major rivers of northern India.

8.10 *offerings, sacrifices*: for the distinction, see BU 1.4.16 n.

he ... is a Brahmin: on the 'true' Brahmin, see also BU 3.5.1.

8.11 *This is . . . that perceives*: see the parallels at BU 3.4.2; 3.7.23; 4.3.23–30.

9.1 *ritual invocation* [nivid]: part of a recitation of praise (*śastra*) to the All-gods. The invocation gives the number of the gods comprehended by the term 'All-gods'. A *śastra*, which is recited by the Hotṛ and his assistants (BU 3.1.2–6 n.), is distinguished from *stotra*, which is sung by the Udgātṛ and his assistants (BU 1.3.28 n.), and always follows the latter. The invocation given in the *Śāṅkhāyana Śrautasūtra* (8.21) reads: 'You who are three and eleven; and three and thirty; and three and three hundred; and three and three thousand.' Our text refers to only the last two numbers.

Yes, of course: in these repeated questions of Vidagdha, I detect the same type of sarcasm I have pointed out above: BU 3.8.5 n.

9.3 *this whole treasure*: probably a reference to material riches. The earth itself bears the epithet *vasudhā* ('wealth-producing'). The Mādhyandina recension adds 'for they provide a dwelling for this whole world'.

9.4 *The ten vital functions* [prāṇa]: see BU 1.5.17 n. The ten are probably the five breaths (see BU 3.9.26) and the five senses.

9.9 *Tyad*: This word is probably related to *tyam* and is the second phoneme of the word *satyam* ('real' or 'truth'). The phoneme *tyad* has acquired the meaning of 'that' or 'the beyond', and thus is used with reference to *brahman* or the ultimate reality beyond the phenomenal world (see TU 2.6). For a discussion of the meanings ascribed to these phonemes, see BU 2.3.1 n.

9.10 *The immortal*: I think the commentator Śaṃkara is right in not taking 'immortal' at face value. He interprets it as 'the essence of food'. I think that the term probably refers to food, here viewed as the source of immortality. The Mādhyandina version has 'women' in place of 'immortal' and omits § 11. The person connected with the body and passions, therefore, is concerned with food and women.

9.15–16 *person in a mirror, in the waters*: the reference is to the reflection of a person in a mirror or in water. See CU 8.7.4; 8.8.1.

9.18 *Poor . . . cat's-paw*: this sarcastic remark is made by Yājñavalkya at the beginning of the questioning in a version of this story preserved in the SB 11.6.3.3. The remark is more apt in that context, because, after Yājñavalkya had driven away the cow, Śākalya became the spokesman for the assembled Brahmins in their attempt to show up Yājñavalkya's ignorance. In this version, the leader of the group is made to speak last, to be defeated, and to lose his life as a result of opposing Yājñavalkya.

9.19 *formulation of truth*: see BU 2.1.1 n.

out-talk: see CU 7.15.4 n.

9.21 *sacrificial gift* [dakṣiṇā]: the gift or payment made by the patron of a sacrifice to the officiating priests. In priestly thinking, this gift took on great significance, often eclipsing the sacrifice itself as the most important element of a sacrifice; the bigger the gift, the more efficacious the sacrifice. We can thus understand why the sacrifice is said here to be based on the sacrificial gift.

9.23 *sacrificial consecration* [dīkṣā]: a special ritual performed not for the priests but for the person who is about to perform a sacrifice as its patron and beneficiary.

9.26 *not—— . . . injury*: see BU 2.3.6 n. Thieme (1968*b*: 720) thinks that this passage, given as prose in our text, was initially perhaps an octosyllabic verse of five lines.

eight abodes . . . eight persons: these are mentioned in §§ 10–17.

providing the hidden connection: the meaning of *aupaniṣada* (lit. 'relating to *upaniṣad*') is unclear. I take it as referring to the person who is at the summit in a hierarchical set of equivalences and is the 'connecting point' for all the other persons; or the one from whom the others proceed (for such meanings of the term *upaniṣad*, see Int., p. lii). Traditionally the term has been translated simply as 'the person taught in the Upaniṣads'.

your head will shatter apart: see BU 1.3.24 n.

9.28 For the interpretation of these somewhat difficult verses, see Horsch 1966, 155–60.

His body hairs: on the seven parts of the body, from the outermost, i.e. hair, to the inmost, i.e. marrow, see Jamison 1986, 167–78.

sapwood: the term *śakarāṇi* (in the plural) literally means 'pieces of wood' or 'splinters', but the context calls for some part of the wood, possibly the soft outer layer, that would resemble and correspond to the flesh of a human body. Further, the comparison of the bones to the inner heartwood (*antarato dārūṇi*, here too in the plural) supports my conjecture.

9.28 *Do not say . . . he dies*: this verse is somewhat obscure and has been subject to different interpretations. The previous verse shows that a tree, when it is cut down, sprouts again from its roots. Does a human possess such a root? The poet says that the human root cannot be the semen, which is comparable to the seeds rather than the roots of a tree. In the case of a man and a tree, the seed turns into a baby or a tree immediately (*añjasā*), even before the father or the parent tree has died. So the semen cannot be viewed as the metaphorical root from which a man grows again after death. Unlike many translators, I take *añjasāpretya* as containing a Sandhi; so I read *apretya* ('before dying') rather than *pretya* ('after death'). The apparent answer to the question, given in the following verses, is that a man does not possess a root from which he can be reborn after death; he is like a tree that has been uprooted.

CHAPTER 4

1.2 *What could a person . . . possibly have*: another possible translation is: 'could it possibly belong to someone who cannot speak?'

one-legged brahman: for this image, see CU 3.18.2–6.

One should venerate: the verb *upa ās-* ('to venerate') has also the meaning of 'to take as', that is, take one thing to be the same as another. The term thus establishes equivalences between components of different spheres, e.g. between bodily components and elements of the cosmos. This meaning is thus very similar to that of other technical terms, such as *bandhu*, and *upaniṣad*: see Int., p. liii.

counterpart (bandhu): see Int. p. lii.

Ṛgveda . . . glosses: for the enumeration of the sciences, see BU 2.4.10n.; CU 7.1.2.

a thousand cows . . . elephants: traditionally the expression *hastyṛṣabhaṃ sahasram* (here and in §§ 3–7) has been translated 'a thousand cows with a bull the size of an elephant'. For reasons given by Hillebrandt (1920, 461–2), I take the first compound as 'elephants and bull'. The term *sahasram* ('thousand'), I think, is a shorthand for *gosahasram* ('a thousand cows'; see BU 3.1.1; the same shorthand is found below at BU 4.3.14–16, 33).

1.3 *breath*: the Sanskrit term *prāṇa* has the meaning of both breath and life. Here, 'for the love of breath' means for the sake of life. What Yājñavalkya wants to point out is that people do things that they should not do in order to obtain a livelihood and thus preserve their life.

1.4 *when they ask . . . as the truth*: on the superiority of an eyewitness account in determining the truth, see also BU 5.14.4.

2.1 *hidden teachings*: the *upaniṣads* Janaka possessed were the six statements told him by various theologians, statements that established equivalences between *brahman* and speech, breath, sight, hearing, mind, and heart. Here again I think that the term *upaniṣad* is used in its primitive sense of hierarchical equivalences. See BU 3.9.26 n.

2.2–3 *Indha, Virāj*: Indha means 'one who kindles', and Virāj means the 'shining' or 'pre-eminent' one. In the waking state they reside in the eyes, while during sleep they meet in the space within the heart (see BU 2.1.17 n.; 4.3). On the person in the eye, see also BU 2.3.5, and on the Hitā, see BU 2.1.19 n. It was a widespread assumption that gods liked cryptic sayings (see BU 3.4.1; AU 1.3.14); see the detailed note of Keith (1909, 232 n. 13) on this subject.

2.4 *this person*: probably refers here to the union of Indha and Virāj in the heart. The directions here make sense if we think of the person as facing the east (cf. BU 1.1.1 n.).

not——: see BU 2.3.6 n.

freedom from fear [abhaya]: this is directly linked to the knowledge of *brahman* at BU 4.3.21; 4.4.25.

These people . . . your service: this idiomatic sentence literally means: 'Here are the people of Videha and here am I!' For a more direct statement of the same, see BU 4.4.23.

3 For a detailed study of the philosophical content of this text (BU 4.3–4), see Hanfeld 1976, 20–70.

3.1 *I won't tell him*: many scholars read *sam enena vadiṣye* and translate, 'I will converse with him.' My translation is based on the reading as *sa mene na vadiṣye*, and it is supported by the reading of the commentator Śaṃkara. I think that this reading makes better sense within the context; what would be the purpose of Yājñavalkya's thinking that he should converse when he was already in Janaka's presence? Neither can the phrase simply mean, 'I will not speak with him', because one would surely not come into the presence of a king and simply refuse to speak. 'I won't tell him', would imply a mental reservation that he will not answer fully any question that is put to him. Yājñavalkya, like many other teachers of his time (see CU 4.4–14), is portrayed as not wanting to reveal his knowledge.

But Janaka exercised the wish Yājñavalkya had granted him. This wish is recorded in the SB 11.6.2.10, where Janaka, after teaching Yājñavalkya the secret meaning of the daily fire sacrifice (*agnihotra*), extracts from him the promise that Janaka would be permitted to ask any question he wanted. In this light Janaka's repeated statements, 'But you'll have to tell me more than that to get yourself released' (§§ 14, 15, and 33; KsU 1.21) and Yājñavalkya's observation, 'The king is really sharp! He has flushed me out of every cover' (§ 33), make sense. This also explains why Janaka spoke first, because Yājñavalkya was keeping silent. Yājñavalkya did not want to reveal what he knew, but Janaka made him do it.

3.7–9 *across both worlds*: the two worlds are the visible world when we are awake and the world of deep sleep. These two meet (*saṃdhyā*) in the twilight zone, the juncture between night and day, which is the state of dream. On fluttering, see SU 3.18; the term *lelāyati* evokes the fluttering of a bird, the flickering of a flame, the trembling of a leaf, or the rustling of the wind (see Brereton 1982, 448 n. 30).

3.12 *goose*: see BU 2.5.18 n.

3.14 *sound asleep*: the term *āyata* literally means 'stretched out'. Some take this word to mean 'suddenly'.

But you'll have . . . yourself released: my translation of this phrase is consistent with my reading of the confrontation between Janaka and Yājñavalkya (see BU 4.3.1 n). Most translators see here a reference to final liberation (*mokṣa*); the phrase would then mean 'Tell me more than that for the sake of liberation.' I do not think this is the correct interpretation, especially because the term *mokṣa* or *vimokṣa* is never used in this Upaniṣad with reference to the final liberation from the cycle of rebirth, while the verb *muc-* is used at BU 1.5.17 for release from a sin, which is often connected with debt and obligation, and at CU 6.16.2 for release of a person charged with a crime.

3.15 *serene realm*: the state of deep sleep.

along the same path: for the paths along which a person travels into the heart during dream time and into the veins of the heart during deep sleep, see BU 2.1.17–19.

nothing sticks to this person: see BU 3.9.26; 4.2.4; 4.4.22; 4.5.15.

3.21 *Now . . . from sorrows*: there appears to be a transition here from the description of dream to that of deep and dreamless sleep. The Mādhyandina recension, in fact, inserts before this passage the sentence 'where as he sleeps . . . no dreams' found at the end of § 19.

3.22 *recluse* [śramaṇa]: in later literature this word becomes a technical term used almost exclusively with reference to non-Brahmanical wandering mendicants. It is unclear, however, whether in this early text the term has the same meaning; it may well refer to Brahmanical religious virtuosi: see Olivelle 1993, 9–16.

ascetic [tāpasa]: refers to those who undertook fierce bodily mortifications. Later literature identifies them with forest hermits.

3.23–31 *Now, he does not see . . . perceive the other*: see the parallel passages at BU 2.4.14; 4.5.15. The Sanskrit is pithy and has been subject to different translations. The intent, I believe, is clear. Although a person in deep sleep does not perceive through the senses, the reason for this is not that he has lost his capacity, that is, his real nature. It is like a fire, which always burns (i.e. has the capacity to burn), but will not burn when there is nothing near it. Thus, the reason he does not see, for example, is not the same as the reason why a blind man cannot see. The self in deep sleep (and after death, see BU 2.4.12; 4.5.13) does not see because there is nothing to see except himself. See Hanfeld 1976, 31 n. 24.

3.33 *Among human . . . highest bliss*: see the parallel passage at TU 2.8.

Yājñavalkya became alarmed: see BU 4.3.1 n. for the possible reason.

4.1 *particles of light*: the reference here, in all likelihood, is to the vital functions themselves. For this comparison, see KsU 3.3.

4.2 *sinking:* literally the term *ekībhavati* means 'he becomes one'. The meaning here is that the vital functions are collapsing inwards and becoming merged into the self or into the single vital breath (*prāṇa*).

He then descends . . . take hold of him: these two phrases are obscure and the readings of the two recensions diverge substantially. I have used the readings of the Mādhyandina recension to emend the Kāṇva by reading *saṃjñānam eva* for *savijñānam eva*, and by placing *saṃjñānam evānvavakrāmati* before *savijñāno bhavati*. The commentator Śaṃkara sees here a reference to the passage of the self into a new body. His interpretation is supported by the use of the prefixes *niḥ* ('away') and *ut* ('up') in the verbs describing the departure of the faculties at death, and by the use of *ava* ('down') with reference to the self acquiring awareness. If that is the case, then the descent of the self into a womb is accompanied by a state of simple awareness (*saṃjñāna*), which develops into full perception (*vijñāna*), followed thereafter by the learning he had previously acquired, the rites (*karma*) he had performed, and his memory.

Karma here may also refer to the effects of his past deeds: see the verse in § 6.

4.3 *As a caterpillar . . . onto it*: Thieme (1968*a*, 60), on the basis of the Mādhyandina recension which omits 'Reaches out to a new foothold', sees here the image of a caterpillar going to the edge of a leaf and building a cocoon around itself, and then emerging from it with a new body.

4.4 *As a weaver . . . more attractive*: the simile here is taken from weaving, possibly the weaving of tapestry (Thieme 1968*a*, 60), and not from metallurgy as assumed by many. Rau (1970, 24–7) has shown that *peśas* refers to coloured weaving material rather than to gold.

4.6 *action*: the term 'action' (*karma*) in this verse appears to have the technical meaning of 'residual effect of past actions' of the *karma* doctrine.

4.7 *When they . . . in this world*: this verse occurs also at KaU 6.14.

4.8–9 *path*: probably refers to the veins of the heart called Hitā, which also contain fluids with these colours: see BU 4.3.20.

4.10 *Into blind . . . in learning*: this verse occurs also at IU 9. The Mādhyandina version reads 'non-becoming' and 'becoming' in place of 'ignorance' and 'learning', a reading found also at IU 12 and viewed as superior by Horsch 1966, 165–6.

4.11 *'Joyless' . . . wise*: a version of this verse occurs at IU 3.

4.14 *While . . . awaits them*: cf. KeU 2.5; KaU 6.4.

4.15 *When a man . . . from him*: cf. KaU 4.5, 12; IU 6. The Mādhyandina recension reads: 'Then he will not have any doubts.' See Thieme 1965, 94.

4.17 *the various groups of five*: the phrase *pañca pañcajanāḥ* may also mean 'the five groups of five', but I think the repetition of *pañca* is meant to indicate an indeterminate number of such groups of five. According to the commentator Śaṃkara, these groups of five may include Gandharvas, ancestors, gods, demons (*asura*), and evil spirits (*rākṣasa*), or the four social classes with the Niṣādas as the fifth. In AB 3.31 the five are given as gods, men, Gandharvas and Apsarases (together), serpents, and ancestors. See the list given in verse 18, to which food is added in the Mādhyandina recension (see BS 1.4.12). For the significance of the number five, see BU 1.4.17 n.

4.18 *The breathing . . . the ancient*: cf. KeU 1.2. For an examination of this sort of expression, see BU 2.1.20 n.

4.19 *With the mind . . . diversity*: cf. KaU 4.10, 11.

4.22 *He does not . . . by bad actions*: cf. KsU 3.8.

dike: this term probably refers to the raised earthen boundaries across paddy-fields that both allow one to walk across wet land and mark the boundaries between properties. The image is transferred to the cosmic sphere where the self is seen as the boundary that keeps the various cosmic entities in their proper places. The term *setu* has been frequently translated as 'bridge' (e.g. Hume 1931), but that is misleading because a bridge spans and connects two pieces of land separated by water, whereas a dike does the opposite; it divides and separates. Thus at CU 8.4.1 a dike is called a 'divider'. See CU 8.4 for a longer account of this image; see also MuU 2.2.5; SU 6.19.

did not desire offspring: see BU 3.5.1.

not ——: see BU 2.3.6 n.

pass across: this expression here and in § 23, I believe, implicitly recalls the earlier image of the self as a dike. Nothing belonging to this word is permitted to cross beyond that dike. This is more explicitly stated in CU 8.4.1–3.

he is not burnt: the term 'burn' (*tapati*) here and in § 23 has both the literal meaning of setting fire to something and the extended meaning of causing harm, as in the slang use of 'burnt'.

4.23 *Ṛgvedic verse*: here and elsewhere in these Upaniṣads I have translated the term *ṛc* as 'Ṛgvedic verse'. Unless otherwise stated, however, these verses are not found in the extant corpus of the Ṛgveda. The term *ṛc* may be a generic reference to 'verse', but I have chosen to interpret it more strictly, especially to distinguish it from the term *śloka* ('verse') also used in these documents (see BU 1.5.1). This verse occurs also at TB 3.12.9.7–8.

He is . . . greatness: I take the pronoun 'he' as referring to the self. Others translate: 'This is the eternal greatness', and assume that greatness is the subject of the entire verse.

It's his trail: on the image of the trail, see BU 1.4.7.

Here, sir . . . your slaves: see BU 4.2.4 n.

5 Another version of this story is given at BU 2.4, where explanatory notes are also given.

5.2 *about to go away*: this version uses the verb *pra-vraj-* for Yājñavalkya's departure from home in place of the more neutral *ud-yā-* of BU 2.4.1. The term *pra-vraj-* acquires a technical meaning with reference to the departure of a wandering ascetic from home. This is one further indication (see also BU 2.4.12 n.;

4.5.15 n.) that this version of the story is somewhat later than the one at BU 2.4.

5.13 *As a mass . . . cognition*: see BU 2.4.12 n. regarding the differences between the two versions.

5.14 *I cannot perceive this*: the reference probably is to the self that Yājñavalkya had just described. See the variant account at BU 2.4.13.

5.15 *About this self . . . injury*: this paragraph (see BU 2.3.6 n.) is clearly not original and is a further example of the editorial emendations inserted into this version (Brereton 1986, 106). This passage is missing in both the version at BU 2.4 and in the Mādhyandina recension of BU 2.5.

CHAPTER 5

2 *Da! Da! Da!*: for similar enigmatic phrases, see CU 3.14.1 n.

3 *Hṛdayam*: this entire chapter is full of phonetic equivalences used for didactic purposes. The connection between *yam* and the verbal root *i-* is less apparent, but in many verbal forms the root exhibits an initial *ya-*, as in *yanti* ('they go').

4 *Clearly, that . . . simply the real*: the first sentence of this passage is very elliptical, and its meaning and especially the antecedents of the pronouns 'that' and 'this' are unclear. I take the meaning to be as follows: that, i.e. *brahman*, is itself, but it *was* this, i.e. this world, here called the 'real'. The statement that *brahman* was this world appears to be cosmogonic, implying that the world originated from *brahman*. See Van Buitenen (1968; 55–7) and Gren-Eklund (1978, 96–8) for other attempts to interpret this sentence.

5.1 *In the beginning . . . who knows this*: the Sanskrit terms for real and unreal carry simultaneously the meanings of true/truth, and false/falsehood. See the parallel at CU 8.3.5 with a somewhat different explanation. I follow the Mādhyaṃdina reading in eliminating the repetition of *brahman*, thus taking Prajāpati as in apposition to *brahman*. According to the Kāṇva reading, the translation is: 'the real created *brahman*, *brahman* created Prajāpati, and Prajāpati created the gods.' On the three syllables of *satyam*, see Jamison 1986, 165–7. In the Mādhyandina recension, the third syllable reads *am*.

5.2 *The person . . . each other*: for parallels, see BU 2.3.5; CU 1.7.5; 4.15.1; 8.7.5.

5.3–4 *svar*: this word is considered to have two syllables (hence the connection to the two feet) because it is pronounced as *su-ar*, the semivowel being converted to its corresponding vowel.

His hidden name: note the phonetic similarity between *ahar* ('day') and *aham* ('I'). On *upaniṣad* as hidden name, see BU 2.1.20 n.

7 *Lightning, cutting*: besides the phonetic similarity between the Sanskrit words, the connection between lightning and cutting may also come from the fact that lightning cuts across the dark cloud.

8 *Svāhā . . . Svadhā*: these are ritual exclamations with no linguistic meaning. Svāhā and Vaṣaṭ are used when oblations are offered to gods, while Svadhā is used in offerings to ancestors. Hanta is a common expression to gain attention in a conversation, meaning something like 'look' or 'come'. It was probably used in giving gifts to people, and its use is prescribed in the first feeding of a child in *Pāraskara Gṛhyasūtra*, 1.19.6.

9 *The fire . . . that noise*: the image is stronger in Sanskrit, which uses the same term, *pacati*, for both cooking and digesting (see BU 1.1.1 n).

10 *Now . . . or cold*: for other descriptions of the passage of a dead person, see BU 6.2; CU 5.3–10. The Sanskrit words for 'heat' (*śoka*) and 'cold' (*hima*) could also mean 'sorrow' and 'snow' (or 'frost').

11 *To suffer . . . austerity*: there is a play here on the verb *tap-*, which can mean 'to be hot', 'to be tormented', and 'to practise austerities'. Sickness, especially a fever, makes one hot and tormented.

wilderness: the reference here is to the fact that the dead are cremated in a wild area outside a village.

12 *food*: the term here possibly has a double meaning: first as the body constituted by food (see CU 6.7; TU 2.1–2), which spoils (rots as a corpse) without the lifebreath, and second as nourishment, without which breath or life withers (see BU 1.3.19 n.).

deities: on the use of this term, see BU 1.3.9 n.

Vi, Ram: the compound *vi-ram-* means 'to cease', 'to be quiet', especially 'to stop talking'. The term has been interpreted as a reference to renunciation. I think it is more likely that the reference is to silence. *Brahman* is often said to transcend speech (TU 2.4), and Śaṃkara in his commentary on the BS (3.2.17) records the episode of Bāṣkali, who asked Bādhva for instruction on *brahman*. The latter remained silent. When asked for the third time, Bādhva said, 'I am telling you, but you do not understand! The self here is silent.' For similar enigmatic phrases elsewhere, see CU 3.14.1 n.

13.1–4 *The uktha . . . world as the kṣatra*: the terms *uktha, yajus,* and *sāman* refer to the ritual texts comprising the Ṛgveda, Yajurveda, and Sāmaveda, all associated with Brahmin priests (see BU 1.3.22–3 n; 1.6.1 n.), while *kṣatra* refers to royal power or the condition of a Kṣatriya (see BU 1.4.11 n.). All these equivalences are based on phonetic correspondences.

14.1 *Gāyatrī*: the name of a vedic metre consisting of three octosyllabic feet. The term also refers (see § 4) to the most famous verse set in that metre, the Sāvitrī verse (see BU 6.3.6 n.).

14.3 *fourth vivid foot*: speculation regarding the absent fourth foot of the Gāyatrī is based on the fact that normally vedic metres have four feet.

in some way visible [dadṛśa iva]: another possible translation of this somewhat ambiguous expression is 'clearly visible'. The SB (11.2.4.1) uses the same expression to compare the full moon and the new moon with the sun.

14.4 *truth is sight*: see BU 4.1.4.

one's breaths: the expression here may also refer to the vital functions (see BU 1.5.17 n.).

14.5 *Anuṣṭubh*: a vedic metre with four octosyllabic feet, as opposed to the three feet of the Gāyatrī.

15 *The face . . . offer to you*: these four verses with slight variations are found at IU 15–18. —(1) The golden dish is the sun's orb. 'For me' is not explicitly stated in the original, but it is strongly implied. The dish that covers may refer to the conception of the sun as the door to the heavenly world: see CU 2.24.4 n.; (3) I take *anilam* ('wind') as breath or the breathing one. The contrast with the body in the next line clearly points to breath as the immortal element in man; (4) 'Sin that angers': I take *juhurāṇa* as 'angering' (from *hṛṇīte*); others take it as 'crooked'.

CHAPTER 6

BU 6.1–3 corresponds to CU 5.1–10. These sections contain three topics: the relative superiority among the vital functions, the rite to achieve greatness, and the story of Śvetaketu's visit to Jaivali. The CU gives the sections in that order, naturally connecting the first two sections with similar themes (see Bodewitz 1973, 273–5). The BU, on the other hand, inserts the Śvetaketu story between them, thereby breaking the natural sequence. For a comparative study of these sections, see Renou 1955, 96–100.

1 For an analysis of this section, see Bodewitz 1973, 269–73.

1.4 *correspondence*: here, I think, the same term, *sampad*, in its nominal and verbal forms, is used with a dual meaning. 'Correspondence' refers to the various equivalences between disparate entities and spheres (*bandhu* or counterpart: see BU 1.1.2 n.) established in this literature, equivalences that are the basis of Upaniṣadic knowledge. The three terms used in §§ 3–5, basis, equivalence, and refuge or abode, are the three ways in which realities of the universe are related to each other: Gonda 1954, 1959, 1969.

1.7–13 *Once . . . they replied*: for another version of this competition, see BU 1.3.2–6 and the note to this.

speech: the reference is not to uttered speech but to the power or faculty of speech.

eye, ear: although I am forced to translate 'seeing with the eye' and 'hearing with the ear' to save the prose, the reference is to the powers of sight and hearing (see BU 1.3.2–6 n).

1.13 *tribute*: the Sanskrit term *bali* can mean either a tribute that a vassal would offer to a king or more generally a ritual offering: see TU 1.5.3; Bodewitz 1973, 270.

1.14 *that breath is food*: literally, the phrase means 'the food of breath', but as Bodewitz (1973, 285 n. 28) has shown, the intent here is to indicate the phonetic/etymological connection between *ana* ('breath') and *anna* ('food') and, therefore, their ultimate identity.

improper food: the term *ananna* literally means 'non-food', but I think that here it is used with reference to items that normally would not be proper food; the reference may be to food given by unclean people (Bodewitz 1973, 285 n. 28) rather than to a suspension of traditional food taboos. A person who knows this secret equivalence between breath and food does not have to perform the customary expiations when he eats food from impure persons (Rau 1957, 37).

2 A version of this story is found in CU 5.3–10 (for a comparison, see Renou 1955, 97–100). A close examination of the two versions shows that the CU version attempts to portray Śvetaketu in a far better light than the BU, where he is depicted as a spoilt little brat. For example, in the CU version Śvetaketu always uses the polite

bhagavan ('my lord'); that version also omits his disregard of Jaivali's invitation to stay (BU 6.2.3) and his arrogant reply to his father's invitation to study under Jaivali (BU 6.2.4). For an analysis of this section, see Bodewitz 1973, 243–53. For other versions of the passage of a dead person, see KsU 1.2–7; JB 1.45–50; the textual tradition of the doctrine of the five fires has been studied by Bodewitz 1973, 110–23, and more recently by Schmithausen 1994.

2.1 *assembly*: this appears to have been a place where the cream of society gathered, where distinguished people spoke on social, political, and theological matters, and where the king gave audience. For an examination of the many terms used for such a place, including *sabhā*, *samiti*, and *pariṣad*, see Rau 1957, 75–83.

Yes: the Sanskrit reads 'OṂ'; on the meaning of this term as yes, see CU 1.1.8–9 n; Parpola 1981, 204.

2.2 *Two paths . . . and sky*: this verse is, with a minor variant, RV 10.88.15. 'Earth and sky': literally, the mother and the father, but the reference clearly is to the earth and sky.

2.3 *Well, well . . . educated*: this is, of course, not a literal translation, which is nearly impossible in the case of this idiomatic and sarcastic statement.

excuse for a prince: the expression *rājanyabandhu* (lit. 'a relative of a king/prince'), I think, is used here pejoratively (cf. CU 6.1.1); see Rau 1957, 68.

2.4 *Gautama*: this is the lineage (*gotra*) name of Uddālaka Āruṇi, the father of Śvetaketu.

2.7 *in the correct manner*: a ritual ceremony was commonly required for a person to be initiated as a pupil of a teacher. We see a rudimentary description of such a rite at CU 4.4.5. For someone being instructed even without such a ceremony, see CU 5.11.6.

2.8 *speaks like that*: the meaning probably is that he spoke very humbly like a vedic student.

2.13 *A fire . . . springs a man*: on sex as sacrifice, see BU 6.4.3 n.

2.14 *Of that fire . . . are the sparks*: the repetitions here are meant to indicate that in the cremation fire the reality of the fire itself replaces the correspondences noted with regard to the other 'fires'.

2.15–16 *The people . . . or snakes*: for parallel passages and similar themes, see CU 5.10.1–6; 4.15.5; BU 5.10; KsU 1.2–7; PU 1.9–10; MuU 1.2.7–11.

people there in the wilderness: this statement does not necessarily imply that these people were some type of forest hermits or ascetics, or that they lived permanently in the wilderness. It only suggests that these esoteric doctrines and practices were carried out in secret outside the villages. See Bodewitz 1973, 237.

venerate: the meaning of this term here is the same as at CU 5.10.1–3; these people accept the equality between two concepts, e.g. austerity and faith; austerity and truth. Here I think Senart (1930, in his note to CU 5.10.1) is right despite the objections of Bodewitz (1973, 253 n. 24). For this extended meaning of veneration, see BU 4.1.1 n. It appears that 'faith' in this context is connected with giving gifts (see CU 4.1.1). It is this meaning of the term that permits the author to contrast the people in the wilderness, who take faith to be something internal (truth here, and austerity in CU 5.10.1), to people in villages, who participate in the external acts of giving. Indeed, in the CU (5.10.3) the contrast is even clearer than in the BU version. The parallel between 'faith' and 'giving' is seen in the Kāṇva and the Mādhyandina versions of BU 4.4.22, where the term *dānena* ('by giving') of the Kāṇva is replaced by *śraddhayā* ('by faith') in the Mādhyandina.

King Soma: probably refers to the moon. The increase and the decrease of the moon refer to its waning and waxing, here explained as caused by dead people going there and becoming the food of gods. This appears to be a recasting of the older belief that the moon contained Soma, the immortal drink of the gods. Coming down to earth as rain, the dead people who were in the moon enter plants, which are eaten by a man, transformed into semen, and deposited in a woman to become a foetus. Further details of the process are given in CU 5.10.3–8.

3 See the comments at the beginning of Ch. 6. A similar rite is given at KsU 2.3. It appears that this rite is meant for a man of the ruling class who wants to attain sovereignty over others of his class: see Rau 1957, 71; Bodewitz 1973, 287 n. 39.

3.1 *preparatory rites* [upasad]: see CU 3.17.1–5 n.

male constellation: there appears to be no consensus in the Indian traditions about which of the twenty-seven or twenty-eight constellations are masculine and which are feminine: see Kane 1962–75, v. 52 n. 754.

an offering of ghee: that the offering is of ghee, even though ghee is not specified, is made clear by the use of the technical term *juhoti* (see BU 1.4.16 n.) and by the parallel passage in CU 5.2.4–5, where the ghee is specified.

3.2 *To the breath, svāhā*: this and the subsequent parallel expressions are lacking in the parallel passages in CU 5.2.5. The reason for this addition, as Deussen (1897) points out, is the editor's desire to connect these to the parallel passages in BU 6.1.1–6 because the sequence has been interrupted by the insertion of BU 6.2. This is the reason why I have added the phrase 'what is meant here is', which is lacking in the original.

3.4 *hiṃ*: on this exclamation, see CU 2.2.1 n.

call, assent: technically called *āśrāvaṇa* and *pratyāśrāvaṇa*, these terms refer to one priest's call *āśrāvaya* (or *om āśrāvaya*) and the other's reply *astu śrauṣaṭ*. See TU 1.8.1 n. For a detailed description, see Kane 1962–75, ii. 1054.

gatherer: see CU 4.3.

3.5 *You are . . . in me*: this sentence is extremely obscure and the translation is very tentative. I have followed the Mādhyandina reading, which is closer to the parallel at CU 5.2.6. The term *āma*, here translated as 'power', literally means 'raw', and may here refer to the raw (uncooked) mixture that is drunk and to raw power. I think the emphasis here is less on the 'meaning' than on the alliterated sound.

3.6 *On that . . . prayers*: the three verses follow each of the three lines of the Sāvitrī verse: 'On that excellent glory of god Savitṛ we reflect, that he may stimulate our prayers' (RV 3.62.10). The difference in syntax between English and Sanskrit makes it difficult to divide the lines into meaningful units; hence the bracketed words. See also Gāyatrī, BU 5.14.1 n. The three verses are RV 1.90.6–8.

Honey: see BU 2.5.

Svāhā: see BU 5.8 n.

lineage: refers to the line of teachers from whom he had received this instruction. Such lineages are appended to the three divisions of the BU (2.6; 4.6; 6.5).

4.1 *Of these . . . semen*: see the parallel passages on essences at CU 1.1.1; 3.1–5. The AA (2.1.3) substitutes 'semen' (*retas*) for 'essence' (*rasa*) with approximately the same meaning: 'The semen of Prajāpati is the gods; the semen of the gods is rain; the semen of rain is the plants, etc.'

4.2 *had intercourse with her*: the expression *adha upāsta* literally means 'venerated from below' (see BU 1.4.11 where the same expression means 'to prostrate oneself'). A pun may be intended here, as a man prostrates himself before a woman in having intercourse with her!

4.3 *Her vulva . . . at the centre*: regarding the comparison between sexual intercourse and sacrifice, see BU 6.2.13; CU 5.8.

4.5 *let the fire . . . its place*: the Mādhyandina recension reads 'fires' (*agnayaḥ* in the plural). I think that reading makes better sense, because the fires probably refer to the vital functions. Their return to their proper places, here allegorized as fire-mounds (i.e. the places where the fires are located during a rite), results in the restoration of the man's strength and virility. The last two lines are variants of AV 7.67.1.

4.6 *Surely . . . to have sex*: in ancient Indian religious law, a husband was obliged to have sexual intercourse during his wife's fertile season, that is, soon after her menses.

4.12 *reverse of the normal*: the reeds are spread out *normally* on the eastern side of the sacrificial enclosure, from the south to the north with their tips facing the east. It is unclear whether all or just some elements of this procedure are inverted, i.e. placed on the western side beginning from the north and ending in the south, and with tips towards the west.

4.14 *I want . . . with ghee*: on the relation between this passage and ancient Indian medical practice, see Wezler 1993.

4.19 *the cooking of the pot of milk-rice* (sthālīpāka): a well-known procedure for cooking rice on the southern fire (see Int., p. xlii) generally used in offerings to deceased ancestors. The verse is RV 10.85.22 with variants.

4.20 *ama, sā*: on these terms and their connection to the Ṛg and Sāman, and to sky and earth, see CU 1.6.1 n. The verse, with variants, is found in TB 3.7.1.9.

4.21–2 *May Viṣṇu . . . tenth month*: these three verses are RV 10.184.1–3. *fire-drills*: see BU 1.4.6 n.

4.23 *As from . . . afterbirth*: the source of these verses is RV 5.78.7–8.

4.27 *Your refreshing . . . to suck*: RV 1.164.49, with lines 2 and 3 reversed.

5.3 *white Yajurvedic formulas*: on the White Yajurveda, see Int., p. xxxi.

Chāndogya Upaniṣad

CHAPTER 1

The context of the various liturgical recitations, songs, and acts that are the special focus of the first two chapters is a Soma sacrifice (*Agniṣṭoma*). A sound knowledge of the procedure and the technical vocabulary connected with this sacrifice is a prerequisite for an adequate understanding of this Upaniṣad. Within the limits imposed by a publication of this kind, I will attempt to provide explanations of that ritual and vocabulary in the notes. For a detailed account of a typical Soma sacrifice, see Caland and Henry 1906; Kane 1962–75, ii. 1133–1212.

1.1 *OṂ — one should . . . of that syllable*: this passage is identical with CU 1.4.1. For the meaning of 'venerate', see BU 4.1.2 n. In all likelihood, the person who is expected to venerate thus is the Udgātṛ priest (Thieme 1968*a*).

High Chant: for its technical meaning as the central and most important section of the five-part Sāman, see CU 2.2.1 n. There the High Chant is preceded by the singing of OṂ. I use the term 'High Chant' in translating the term *udgītha*, taking 'high' to mean the chief and most important. It also permits the reader to see how this meaning can blend into the meaning of high as a spatial term. So, the High Chant can be compared to the sun that 'rises high' (*udeti*) at CU 1.3.1.

1.2 *The essence . . . High Chant*: for parallel passages, see BU 6.4.1 n.

1.8–9 *Clearly, this syllable . . . High Chant*: the context in which OṂ is said to mean assent is the ritual. Parpola (1981) discusses the scholarly debate on the meaning and etymology of OṂ and argues that the Sanskrit term OṂ is derived from the Dravidian term *ām* ('yes') and that the Sanskrit term also indicated assent or approval in ordinary speech. The priests (see BU 3.1.1 n. and Int., p. xlii) are not identified in the original Sanskrit; I have included them in the translation to make the meaning clear. On the assent and call of the priests, see BU 6.3.4 n.

1.10 *hidden connections*: on this meaning of *upaniṣad*, see BU 3.9.26 n. and Int., p. lii.

2.7 *smashed to bits*: although a clod of earth is not specified here in the original Sanskrit, it is doubtless implied, while it is explicitly mentioned in the parallel passage at BU 1.3.7.

2.9 *Therefore . . . vital functions*: one may also translate: 'Whatever one eats or drinks with that [breath], one nourishes thereby the other vital functions.' I think, however, that the author assumes (rather than states explicitly) that one always eats and drinks (i.e. swallows) by means of the breath within the mouth (see BU 1.3.17). The fact that one nourishes all faculties by eating and drinking is seen as another indication that breath is superior to all others.

one leaves . . . wide open: if we follow Böhtlingk's (1889*b*) emendation (followed by Senart 1930) *utkrāmanti* (plural 'they depart'), then the subject of the final sentence would be the vital functions. At the end, that is when one dies, the mouth is left wide open because the vital functions went out through it in an effort to find the breath within the mouth from which they obtain nourishment. The sentence, however, makes sense without the emendation; the one who fails to find it is the same as the one who eats and drinks, that is, the self.

2.10–12 *Aṅgiras venerated . . . from the mouth*: for these phonetic etymologies, see BU 1.3.8 n.

2.14 *And, indeed . . . as this syllable*: this parallels CU 1.1.8 and implies the identification of the syllable OṂ with the breath within the mouth, both of which are identified with the High Chant.

3.1 *One should . . . darkness*: see the parallel passage at CU 1.11.7.

3.2 *This breath . . . so is that*: the text uses just the deictic pronouns 'this' and 'that' ('This and that are the same'), a feature common in these oral compositions: see BU 1.2.2–3 n.; 1.4.6 n.

shine, shining back: the meanings of the terms *svara* and *pratyāsvara* as applied to the sun are unclear. I have taken these two words to be related to the verb *svar*- 'to shine', although there is clearly a word play here (*svara* as sound and *svara* as light).

3.5 *churning a fire*: see BU 1.4.6 n.

3.7 *eat his own food*: on the significance of this image, see BU 1.2.5 n.

3.9 *supplies the lyrics*: Sāman refers to a verse as it is sung; the Ṛgvedic verses supply the lyrics to nearly all of the Sāmans.

3.10 *arrangement* [stoma]: refers to the repetitions of the different parts of the verses when they are actually sung. These repetitions number from three to forty-eight and are done in a set of patterns called *viṣṭuti*. Thus, for example, to increase three verses (x, y, and z) to fifteen there could be three patterns of repetition: 1. x x x y z; 2. x y y y z; 3. x y z z z. See Kane 1962–75, ii. 1182–3.

4.2 *covered it*: in the original Sanskrit, the verb does not have an object, so it is unclear what or whom they covered. Others translate 'they covered themselves', but this is unlikely because the verb is active. They may have covered the Veda (which consisted of words) with metres (*chandas*), thus giving the name *chandas* also to the Veda as such. So the statement 'gave the name to . . . true nature of the metres,' may mean at the same time: 'gave the name to . . . true nature of the vedic texts' (see BU 1.2.1 n.).

4.4–5 *syllable*: on its two meanings, see BU 3.8.8 n.

5.1 *it makes the sound* OṂ: the meaning is not altogether clear. It could refer to the ritual acclamations to the rising sun (see CU 1.11.7; 3.19.3); then the sound is actually not made by the sun but only accompanies the rising sun (for the association between OṂ and the rising sun, see Parpola 1981). In another context, Parpola (1981, 205) suggests that the very upward movement of the sun may have been interpreted as a sign of assent (see CU 1.1.8–9 n.) parallel to the waving of the head or hands and thus figuratively as OṂ.

5.5 *So, then . . . improperly*: the argument here is the following. The Hotṛ priest is not allowed to sing the High Chant; only the Udgātṛ can sing it. If the High Chant is essentially OṂ, however then the Hotṛ priest can rectify the faulty singing of the High Chant by the Udgātṛ priest, because the Hotṛ can recite OṂ.

6.1 *overlaid*: the reference is to the Ṛgvedic lyric set to the Sāman tune, on the one hand, and to the laying of the fire upon the earth: see CU 1.3.9 n. The same image is carried into the other equivalences in the subsequent paragraphs.

Sāma: the nominative form of the stem *sāman* is here viewed as a compound of *sā* and *ama*. Grammatically, the former is feminine and the latter masculine; there may be a play here on the grammatical genders of the two, Sāman being viewed as a fertile union of the male and the female. See CU 1.1.6.

6.8 *High Chanter*: i.e., the Udgātṛ priest; see BU 1.3.28 n.

7.5 *Recitation* [uktha]: see BU 1.6.1 n.

formulation of truth (*brahman*): see BU 2.1.1 n.

8.5 *for heaven . . . sung*: the place from which the Sāman is sung is a special area of the sacrificial enclosure (see Kane 1962–75, ii. 1167), here identified with the heavenly world.

8.6 *head will shatter apart*: see BU 1.3.24 n.

9.3–4 *world*: on possessing a world, see BU 1.3.28 n.

10.3 *leftovers*: what is actually left on a plate or cup after someone has eaten or drunk off it. Such food and water are considered extremely impure.

10.8–11 *Udgātṛ priests*: in the plural, the reference is to the Udgātṛ and his assistants, Prastotṛ and Pratihartṛ: see Int., p. xlii.

area designated for it: see CU 1.8.5 n.

Introductory Praise, High Chant, Response: three of the five parts of a Sāman explained at CU 2.2.1 n. The rest of this chapter, and the whole of Ch. 2, are devoted to drawing out hidden meanings and connections between the parts of a Sāman and various cosmic and bodily entities.

11.5 *all these beings . . . towards breath*: this statement is generally translated: 'all beings enter [into life] with breath and depart [from life] with breath' (Hume 1931). I think the term *abhisaṃviśanti* has more the meaning of entering or gathering around a leader (see BU 1.3.18; CU 3.6–10; TU 3.1). The meaning of *abhyujjihate* is less clear; I take it as reinforcing the first term rather than implying a contrary meaning. The following two equivalences (between sun and High Chant, and food and Response) are based clearly on the phonetic similarity of the activities with regard to the sun and food. Here the phonetic similarity appears to be with the word *prāṇa* ('breath') itself.

11.7 *when the sun . . . sing to it*: parallel passage at CU 1.3.1. The singing probably refers to both the liturgical prayers addressed to the rising sun and the noise of people and animals, especially the singing of the birds, that accompany sunrise (see CU 1.5.1 n.).

12.4 *Bahiṣpavamāna*: a special hymn of praise. To sing it the priests, led by the Adhvaryu, proceed stealthily towards the northern part of the sacrificial enclosure one behind the other, their heads bent and each priest holding on to the shoulders of the one in front of him. This manner of walking is expressly stated to be in imitation of deer hunting, the deer in this case being the sacrifice itself. See Kane 1962–75, ii: 116–67.

13.3 *The thirteenth . . . unexplained*: this obscure and difficult passage is discussed by Gren-Eklund 1978, 45–9.

13.4 *hidden connections*: see BU 3.9.26 n. and Int., p. lii; parallel at CU 1.3.7.

CHAPTER 2

1.1 *the Sāman chant in its entirety*: that is, all five parts of a Sāman: CU 2.2.1 n. Much of the earlier sections of Ch. 1 was devoted to just one of those parts, the High Chant. The extensive word play in this section is based on the meanings of the several homonyms of *sāman* and the many contextual meanings of *sādhu*, both as a substantive and as an adverb.

2.1 *fivefold Sāman chant*: the Sāman used as a hymn of praise at a Soma sacrifice consists of five parts sung by the three Sāmavedic priests, Udgātṛ, Prastotṛ, and Pratihartṛ. The five parts are: Introductory Praise (*prastāva*), High Chant (*udgītha*), Response (*pratihāra*), Finale (*upadrava*), and Concluding Chant (*nidhana*). In the fivefold division given here, however, the initial *hiṃ* (referred to as the *Hiṃ*-interjection, even though it is pronounced *huṃ*, see CU 2.8.1) of the Introductory Praise is regarded as the first division, and the Finale is assimilated into the Response. Later, at CU 2.8–10, the fivefold Sāman is further subdivided into seven by treating the initial interjection *huṃ*, the Response, and the Finale as separate parts, and by considering the OṂ which opens the High Chant as a distinct part called Opening (*ādi*). The first verse of the Bahiṣpavamāna hymn (BU 1.3.28) reads: *upāsmai gāyatā naraḥ pavamānāyendave | abhi devān iyakṣate* | (RV 9.11.1). It is sung in five parts (a numeral indicates the length of prolation of the preceding vowel):

Introductory Praise (by Prastotṛ): *huṃ | upāsmai gāyatā narom* |
High Chant (by Udgātṛ): *oṃ | pā(2)vā(2)mānāyendavā(2) abhi devam iyā (1 2 1 2)*
Response (by Pratihartṛ): *hum ā(2)*
Finale (by Udgātṛ): *kṣāto*
Concluding Chant (by all three): *sā(3 4 5)t*

For further information, see Kane 1962–75, ii. 1166–74.

4.1 *When the easterly . . . flow westwards*: the reference here is to the rivers of northern India, most of which flow from the Himalayas either towards the east, e.g. the Ganges, or towards the west, e.g. the Indus.

7.1 *most extensive*: the exact sense of the Sanskrit term *parovarīyas* is somewhat unclear. It may have simultaneously the meanings of extensive and excellent. For an analysis, see Gren-Eklund 1978, 94–5 (although I think she is reading too much into this term).

8.1 *sevenfold Sāman*: see CU 2.2.1 n.

Hiṃ-interjection: as pointed out earlier (CU 2.2.1 n.), even though the interjection is pronounced *huṃ*, it bears the title *Hiṃ*.

9.5 *Gods are linked to it*: on the use of the High Chant by the gods, see BU 1.3.

Prajāpati's children: see BU 1.3.1 n.

10.3–4 *Ud.gī.tha ... the same as those*: when three syllables are taken from the two to make them equal, one syllable is left over. But the Sanskrit word for 'syllable' is *akṣara*, which word also has three syllables, making the one syllable left over equal to the other two! Since the word *nidhana* also has three syllables, all these terms are equal to each other.

10.5 *With twenty-one ... from sorrow*: 'Twenty-one' refers both to the number of syllables in the words and to cosmic phenomena, i.e., 12 months, 5 seasons, 3 regions (earth, intermediate region, sky), and the sun (SB 1.3.5.11). The vault of the sky (*nāka*) is located toward the nocturnal zenith, near the North Pole above the Milky Way (as observed in northern India). Witzel (1984) has described these astronomical features in detail with maps and graphs.

11.1 *Gāyatra*: the names of the Sāmans, such as Gāyatra and Rathanthara, mentioned in §§ 11–20 refer to specific Sāmans sung at specific moments during the Soma sacrifice. In a typical Soma sacrifice there are twelve such Sāmans.

woven: on the weaving metaphor repeatedly encountered here and in subsequent paragraphs, see BU 3.6.1 n.

11.2 *big man*: I use this expression here and elsewhere in the sense it has been employed in anthropological literature, that is, a man who has made himself rich, important, and influential in his community not because of birth (ascribed status) but because of his own efforts.

big-minded: there is a play here on 'big' (*mahān*). The expression means both 'magnanimous' and 'haughty'.

12.1 *churns the fire-drill*: see BU 1.4.6 n.

19.1 *The Hiṃ-interjection ... bodily parts*: on these five standard bodily parts, see Jamison 1986, 167–78.

20.1 *deities*: see BU 1.3.9 n.

21.1 *glittering specks*: probably the dust particles floating in the air that glitter in the sun.

the Whole: see BU 1.4.9–10 n.

21.3–4 *There is ... to him*: the manuscript tradition of numbering paragraphs, as well as modern editors and translators, have not recognized that the first two sentences of § 4 form the last two lines of this verse in the unusual metre with 9, 11, 9, 11 syllables in each line (Horsch 1966, 173–4). The term 'Whole' in the verse is the same as 'all' (*sarvam*) and in the original parallels 'all the quarters'.

22.5 *with an open passage ... articulation*: the technical term *vivṛta* refers to the 'internal effort', that is, the manner of articulating vowels and spirants. When the articulator closes the passage between it and the place of articulation, it completely stops the outgoing breath and produces the stops. When, on the other hand, the articulator comes close to the place of articulation but does not actually touch it, creating a passage for outgoing air, it is called *vivṛta*; this form of articulation is used to create the open sounds of the spirants. There are three spirants in Sanskrit: dental, palatal, and retroflex. They are produced at the same places as the corresponding stops, but when spirants are pronounced the tongue remains close to but does not touch the place of articulation. The text recommends that the spirants should be pronounced in that 'open' manner, without making them too weak ('swallowing') or too strong in their hissing quality ('ejecting'), suggesting that they are pronounced in a smooth continuous manner.

22.5 *pronounce all the stops*: although the technical term *sparśa* means a stop, here it probably covers the semivowels as well (the articulator of the latter being called *īṣatspṛṣṭa*). I follow Śaṃkara and the opinion of George Cardona (private communication) in accepting the reading *anabhinihitāḥ*, rejecting Böhtlingk's emendation, both because the former is the *lectio difficilior* and because it makes perfect sense. The meaning is that while pronouncing a consonant one should hold the sound for a split second before pronouncing the following sound so that the two can be heard by the listener as separate sounds. I thank George Cardona and Madhav Deshpande for their insightful and learned comments on this difficult passage.

23.1 *There are three . . . immortality*: this passage has often been cited as early evidence for the system of the orders of life (*āśrama*). It is at best, however, only representative of the theological innovations that finally gave rise to that system: see Sprockhoff 1981: 80–2; Olivelle 1993, 106–11. My translation of this passage is based on taking *dharmaskandhāḥ* as a possessive compound (*bahuvrīhi*); this interpretation is supported by the contrast drawn between it and *brahmasaṃsthaḥ*, 'a person who is steadfast in brahman'. In the vedic literature *skandha* means either the upper torso (shoulder area of the upper back) or the trunk of a tree. Even in later literature compounds with *skandha* as the final member regularly refers to a person or tree with a particular type of *skandha*. Thus we have *dīrghaskandha* (tree 'with a long trunk') as the name of a particular tree, and *siṃhaskandha* ('lion-shouldered') as a descriptive epithet of a strong man. Traditionally this passage has been translated: 'There are three branches of the Law.'

that is . . . teacher's house: both Böhtlingk (1889*b*, 99) and Senart

(1930, 28) take this phrase to be a gloss and omit it. I think they are right in considering it a gloss but keep it in the translation because it is part of the received text of the CU.

worlds earned by merit: the term *puṇya*, here translated as 'earned by merit' can also mean 'pure' or 'pleasant'.

steadfast in brahman: the term *brahman* here probably refers to the syllable OṂ, which is the subject of discussion in the first two chapters of the CU, or means 'formulation of truth' (see BU 2.1.1 n.).

23.2 *incubated the worlds*: in many cosmogonies the application of heat precedes the emergence of created beings. The image here is undoubtedly borrowed from the hatching of an egg, where the creator sits upon the material of creation to incubate it, like a hen upon her eggs. See, for example, CU 3.1–5; 4.17; AU 1.1.4; 1.3.

bhūr, bhuvas, svar: these syllables, bearing the general name 'Calls' (*vyāhṛti*), are both sacred sounds and the names for the earth, the intermediate region, and the sky, respectively.

23.3 *As all the leaves . . . pin*: the leaves here probably refer to the leaves of a manuscript. These manuscript leaves were made with a variety of materials, including palm leaves and birch bark. To bind the separate leaves together with a string, one or two holes were bored through them (Thieme 1968*a*, 17). It is this image that the text is using to show how all of speech is penetrated by OṂ. If this interpretation is right, then it is an important piece of evidence both for writing in India and for the relative age of the final redaction of this Upaniṣad.

24.1 *formulations of truth*: see BU 2.1.1 n.

Since the morning . . . All-gods: for the relationship between these groups of deities and the three pressings of Soma, see CU 3.16. The 'pressing' refers to the crushing of the stems of the Soma plant to obtain the juice that is to be offered in sacrifice.

24.3 *the command*: is given by the Adhvaryu to the Hotṛ, who recites the litany sometime before daybreak of the last (normally the fifth) day of the Soma sacrifice, when the Soma is pressed. The number of verses in the litany varies but is generally over 100.

the householder's fire: one of the three main fires used in a vedic sacrifice (see Int., p. xlii; Fig. 3, p. xliii). It is located on the western side of the sacrificial enclosure; the patron of the sacrifice sits behind (i.e. to the west of) that fire.

24.4 *door to the world*: this door is identified as the moon (KsU 1.2) and as the sun (CU 8.6.5; IU 15). Witzel (1984, 223, 233) has argued that the door to the heavenly or the 'brilliant' world, i.e. the Milky

Way of the northern Indian winter–spring nights, is the mouth of the two arms projecting towards the east from the Milky Way (see Int., p. xlvi). This Sāman and its four subsequent variations are sung with the prolation of certain vowels and the insertion of interjections (see CU 2.2.1 n.). I give here the original Sanskrit with the length of prolations indicated by numerals in order to give the reader some idea as to how it was sung: *lo(3)kadvāram apāvā(3)rṇū(3 3)* | *paśyema tvā vayaṃ rā(3 3 3 3 3) hu(3)m ā(3 3)jyā(3)yo(3)ā(3 2 1 1 1)* |

24.5–16 *Vasus, Rudras, Ādityas, All-gods*: these deities are probably viewed as presenting to the patron the world connected with the different pressings of Soma. For All-gods, see BU 3.1.9 n.

24.7 *Āgnīdhriya fire*: is associated with the Āgnīdhra priest, an assistant priest responsible for maintaining the sacrificial fires. This fire is kept within his special shed located on the north side, half inside and half outside the sacrificial enclosure.

CHAPTER 3

1.1 *Cross-bar*: probably refers to the branch on which the bees build their hive. It is difficult to understand completely these images without a knowledge of the apiary culture of the time.

glittering specks: see CU 2.21.1 n.

1.2 *immortal waters*: are located in heaven; the reference probably is to the Milky Way (Witzel 1984).

1.3 *incubated*: on the cosmogonic aspects of heating, see CU 2.23.2 n. The image here is that of a bee sitting within a flower, which can be compared to a hen sitting on the eggs. The 'incubation' by the bee converts the contents of the flower into honey, that is, nectar.

essence [rasa]: the Sanskrit term carries a liquid image, for example, the sap of a tree. This liquid image is important for understanding the imagery in this passage on the honey of the gods.

foodstuff [annādya]: see BU 1.3.17 n.

1.4 *red appearance*: on the meaning of *rūpa* as visible appearance, see BU 1.4.7 n.

4.1–2 *Collections of Histories*: regarding this and the other texts mentioned here, see CU 7.1.2 n.

5.1 *secret rules of substitution*: see BU 2.3.6 n.

formulation of truth: *brahman* here, in all likelihood, refers to formulations (BU 2.1.1 n.) such as those termed *upaniṣad*. See also CU 1.7.5.

6.2 *appearance*: the appearances referred to here and in the subsequent passages are the different colours of the sun created by the flow of the essences of the different Vedas.

6.4 *achieve dominion*: in speaking of the dominion achieved over the three classes of gods, this and the subsequent passages pick up the theme introduced in the question at CU 2.24.1–2.

11.2–4 *formulation of truth*: this, I think, is the meaning of the term *brahman* here, especially because it is something that is uttered and taught (see Thieme 1952, 119), although other meanings, especially 'the unchanging whole', may also be present.

12.1 *Gāyatrī*: see BU 5.14.1 n.; 6.3.6 n.

12.5 *six types*: refer probably to creation (beings), speech, earth, body, heart, and vital functions that are identified with Gāyatrī. The four quarters (literally 'feet', *pada*) may refer to the four quarters of the cosmic person cited in the subsequent verse.

12.6 *Such is . . . in heaven*: RV 10.90.3 with variants.

12.9 *full and non-depleting*: see parallel at BU 2.1.5 and the note to this.

13.1 *deities*: here means the senses; see BU 1.3.9 n.

foodstuff [annādya]: here and in § 3, see BU 1.3.17 n.

13.7 *far above . . . blazing fire*: for a similar image, see BU 5.9.

14.1 *jalān*: this term is a hapax and, as far as we know, has no meaning. It is also unclear whether the initial *taj* (= *tat*) should be taken as part of the expression (i.e. *tajjalān*) or as a separate demonstrative pronoun referring back to *brahman*. The commentator Śaṃkara himself could find no meaning for it and construed it as an acronym indicating that everything proceeds from (*ja*), dissolves into (*la*), and lives by (*an*) *brahman*. In all likelihood, as Deussen in his translation has pointed out, this is one of the several 'meaningless' expressions relating to the ultimate being that become meaningful only within the esoteric Upaniṣadic doctrines: see *neti* (BU 2.3.6); *dadada* (BU 5.2); *viram* (BU 5.12); *saṃyadvāma* (CU 4.15.2), *idandra* (AU 1.3.14); *tadvanam* (KeU 4.6). In most of these cases the subsequent explanation functions as a commentary and reveals at least part of the meaning. Here, however, no such commentary appears to be provided. The emendation of Böhtlingk, *taj jānāni* ('I will get to know'; see Thieme 1968*a*, 39), is problematic because one fails to see how such a common form could have been corrupted into a meaningless jumble.

So . . . resolve: the meaning appears to be that a man should resolve to understand himself in the manner described in the rest of the passage.

14.2–3 *This self . . . put together*: for parallel descriptions, see BU 5.6; CU 3.13.7; 8.1.3; KaU 2.8, 20; MuU 2.2.9; SU 3.20.

15.3 *so-and-so*: here the father would state the names of all his sons.

bhūr, bhuvas, svar: refer to the earth, intermediate region, and sky; see CU 2.23.2 n.

16.1 *morning pressing*: regarding the Soma pressing and the Gāyatrī metre, see CU 2.14.1n. The Vasus are identified with the morning pressing because there are eight Vasus, and there are eight syllables in each of the three feet of the Gāyatrī metre.

To this, therefore, are linked: here and in the subsequent paragraphs, the meaning of this phrase probably is that the Vasus (as the parallel deities in the other paragraphs) are linked to both the pressing and to the corresponding period of a man's life.

16.3 *Triṣṭubh metre*: has four feet with 11 syllables in each (making a total of 44), and there are 11 Rudras as well.

16.5 *Jagatī metre*: has four feet with 12 syllables in each (making a total of 48), and there are 12 Ādityas as well.

17.1–5 *When a man . . . his death*: here various aspects of living are equated with central elements of a Soma sacrifice: a man is consecrated (*dīkṣā*) prior to undertaking a sacrifice; various preparatory rites (*upasad*) are performed daily between the day of consecration and the day of the Soma pressing; 'chants' and 'recitations' refer to singing of the Sāmans by the Udgātṛ and his assistants and to the recitations of Ṛg verses by the Hotṛ; a sacrifice ends with the distribution of gifts (*dakṣiṇā*) to the priests and the final ritual bath (*avabhṛtha*) by the patron of the sacrifice.

17.5 *He will press . . . He has pressed*: these phrases have the additional meanings of 'he will procreate' and 'he has procreated', and thus tie in with the statement that the sacrifice is the regeneration of the sacrificer.

17.6 *After Ghora . . . by breath*: on the interpretation of this somewhat difficult passage, see Ickler 1973, 76–8.

17.7 *Then they . . . the sky*: RV 8.6.30, cited in the original Sanskrit only by the first foot (*pratīka*).

Far beyond . . . have gone: RV 1.50.10 with some modifications.

18.1 *venerate*: see BU 4.1.2 n. A comparison with the opening statement of the next section (CU 3.19) shows that 'venerate' here must mean something close to 'substitute' or 'take as an equivalent'.

divine sphere: see BU 1.3.9 n.

substitution: I think the term *ādiṣṭa* (here and in § 2) is used again in the technical grammatical sense (see Thieme 1968*b*, 719). The meaning then is that both the individual level (body) and the universal level (divine sphere) are candidates for applying the principle of substitution. It results in the elements of the two levels being equivalent to each other, since they are all equal to *brahman*. The rule of substitution (see BU 2.3.6 n.), therefore, obliterates the difference between the two spheres, a central goal of Upaniṣadic arguments.

18.2 *four-legged*: on the four legs of *brahman*, see BU 4.1.2 f.; CU 4.5–8.

19.1 *non-existing*: the exact meaning of *asat* ('non-existent') and its contrast with *sat* ('existent') has been much debated. That the 'non-existent' was the primordial state of the universe prior to the creative process appears to have been an ancient belief (RV 10.72.2; 10.129.4). This view is rejected explicitly by Uddālaka Āruṇi at CU 6.2.1. In the cosmology where the 'existent' develops from the 'non-existent', the latter term, in all likelihood, refers to a state of affairs where the distinct parts of the universe, especially the separation of earth, atmosphere, and sky, had not yet emerged and where the totality was in a state of chaotic confusion. The term 'existent,' on the other hand, refers to the existent universe: see also BU 2.3.1 n. It is, however, anachronistic to hypostetize these terms and to see in them cosmic principles. Hence, I have opted to translate them as 'what is non-existing' and 'what is existing'. The second sentence, 'and what is existing was that', is also problematic. I think it may mean something like this: 'and that was what the existent was at that time', that is, the existent then did not have the structure that it now has, as then there was no earth, sky, atmosphere, or sun.

CHAPTER 4

For detailed studies of the episode of Jānaśruti and Raikva (CU 4.1–3), see Lüders 1940*b*; Hauschild 1968.

1.1 *totally devoted to giving*: whether we take the expression as *śraddhādeyaḥ* (which I prefer; it parallels the Buddhist Pāli *saddhādeyya: Dīgha Nikāya* I.5) or adopt the emendation *śraddhādevaḥ* (Böhtlingk 1889*b*; Senart 1930), the meaning appears to be that he was a man who was totally devoted to the rites of hospitality. Regarding the relation of *śraddhā* ('faith') to giving gifts, see also BU 6.2.15–16 n.

1.3 *why do you . . . the gatherer*: I follow the conjecture and interpretation of Ickler 1973, 71.

gatherer [sayugvan]: this is probably a technical term of the dice game referring to the method of gathering up the winnings. The game had four possible throws: Kṛta (4), Tretā (3), Dvāpara (2), and Kali (1). The bet of each of the two players was divided into five equal parts, thus creating ten divisions. Each higher throw would take its own number of divisions, plus those of the ones below it. Thus Kali would get one; Dvāpara would get 2 + 1; Tretā 3 + 2 + 1; and Kṛta, 4 + 3 + 2 + 1. Thus the highest throw, Kṛta, gathers to itself all the lower throws and becomes ten (CU 4.3.8). See Lüders 1907, 61–2; 1940a, 368–70; Falk 1986, 119.

1.5–6 *Jānaśruti . . . Raikva knows*: this passage is very unclear. Most translators take the three statements as questions and answers between King Jānaśruti and his steward, paralleling the conversation between the geese. Hauschild (1968, 350–1) has shown the inadequacy of this interpretation. I follow him in accepting this section as a quotation, that is, as a recounting by Jānaśruti of what he had heard. Implicit here is the fact that he failed to understand the meaning of what the geese had said. Hauschild, however, thinks that Jānaśruti is asking the steward whether it was the steward who had said these to him. I find no support for this in the text itself, which clearly states that Jānaśruti had 'overheard' the geese; so, he could not have had any doubt about who said it. If a steward was an informal counselor to a king, then the composer of this story must have expected his audience to know why the king recounted what he had heard; he wanted the steward to explain it. That may be the reason why the steward immediately went in search of Raikva.

1.7 *non-Brahmin*: I follow the emendation *abrāhmaṇa* ('non-Brahmin') proposed by Rau in Ickler 1973, 82.

2.4–5 *Raikva, here . . . swindled me*: I have followed the conjectures and interpretation of Ickler (1973, 53–5) in translating these obscure exchanges between Jānaśruti and Raikva. Raikva's final response probably means that Jānaśruti could have cheated him of his knowledge by just giving his daughter; he is relieved not to have been so cheated and to receive the wealth as well.

3.1 *gatherer* [saṃvarga]: again a technical term from the game of dice (Lüders 1940*a*, 375–6) with a meaning identical to that of 'gatherer' (*sayugvan*): see CU 4.1.3 n. It is used here with an extended meaning indicating the hierarchy of cosmic and bodily elements, where the superior ones gather up the inferiors.

3.4 *deities*: see BU 1.3.9 n.

3.5 *Once . . . give him any*: on the interpretation of this episode, which is found also in JU 3.2, see Geib 1976, 228–9.

3.6 *One god . . . mighty ones*: the one god is breath, and the four are the other vital functions, i.e. mind, sight, hearing, and speech. This is clearly a riddle that the student expected the two men to solve. The implication is that if they were unable to solve it, then the student, being their master, had a right to expect food from them.

3.7 *He's the self*: the term 'self' (*ātman*) here probably refers to breath rather than to the self or the body (see Geib 1976, 229). The 'breath of gods' is the wind.

3.8 *The former five and the latter five*: fire, sun, moon, water, and wind; and speech, sight, hearing, mind, and breath. These are then compared to the highest throw of the dice, which is ten (see CU 4.1.3 n).

Virāj: as Falk (1986, 119–24) has shown, Virāj here refers to the Virāj metre essentially consisting of 10 syllables, which is here identified with the highest throw of the dice, Kṛta, which likewise consists of 10 when it takes in the lower throws.

sinks his teeth: I follow Lüders (1940*a*, 377) in reading *daṣṭam* ('bite' or, in an extended sense, 'capture a prey by sinking the teeth into it') in place of *dṛṣṭam* ('seen'), which, within this context, makes absolutely no sense.

4–9 For a detailed study of the episode of Satyakāma Jābāla (CU 4.4–9), see Lüders 1940*b*.

4.2 *a lot of relationships*: a reference to the many men she had had in her youth (Ickler 1973, 58–9).

Jābāla: is here a matronymic, 'son of Jabālā'.

4.5 *Who but a Brahmin*: even in literature earlier than the CU we find instances where the status of a Brahmin is defined in terms other than mere birth. A verse found in both the MS (4.8.1) and the KS (30.1) asks: 'Why do you enquire about the father or the mother of a Brahmin? When you find learning in someone, that is his father, that is his grandfather.'

Fetch some firewood: the purpose is to feed the teacher's sacred fire; this rite signals the placing of oneself under a teacher as a pupil: see BU 6.2.7 n.

5.2 *quarter*: the Sanskrit *pāda* means both leg/foot and quarter. For the image of the four legs (= quarters) of *brahman*, see also BU 4.1.2 f.; CU 3.18.2.

5.2–3 *Far-flung*: the Sanskrit term *prakāśavān* may also mean 'shining' or 'resplendent'. I follow Thieme (1968*a*, 7) in taking it as referring to the wide extent of *brahman*, although there may be a play here on both meanings, especially when a man who knows this is said to be *prakāśavān* in this world, meaning that his power and fame would extend widely in the world.

8.3–4 *Abode-possessing*: on the abode and its relationship to the vital functions, see BU 4.1.2–7.

10.3 *afflicted*: the Sanskrit says simply that Upakosala stopped eating 'because of sickness', without specifying the ailment. The reference to 'desires lurking in the heart' contained in his response to his teacher's wife may indicate that the sickness had to do with problems of a sexual nature, because a student had to be permitted to return home by his teacher before he could get married.

11.1 *householder's fire*: see CU 2.24.3 n.

11.2 *provides himself with a world*: see BU 1.3.28 n.

12.1 *southern fire*: is located to the south of the other two fires, but closer to the householder's fire, and is used for cooking rice and, therefore, also called *anvāhāryapacana* (see Fig. 3, p. xliii).

13.1 *offertorial fire*: is the fire in which the sacred oblations are put. See Int., p. xlii.

15.1 *person in the eye*: for parallels, see BU 2.3.5; 5.5.2; CU 1.7.5; 8.7.5.

15.5 *whether they . . . human condition*: for parallels, see BU 6.2.15–16 n.

16.2 *One of those . . . speech*: on the four priests, see BU 3.1.2–6 n.

the morning litany: see CU 2.24.3 n.

16.3–4 *pauper, rich man*: on the opposing categories of pauper (*pāpīyān*) and rich man (*śreyān*), see Rau 1957, 32–5 and BU 1.4.11 n.

17.1 *incubated*: see CU 2.23.2 n.

17.2 *essences*: on the liquid nature of essence, see CU 3.1.3 n.

17.3 *bhūḥ, bhuvaḥ, svaḥ*: see CU 2.23.2 n.

17.4 *he should make an offering*: the person who performs this offering to mend the sacrifice here and in the subsequent paragraphs is the Brahman priest, thus connecting this section to CU 4.16.2–4.

17.7 *salt*: the meaning of *lavaṇa* here is uncertain. In general, it means 'salt', but in this context it must refer to some chemical used to mend gold. On this passage and on parallel passages in the Brāhmaṇas, see Rau 1973, 30.

17.9–10 *Wherever it turns*: the meaning probably is 'wherever the sacrifice turns'. On this difficult verse, see Horsch 1966, 175–7.

CHAPTER 5

1–2 See the parallel passage at BU 6.1, where most of the notes are given.

1.12 *a fine horse . . . tethered*: on the precise meaning of this passage, see Wezler 1982. The image is that of a powerful horse tied with ropes to stakes. As it begins to gallop away it would exert a sudden and violent jerk on all the stakes and finally tear them up. It is the initially violent tug that is the point of comparison. The breath had not departed but was just beginning to set off; this caused a violent and sudden tug at the other vital functions, which prompted them to beg the breath not to depart.

1.15 *Surely . . . all these*: this passage gives the reason why the vital functions, including the senses, are called *prāṇa* (lit. 'breath') in Sanskrit: see BU 1.5.17 n.

2.1 *nothing that is not food*: the meaning of 'not food' probably is that nothing is improper and unclean food for him. See the comments at BU 6.1.14 n. On the open name, see BU 3.4.1; 4.2.2. The intent appears to be that *ana* is the name of breath that makes a clear connection between breath and food (*anna*), whereas in its more common name *prāṇa* the connection is hidden.

2.2 *Then he asked . . . remain naked*: the reference here is to the ritual practice of sipping some water before and after a meal (see BU 6.1.14). The verb for 'surround', *paridadhati* also means to wear clothes.

2.3 *After telling . . . new leaves*: see parallels at BU 6.3.7–12.

2.4–9 *Now, if . . . dream vision*: see the longer parallel passage at BU 6.3.

2.4 *sacrificial consecration*: see BU 3.9.23 n.

svāhā: see BU 5.8 n.

2.6 *slides back stealthily*: see CU 1.12.4 n.

You are power . . . your side: the translation of the sentence is tentative (see Ickler 1973, 91; Bodewitz 1973, 274). In another context the obscure word *ama* is taken as the second part of the word 'Sāma': see CU 1.6.1 n.

2.7 *We choose . . . for ourselves*: this verse is a variation of the Sāvitrī verse. On the recitation here of the Sāvitrī verse, see BU 6.3.6 n.

2.8 *unresistant*: may imply that he should let himself fall asleep and not attempt to keep awake. This ties in with what follows, for it is in a dream that he will see a woman.

3–10 See the parallel account of this episode at BU 6.2, where most of the notes are given.

3.5 *As you report . . . to you*: the father's reply is extremely unclear; the reading is probably corrupt. I have followed Böhtlingk's plausible emendations, which, however, do not make it much more clear.

9.2 *appointed time*: I follow the emendation *diṣṭam itaṃ* in place of *diṣṭam itaḥ* (Ickler 1973, 64) in translating: 'when he has reached his appointed time'.

10.1–3 *venerate*: see BU 6.2.15–16 n.

10.3 *Gift-giving . . . to priests*: the meaning probably is that these people equated the virtue of generous giving to the sacrificial offerings to gods and sacrificial fees to priests. This fixation on sacrificial activities among people living in villages is also the theme of the parallel passage in BU 6.2.16 and MuU 1.2.7–10.

10.5 *residue* [sampāta]: this term has often been interpreted within the context of the *karma* theory as referring to the residue of merits. It is, however, clear that the term, which generally refers to the residue of a sacrifice, refers here to the residue of Soma/moon as the gods eat it. When it is completely gone, then the people return in the form of rain. This meaning is clear also in the parallel passage at BU 6.2.16, where it is said that the people return after the gods have completed their feeding.

10.6 *from him one comes into being again*: the meaning and grammar of this phrase are somewhat unclear. The commentator Śaṃkara takes it to mean that the person is born resembling the man who deposited him as semen, i.e. his father.

10.8 *As a result*: the reference is to the question at CU 5.3.3.

A man should . . . himself from that: that is, from getting into a 'foul womb' by committing crimes specified in the verse (see Thieme 1965, 94).

11 A possibly older version of this story is found in SB 10.6.1, and it is the likely source of the CU version. In the SB the topic is the Vaiśvānara fire, which is here recast as the search for the Vaiśvānara self.

11.2 *the one common to all men* [vaiśvānara]: here and in the subsequent passages, this Sanskrit term is also the name of a fire (see BU 1.1.1 n.) that is the subject of the SB version of the story. The phrase could also be translated: 'studying the self as the Vaiśvānara fire'. I think that the parallel between the self and the Vaiśvānara fire, especially in its reference to the sun, runs through this entire section.

11.7 *carrying firewood*: part of the ceremony of initiation as a pupil. See BU 6.2.7 n.

12.1 *brightly shining self*: there is clearly a phonetic connection between 'brightly shining' (*sutejas*) and the ceaseless pressing of Soma (*suta, prasuta, āsuta*). It is unclear, however, whether *sutejas* is a corrupt reading for *sutatejas* ('splendour of Soma'), the reading found in the parallel passage in the SB 10.6.1.8, as assumed by Böhtlingk in his edition of CU; see Senart's (1930) comments in his note on this passage.

12.2 *You eat food*: here and in the following paragraphs, this expression has a pregnant meaning: he becomes an eater of food (i.e. gains power over others), rather than becoming food that is eaten by another (i.e. becomes subservient to another). On the significance of this image, see BU 1.2.5 n.

shattered apart: see BU 1.3.24 n.

13.1–2 *dazzling* [viśvarūpa]: for this meaning, see BU 1.4.7 n. On this passage, see Bodewitz 1985, 16–17; Rau 1973, 54. I have translated the term *cakṣuḥ* here and in CU 5.18.2 as 'eye', even though the term generally refers to sight or the visual power (see BU 1.3.2–6 n). The parallel with the other physical parts of the body makes it clear that here the reference is to the physical eye rather than to the power of seeing. The attribute 'brightly shining' or glittering also fits better with the physical eye.

18.1 *beyond all measure*: the meaning of the term *abhivimāna*, which I have translated 'beyond all measure' following Böhtlingk's conjecture *ativimāna*, is unclear. But the image of the self as both infinitesimally small and unimaginably large is common in this literature: see CU 3.14.1; KaU 4.12–13; 6.17; SU 5.8.

18.2 *Now, of this self... the mouth*: this summary of the incomplete identifications of the self made in the preceding paragraphs shows clearly the close association of the two meanings of *ātman*, as body and as self. Even though the translation has to necessarily choose between these two meanings, the original Sanskrit keeps these two dimensions of the term tightly together. See Int., p. xlix; BU 1.1.1 n.

18.2 *householder's fire*: on the three fires, see Int., p. xlii.

19–24 *The first morsels . . . all the beings gather*: what is described here is the offering of food in the five breaths of man conceived of as five fires. Thus, this ritual offering is called 'the fire sacrifice in the vital breaths' (*prāṇāgihotra*). For a discussion of this and parallel passages, see Bodewitz 1973, 264–9. For a detailed account of this rite, which becomes especially important in later Brahmanical ascetic traditions, see Bodewitz 1973, 213–343.

svāhā: see BU 5.8. n.

23 *the up-breath . . . wind becomes satisfied*: some editions read: '. . . the up–breath is satisfied, the skin becomes satisfied; when the skin is satisfied, the wind becomes satisfied.' The section on the skin is also lacking at CU 3.13.

CHAPTER 6

1.1 *Āruṇi*: the same person as Uddālaka Āruṇi, who appears in somewhat unflattering roles elsewhere in the Upaniṣads: BU 3.7; 6.2; CU 3.11.4; 5.3–10; 5.11; 5.17. This is the place where he appears as the teacher of Upaniṣadic doctrine.

kind of Brahmin . . . birth: on the expression *brahmabandhu* ('a Brahmin only by birth'), see BU 6.2.3 n.

1.3 *you must have surely asked*: I follow Speyer's conjecture *aprakṣyaḥ* for the manuscript reading *aprakṣyāḥ*. See Hamm 1968–9, 150 n. 6; Morgenroth 1970, 34–6.

rule of substitution: see BU 2.3.6 n.

1.4–6 *the transformation . . . a name*: the nominal phrase *vācārambhaṇaṃ vikāro nāmadheyam* has been the subject of much scrutiny and debate. Edgerton (1965) takes the final word as the subject, and translates: 'the appellation (of individual manifestations; of any particular product of iron) is a verbal handle, a modification.' I follow those (Böhtlingk 1889*b*, Hume 1931, Senart 1930, Hamm 1968–9, Hanfeld 1976) who take 'modification' as the subject. Thieme (1968*a*, 44–5) takes the three terms as standing in apposition to an implied subject. Senart and Hanfeld resort to Thieme's syntax at CU 6.4 where the same phrase occurs, because the context there appears not to favour taking this phrase as an independent sentence. Thieme thinks that in each sentence the referent is the respective example (lump of clay, copper trinket, or nail-cutter); thus the meaning is that when we say something is a nail cutter, that term is merely a verbal handle, the reality being that it is just iron. I think that van Buitenen's (1955, 1958) attempt to relate *vācārambhaṇam* to cosmological speculations concerning Speech is a forced over-interpretation. The phrase is more easily explained, because *ārambhaṇa* is regularly used in the Upaniṣads with the meaning of support or foothold, especially the lack of such a support in the atmosphere: CU 2.9.4; BU 3.1.6. I think Edgerton (1965) is right when he translates it as 'verbal handle'.

1.7 *illustrious men*: the reference is to the former teachers of Śvetaketu; or it may be merely a majestic plural, and the reference may be to his teacher in the singular.

2.1 *existent, non-existent*: see CU 3.19.1 n. The exact opposite doctrine is presented at CU 3.19.

2.3 *Whenever it is hot . . . water is produced*: see Edgerton 1915; Morgenroth 1970, 36–7. Edgerton (1965) translates: 'Therefore, wherever it is hot, a man surely sweats, just because of the heat; on this basis water is produced.' Thieme (1968*a*, 46) thinks that a phrase, given here in brackets, has been omitted: 'Whenever it is hot therefore, [there arises from it rain] or a man perspires.' This interpretation ties in with the rising of food from rain in the next sentence and has a parallel in CU 7.11.1.

3.1 *only three sources . . . from sprouts*: the references here are to the birth from eggs; live birth from a mother; and the growth of plants from seeds. It appears that these three origins are related to the three primary entities: the hatching of eggs to heat, live birth to water, and sprouting to food. For a longer enumeration, see AU 5.3.

3.2 *deity*: that is, the 'existent' that was there in the beginning.

three deities: I do not think that the three types of creatures born from eggs etc. are meant here, as assumed by Hamm (1968–9, 151 n. 20). The parallel passage at CU 6.4.7 shows that they are heat, water, and food (for the extended meanings of 'deity', see BU 1.3.9 n).

3.3 *make each of them threefold*: Edgerton (1965) is right in thinking that the triplication is done by adding to each the other two, thus producing in the concrete the various combinations of all three. Another form of triplication is given in CU 6.5.

4.1–4 *the character of fire* [agnitvam]: indicates both what makes fire fire, i.e. the individual nature of fire and the name 'fire' that we ascribe to it (see BU 1.2.1 n.). So, one gets at the reality of fire not by saying, 'It's a fire', but by saying, 'Its the three appearances'. The same applies to the parallel expressions with reference to the sun, moon, and lightning in the subsequent paragraphs. The effort of van

Buitenen (1958, 297) to trace here a cosmology is mistaken, especially because it is founded on assuming *agneḥ* to be a genitive, when it is, in fact, an ablative, as demonstrated by the parallels *ādityāt* and *candrāt*. He is, however, right to point out that no illusionistic or monistic philosophy is implied here; the fire is not unreal, but its more basic reality is the three appearances. Here again we are dealing with the equivalences and substitutions that are at the heart of Upaniṣadic teaching: see BU 1.1.2 n.; 2. 3. 6 n.

4.7 *indistinct*: means something whose colour cannot be easily discerned as red, white, or black.

5.3 *eats heat*: the fact that one eats *tejas* ('heat') shows the concrete nature of this entity. The implication may well be, as Thieme has pointed out, that 'heat' is 'eaten', that is, absorbed into the body, through the medium of eating hot food.

7.3 *Out of a huge . . . all that much*: on the various translations of this difficult passage, see Ickler 1973, 38–9.

7.6 *And he did . . . from him*: this sentence brackets the section that began at CU 6.4.7.

8.1 *sleeping*: on a somewhat different etymology of 'sleeping' related to vital breaths rather than to the existent, see SB 10.5.2.14.

8.3 *hunger*: here (and in the parallel passage in § 5) the correspondences are based on the word for hunger *aśanā* or *aśanāyā*. The two final syllables, *nāyā* (here converted to *nāya*) can be related to the verb *nayati* ('to lead' or 'to drive'). Thus, a cattle-driver is *gonāya*. Hunger, therefore, can be seen as meaning 'driver of food' (*aśa*). Thus the water is both food-driver and hunger, and heat is both water-driver and thirst.

as a bud . . . without a root: the contrast between bud and root is, beyond the image, the contrast between an effect and its cause. What 'this' stands for is unclear. Traditionally it has been taken as a deictic pronoun referring to the body. Edgerton (1965) and Hamm (1968–9), however, prefer to take hunger as the referent, hunger being caused by the water carrying away the food. I still prefer the traditional interpretation, because in the other the symmetry is broken: the absence of food causes hunger, whereas it is the presence of water, heat, and the existent that produces food, water, and heat, respectively.

8.6 *I have already . . . threefold*: here ends the section that began with the last sentence of CU 6.4.5.

highest deity: that is, the existent: see CU 6.3.2 n.

8.7–16.3 *that's how you are*: in interpreting the famous saying *tat tvam asi*, that has been traditionally translated as 'That art thou', I follow the insightful study by Brereton (1986). He has shown that in the phrase *tat tvam asi*, according to the rules of vedic syntax, the neuter pronoun *tat* ('that') cannot stand in apposition to a masculine noun or pronoun (here *tvam*, 'you'), even when the antecedent of 'that' may be a neuter word. Thus, if the author had wanted to assert the identity between 'that' and 'you', he would have used the masculine of 'that'; the phrase would then read *sa tvam asi*. Brereton has convincingly argued that the pronoun *tat* ('that') cannot refer either to *sat* ('existent') or to *aṇiman* ('fine essence'), and that this entire paragraph has migrated to sections 8–11 and 13–16 from its original place at the end of section 12, thus becoming a refrain. The phrase, therefore, does not establish the identity between the individual and the ultimate being (*sat*), but rather shows that Śvetaketu lives in the same manner as all other creatures, that is, by means of an invisible and subtle essence. It may also (and here I depart somewhat from Brereton), to some degree, indicate the cause of his existence, just as at CU 6.12.2 the finest essence of the seed is said to be the reason for the tree's existence. In using the term 'how' I attempt to capture both these meanings: that is how you came to be, and that is how (the way) you exist. Brereton (1986, 109) writes: 'First, the passage [CU 6.12] establishes that the tree grows and lives because of an invisible essence. Then, in the refrain, it says that everything, the whole world, exists by means of such an essence. This essence is the truth, for it is lasting and real. It is the self, for everything exists with reference to it. Then and finally, Uddālaka personalizes the teaching. Śvetaketu should look upon himself *in the same way*. He, like the tree and the whole world, is pervaded by this essence, which is his final reality and his true self' (original emphasis). For a similar statement regarding the sap by means of which the ultimate Person lives in all creatures as their inner self, see MuU 2.1.9.

10.1 *The easterly ones . . . just the ocean*: for the easterly and westerly rivers, see BU 3.8.9; CU 2.4.1. As Edgerton (1965) has pointed out, rightly I believe, the two oceans are the heavenly one and the earthly (Indian) ocean. Witzel (1984, 262) interprets it as referring to the movement of the celestial rivers located in the Milky Way, from the east to the north and from the west toward the south. As Witzel has shown, the vedic Indians regarded the Indus and Ganges river systems as connected to the celestial rivers of the Milky Way.

10.2 *when all these . . . reaching the Existent*: I have followed Edgerton (1965) and Ickler (1973, 21). Others translate: 'although all these creatures have come from the Existent, they are not aware: "We have come from the Existent." '

11.1 *its living sap would flow*: others translate: 'being alive, its sap would flow.' The participle *jīvan* ('living') is better viewed as qualifying the implied sap (so Thieme 1968*a*, 52); it is the sap that gives life to the tree. It is this sap that is then referred to as 'the living essence (or self)' (*jīvātman*) which pervades the tree and gives it life and as the 'life' that sometimes leaves one of its branches.

11.3 *this, of course, dies*: the referent of 'this' is unclear. It may refer to anything in the world that is bereft of life (e.g. a branch, a tree, a body); more likely, however, it is a diectic pronoun referring to the body of the speaker.

12.2 *look how . . . stands here*: I follow Hamm (1968–9, 157 nn. 65–6) in reading *mahānyagrodha* (as a compound: 'huge banyan tree') and in taking *evam* ('in this manner') as an adverb of manner qualifying the verb. I think, in the colloquial context of the conversation, it invites the listener to be amazed at how such a large tree is sustained by such a small and invisible essence; hence my translation 'look how'. Most translators take the verb *tiṣṭhati* ('stand') to have the meaning of 'arise'. The sense of the statement then is that the large banyan tree has grown from a tiny seed. Although this sense is not excluded, I think the focus of Uddālaka's example is to show what sustains the large tree, what is the ultimate essence of that tree, rather than where it originally came from (Brereton 1986, 105). This meaning also corresponds to the point made by the earlier example that saw the sap as the bearer of life to the tree.

13.2 *Throw it out . . . right there*: I follow Edgerton (1965) in understanding this passage the following way. The son would throw the salt water on the ground (Edgerton suggests a slab of stone). When the water evaporates, the dissolved salt would become visible again, showing that even though it was invisible, it was all the time present in the water. This assumes the reading to be *abhiprāsya* ('throw out') rather than *abhiprāśya* ('eat'). All other interpretations, I feel, are forced in comparison and do not support the point Uddālaka wants to make through this example.

14.1–2 *he would drift . . . or the south*: I follow Edgerton's (1915, 243) convincing argument for omitting the western direction, missing also in some manuscripts. The point, of course, is that, Gandhāra being in the west, he would actually end up there if he wanders towards the west! Indeed, that must be the direction pointed out by the man who removed his blindfold.

There is a delay . . . I will arrive: on the difficulties associated with this statement, see Edgerton 1915, 244–5; Hanfeld 1976, 133 n. 19. In spite of Edgerton's argument, I think that this sentence is a direct quote reflecting the thought of the pupil. I take the opening *tasya* ('of this' or 'his') as standing for *tasya mama* ('for me here'). What he is freed from is not specified, some taking it as the body and others, correctly I believe, as ignorance. The last word *sampatsye*, if it parallels *upasampatsye* used with reference to the arrival of the man who had been blindfolded in Gandhāra, would mean 'arrive'. But in CU 6.15 the same verb is used with the meaning of uniting or merging. Both meanings may well be hinted at here. Where he will arrive or into what he will merge is also left unstated; in all likelihood, it is the existent, which is the focus of all these discussions. The meaning appears to be: 'This state of affairs will go on for a while before I am released; but then I will arrive!'

15.1 *highest deity*: see CU 6.8.6 n.

16.1–2 *a manacled man . . . he is released*: for a discussion of this example, see Edgerton 1915, 245–6. The reference here, clearly one of the oldest in Indian history, is to the fire ordeal for ascertaining the guilt or innocence of the accused.

16.3 *And he did . . . from him*: this sentence brackets the section that began at CU 6.8.1. See CU 6.7.6 n.

CHAPTER 7

1.1 *Come to me with what you know*: this must be a play on the fact that normally a pupil approached the teacher with firewood in his hand (see CU 4.4.5 n.). The meaning, of course, is that Sanatkumāra wanted Nārada to tell him what he already knew.

1.2 *I have studied . . . serpent beings*: on this list of 'sciences', see Horsch 1966, 9–42; Faddegon 1926. The original meaning of some of these entries is clearly uncertain, and the interpretations of later commentators are often anachronistic. I take *vedānāṃ vedam* ('Veda of the Vedas') as appositional to *pañcamam* ('fifth'). Traditionally this phrase has been taken as a separate item, with the meaning of 'grammar'. The meaning of *ekāyana* (lit. 'point of convergence,' see CU 7.5.2) is uncertain (Horsch 1966, 37). The commentator Śaṃkara's interpretation as 'statecraft' (*nītiśāstra*) is clearly anachronistic. I follow Faddegon (1926, 52) in taking the term as the opposite of *vākovākya* ('speech and reply' or 'dialogue'); it would then mean an uninterrupted speech. 'Science of the gods' (*devavidyā*) is again a guess; the term may mean the knowledge of myths. 'Science of ritual' (*brahmavidyā*): here again the meaning is uncertain; *brahma* may refer to the Veda, Brahmins, the god Brahmā, or the absolute *brahman*. I take it as related to the vedic ritual, in contradistinction to the science of government (*kṣatravidyā*). 'Science of spirits' (*bhūtavidyā*) probably refers to the science associated with exorcism. 'Science of heavenly bodies' (*nakṣatravidyā*) is the knowledge of the movement of stars and the lunar mansions and would include what we call today astronomy and astrology. 'Serpent beings': I take the compound *sarpadeva-janavidyā* as referring to a single science; others divide it and interpret it as the sciences dealing with snakes and with demonic beings of Indian mythology. In any case, this science deals with beings who are divine/demonic and conceived of as serpents. For other similar lists, see BU 2.4.10; 4.1.2; 4.5.11.

1.3 *pass across, take across*: these expressions take up the common image of this world of suffering as a fearsome body of water (river, ocean). Safety and freedom from sorrow lie on the opposite shore, and a person must cross the river to reach them.

1.4 *venerate*: see BU 4.1.1 n.

4.1 *Intention*: the Sanskrit term *saṃkalpa* contains a very elusive concept. It refers first to intention, will, or purpose; in a more ritual sense, to the public declaration of one's intention to perform a rite. Its verbal equivalents, on the other hand, have a wider range of meanings, including the formation, the ordering, and the coming into being of something. I think this passage is not a metaphysic of intentionality in creation; rather it is another example of the phonetic equivalences we have seen repeatedly in these documents. The use of the same term for the origin of things gives priority to intention over the mind and other functions. This is, nevertheless, an ambivalent passage that is difficult to translate adequately.

7.1 *Perception* [vijñāna]: the reference here probably is to the correct perception and insight into things.

15.1 *lifebreath gives lifebreath and gives to lifebreath*: the meaning is not altogether clear. I take it to mean that the one who gives is lifebreath; what is given (the gift) is lifebreath; and the one to whom it is given is also lifebreath. The commentator Śaṃkara is right, I think, in stating that the meaning of this paragraph is that all things, usually distinguished into author, action, result, etc., are nothing but lifebreath.

15.3 *When their . . . burn them up completely*: the reference here is to the cremation of a dead relative.

15.4 *for only breath becomes all these*: occurring also at CU 5.1.15, this phrase indicates the superiority of lifebreath over 'these', namely, all other vital functions.

a man who out-talks: I think the term *ativādin* ('one who out-talks') is used here with a double meaning. In its positive meaning, it refers to a person who is smart enough to win a debate (used in this sense in BU 3.9.19). Such a person, however, may just be a fast talker and full of hot air, but in reality not very wise. At MuU 3.1.4 also I think the term is positive, even though the usual way of reading the text makes it out to be negative (see my note on this). In this passage, there appears to be a play on these two meanings. When people say that he is an *ativādin* (second meaning), he should reply that he is indeed an *ativādin* (first meaning, explained in CU 7.16.1).

20.1 *produce*: the meaning of *nistiṣṭhati*, here translated as 'produce', is unclear. The same term is used at CU 6.9.1 with reference to the production of honey by bees. Perhaps the meaning is that a man must first have produced wealth before he can have faith, because faith here is not merely something internal but a virtue demonstrated in hospitality rites to human and divine guests (see BU 6.2. 15–16 n.), rites that require wealth.

21.1 *act*: the reference may be to ritual action (so Senart), but in this context the term probably has a broader meaning, because one cannot produce anything without acting.

22.1 *well-being* [sukha]: the exact meaning of this term here is unclear. It probably includes prosperity, health, and comfort; in general, what we would call 'being comfortably off'.

25.1 *Plenitude*: the original has a pronoun *saḥ* ('he, that') in place of 'plenitude'. I have used the latter in the translation first to make the antecedent clear (Sanskrit pronouns are notoriously vague with respect to their antecedents: see Note on the Translation) and second to indicate some of the force of the repeated pronoun in Sanskrit, paralleling the repetition of 'I' and 'self' in the subsequent passages.

extends over this whole world: on this translation of *sa evedaṃ sarvam* (and its parallels in the other two passages), see Brereton's (1986, 102 n. 13) remark that there appears to be here an ellipsis of a verb of motion ('extend'), the type of verb found in the similar passage at MuU 2.2.12.

substitution: see BU 2.3.6 n.

25.1 *the word 'I'*: the term *ahaṃkāra*, which I have translated as 'the word "I"' takes on a more technical meaning in later philosophical traditions, especially Sāṃkhya, where it refers to the principle of psychological individuation (ego) of a person. I doubt whether these early occurrences of the term have any such technical meaning. On this passage, see van Buitenen 1957*a*, 19–20.

26.2 *It is single*: the reference is probably to the self. The numbers may have some esoteric meaning, or they may be intended, as the commentator Śaṃkara thinks, merely to point out the numerous ways in which the self is manifested within the world (see SU 1.4).

one's being [sattva]: this term takes on a technical meaning in later philosophical traditions, and van Buitenen (1957*b*, 106) takes it to mean 'a person's capacity of [for?] release'. I take it to mean something more simple, such as the physical being of a person. When it is nourished by good food, it makes one's intellectual powers and memory sharp (see, for example, CU 6.7.1–5).

Skanda: in later mythology, Skanda is the god of war and a son of Śiva. It is, however, unclear whether the term is used in this sense in this early text.

CHAPTER 8

1 The exact antecedents of the numerous pronouns used in this section are very unclear. This problem is examined in detail by Ickler 1973, 80–2. I have followed her interpretation and made the antecedents explicit in the translation itself, for repeating the pronouns alone would make it unintelligible to the reader.

1.1 *this fort of brahman*: traditionally interpreted as the body.

small lotus: the heart. The reference is to the space within the heart: see BU 4.2.2; 4.4.22; 5.6.

1.2 *But what is . . . to perceive*: given the adversarial nature of the questions posed, it is likely that the question means: 'What could there possibly be in such a small space that one should want to discover it?' In other words, the questioner seems to be implying that nothing of great significance could be in such a small space. This explains why the responder immediately shows how that small space is as vast as the universe.

1.3 *What belongs here to this*: the antecedent of 'this' has been taken by some to be a man in general (e.g. Hume: 'both what one possesses here and what one does not possess') and by others to be the body (so Thieme 1968*a*, 41). I have followed Ickler (1973, 81) in taking the referent to be the space around us, to whose vastness the space within the heart was compared at the beginning of the answer.

1.4 *the whole world . . . all desires*: as Ickler (1973, 82) points out, the three items listed here correspond to the longer list in the previous paragraph: the whole world = earth, sky, fire, etc.; all beings = what belong to the space around us; all desires = what does not belong to space.

3.2 *by going there . . . located there*: the antecedent of 'there' is probably the space within the heart dealt with in CU 8.1.

3.5 *three syllables*: the constituent syllables of *satyam* are identified as *sa, ti,* and *yam*, but in the explanation it becomes clear that they are actually viewed as *sat, ti,* and *yam.* The syllable *yam* is related to 'joining' because the verbal root of the latter is *yam-*. For another explanation of the term, see BU 5.5.1.

4.1 *dike*: on the image of a dike as a divider, see BU 4.4.22 n.

5.1–4 *Now, what . . . in all the worlds*: on the phonetic equivalences in this long passage, see Sprockhoff 1981, 59 n. 118. On the landscape of the world of *brahman*, see KsU 1.3. Airaṃmadīya probably refers to the abundance of water. Somasavana means that from which Soma is pressed. Aparājita = invincible; Prabhu = ruler (in KsU the hall is called Vibhu).

6.1 *veins of the heart*: see BU 4.3.20; 4.4.8–9; KsU 4.19.

6.3 *sound asleep*: on the explanation of dreamless sleep, see BU 2.1.18–19; 4.3.9–20; KsU 4.19.

6.4 *Now, when . . . recognize them*: for a parallel passage, see CU 6.15.1.

6.5 *door to the farther world*: see CU 2.24.4 n.

6.6 *One hundred . . . all directions*: also occurs at KaU 6.16.

7.2 *gods and demons*: as children of Prajāpati, see BU 1.3.1 n.

carrying firewood: see CU 4.4.5 n.

7.3 *So, you . . . seeking that self*: the vulgate reading (*icchantāv avāstam*) has the verb in the second person dual. This causes a problem if the phrase is spoken by Indra and Virocana, in which case the verb should be in the first person dual. Thieme (1968*a*, 31) reconstructs the phrase into a first person singular (*icchan avatsam*): 'I have lived', while Böhtlingk (1889*b*) and Senart (1930) regularize the verb as a first person dual (*avātsva*). I have resolved the difficulty by reading this phrase as Prajāpati's response to the speech made by the two. The lack of an *iti*, which closes a quotation, at the end of that speech makes my reading somewhat tentative, but it avoids the necessity of textual emendations.

7.4 *person . . . in the eye*: see BU 2.3.5 n.

8.4 *correspondence*: the term *upaniṣad* is used here with the technical meaning of 'correspondence', that is, a teaching that establishes a hierarchical correlation and identity between two disparate things. See BU 1.1.2 n. and Int., p. lii.

10.2 *it is not killed . . . lame*: see the parallel at CU 8.1.5, and Ickler's comments (1973, 48, 85–6).

Nevertheless, . . . even cries: on the experiences in a dream, see BU 4.3.20.

11.1 *perceive itself fully*: on the term *saṃprati* in connection with knowledge, here translated as 'fully' (i.e. to know something completely), see KsU 1.4a; AA 2.3.1, 4, 6.

11.3 *but only under . . . five years*: on this difficult phrase, see Ickler 1973, 75; Senart 1930, 118 n. 1.

12.3 *this deeply serene . . . person*: see the parallel at CU 8.3.4.

13.1 *Rāhu's jaws*: Rāhu is a demon who is regarded as causing the eclipse of the sun and the moon by periodically swallowing them.

14.1 *the grey and toothless state*: the reference is to the debilitating effects of old age.

15.1 *All this . . . children*: this is an abbreviated form of the account of the teacher–pupil lineage given extensively elsewhere: see BU 2.6; 4.6; 6.5.

except for a worthy person: the phrase *anyatra tīrthebhyaḥ* is somewhat ambivalent. It has been translated as: 'except at sacrifices', 'except at holy places', and 'except in the prescribed manner'. The term *tīrtha* can mean all these. The hospitality shown to honoured guests included the slaughter of a good animal for their food.

Taittirīya Upaniṣad

CHAPTER 1

1 *May Mitra . . . long strides*: RV 1.90.9. On the three long strides of Viṣṇu, see KaU 3.7 n.

I will proclaim you: I think that 'you' of this sentence is implied in the next two also. Others translate them simply as 'I will proclaim the right! I will proclaim the true!'

teacher [lit. 'speaker']: according to the traditional interpretation, it is the pupil who recites this invocation. So 'the speaker' refers to the teacher, and 'me' refers to the pupil.

2 *quantity*: the length of time required to pronounce a vowel. One unit is the length required to pronounce a short vowel. Three lengths are recognized: the short, the long (two units), and the prolate (three units).

strength: the force with which a particular syllable is articulated.

articulation: defined as the recitation of the Veda at a medium speed (*madhya*), as opposed to the fast (*druta*) and the slow (*vilambita*), the latter being used when a teacher is instructing a pupil.

connection [saṃtāna]: refers to the modifications of sounds in speech or recitation by the influence of contiguous sound or sounds, a process more commonly referred to as *sandhi*. When a text is so 'connected', that is, presented in the way that it is pronounced, it is called *saṃhitā*, a term used with regard to the normal arrangement of the vedic texts.

3 A very similar passage is found in AA 3.1.1.

3.1 *hidden connection*: on this meaning of *upaniṣad*, see BU 3.9.26 n.; Int., p. lii.

combination [saṃhitā]: refers both to the modifications of sounds earlier referred to as 'connection' (TU 1.2. n.) and to the vedic texts in their normal arrangement incorporating those modifications, that is, the phonetic changes caused by *sandhi*. In general, the initial sound of a word modifies the final sound of the preceding word. These combinations within the realm of speech are here extended to cosmic and bodily realities, thus establishing connections among various entities. The sexual metaphor inherent in these correspondences is evident in the examples, especially that of the mother, father, and child.

3.4 *food-supply*: see BU 1.3.17 n.

4.1 *dazzling* [viśvarūpa]: see BU 1.4.7 n.

vedic hymns: here include all vedic texts, including the prose liturgical formulas of the Yajurveda.

Indra: commentators take this to mean the syllable OṂ, generally viewed as the essence of the Vedas. But see the other esoteric meanings of Indra in BU 4.2.2; AU 1.3.14; TU 1.6.

brahman's chest: see CU 3.15.1.

5.1 *other deities*: that is, the other Calls: see BU 1.3.9 n.

5.3 *four sets of four*: the four Calls are divided four ways: worlds, lights, vedic recitations, and breaths, thus giving rise to four sets of four within their cosmic correspondences.

6.1 *space within the heart*: see BU 2.1.17 n.

hangs like a nipple: that is, the uvula. It appears that the person within the heart passes through this passage in going from the heart to the crown of the head.

7.1 *Skin . . . Marrow*: on the five components of the body, see Jamison 1986, 167–78. As Jamison has shown, the Sanskrit word here for skin, *carma*, is used in the earlier literature to refer to the hide of an animal rather than to the skin of a living being. Its substitution here for the older *tvac* indicates the lateness of the TU.

fivefold: on the significance of five, see BU 1.4.17 n.

8.1 *the Adhvaryu priest says OṂ*: the instruction of the Adhvaryu to his assistant, the Āgnīdhra, takes the form *ā śrāvaya* or *o śrāvaya* (sometimes also *oṃ śrāvaya*). Here the initial 'o' is seen as equivalent to OṂ. See BU 6.3.4 n; CU 1.1.8–9 n. The sounds *oṃśom* are contained in the Hotṛ priest's call to the Adhvaryu before reciting a hymn of praise (*śastra*), and the Adhvaryu response (*pratigara*) to this call also begins with OṂ. For these technical terms, see Kane 1962–75, ii: 1054, 1179–80.

10.1 *I am the shaker . . . and wise*: this verse is very obscure. The meaning of the hapax *rerivan*, here translated as 'shaker', is unclear; Śaṃkara's interpretation as 'cutting' the tree of transmigratory existence (*saṃsāra*) is anachronistic.

11.4 *rule of substitution*: see BU 2.3.6 n.

CHAPTER 2

1 *cavity*: (or 'cave') here and elsewhere in these documents refers

most commonly to the open space within the heart: see BU 2.1.17n. On the interpretation of this verse, see Horsch 1969, 160.

together with the wise brahman: the meaning of this phrase is not altogether clear. On its ambiguity, see Beall 1986.

a man here . . . he rests: the description of a man in this and the subsequent paragraphs relates also to the fire-altar built to resemble a bird with extended wings. Thus the word for sides (*pakṣa*) also means wing, and the word for bottom (*puccha*) means also the tail.

2 *all herbs*: the expression *sarvauṣadham* could mean both 'all herbs' and 'all medicine'; some have translated the expression as 'panacea'. See, however, the use of the same expression in SB 7.2.4.14 with the meaning 'all herbs'. See the parallel expression 'all life' in § 3.

From food . . . they grow: on the way beings come into being through food, see also BU 6.2.9–13 and the parallels cited in BU 6.2n.

It is eaten . . . food: the Sanskrit word for 'food' (*anna*) is etymologically related to the word for eating (*ad-*).

3 *Of that, this here . . . the former*: this expression, here and in the following sections, is elliptical, and its meaning is not altogether certain. I take it to mean that the self under discussion (here, the self consisting of breath) is to be regarded as the embodied self *vis-à-vis* the self previously discussed (here, the self consisting of food); thus the former belongs to, or is contained in, the latter. In other words, a human being is like an onion with five layers. Each outer layer acts as a body to each inner layer, which is the self enclosed by the former.

rules of substitution: see BU 2.3.6 n; here the expression probably refers to a class of vedic texts or formulas containing such rules.

6 *Tyat*: see BU 2.3.1n; BU 3.9.9 n.

7 *well-made*: on man's body being 'well-made', see AU 1.2.3.

8 *The fear . . . the fifth*: parallel in KaU 6.3.

analysis of bliss: on the gradation of bliss, see BU 4.3.33.

CHAPTER 3

1 *practised austerities*: the expression *tapo 'tapyata* has also the meaning of heating oneself or incubating, especially within cosmogonic contexts: see TU 2.6; CU 2.23.2 n.

6 *big man*: for the meaning of this expression here and in the following paragraphs, see CU 2.11.2 n.

7 *not belittle food*: the rule that one should not belittle food implies that one should eat food and thus parallels the rules given in §§ 8–9. This rule probably contrasts with the teaching of Bhṛgu, whose practice of austerity may have included fasting.

8 *Water is food . . . based on food*: the opposition here may be between both water and fire, and the heavenly waters and the heavenly lights, especially the sun.

10.1 *When he makes . . . final portion*: the precise meanings of the expressions that I have translated as 'the first portion' (*mukhataḥ*), 'the middle portion' (*madhyataḥ*), and 'the final portion' (*antataḥ*), are unclear; even the commentators give conflicting interpretations. They may refer to the times of a person's life (youth, middle age, and old age) or to the time of day when food is prepared for guests (morning, midday, and evening). The commentator Śaṃkara takes these expressions to refer to the quality of the place and the time when the food is given, and of the recipient of the gift, *mukhataḥ* being the highest and *antataḥ* being the lowest.

10.2 *In speech . . . as totality*: the meaning of these elliptic phrases is far from clear. The meaning probably is that one should venerate (that is, recognize the correspondence) *brahman* as the various powers resident in speech etc.

rest [kṣema]: is associated with people who settle a land and live there; this is contrasted in the Vedas to 'activity' (*yoga*) associated with people (*yāyāvara*) who venture out to conquer new land. Activity is generally viewed as superior to rest: Rau 1957, 14.

10.4 *venerate it as brahman*: the meaning of *brahman* here is unclear. It may refer to a 'formulation of truth' (see BU 2.1.1 n) possibly used as an incantation for attaining a wish, such as killing one's foes mentioned in the next sentence. In this case, 'possess *brahman*' may imply skill in the knowledge and use of such incantations.

Dying around brahman: see AB 8.28 and KsU 2.11–12.

10.6 *I am . . . the light in the firmament*: I read *suvar na jyotīḥ* and take the lengthening of the final *ī* as a prolation of the last syllable (the word is *jyotiḥ*). Some commentators (e.g. Sāyaṇa on TA 4.40) read *suvarṇajyotīḥ* ('possessing a golden light').

anyone who knows this: this subordinate clause is left dangling without a main clause. I take it with an implied connection to the subject of the preceding section, including the song: a man who knows this will be like the man just described. If one connects this clause with the preceding *suvar na jyotīḥ*, then the translation would be 'Anyone who knows this will be like the light in the firmament [*or* possess a golden light].'

Aitareya Upaniṣad

CHAPTER 1

1.2 *the flood . . . the waters*: the term *ambhas* ('flood' or 'water') appears to indicate the celestial waters above the firmament as opposed to *āpaḥ*, the terrestrial waters. On the 'glittering specks', see CU 2.21.1 n.; here they indicate the region between sky and earth where the shining specks of light are seen.

1.4 *a mouth was hatched*: on the image of creation as the hatching of an egg (cf. CU 3.19.1) through incubation, see CU 2.23.2 n.

2.1 *these deities*: see BU 1.3.9 n.

It afflicted him: the antecedents of these pronouns are unclear. The meaning probably is that the ocean afflicted the self with hunger.

2.3 *well made*: see TU 2.7.

2.5 *Find one for us also*: I follow Böhtlingk's (1890) reading of *api prajānīhi*, which parallels the request of the other deities in § 1; the request here too is for a dwelling in which hunger and thirst can eat food.

3.3 *sought to escape*: I follow Böhtlingk's (1890) reading of *atyajigāṃsat*.

3.11 *then who am I*: this question appears to be a search for the identity of the self (*ātman*). It is not identified with the functions of any of the organs, a point made explicit in AU 3.

3.12 *So he split . . . that gate*: see the parallel at TU 1.6.1. In a similar context, the AA 2.1.4 depicts *brahman* as entering the body through the tip of the foot.

that is the heaven of pleasure [nāndana]: the exact meaning is unclear; the antecedent of 'that' is probably the name (*nāma*), and there may be a play on *nāma* to connect it with *nāndana*.

this is one . . . the third: the deictic pronoun 'this', repeated three times here, is, as we have seen, an indicator of the oral nature of the text. The three are probably the crown of the head (= deep sleep, the heaven of pleasure), the middle of the body or the navel (= atmosphere, state of dream), and the feet (= earth, the waking state). A similar correlation is found in the creation hymn RV 10.90.14.

3.13 *that man*: the reference is to the cosmic man of AU 1.1.3–4.

utmost: the meaning of *tatama* is extremely obscure. The

commentator Śaṃkara takes it as *tatatama* 'most widespread'. I have taken it to be sort of superlative, indicating the utmost there is.

This I have seen: probably refers back to the very beginning where 'this' (*idam*) refers to the totality of what is here. The meaning is that, seeing the man who is *brahman*, one has seen all there is here.

3.14 *Idandra*: this name is here derived from *idam* ('this') and the verb *adarśam* ('I have seen'), which was what the creator, here identified with Indra, spoke (see CU 3.14.1 n.).

gods love the cryptic: see BU 4.2.2 n.; see also BU 3.4.1.

CHAPTER 2

1–3 *At the outset . . . second birth*: for the cycle from death to rebirth, a cycle within which a person passes a period of time as semen, see BU 6.2.8–16; CU 5.4–10. Here, however, we have a much older and a somewhat different concept of a man being born again in the wife through his semen. On this subject and on the connection between a son and the securing of a world, see Olivelle 1993, 41–6. Note the varying, but intertwined, meanings of the term *ātman* in this passage (see BU 1.1.1 n.). The father takes care of the child even before its birth, probably through the sacramentary rites (*saṃskāra*), several of which are performed during pregnancy.

4 *And he . . . holy rites*: the reference here is to the son, his very self, who will carry on the ritual activities of the family after the death of the father. The father, after his death, will be reborn (his third birth). This is an interesting combination of the two types of rebirth theories of ancient India: rebirth as the son and rebirth in another life after death.

5 *I knew . . . flew away*: RV 4.27.1.

CHAPTER 3

1 *Who is this . . . venerate*: this initial phrase is rather unclear. Others have taken it as two sentences: ' "Who is this?" We worship him as the self.' The opening word *kaḥ*, although generally taken as the interrogative 'who', is also another name for the creator god Prajāpati. In that case, the translation would be: ' "This self is Prajāpati"—so it is that we venerate [the self].' A very similar statement occurs at JB 1.18 (Bodewitz 1973, 54), where the word *kaḥ* explicitly refers to Prajāpati. The term 'venerate' (*upa-ās-*) may indeed have the meaning of correspondence (see BU 4.1.2 n.). Then

the question becomes, in fact, a search for things that would correspond to the self.

2 *awareness . . . Desire*: the exact meanings of 'awareness' and the other mental functions and their distinctions from each other are very unclear. I do, however, attempt to distinguish *prajñā*, which means knowledge, from *prajñāna*, which refers to the act of knowing, or cognition. The general point of the passage is that no single aspect of the cognitive powers of man can be viewed as the self.

3 *immense beings* [mahābhūtāni]: this term has the technical meaning of primary elements (earth, water, fire, air, and ether) in later philosophies, but here, I think, they refer to the five large and expansive beings, as opposed to the small individual entities.

those born from eggs . . . sprouts: see CU 6.3.1 n.

4 *he went up*: according to the commentator Śaṃkara, 'he' refers to Vāmadeva (AU 2.5–6).

Kauṣītaki Upaniṣad

CHAPTER 1

Another version of the story of Śvetaketu, with Jaivali Pravāhaṇa as the king, is found at BU 6.2, CU 5.3–10, and JB 1.17–18.

1 *Citra Gāṅgāyani*: a variant reading for Gāṅgāyani is Gārgāyaṇi (BU 4.6.2).

Son of . . . another road: Citra's question is extremely elliptical, possibly an enigmatic question, and the problems of interpretation are compounded by the probability of textual corruption. The translations have varied greatly. I think that, on the whole, the question is directed at the two paths described later.

closed door: the term *saṃvṛtam* refers to something closed, for example, the enclosure of a cowpen (Frenz 1968–9, 82 and105). Here, however, I think that it refers to the closed door represented by the moon (KsU 1.2). See also CU 2.24.4n. for the association of the door to heaven with the Milky Way.

I fear . . . false world: this statement is not altogether clear, but I think its thrust is that Citra wants to know whether Śvetaketu is knowledgeable enough, for otherwise he may end up placing Citra in a false world (*aloka*) through the sacrifice.

I'll ask my teacher: Śvetaketu is referring here to his father, Uddālaka Āruṇi, whose lineage name is Gautama (see BU 6.2.4n.).

Even I . . . give us: the father's reply is unclear and has been subject to various interpretations. I take it to mean that Āruṇi wants to return to the sacrifice that had been suspended and to learn from the 'outsider', that is, someone who is not a Brahmin, the answers to the questions. 'After we have performed our vedic recitation' may also be a reference to placing themselves as students under Citra.

sacrificial arena [sadas]: a shed erected in the western section of the larger sacrificial enclosure (*mahāvedi*) during a Soma sacrifice. The seats for several of the priests are located in this shed.

carrying firewood: see CU 4.4.5n.

Let me . . . it clearly: parallels to this exchange between a Brahmin and a Kṣatriya are BU 2.1.15; KsU 4.19.

formulation of the truth: see BU 2.1.1n.

not succumbed to pride: Āruṇi invites his son to come, but, although the text is silent on this point, it is clear that, just as in the parallel narratives in BU and CU, Śvetaketu declined that invitation out of pride, which explains Citra's satisfaction that Āruṇi has not succumbed to pride.

2 *door to the heavenly world*: see CU 2.24.4 n.

The semen . . . I am you: on these somewhat difficult verses, see the comments of Bodewitz 1973, 54–61. In the JB (1.18), which was probably the original context of these verses, it is the seasons that lead the dead man to immortality, which explains why the verses are addressed to the seasons and not to the moon (see also KsU 1.6). The fifteen parts refer to the digits of the moon, while the comment 'who is born' may refer to the fact that the moon is being born continuously, although the words *prasūta* ('born') and *prasuta* ('pressed', i.e. Soma) are often connected in these texts (see Renou 1948, 18 n. 19; Bodewitz 1973, 59 n. 20). All these epithets refer to the moon, from whom the semen (in the form of rain) is gathered. The 'father of twelve parts' is the year with twelve months. The man considers himself to be born as the thirteenth, or the intercalary month, and the one who gives birth to him is the year, his real divine father, as opposed to the 'agent' who is his earthly father. The thirteenth month is often identified with the year and the sun, and therefore with immortality: see Bodewitz 1973, 59–60 nn. 24–5.

3 *in this world . . . Amitaujas*: on the term Āra and its possible connection with *araṇya* ('wilderness'), as well as some of the items located in the world of *brahman*, see CU 8.5.3. Muhūrtas are a division of time, approximately 48 minutes. Vijarā means 'undecaying' or 'ageless', and the alternate reading *viraja* means 'pure'. The meanings of Ilya and Sālajya are uncertain; if Ilya is connected to *ilā*, it would mean speech or earth. Aparājita = invincible. Vibhu = extensive (in CU the hall is called Prabhu); Vicakṣaṇa = radiant or far-shining; Amitaujas = unlimited power.

4*a* *as a man . . . days and nights*: days and nights are viewed here as a pair of wheels that turn with the passage of time. As Witzel (1984, 230; see the diagram of the two wheels on p. 277) points out, the wheel of the day has two sides, the one that is bright and seen during the day, and the other that is dark during the night. The night, likewise, has bright and dark sides, seen during the night and day, respectively. When one is on top of heaven one sees these two wheels spinning beneath him.

pairs of opposites: heat and cold, pleasure and pain, and other such pairs.

4*b* *The beloved Mānasī . . . on to brahman*: Mānasī means 'belonging to the mind', and Cākṣuṣī means 'belonging to sight'. These appear to be personifications of the mental and visual capacities of perception. This is an extremely difficult and possibly corrupt passage; Frenz (1968–9, 107 n.7) confesses that he does not understand it. Thieme (1951–2) thinks that this passage is set in metre, and I have generally followed his emended text. Thieme takes the dual *jagatī* to refer to heaven and earth.

5 *the throne Vicakṣaṇa . . . pillow is prosperity*: the names given to various parts of the throne and the couch are the names of different Sāman chants used during the Soma sacrifice: see CU 2.11–21 and the note to this. There is a similar connection established between the throne of Indra and the ritual texts at AB 8.12. On the High Chant, see BU 1.3.1 n. On the throne and the couch and their construction, see Rau 1957, 125–6. On the construction of the throne at a king's anointing, see AB 8.5. On the 'second cover' I follow the reading of Rau: *aparaś cayaḥ*. The man coming to the couch is said to mount it 'first with his foot'. The meaning may be that he climbs placing one foot (right?) on the couch first. The AB 8.6 says that the king mounts the throne with the right knee first, and then the left.

5–6 *Who are you . . . you are this whole world*: on the question and the answer, see KsU 1.2. The term *satyam* is here considered to be composed of *sat* and *tyam*. On this explanation of the term *satyam*, see BU 2.3.1–5 and BU 2.3.1 n.

7 *He consists of brahman*: the term *brahman* may here mean specifically 'the formulation of truth': see BU 2.1.1 n.

By what means . . . feminine names: the reason for the connection between masculine, neuter, and feminine names, and breath, mind, and speech, is the gender (masculine, neuter, and feminine, respectively) of the terms for these in Sanskrit.

CHAPTER 2

1 *Kauṣītaki*: this person, after whom this Upaniṣad is named, also appears at CU 1.5.2.

And, indeed . . . a maid: this paragraph is missing in some manuscripts and is relegated to the notes in Limaye and Vadekar's (1958) edition.

all these deities: the deities who bring offerings are the vital functions (BU 1.3.9 n.), a subject that is described in greater detail at BU 6.1.7–14. The term *bali* here probably means offerings given voluntarily, but it can also mean a tribute paid to a king (BU 6.1.13 n.).

3 *the capture of 'an identical object of value'*: for a similar ritual for obtaining a wish, see BU 6.3. The meaning of *ekadhana* is not altogether certain. It may mean an exceptionally valuable thing, a particular object of value, or even a valuable object belonging to a particular person. Since the rite involves the capture of an object from another person, I take it to mean the same valuable thing that two people have set their hearts on, and which both are trying to obtain.

svāhā: see BU 5.8 n.

4 *divinely secured love*: means love secured through the ritual offerings to the vital functions as described in the previous section.

5 *the control of Pratardana*: Bodewitz (1973, 239–40) is right in rejecting any connection between this and either yogic exercises or the rite of offering in one's breath (*prāṇāgnihotra*). It is unclear why this correspondence between breathing/speaking and the fire sacrifice is called 'the control of Pratardana' (*saṃyamanaṃ* [or *sāṃyamanam*] *prātardanam*). Bodewitz, taking a cue from Sāyaṇa's commentary on AA 3.2.6, suggests the reading *sāyaṃtanaṃ prātastanam* ('morning and evening'), although Bodewitz himself acknowledges that this does not solve all the problems, because this sacrifice takes place all the time and not just in the morning and the evening. Pratardana appears again at KsU 3.1.

he offers his breath in his speech: on breathing and speaking as a fire sacrifice, see JB 1.20; 2.50; AA 3.2.6.

6 *Uktha*: see BU 1.6.1 n.

One should venerate . . . bow down to him: on 'venerate': see BU 4.1.2 n. Note here the phonetic connections established between Ṛg (= ṛc), Yajus, and Sāman and the corresponding activities of all beings.

Recitations of Praise: see BU 3.9.1 n.

Adhvaryu priest: on the three types of priests, see Int., p. xlii.

weaves upon it: on the weaving metaphor, see BU 3.6.1 n.

7 *Sarvajit*: this epithet means 'all-conquering'.

Wearing . . . position: I take the term *yajñopavīta* to mean the manner of wearing the upper garment, actually a shawl or cincture. I doubt that the custom of always wearing a sacred string, a common and obligatory practice in later Brahmanism, had come into practice during the period of the composition of this text (see Kane 1962–75, ii: 287–91). In the 'sacrificial position', i.e. during sacrifices to the gods, the garment is worn as a loop from the left shoulder to the right waist, whereas during offerings to ancestors it is worn from the right shoulder to the left waist.

one who gathers: on the doctrine of 'gatherer', see CU 4.3.1–4 and 4.3.1 n.

8*a* *My heart . . . misfortune*: the heart is here compared to a good piece of firewood, and in this context it appears clear that the moon is implicitly compared to a fire. The term *adhiśrita* ('placed') is used frequently in the technical sense of putting wood or other offerings into a fire.

8*c* *Swell up . . . highest glory*: these two verses are RV 1.91.16, 18.

That tiny drop . . . make us swell: TS 2.3.5.3 (= TS 2.4.14.1). The Sanskrit text cites only the opening lines of these three verses (*pratīka*), a common practice in Brahmanical literature where the readers/listeners are expected to know these verses by heart; unable to presuppose such knowledge in my reader, I have chosen to give the entire translation of the verses. In the original context these verses are addressed to the Soma drink, but here Soma is identified with the moon (see KsU 2.9). On the moon swelling by meaning of the lifebreaths of people, see KsU 1.2.

9 *eat the kings*: 'king' refers to the Kṣatriya class. On the classes of ancient Indian society, see Int., p. xxvi. On the metaphor of food and eater, see BU 1.2.5 n.

Do not waste away: the reference is to the waning of the moon, in the manner opposite to the swelling described in the previous section.

10 *sniff his son's head*: kissing the son's head here is done in a manner similar to what an animal does to its young, and refers especially to sniffing and to the breathing upon (hissing) the calf (see Hopkins 1907). This is the intent of the final statement that the father makes the sound '*huṃ*' just like a cow over her calf (see CU 2.2.1 n.). A similar rite is described in several Gṛhya Sūtras: *Āśvalāyana*, 1.15.9 and the parallels given in Oldenberg 1892, 302.

From my body: see BU 6.4.9.

You're my self: a variant reading, found also in the Gṛhya Sūtras, translates: 'You are my self bearing the name "son".'

O Indra . . . sons: RV 3.36.10, with the reading *asme* ('for us') in place of *asmai* ('for him'). This and the next two verses are cited in the original Sanskrit by their first lines only.

Grant him . . . of his life: RV 2.21.6. Here too I have replaced *asme* with *asmai*, following the pattern of the previous verse.

10 *the sound huṃ*: within the Soma ritual this sound is technically called *hiṃ* (CU 2.1.1 n.), and here it is compared with the low of a cow.

11 *dying around of the deities*: the dying around *brahman* is described in AB 8.28; see also TU 3.10.4.

12 *all these deities*: see BU 1.3.9 n.

both the mountain ranges: the southern is the Vindhyas, and the northern is the Himalayas.

13 *arguing for its own pre-eminence*: on the relative superiority of the vital functions, see BU 1.3.2–6 n.

14 *father–son ceremony*: for another version of this rite, see BU 1.5.17 and the note to this.

bliss, delight, and procreation: the reference is to sexual activity; see TU 3.10.3; KsU 1.7; 3.5–8.

live as a wandering ascetic: the word *pari-vraj-* ('to wander about') is used here probably as a technical term for living the life of a wandering ascetic (see BU 4.5.2 n.).

CHAPTER 3

1 *as a result of war and valour*: it is part of the ancient Indian warrior ethic that death in battle assures a warrior a place in heaven. That is how Pratardana got to Indra's abode.

I killed . . . in the process: the exploits about which Indra boasts here are part of his mythic history. These episodes came to be viewed in later times negatively as the sins of Indra. Tvaṣṭṛ was Indra's father, whom he slayed after drinking Soma (Macdonell 1898, 57). The killing of the Arunmukhas and the episode of throwing the Yatis (by some, mistakenly I believe, identified as ascetics) to hyenas are recorded in AB 7.28; for a detailed and convincing new interpretation of this myth, see Jamison 1991, 45–130. Prāhlādīyas, Paulomas, and Kālakāñjas are types of demons. This passage takes a different slant and shows why these sins did not taint Indra.

2 *attains immortality in this world*: the meaning probably is that when breath is present it keeps death away in this world.

3 *But only the breath*: on the pre-eminence of breath, see BU 1.3.2–6 n.

Uktha: see BU 1.6.1 n.

Whole: see BU 1.4.9–10 n.

When a man is sick . . . that it departs: for the example of a sleeping man, see KsU 4.19–20; PU 4; and for the dying man see BU 4.4.1; CU 6.15.1. The relation of speech to names, corresponding to the senses and their objects, must be seen within the broader category of 'name and visible appearance', which comprehends physical realities: see BU 1.4.7.

4 *Speech releases . . . depart from it*: the previous passage shows how, becoming unconscious, the various vital functions merge into breath. This passage indicates what happens when a person regains consciousness. Each vital function 'releases from this', that is, from breath, the corresponding object, and the awakened man is able to perceive those objects through the vital functions.

Next . . . become one: this sentence is an introduction to the following passages, which intend to show how all beings 'become one', that is, become united in intelligence as their source.

5 *particle of being* [bhūtamātra]: this term should perhaps be understood within the line of thought that developed into the Sāṃkhya cosmology with its doctrine of subtle elements (*tanmātra*).

7 *For without intelligence . . . any name*: the connection between 'intelligence' (*prajñā*) and 'perceiving' (*pra-jñā-*) is clearer in Sanskrit because of the identity of the terms. 'Perceiving' here has the sense of making someone aware of a sensory perception.

8 *It is not the speech . . . the one who thinks*: on perceiving the subject rather than the external products, see BU 2.4.7–9; 4.5.8–10.

visible appearance: see BU 1.4.7 n.

It does not become more . . . from these worlds: on being unaffected by action, see BU 4.4.22.

CHAPTER 4

1 *Gārgya Bālāki . . . widely travelled man*: for a variant of this story, see BU 2.1 and the notes to this. The term *saṃspṛṣṭa* (variant *saṃspaṣṭa*) is obscure; my translation 'widely travelled' follows Frenz and is a conjecture based on the context. For the names of the regions see the List of Names and Fig. 2.

2 *The great . . . the left eye*: this passage appears to be a summary list of the items that in the subsequent sections Bālāki assumes to be *brahman*. Frenz (1968–9) rightly assumes that this must be a later addition by way of a table of contents.

3 *It is that person in the sun*: here and in the subsequent passages it is

clearly implied that Bālāki venerates (see BU 4.1.2 n.) these items as *brahman*.

10 *essence of truth*: a variant here reads 'the essence of radiance (*tejas*)'.

divine sphere: see BU 1.3.9 n.

16 *propagates himself*: here probably has a spectrum of meanings, including 'getting a new life' through his children and heaven, and 'becoming prosperous/famous' through livestock, wealth, and fame.

19 *In vain*: it may also mean under false pretext.

carrying firewood: see CU 4.4.5 n.

20 *Then these become . . . the worlds*: see the parallel passages at KsU 3.3 and BU 1.4.7 for notes.

these other selves: probably refer to the vital functions.

For as long as . . . all the gods: for the allusion to the knowledge of Indra and of the gods, see CU 8.7–14; 1.2; BU 1.3.

Kena Upaniṣad

CHAPTER 1

2 *That which . . . from this world*: see the parallel verse in BU 4.4.18. For an examination of this sort of expression, see BU 2.1.20 n.

3 *so have we heard . . . to us*: this refrain occurs also in IU 10 and 13.

4 *venerate*: in the refrain here and in subsequent verses, see BU 4.1.2 n.

CHAPTER 2

1–5 *If you think . . . from this world*: this entire section appears to be a discourse. Some think that it is a dialogue between a teacher and a pupil. The syntactic problems and general obscurity of the first few paragraphs (they almost look like riddles) make it difficult to demarcate the sections spoken by the two or even to conclude that it is in fact a dialogue. These obscurities make any translation very tentative, and mine assumes that the entire section is a discourse by a teacher to a pupil.

2 *I do not . . . not know*: this verse is elliptic and obscure. In general, the meaning appears to be that we do know the visible appearance of *brahman* in this world. This appears to be the meaning of 'Who of us knows that, he does know that.' But there is a deeper aspect of *brahman* (the part among the gods?) that is so far beyond human perception that we do not even know that we do not know it.

CHAPTER 3

1 *victory*: the reference is probably to the victory of the gods over the demons (see BU 1.3).

2 *Brahman*: although at some level personified, *brahman* is presented as both grammatically neuter and in some ways a principle or a truth (see BU 2.1.1 n.), rather than a person. Hence, I use the pronoun 'it' with reference to *brahman*.

CHAPTER 4

2 *close contact with it*: manuscripts add: 'for they were the first to recognize it as *brahman*'. I think this phrase has been copied from

§ 3, where it fits the context. Here, on the other hand, the phrase is completely out of place, because Fire and Wind did not recognize it as *brahman*. Further evidence for its migration from § 3 is provided by the fact that in the Sanskrit the word 'first' is in the singular and the verb 'recognize' is in the third person singular (as in § 3 with reference to Indra), while the subject has been changed to the plural 'they', creating an anacoluthon. For these reasons, I have omitted the phrase from the translation.

4 *Here is its . . . blink*: this is a somewhat obscure passage (see Thieme 1968*b*, 721–2). The intent appears to be to show phenomena in the cosmic and the individual spheres that can represent (be substitutes for) *brahman*. On substitution, see BU 2.3.6n. On the flash of lightning, see BU 2.3.6. The sudden flash of recognition in the mind is here likened to a flash of lightning that makes people exclaim 'Ah!'

6 *tadvana*: the meaning of this expression is quite unclear. If *vana* means 'wood', then the meaning is 'the wood (i.e. material) of that (i.e. *brahman*)'. Others take *vana* as 'desire' or 'love'. Then the meaning is 'one who has love for that'. The latter appears to be the intention of the author when he concludes that when someone knows this name people will 'long for' him; *vana* is here connected with the verbal root *vāñc*- ('to desire or long for'). I am inclined to think that this too is an esoteric term without a specific semantic meaning: see CU 3.14.1n.

Kaṭha Upaniṣad

CHAPTER 1

1–4 The three prose passages (§§ 1,2,4) of this section are taken verbatim from TB 3.11.8.1. The episode of Naciketas is narrated in the TB (3.11.8.1–6) to teach the origin and significance of a special fire-altar bearing the name Naciketas. Bodewitz (1985, 8–10) has demonstrated that the expression *agnir nāciketaḥ* (lit. 'Naciketas-fire') refers not to a type of ritual fire, but to a special type of fire-altar that is constructed during a sacrifice. The story, as told in TB, begins with a sacrifice offered by the father of Naciketas at which all the father's possessions were given away as sacrificial gifts. The boy, assuming that he too is to be given away, irritated his father by asking three times: 'To whom will you give me?' The father, in exasperation, says: 'To death'. He could not take back his words, but tells Naciketas that, when he goes to Death's residence, the latter will be away and that Naciketas will remain there without food for three days (here Death is both death and the god of death, who has many names and epithets, including Yama and Vaivasvata). It is, of course, a great discourtesy to let a Brahmin guest remain in one's house without food. The father instructs the boy on what to say when Death returns. When, after returning home, Death asks him how many days he has been there, Naciketas replies: 'Three.' Death: 'What did you eat the first night?' Naciketas: 'Your children.' Death: 'What did you eat the second night?' Naciketas: 'Your livestock.' Death: 'What did you eat the third night?' Naciketas: 'Your good works.' To redeem himself Death grants Naciketas three wishes. His first wish is that Death should return him to his father's house alive; the second, that he be taught how sacrifices and good works can be made not to decay; and the third, that he be taught how to ward off repeated death (see BU 1.2.7 n.). The answer to the last two is the construction of the Naciketas fire-altar. The KaU expands on this story, but its main focus is on the second and the third wish of Naciketas.

1–2 *Uśan . . . led away*: I take Uśan as the personal name of Vājaśravas. Others take it to mean 'desirous' and have to assume an implied object of his desire, either heaven (Rau 1971) or the fruit of the sacrifice (Edgerton 1965). The ritual giving of all one's possessions took place at the conclusion of a specific sacrifice called 'Sacrifice of All' (*sarvamedha*). This explains the reference to the cows given as sacrificial gifts to the priests who assisted at this sacrifice.

3 *They've drunk . . . as gifts*: the significance of this statement is not altogether clear. I take it as a sarcastic remark, meant both to indicate the uselessness of such sacrificial gifts and to hint at the hypocrisy of people who gave the worst of their flock as gifts. I take the term *nirindriya* as a reference to sterility (following its usage in TS 2.5.6.4; TB 1.5.3.3; BU 6.4.4), although it can refer more generally to bodily weakness. On joyless worlds, see BU 4.4.11 (cf. also IU 3).

5 *Naciketas reflects*: the identities of the different speakers here and in the subsequent passages are not specified in the Sanskrit text. Although these identities are not always certain, I have given the probable ones within brackets in the translation.

6 *Look ahead . . . after us*: the Sanskrit is very succinct, and the translation is somewhat free. In the previous verse Naciketas says that he is the first of many, i.e. of those who will die after him, and the middlemost of many, i.e. of those who have died before him. Here, the voice says in effect that all men must die and be born again, like seeds of grain.

7 *A Brahmin guest . . . appease him*: the reference here is to Naciketas, who has come to Death's house as a guest. 'Fire in all men' is Agni Vaiśvānara (BU 1.1.1 n.).

9 *Three nights . . . any food*: Death comes home and finds that Naciketas has been there for three nights. This verse presupposes the questions and answers found in the TB narrative (see KaU 1.1–4 n.).

11 *Auddālaka Āruṇi*: this reference has caused some problems. I take it (with Edgerton 1965 and Rau 1971) as a separate sentence and Auddālaka Āruṇi ('son of Uddālaka Āruṇi') as a reference to Naciketas. Others (e.g. Renou 1943) take this line to be syntactically connected to the first and Auddālaka Āruṇi as a reference to the father of Naciketas. They emend the final word *prasṛṣṭaḥ* to *prasṛṣṭe*. The translation would then be: 'Auddālaka Āruṇi will be affable in the future, just as before, towards you dismissed by me.'

12 *no fear of old age or you*: I follow Rau (1971) in reading *tvan* (= *tvat*) *na jarāyā*.

13 *studying*: the implication is that Death is an expert in this knowledge, an expression used also elsewhere: CU 5.11.4–6.

fire-altar: the Sanskrit *agni* ('fire') here and in what follows has the meaning of 'fire-altar' (see KaU 1.15), a structure that is built with bricks during a particular sacrifice called Agnicayana (Bodewitz 1985, 8–10, 25).

who has faith: the faith that Naciketas has is in the efficacy of the sacrificial ritual.

15 *the beginning of the world*: the meaning appears to be that the fire-altar ritually builds the entrance to the heavenly world for the sacrificer.

16 *glittering*: on the meaning of *anekarūpa* (lit. 'of many forms') as 'glittering' (or dazzling), see BU 1.4.7 n.

disk of gold: the meaning of *sṛṅkā*, a term found only in the KaU, is unclear. It is undoubtedly something precious, probably made of gold. Some have taken it to be a necklace or a chain. I think the argument of Bodewitz (1985) for taking it as a gold plate or disk that could be worn on the breast is convincing. Its connection with the orb of the sun is clear, and it appears to have been an object deposited under the fire-altar during its construction.

17 *three-Nāciketa man*: the term *triṇāciketaḥ* has been interpreted as one who has kindled or is equipped with the three Nāciketa fires. I have taken it as an epithet of a man connected with the three Nāciketa fire-altars. Bodewitz (1985, 13–14) has shown that the fire connected with the Nāciketa fire-altars is just one and not the three usual vedic fires. So the 'three' here probably refers to the fact that a person who truly understands the Nāciketa fire-altar constructs it in its three dimensions: the ritual, the macrocosmic, and within the individual ('in the cave of the heart').

Perceiving . . . unending peace: this passage poses serious difficulties. I follow Bodewitz (1985, 24). The point appears to be that the man sees the ritual identity between the disk of gold to be deposited and the *brahman*, who is the god to be adored in the form of the sun as it is being born, i.e. rises in the east. The expression *brahma jajña* (= *jajñāna*) is a reference to the ritual formula at AV 4.1.1 (Rau 1971, 162), which is recited at the construction of the fire-altar.

29 *transit*: that is, the passage from this world to the next at death, which is the focus of the third wish of Naciketas.

CHAPTER 2

3 *You have looked . . . wealth*: the meaning, as Bodewitz (1985, 20–1) has pointed out, is that even though Naciketas accepted the gold disk, he did so not to get wealth but as an item to be used in the ritual of constructing the fire-altar.

5 *Wallowing . . . blind*: parallel in MuU 1.2.8.

6 *transit*: see KaU 1.29 n.

7 *Many do not . . . taught it*: I follow the emendations suggested by Rau (1971, 173): dropping *api* ('even') in the first line, and the reading *kuśalo 'nuśiṣṭaḥ* for *kuśalānuśiṣṭaḥ* ('taught by a skilful man'). The antecedent of 'it' here and in the next verse is unclear. Many take the reference to mean the true self (*ātman*), while Rau (1971, 164 n. 16) takes it to be the doctrine (*dharma*) regarding what happens to a man who dies given in KaU 1.21. Rau is on the right track, but it is not necessary to go back all that way, since the 'transit' (*sāmparāya*) from this world to the next is mentioned in the preceding verse. I have made this reference explicit in the translation.

8 *For it is . . . reason*: there appears to be a play on words here. The term *aṇu* can mean both fine/subtle (see KaU 2.13, 20) and an atom, while *pramāṇa* means both size and a means of valid knowledge, such as perception or inference. So, the phrase may also mean, 'more subtle than subtle means of knowledge'. The intent, in any case, is to show that reasoning alone cannot reveal the path of the dead.

13 *drawn it out*: see KaU 6.17.

point of doctrine: the meaning of *dharmyam*, which I have translated as 'point of doctrine', is unclear. But it cannot be very different from the meaning of the term *dharma* (also said to be subtle, *aṇu*) at KaU 1.21 and from its usage in the next verse, KaU 2.14.

18 *The wise one . . . is killed*: the wise one is the self (*ātman*). From here the discussion shifts to the nature of the self in so far as it is different from the body and survives death. As Rau (1971, 166) has pointed out, the older part of the text containing the dialogue between Naciketas and Death ends here, although it appears that the later editors intend to place what follows also in the mouth of Death (see, for example 4.15). On this and the following verse, see the parallels in BhG 2.19–20.

20 *Finer than . . . the self*: see the parallels in SU 3.20.

23 *chooses*: for my textual emendation here, see MuU 3.2.3 n.

CHAPTER 3

1 *five fires*: see Int., p. xlii.

Shadow and Light: 'shadow' refers to the person in the heart, and 'light' to the person in the firmament. The intent is to show the correspondence between the cave of the heart and the highest heaven.

2 *dike*: see BU 4.4.22n.

danger: with Rau (1971, 174), I read *bhayam* ('danger' or 'fear') in place of *abhayam* ('fearless') both because it makes better sense and because it restores the metre.

7 *final step*: here refers to the highest step of Viṣṇu referred to in verse 9. The three steps of Viṣṇu is a recurrent theme in the Vedas. His third and highest step is in the farthest heaven, the most desirable place for gods and men. The three steps are in some way related to the movement of the sun through the three regions of the universe. To these three steps is connected the myth of the dwarf Viṣṇu in the Brāhmaṇas (see SB 1.2.5). The gods having been defeated, the demons (*asura*) were in the process of dividing the earth. The gods went there to get themselves a share, and the demons allowed them the area Viṣṇu would lie on. In later versions of the myth Viṣṇu is allowed as much territory as he could encompass in three steps. The dwarf Viṣṇu assumes his normal size, placing one step on earth, a second in the intermediate region, and the third in the highest heaven, thus winning the entire universe for the gods.

round of rebirth: this is the earliest usage of the significant term *saṃsāra* in the early Upaniṣads. It occurs again in SU 6.16.

11 *immense self*: may correspond to the *mahat*, which is the first product evolved out of *prakṛti*. Thus in verse 15 the ultimate state is said to be beyond this *mahat* ('immense').

the unmanifest: the reference is probably to the Sāṃkhya cosmological principle of primal nature or *prakṛti*, from which all material objects evolve. The ideas and terminology of this section of the KaU bear some resemblance to Sāṃkhya, although not in its classical form (see Horsch 1965, 475).

person: opposed to the material nature and entrapped by its products is the spiritual 'person' or *puruṣa*.

15 *no appearance*: see BU 1.4.7n.

16–17 *The wise man . . . eternal life*: these two verses appear to be a later addition to praise the importance of this text and to show the rewards for its recitation.

CHAPTER 4

3 *what then is here left behind*: see KaU 5.4.

5 *it does not seek*: the antecedent of 'it' appears to be the self (KaU 4.12). Cf. BU 4.4.15; IU 6.

6–7 *He who was . . . abiding there*: these two verses are very obscure and possibly corrupt. Rau (1971, 168) leaves them untranslated, calling them untranslatable and corrupt. My translation is, of course, very tentative. 'Heat' and 'the waters' refer to the primordial cosmic forces that were part of the cosmogonic process.

9–11 *From which . . . diversity*: the meaning is that the sun rises from and sets into the ritual fire. Thus the ritual sphere down here is identified with the cosmic sphere up above. When one understands this correspondence (see Int. p. lii), one sees the unity behind the apparent diversity in the world. For verse 9, see BU 1.5.23; and for the last two lines of verse 10 and the first two of 11, see BU 4.4.19.

12 *A person . . . himself*: the meaning is that the 'person', that is the ultimate self, does not hide himself from a man who knows him close at hand (see KaU 4.5).

14 *laws*: the term for 'laws' is *dharma* (here in the plural). Many have considered this evidence of Buddhist influence on the KaU. But as Horsch (1968, 472–5) has shown, the term here refers to the diversity of ritual and moral rules that govern a Brahmin's life. The term is used in a very similar way at BU 1.5.23.

CHAPTER 5

1 *fort with eleven gates*: the fort is the body (see BU 2.5.18), and the eleven gates are the two eyes, two nostrils, two ears, mouth, anus, urinal opening, navel, and the cranial opening (see TU 1.6.1; AU 1.3.13). The fort is said to have nine gates, when the last two are omitted (see SU 3.18).

2 *The goose . . . truth*: with minor variants, found in RV 4.40.5. According to its explanation in SB 6.7.3.11, the reference is to the various aspects of fire: e.g. goose = sun (see BU 2.5.18 n.); Vasu = wind; *hotṛ* and guest = ritual fire.

3 *Dwarf*: see the characterization of the self as the size of a thumb at KaU 4.13.

9–10 *As the single . . . of each*: the fire that enters living beings is either the digestive fire or the fire that keeps the body warm, while the wind is the breathing of living beings.

12 *The one . . . happiness*: cf. SU 6.12.

13 *The changeless . . . bliss*: cf. SU 6.13.

15 *There the sun . . . light*: = MuU 2.2.10; SU 6.14.

CHAPTER 6

1 *Its roots . . . ever pass*: cf. KaU 5.8.

4 *If one . . . worlds*: this verse has created difficulties to both ancient commentators and to modern translators. For a discussion of them, see Rocher 1973. The difficulties stem from the assumption that the knowledge of *brahman* in this world should *not* lead to another body but to liberation. One may, however, question whether such an assumption can be made with regard to the Upaniṣads (see, for example, KaU 5.7). Some emend *sargeṣu* to *svargeṣu*, and translate 'within the heavenly worlds'.

6 *The separate nature*: the meaning is that a wise man should recognize that the senses are different from the self both in their nature and in their coming into being at birth and their ceasing to be at death.

7 *Higher than the senses . . . unmanifest*: see the parallel at KaU 3.10. 'Intellect' (*buddhi*) of that passage is replaced by 'essence' (*sattva*) here. It is unclear whether the latter is another term for the former (in Sāṃkhya cosmology the intellect is constituted predominantly by the quality of *sativa* or goodness/light), or a new category that replaces it.

9 *His appearance . . . immortal*: the meaning is that one becomes capable of knowing him only with one's heart, spirit, and thought. See SU 3.13; 4.20.

Īśā Upaniṣad

In his detailed study of the first 14 verses of the IU, Thieme (1965) has attempted to demonstrate that the text consists of four separate discussions (I = 1–3; II = 4–6; III = 7–11; IV = 12–14) carried out by two adversaries with opposing views, with statements of principle, objections, and answers. I give here the identities of the speakers of each verse, according to Thieme: I: 1 = statement, 2 = objection, 3 = answer; II: 4–5= objection, 6 = answer; III: 7–8 = statement , 9–10 = objection, 11 = answer; IV: 12–13 = objection, 14 = answer. Although Thieme's suggestion is intriguing (the text may, indeed, present some views that the author goes on to refute), I am not convinced that this little text intends to present such a complicated argument. Regarding the first verses of the IU, see also Sharma and Young 1990.

1 *So you . . . abandoned*: some take this to mean that one can eat, or more generally enjoy or use, what has been abandoned by the Lord, namely, what is without life or is dead. Under this interpretation, the statement amounts to an injunction not to kill living beings for food (Thieme 1965). Others think that the injunction refers to ascetics who must eat what has been given (i.e. abandoned) to them by others.

2 *Just performing . . . on you*: the meaning appears to be that one should perform works, especially rites, because one is obliged to do so and not out of any desire for their results. This is the major point of the discussion on renunciation in the BhG. 'Hundred years' is the standard expression for the full life span of a human being. So the meaning is that a man should desire to live his full life devoted to performing his duties. I follow Thieme (1965, 90) in dropping the final *nare* of this verse and in interpreting *asti* ('he/it is') as an idiomatic expression indicating that the statement made is, indeed, a fact.

3 *Demonic*: it is tempting to read *asūryāḥ* ('sunless') in place of *asuryāḥ* ('demonic'). Given that the demons are often connected with the night and gods with the day, both expressions may suit this context.

who kill the self: the expression *ātmahanaḥ* has caused much controversy (see Sharma and Young 1990) and has been interpreted differently depending on the value given to the term *ātma-*. If we exclude the allegorical interpretation of some commentators, who take the expression to mean 'those who do not know the self', two major interpretations have been offered. Some see this as referring to suicide ('who kill themselves'), taking the latter term to be a reflexive pronoun. Others (Thieme 1965) take it as a reference to killing living beings; here *ātman* would refer to a living body and, thus, to a living being (see BU 1.1.1 n.). My translation deliberately leaves open both possibilities.

4 *the one*: compare the repeated use of the term 'one' (*eka*) in the SU. The pronouns used here and in the subsequent verses are neuter and may refer to *brahman*, although the exact meaning of that term in this context is far from clear (see the use of this term in the SU).

Mātariśvan: generally identified with the wind. See PU 2.11 n.; Thieme 1965, 93–94.

6 *When a man... from him*: cf. BU 4.4.23; KaU 4.5. 'It will not hide': i.e. the self, here viewed as the universal self present in oneself and in others, will not hide itself from such a man.

7 *When ... oneness*: I take the antecedent of the correlatives *yasmin* ('in which') and *tatra* ('regarding that') as the self (*ātman*), also used similarly in the locative in the previous verse. On the translation of this difficult verse, see Thieme 1965, 94–5.

8 *He has reached*: the antecedent of 'he' is unclear; it probably refers back to the 'self'.

seed: (or semen: *śukram*) probably refers to the germ of creation; the term could also mean 'bright'.

riddled by evil: see BU 1.3.1–18.

through endless years: following Thieme (1965, 95), I take out the expression *yathātathyataḥ* from the last line. With it, the sentence would translate: '... objects as they are in reality through endless years'.

10 *It's far different*: the antecedent of 'it' (neuter) is unclear; it probably refers back to the 'one' in verse 4.

12 *non-becoming, becoming*: the exact meanings of 'becoming' (*sambhūti*) and 'non-becoming' (*asambhūti*) are unclear. The use of the term 'destruction' (*vināśa*) in verse. 14 as a synonym of 'non-becoming', however, points in the direction of the belief that after death there is no further existence. In that case, the opposite, i.e. 'becoming', must mean the belief in the continued existence after death, probably in the sense of rebirth.

15–18 *The face ... offer to you*: these verses are found at BU 5.15, where notes are given.

Śvetāśvatara Upaniṣad

CHAPTER 1

1 *What is the cause of brahman*: others translate this question as: 'What is the cause? *Brahman*?' The assumption there is that *brahman* is a possible answer to the first question. I think, however, that the first verse contains only questions, and the second, possible answers. So the first question relates to the cause of *brahman*, here probably taken as the totality of the world (see verses. 6, 12) or Primal Matter (*prakṛti*, see Int., p. xlviii), rather than to a cause in the abstract.

Why were we born: the question is about the reason or cause rather than the purpose of our birth; the term could also mean 'whence' or 'from where'.

Governed by . . . situation: this question refers to the one who governs the process of rebirth in which people are born in different situations, some pleasant and others painful.

2 *Should we . . . and pain*: the author here gives several answers to the questions posed in verse 1, possibly answers that were given in various contemporary schools of thought (for his own answer on the cause, see SU 6.9). 'Source of birth' (lit. 'womb') probably refers to the different wombs a person may enter during the rebirth process (see verse. 5) which will determine the way he is at present. This, and the next answer, i.e. the person (*puruṣa*, probably in the Sāṃkhya sense of the conscious and spiritual principle in a human being), may be answers to the last question. The last sentence may also be translated: 'Even the self has no power over what causes pleasure and pain.'

3 *Those who . . . self*: this succinct verse has been subject to various interpretations. I follow Rau's (1964), which is closer to the syntax and fits with what follows. The term *sva-* ('own') in the compound *svaguṇaiḥ* ('by own qualities') is a reflective and can only refer back to the subject of the sentence, the anonymous 'those', and not to 'God', as assumed by some. Some also interpret the compound *devātmaśakti* as 'the self-power (or inherent power) of God'. Rau's interpretation assumes that the compound refers to the three cosmic principles—God, self (i.e. the individual soul), and power (i.e. the material principle called *prakṛti* in Sāmkhya cosmology)—which are the subject of discussion later in the chapter (see e.g. verses 6–12). The final statement refers to the theistic assumption of the

document, namely, that it is God alone who oversees every cause that operates within the universe. From 'time' to 'self' refers back to the list of causes given in verse 2.

4–5 *We study it . . . five sections*: see Johnston 1930 for a detailed study of these two verses. On the term 'study', with reference to those who have expertise in something, see KaU 1.13 n.; CU 5.11.2. The terms 'wheel' and 'river' are not given in the text, but are strongly implied by the adjectives; note also the expression 'wheel of *brahman*' in verse 6. I give here the traditional understanding of these numbers: one rim = primal nature or *prakṛti*; threefold = the three qualities (*guṇa*) of Sāṃkhya, i.e. goodness (*sattva*), energy (*rajas*), and darkness (*tamas*); sixteen tips = five elements, five organs of perception, five organs of action, and the mind; fifty spokes = the fifty dispositions (*bhāva*) of Sāṃkhya listed in the *Sāṃkhyakārikā*, 47; twenty counter-spokes = ten organs of perception and action and their respective objects, or, according to Johnston (1930, 858), the five elements, five objects of perception, and the ten organs of perception and action; six sets of eight = (1) five elements, intellect, ego (*ahaṃkāra*), and mind; (2) eight elements of the body: outer skin, inner skin, blood, flesh, fat, bone, marrow, and semen; (3) eight yogic powers: the power to become extremely small, extremely large, or extremely light, power to obtain anything, total freedom of will, power to subdue all to one's will, lordship, and power of suppressing desire (eight different results of yoga are listed at SU 2.13); (4) eight dispositions: righteousness and unrighteousness, knowledge and ignorance, detachment and non-detachment, superhuman power and lack of such power; (5) eight divine beings: Brahmā, Prajāpati, Devas, Gandharvas, Yakṣas, Rākṣasas, Ancestors, and Piśācas; (6) eight virtues: compassion, forbearance, lack of jealousy, purity, ease, generosity, auspiciousness, and absence of desire. One rope = desire ['of many forms' (*viśvarūpa*): although in general this term means glittering (see BU 1.4.7 n.), in this context it probably means the multiple ways in which the single rope of desire manifests itself; this interpretation of the rope image is challenged by Johnston 1930, 859]; three paths = righteousness, unrighteousness, and knowledge, though Johnston (1930, 859–60) views the paths as referring to the three ways to liberation, i.e. knowledge, yoga, and devotion (*bhakti*); two causes = good and sinful actions (the delusion regarding the 'one' refers back to the 'one' (verse. 3) who governs all the causes: Johnston (1930, 860–61) sees here a reference to the Sāṃkhya ignorance where the self regards the two, *puruṣa* and *prakṛti*, as just one); five sense organs: following Rau (1964, 28), I take *srotas* as 'sense organ', but the term literally means a stream and both meanings are probably intertwined here; I follow Johnston's (1930, 863) emendation *-nakrām* ('crocodile') for *-vakrām*; five sources of birth: traditionally viewed as the five elements (see Johnston's (1930, 864–72) long excursus), but they may be the types of births that a person may have during the rebirth process (cf. SU 1.2; BU 4.4.17 n.); five types of perception = those arising from the five senses; five whirlpools: the term may also mean 'back-currents' and refer to the path of rebirth which has five stages (BU 6.2.9–13; Rau 1964, 28); [traditionally, however, the five are viewed as the five objects of the senses]; five types of sorrow = suffering associated with residence in the womb, delivery, old age, sickness, and death, while Johnston (1930, 872–3) takes them to be the five sense objects; fifty ways may be the same as the fifty spokes of verse 4, but the reading here may be corrupt (Johnston 1930, 873–4); five sections = ignorance, sense of ego, love, hate, and attachment.

6 *goose*: here and elsewhere in the SU is either a symbol for the individual soul (see BU 2.5.18 n.) who circles around (i.e. is reborn repeatedly) in the wheel of *brahman* (i.e. existence subject to rebirth, *saṃsāra*) or of God (SU 6.15).

impeller: refers to God who sets the wheel in motion.

from there: that is, from the wheel of *brahman*.

To immortality: the concluding statement here and in verses 7–11 refers to the liberation of the self.

7 *oneself, the foundation*: I follow Rau's (1964, 44) emendation *svaḥ pratiṣṭhā-* for *supratiṣṭhā-*. 'Oneself' (*svaḥ*) is the *ātman* or individual self; 'foundation' is *prakṛti*; and 'imperishable' is God.

from the womb: that is, from repeated births.

9 *the one is Lord and the other is not the Lord*: 'Lord' and 'not the Lord' of this expression here and elsewhere in this Upaniṣad have also the meanings of 'powerful/free' and 'impotent/not free'. These two refer to the individual self (*ātman*) and God.

unborn female: that is, *prakṛti* (see SU 4.5). In the original Sanskrit 'female' and 'male' are expressed merely by the grammatical gender of the term 'unborn'.

displaying every form: I have previously translated the term *viśvarūpa* (see BU 1.4.7 n.) as 'dazzling'. In later texts such as the SU, however, the term probably has the meaning 'displaying every form'. This is demonstrated well in the famous transfiguration of

Kṛṣṇa in the BhG (ch. 11), where all the forms, i.e. all beings, are seen in the body of Kṛṣṇa. I still think that the term continues to refer to the luminescent conception of the self in its relationship to the sun (see, e.g., SU 5.8, where the Lord is compared to the sun; Bodewitz 1985, 17).

he finds: these words are not in the Sanskrit but are strongly implied.

10 *primal source* [pradhāna]: this is another term for primal matter or *prakṛti*.

Hara: the meaning of this term is unclear. In later times, it is an epithet of Śiva. Rau (1964, 29) takes it to mean 'glow' (*Glut*) and refers to *śukra* ('bright') of SU 4.2.

11 *blemishes* [kleśa]: are five in number: ignorance, sense of ego, love, hate, and attachment.

in the absolute . . . fulfilled: an alternative translation is: 'He becomes isolated [i.e. liberated] and his desires are fulfilled,' if we take *kevala* as a nominative (*kevalaḥ*) rather than a locative (*kevale*), both being possible according to the rules of sandhi.

12 *This*: the reference is to the three (God, self, and *prakṛti*) that was discussed in SU 1.3, 7, 9–10, and is called at the end 'threefold *brahman*'.

within one's body: I take *ātman* here as a reference to one's body in light of the statements in the subsequent verses (see BU 1.1.1 n.).

When the enjoyer: here I follow Rau's (1964, 44) emendation *bhoktā* for *bhoktāram*. In the next verse, indeed, it is the self that perceives 'both', i.e. God and objects of enjoyment, *prakṛti*.

13 *When a fire . . . tinder*: the image here is the production of fire by using a fire-drill (see BU 1.4.6 n.; KaU 4.8). The womb is the depression on the lower slab into which the drill is inserted and twirled to produce fire. 'Essential character' (*liṅga*) appears to refer to the essential element of fire, which remains within the fire-drill even when its visible form is extinguished. In later thought the term *liṅga* has the technical meaning of 'subtle form'.

one can grasp both: that is, God and *prakṛti* mentioned is the previous verse.

14 *the hidden thing*: probably the fire hidden in its source, the fire-drill.

15–16 *water in the river-bed*: the reference probably is to water hidden under a dried-up river-bed. The point of all these images is that in every case one has to engage in a strenuous activity (crushing the sesame seeds, churning the curds, or digging up the river-bed) to obtain what is hidden therein.

one grasps that self: here 'self' refers to God, who was the subject of discussion in the preceding verses.

CHAPTER 2

Verses 1–5 are, with some variants, TS 4.1.1.1–2 (where verses 2 and 3 are transposed). In that context these verses are part of a group of eight verses recited while the Adhvaryu priest makes an offering of eight parts. The references to yoking in these verses probably reflects the actions that follow immediately, namely the yoking of a horse to bring freshly dug clay to construct the fire altar. Verses 4–5 are also RV 5.81.1 and 10.13.1, respectively.

1 *recognized the fire as the light*: I see the term 'recognize' (*nicāyiya*) as referring to the perception of the identity between two things (see its use at SU 4.11; Bodewitz 1985, 24). 'Light' (see verse 3) here may refer to the heavenly light (sun?), which is identified with the earthy fire. According to another interpretation, one could translate: 'having recognized its light, brought the fire here from the earth'.

2 *With minds . . . heaven*: this verse lacks a verb, but given the context of offering oblations, 'make the offering' must be implied here.

5 *formulation*: the exact meaning of this term (*brahman*: see BU 2.1.1 n.) here and in verses 7–8 is unclear. It probably refers to some type of verbal formulation, and especially in verse 8 may refer to the syllable OṂ.

6 *Where the fire . . . born*: the fire is churned by twirling the fire-drill (BU 1.4.6 n.) and by blowing on it. This blowing must be intended by 'wafts' (I follow Rau's reading of *abhivyajyate* for *abhiyujyate*). The reference is clearly to a Soma sacrifice.

7 *By means . . . else's lot*: this is a very obscure verse (see parallel at RV 6.16.17–18) and the translation is tentative. I follow Hauschild (in Rau 1964, 31) in translating the last sentence, which is elliptic.

8 *the three sections*: namely, head, neck, and chest (see BhG 6.13).

9 *in here*: used deictically to refer to the chest or the body.

that wagon yoked to unruly horses: for this simile see KaU 3.3–6; the expression 'that wagon' may indeed be a reference to this well-known simile.

10 *noiseless*: I follow Johnston's (1930, 877–8) emendation *-vivarjite' śabda-* ('noiseless').

12 *When earth . . . suffering*: I follow Rau's (1964, 44) emendations *-khe samutthite* and *duḥkham* ('suffering') for *mṛtyuḥ* ('death').

14 *Just as a disk . . . from sorrow*: the Sanskrit term *bimba*, here translated as 'disk', probably refers to a round metal disk of some sort that may have served as a mirror. The Sanskrit term here translated tentatively as 'cleaned well' is unclear, with readings *sudhāta, sudhānta,* and *sudhauta*. The meaning of 'solitary' (*eka*, lit. 'one') is unclear; it may refer to the liberated condition viewed as 'solitary' (*kevala*) within Sāṃkhya.

15 *sees here*: the term 'here' may refer either to this world or to the body of the yogin.

objects [tattva]: the reference here may be to the material principles of Sāṃkhya cosmology.

16 *This God . . . towards men*: = VS 32.4.

face everywhere: this and the similar expressions regarding eyes, hands, and feet in SU 3.3 indicate that God's powers are present everywhere, or extend in every direction (see SU 3.14, 16). These expressions do not necessarily indicate the presence at this early time of the later iconographic representation of such powers in gods with multiple heads, hands, and feet.

17 *He who . . . Adoration*: = TS 5.5.9.3, with variants.

CHAPTER 3

2 *he stands . . . towards men*: I follow Rau's (1964, 44) emendation: *pratyaṅ janāṃs tiṣṭhaty antakāle*.

3 *Eyes . . . one God*: = RV 10.81.3, where the god creating the world is Viśvakarman ('All-maker'), the divine smith. The image is that of a smith who uses his two hands to work the metal and fans the fire with 'wings', which were probably some sort of fans made with feathers.

4 *Who, as . . . intelligence*: cf. SU. 4.12. I follow Rau's addition (*metri causa*) of *deva* ('god') before *rudra*. Hiraṇyagarbha, lit. 'golden germ', is viewed as a universal egg from which the entire creation hatched.

5–6 *That form . . . or beast*: = TS 4.5.1.1–2.

7 *higher than that*: the meaning appears to be that God is higher than the parts of the world described above, the totality of which constitutes *brahman*.

8 *I know . . . getting there*: = VS 31.18; cf. SU 6.15.

9 *This whole . . . in heaven*: = TA 10.10.3.

10 *What is . . . awaits them*: cf. BU 4.4.14. 'Higher than that': see SU. 3.7 n.

11 *Benign One*: that is, Śiva, but the term *śiva* at this time is probably just an epithet rather than another name for Rudra.

12 *real, attainment*: these two terms here, according to Rau (1964, 34), have the technical Sāṃkhya meanings of the 'quality of goodness' (*sattvaguṇa*) and 'yogic attainment' (*siddhi*, i.e. extraordinary powers), respectively.

13–14 *The Person . . . beyond it*: cf. SU 4.17; KaU 6.9.

the size of a thumb: see KaU 4.12; 6.17.

14–15 *The Person . . . through food*: these are the opening two verses of the famous hymn of creation, Puruṣasūkta, RV 10.90.1–2. The last sentence of verse 15 is elliptic and has been subject to diverse interpretations.

16 *With hands . . . world*: = BhG 13.13. There is a shift in the subject of the sentence here from the masculine to a neuter pronoun (*tat*, 'it'). Within the BhG the reference is to *brahman*.

17 *That which . . . every sense*: = BhG 13.14.

18 *fort with nine gates*: see KaU 5.1 n.

goose: see BU 2.5.18 n.

20 *Finer than . . . from sorrow*: see KaU 2.20. 'Heart' is here literally 'cavity', which is a synonym for the heart, see TU 2.3.1 n.

21 *the one . . . of birth*: this half of the verse is elliptic and obscure. My translation is tentative and follows Rau's (1964, 35) interpretation.

CHAPTER 4

1 *in whom . . . the end*: this phrase is corrupt in the original. Rau (1964, 45) suggests the emendation: *saṃ cādāv eti vi cānte sa devaḥ*. I have followed the reading suggested by Joel Brereton (private communication): *vi cānta eti viśvam ādau saṃ caiva* (see the parallel at SU 4.11). The expression clearly refers to the fact that God is the origin and the final dissolution of all beings (see SU 4.12).

2 *The fire . . . Prajāpati is that*: = VS 32.1 with variants. Even though the use of the neuter pronoun *tat* ('that') in apposition to masculine nouns violates vedic syntax (see CU 6.8.7–16 n.), I think in this late text they are used in apposition, especially because the following verses also seek to establish identities.

3 *You are a woman . . . direction*: = AV 10.8.27.

5 *One unborn . . . her pleasures*: this verse plays on the *double entendre* of the masculine *aja* ('unborn' and billy goat) and the feminine *ajā* ('unborn' and nanny-goat): see SU 1.9. The sexual metaphor is explicit. In its cosmological meaning, the 'unborn male' is the soul and the 'unborn female' is *prakṛti*. The three colours are standard references to the three qualities (*guṇa*) of *prakṛti*: goodness (*sattva*), energy (*rajas*), and darkness (*tamas*). The unborn male who leaves his partner refers to the liberated soul.

6–7 *Two birds . . . disappears*: these two verses are MuU 3.1.1–2, to which notes are given. The first verse is RV 1.164.20.

8 *The syllable . . . do know it*: = RV 1.164.39. The term *akṣara* means both 'imperishable' and 'syllable', especially the sacred syllable OṂ. Often, as here, there is a play on this double meaning. 'Ṛg' in the singular here may refer to the class of sacred verses included within the Ṛgveda.

9–10 *Metres* [chandāṃsi]: this may also be a more general reference to vedic hymns.

illusory power [māyā]: this is an early use of this term as a cosmic category, although it probably means here more a 'trick' or 'magic' than a cosmic illusion, as in later philosophies that denied the existence of the world. This magic is used by the 'illusionist' (i.e. the Lord as magician) to create the world in which 'the other' (i.e. individual souls) are trapped.

primal matter [prakṛti]: see SU 1.1 n.

11 *Who alone . . . unending peace*: cf. KaU 1.17 (Bodewitz 1985, 14 n. 24); SU 4.1.

12 *Who, as the source . . . intelligence*: cf. SU 3.4 and the note to this.

14 *disorder*: the reference is possibly to the primordial waters (Rau 1964, 37).

displaying various forms [anekarūpa]: see SU 1.9 n.

Benign One: see SU 3.11 n.

15 *seers*: I follow Rau's (1964, 45) emendation (*metri causa*) of *ṛṣayo* ('seers') for *brahmarṣayo* ('Brahmin seers'); the qualifier *brahma* is probably a later gloss.

17 *That God . . . immortal*: cf. SU 3.13.

maker of all: this may also be a reference to the god Viśvakarman (cf. SU 3.3 n.).

18 *When there was darkness*: I think the reading *yad ā tamas* ('when

there was semi-darkness') in place of *yadā tamas* suggested by Böhtlingk (Hauschild 1927, 26) is unnecessary. Darkness refers to the primordial time without the celestial lights. That darkness is different from night; the distinction between day and night is not based on the opposition between light and darkness but between the daytime sky dominated by the sun and the night sky with the moon and the stars, especially the Milky Way (see the image of the two wheels of a cart applied to day and night in KsU 1.4*a* and the note to this). When nothing of the present universe was in existence, the Benign One (cf. SU 3.1 n.) alone existed.

The excellent [*glory*] *of Savitṛ*: these are the first words of the Sāvitrī verse (RV 3.62.10; see BU 6.3.6 n.).

19 *likeness*: this is the only occurrence of the term *pratimā* ('likeness') in the Upaniṣads. The meaning is that it is not possible to create an image or portrait of him, especially in the light of what is said in the very next verse.

20 *His appearance . . . immortal*: cf. KaU 6.9.

21 *He is . . . face of yours*: I follow the emendations suggested by Rau (1964, 45). The author probably refers to himself, or includes himself, in the phrase 'some man'.

22 *Do not hurt . . . your seat*: = RV 1.114.8 with a variant.

CHAPTER 5

1 *fort*: see BU 2.5.18 n.

2 *womb after womb*: see SU 1.7 n.

carried this Kapila: possibly a reference to the seer who is traditionally viewed as the founder of the Sāṃkhya tradition. The 'carrying' implies that he is pregnant with Kapila. In light of the next verses, the term *kapila* ('red') may also refer to the sun. Cf. RV 1.164.4; 4.27.1.

3 *Spreading . . . the whole world*: I follow Rau's (1964, 45) emendation *patayati tatheśaḥ* of this otherwise corrupt verse. The net may refer to the rays of the sun which are spread out in the morning and gathered in at night.

4 *draught-ox*: an epithet of the sun.

wombs and inherent natures: a reference to the putative causes listed earlier at SU 1.2 (cf. SU 6.1), and the plural may merely indicate that the many items in that list are here included.

5 *by his inherent nature*: I follow Rau's (1964, 45) reading *svabhāvāt* ('by his own nature') for *svabhāvam*.

qualities: the three qualities (*guṇa*) of *prakṛti* (see SU 4.5 n.), which the creator distributes among the created objects.

6 *It is hidden . . . immortal*: I follow Rau's (1964, 45) emendation *brāhmaṇā* for *brahmā*, because it fits the context and restores the metre. I also emend *vedate* to *vedata* (imperative 2nd person plural), which is also required by Rau's translation. In a late text such as the SU, the term *upaniṣad* (in the plural) probably refers to the vedic texts of that name (see Int., p. liii).

7 *Displaying every form*: see SU 1.9 n.

three paths: see SU 1.4–5 n. The reference here is to the migration of the self from one existence to another.

10 *It is neither . . . obtains*: the meaning is that the self acquires the gender of the body to which it becomes attached.

11 *The birth . . . its actions*: I follow Rau's (1964, 45) emendation *-homair* ('through the offerings') for *-mohair* ('through delusions'). This is a reference to the doctrine of the five fires in BU 6.2 and CU 5.3–10. The first part concerns the birth of the body caused by sexual activity (this must be the meaning of the three offerings: intending to have sex, touching, and seeing the woman) and its growth through food and drink. The term *vṛṣṭi* literally means 'rain' and may refer to the rain as one step in the transmigratory process. I take it as 'impregnation' because in this section the discussion is not about transmigration (the focus of the second part) but about the birth and growth of the body.

12 *their union*: that is, the union with another body during the process of rebirth.

13 *Who is without . . . fetters*: cf. SU 4.14.

14 *who is called 'Without-a-Lord'*: I have taken *anīḍ-* in the compound *anīḍākhyam* to mean 'one who has no Lord', i.e. one who rules over all but has no one to rule over him (Rau 1964, 40; see SU 6.9). As *anīḍa* it would mean 'without a nest [abode]'; and as *anīḍā*, 'one who is without praise', i.e. one who cannot be adequately praised.

CHAPTER 6

1 *Some wise . . . around*: this refers back to SU 1.2 that discussed the cause of the universe or, as the SU calls it, the wheel of *brahman*.

2 *without qualities*: I follow Rau's (1964, 45) emendation *'guṇī* (i.e. *aguṇī* 'without qualities') for *guṇī* ('with qualities').

work of creation: the term *karma* ('work') here and in the subsequent verses refers to the creation viewed as the handiwork of God.

3–4 *After completing ... those realities*: these two verses are a mess with an impossible syntax. I think Rau (1964, 40) is right in taking the two as a syntactic whole. I do not follow his textual emendation, however. The general meaning is that when God has created and then withdrawn the entire creation into himself, one sees that he is distinct from all the created 'realities', which term here refers to the constituents of the world. The meaning of the numbers is unclear but they most certainly derive from early Sāṃkhya speculation. 'One' may be either the Person (*puruṣa*) or Primal Matter (*prakṛti*). 'Two' is traditionally viewed as the world and the unmanifest. 'Three' is the qualities. 'Eight' probably refers to the first eight evolutes of *prakṛti*, namely, intellect, ego, mind, and the five elements.

5–6 *One sees ... all beings*: I follow the logical rearrangement of these two verses by Rau (1964, 41): first verse = 5ab, 6ab; second verse = 5cd, 6cd. The second verse, as rearranged, is syntactically connected with verse 7. 'Tree' here refers to the manifest universe: cf. SU 3.9; 4.6.

9 *overlords of the sense organs*: the reference could be to the breaths or to the individual souls.

10 *primal source*: see SU 1.10 n.

11 *overseer*: can mean supervisor and/or eyewitness.

work: here refers to the creation (see SU 6.2 n.).

spectator: Rau (1964, 46) reads *cetā* for *cettā*, and translates as 'revenger'.

12 *the one controller ... happiness*: cf. KaU 5.12.

13 *The changeless ... fetters*: cf. KaU 5.13. The expression *sāṃkhyayogādhigamyam* may also be translated: 'to be comprehended through Sāṃkhya and Yoga (or Sāṃkhya-Yoga)', or 'to be comprehended through the application of analysis'. It is unclear whether the terms Sāṃkhya and Yoga had at this time the technical meaning of a system of thought.

14 *There the sun ... his light*: = KaU 5.15; MuU 2.2.10.

15 *goose*: see SU 1.6 n. Second half of the verse is SU 3.8.

16 *individual souls*: the expression *kṣetrajña* literally means 'knower

of the field', i.e. the soul as the one who is conscious of the unconscious products of primal matter, here viewed as a 'field'.

17 *He who . . . becoming the Lord*: I follow Rau's (1964, 46) emendation transposing the correlative pronouns *sa* and *ya*. The last sentence imitates SU 3.8; 6.15.

19 *dike*: see BU 4.4.22 n. It may well be that in a late text such as this the term *setu* may have already acquired the meaning of 'bridge'.

21 *to those . . . order of life*: many scholars have assumed, I believe mistakenly, that the expression *atyāśramibhyaḥ* ('to those who had passed beyond their order of life') refers to those who had passed beyond the four stage of life known as the *āśramas*. The term *āśrama* here means just the householder's life, and the expression refers to ascetics who have moved beyond the household life. See Olivelle 1993, 23.

23 *Noble One* [mahātman]: the reference here is probably to Śvetāśvatara.

Muṇḍaka Upaniṣad

CHAPTER 1

1.1 *Brahmā arose*: a distinction appears to be made here between Brahmā (a masculine noun), the first of the gods, and *brahman* (a neuter noun), the knowledge of which Brahmā taught, a knowledge that leads to immortality. The neuter *brahman* may refer to 'the formulation of truth' (see BU 2.1.1 n.) and/or to the absolute reality. What relation, if any, this *brahman* has to Brahmā is unclear.

1.3 *prescribed manner*: refers to the ritual accompanying a pupil's placing himself under the guidance of a teacher: see BU 6.2.7 n.

1.4 The rest of the Upaniṣad is presented as the answer of Aṅgiras. I have not placed the entire text within quotation marks, however, because in these verse Upaniṣads the initial dialogue is merely a literary device to present the text as the teaching of a divine or sage being—a practice common in later works such as the Dharmaśāstras and the Purāṇas. The text itself does not contain any indication that it is really a dialogue.

1.5 *Ṛgveda . . . astronomy*: on these texts and sciences, see CU 7.1.2 n.

1.7 *As a spider . . . living man*: for similar images, see BU 2.1.20.

1.8 *Through heat . . .* : here begins, I think, an argument (extending up to verse 2.6) for the efficacy and superiority of ritual activity. This opinion is rejected by the author at MU 1.2.7. The term *tapas* may mean both heat and austerity: see TU 3.1 n.

1.9 *appearance* [rūpa]: see BU 1.4.7 n.

2.2 *When the flame . . . ghee*: the main offering at some major sacrifices, such as the new-moon sacrifice, is offered between two pourings of ghee into the fire, technically called *ājyabhāga*. After the ghee is poured the flame of the fire blazes, and it is into this blazing fire that the main offering is made.

2.3 *four-month sacrifice*: is one offered after every four months, that is, at the beginning of each season (spring, rains, autumn).

offering to all the gods [vaiśvadeva]: is part of every sacrifice (see BU 3.1.9 n).

2.4 *glittering*: (with Hertel read *viśvarūpī* in place of *viśvarucī*) see BU 1.4.7 n.

2.5 *When a man . . . reside*: the context is the death of a man. He has been brought to the funeral pyre and is surrounded by the seven flames of fire. These flames, in the form of the rays of the sun, carry the dead man to the world of *brahman*.

2.7 *Surely, they are . . .* : here begins the author's reply to the ritualist's arguments, which began at MuU 1.1.8.

eighteen forms: it is unclear what these eighteen forms are. Some take them as texts in which the sacrificial doctrine is spelled out, and identify them with the Saṃhitā, Brāhmaṇa, and the ritual sūtra of the four Vedas (= 12), plus the six ancillary sciences (see MuU 1.1.5). It seems more likely, however, that the reference is to types of sacrifice, such as the new-moon and the full-moon sacrifice mentioned earlier in verse 2, and not to ritual texts.

2.8 *Wallowing . . . blind*: see KaU 2.5.

2.9 *Wallowing . . . to a close*: their stay in heaven comes to a close when the ritual merit that took them there becomes exhausted. The aim of this entire section is to show the temporary nature of any happiness won through ritual activities.

2.10–11 *Deeming . . . immutable self*: a more detailed version of this contrast between people given to rites, who live in villages, and those given to ascetic practices, who live in the wilderness, is given in BU 6.2.15–16 and CU 5.10. 'Gifts' (*pūrta*) refer especially to the gifts to officiating priests at a sacrifice (see CU 5.10.3). 'Sacrifices and gifts' of ordinary people are contrasted here with 'penance and faith' of those in the wilderness.

2.12 *What's made . . . unmade*: the pithy saying *nāsty akṛtaḥ kṛtena* literally means 'There is no unmade through made.' The term *kṛta* can mean 'made', 'done', or 'created' and refer to both normal and ritual action (*karma*). Thus 'unmade' (*akṛta*) can also mean what is not subject to or produced through rites. The worlds that one obtains through rites are *kṛta*, while the immortal self in *akṛta*.

firewood in hand: see CU 4.4.5 n.

2.13 *To that . . . imperishable*: this concluding verse may refer back to MuU 1.1.3. Then the student is Śaunaka and the teacher is Aṅgiras.

CHAPTER 2

1.4 *His head . . . every being*: this verse echoes the creation hymn of RV 10.90. This entire chapter appears to be a reinterpretation of that ancient hymn of creation.

1.5 *From him comes . . . creatures*: this is a very brief statement of the doctrine of the five fires, explained in detail in BU 6.2.9–14; CU 5.4–9.

1.8 *The seven breaths . . . spring*: the seven flames are mentioned in MuU 1.2.4; see also PU 3.5. The seven worlds probably refer to the ancient three (earth, intermediate region, and sky), to which were added in later mythology four others: Mahas, Janas, Tapas, and Satya (identified with the world of Brahmā). The identities of the other sets of seven are less clear. For the cave or space within the heart, see BU 2.1.17 n.

1.9 *the sap . . . self*: for the image of the sap by which a plant lives, see CU 6.8.7–16 n.; 6.12.2 n.

1.10 *All this . . . Person*: these words of this verse recalls the opening words of RV 10.90.

2.3 *weapon of upaniṣad*: the precise meaning of the term *aupaniṣada* (lit. 'relating to or derived from *upaniṣad*') is unclear. The following verse identifies the weapon as OṂ; so OṂ must be viewed here as showing the hidden connection between *brahman* and the self (see Int., p. lii).

veneration: for the meaning, see BU 4.1.2 n.

2.4 *He will . . . the target*: my translation is somewhat free. The pithy Sanskrit literally means: 'Like the arrow, he will be made of that (or same as that).' The meaning appears to be that as the arrow embedded within the target becomes lodged within it and thus becomes one with it, so the person enters into *brahman* and becomes the same as *brahman*.

2.5 *woven*: see BU 3.6.1 n.

breaths: here the term may have the meaning of 'senses' (see BU 1.5.17 n.).

dike: see BU 4.4.22 n.

2.6 *Where the veins come together*: the reference is to the space within the heart; see BU 2.1.19 n.

like spokes: the vulgate reads, 'like spokes at the hub', an addition that is probably a gloss. For this image, see BU 2.5.15; PU 2.6; 6.6.

2.7*a* *fort*: see BU 2.5.18 n.

2.7*b* *breaths*: meaning the senses; see MuU 2.5.

2.8 *the high and the low*: the reference is to the two abodes of the self, in the city of *brahman* in the sky and in the heart. Works here refer especially to ritual actions, although they are possibly not limited to them.

The knot of one's heart: see KaU 6.15.

2.9 *In that . . . of lights*: the high golden container or bucket may be a reference to the area around the Pole Star (see BU 2.2.3 n.). This may also be a reference to the 'city of *brahman*' in the sky in verse 7*a*. *Brahman* thus would refer to the Pole Star fixed firmly in the sky and shining brightly without changing. 'Partless' would then refer to the fact that this star does not wax and wane like the moon (Rau 1965, 223).

2.10 *There the sun . . . with his light*: see KaU 5.15; SU 6.14.

2.11 *Brahman alone . . . widest extent*: on the interpretation of the verse, see Brereton 1986, 102 n. 13; cf. CU 7.25.1.

CHAPTER 3

1.1 *Two birds . . . looks on*: = RV 1.164.20. This and the next verse are also in SU 4.6–7.

1.2 *by her who is not the Lord* [anīśayā]: this expression probably refers to the female cosmic power, that is, *prakṛti*, which is distinct from the Lord and which is the cause of human ignorance. The opposition between the two principles is more pronounced in the SU.

1.3 *highest identity*: the expression may also mean 'identity with the highest' (Rau 1965, 224). There may also be a play here on the term *sāmya*, which, besides identity, can also mean calmness in the yogic sense (see BhG 5.19; 6.33).

1.4 *thereby a man who out-talks*: I read *bhava tenātivādī* in place of *bhavate nātivādī*, and take this as a positive rather than a negative sentence (Rau 1965, 224). On 'out-talking' as a virtue, see CU 7.15.4 n.

active man: refers to one who engages in ritual and other activities; but this man performs these acts by his dallying with the self (*ātman*).

2.1 *what is here bright* [śukram etat]: the meaning of *śukram* is unclear, since it can mean both 'bright' and 'semen'. The term clearly relates to *śubhram* (also meaning 'bright') of the second line. The meaning could be that wise men go beyond the celestial lights, or, according to the traditional explanation, that they go beyond the semen, i.e. they are not reborn.

2.2 *One who hankers . . . very world*: here too, actions refer primarily to ritual actions (see MuU 2.2.8 n.). On the lack and fulfilment of desires, see BU 4.4.6.

2.3 *chooses*: with Rau (1965, 225), I read *vṛṇute* ('chooses') in place of *vivṛṇute* ('reveals'); see KaU 2.23.

2.4 *without the marks*: the term *aliṅga* is probably used here in a technical sense to indicate the proper marks of an ascetic (Johnston 1930, 863). The meaning appears to be that austerity when undertaken improperly does not lead to the understanding of the self.

by these means: that is, through strength, careful attention, and austerity undertaken properly.

brahman-abode: that is, the cavity in the heart of the man who knows. The abode of the heart here corresponds to the heavenly abode of *brahman* noted at MuU 2.2.7*a*, 9.

2.5 *All*: = 'Whole', see BU 1.4.9–10 n.

2.6 *Vedānta*: the reference here is probably to the Upaniṣads, which by the time of the MuU probably constituted a body of literature distinct from the earlier collections dealing with the ritual (cf. MuU 1.1.5).

renunciation: the Sanskrit is *saṃnyāsa*, one of the earliest occurrences of this term with this technical meaning (see Olivelle 1991).

2.7 *fifteen parts*: the reference is to the fifteen functions of a person, possibly the five senses, the five breaths, and the five organs of action.

all the senses . . . divinities: the senses (here called 'divinities', see BU 1.3.9 n.) return to the cosmic entities to which they correspond (see BU 3.2.13).

2.8 *As the rivers . . . highest*: see CU 6.10.1; PU 6.5.

2.10 *offer for themselves*: that is, people who offer sacrifices for their own benefit, but do not act as hired priests at sacrifices performed by other patrons.

lone seer: his identity is unclear. He is identified with breath in PU 2.11, and with Pūṣan in IU 16. If it is breath, then 'offering for themselves' may refer to the offering of food in the breath (*prāṇāgnihotra*).

head-vow: this may refer to the shaving of the head (*muṇḍana*) hinted at by the title of the Upaniṣad.

Praśna Upaniṣad

QUESTION 1

1 *carrying firewood*: see CU 4.4.5 n.

4 *he heated himself*: on the significance of heat in creation and its relation to austerity, see BU 1.2.6; CU 2.23.2 n.; TU 3.1 n.

couple: this term has clear sexual connotations here, the Sanskrit terms for substance (*rayi*) and lifebreath (*prāṇa*) being feminine and masculine nouns, respectively. It is their union that produces creatures. The term *rayi* generally means wealth or property, but in its usage here as a cosmological category it appears to have a wider significance. Many have translated the term as 'matter'. In adopting the translation 'substance' (without any Aristotelian connotations) I am attempting to capture both the meanings of this term: matter and wealth.

7 *fire common to all* [vaiśvānara]: see BU 1.1.1 n.

dazzling [viśvarūpa]: see BU 1.4.7 n.

8 *Golden . . . created beings*: the syntax and grammar of this verse is far from clear, with the first two lines (*pāda*) either connected with a phrase outside this verse or connected with the last two with 'broken syntax' (Salomon 1991, 58). Grammatical irregularities, studied by Salomon (1991), are a common feature of this Upaniṣad.

9 *two courses*: on the two courses of the sun, and on this passage in general, see BU 6.2.15–16; CU 5.10.

best action: the meaning of *kṛtam*, here translated as 'best action', is unclear. It may mean ritual action, and evoke also the winning throw of the dice (see CU 4.1.3 n.). This term is substituted here for *dattam* ('gift') of CU 5.10.3. Read differently, the phrase also may mean: 'those who venerate offerings to gods and priests, thinking "That's enough!ē'

10 *stoppage* [nirodha]: this is a technical term in Yoga, meaning the cessation of mental activities that marks the state of final liberation. The term is also related to *nirvāṇa*, which in Buddhism signifies the final cessation of phenomenal existence that marks the liberated state.

11 *Some call . . . six spokes*: this rather obscure verse is taken from RV 1.164.12, a hymn full of enigmas and riddles. The one on the far side may refer to the sun, and the one on the near side to the moon or

possibly to the sacrifice, at least within the context of the PU. Five and twelve forms probably refer to the five seasons and the twelve months. The reference of the seven wheels and six spokes is unclear; this may be a reference to the chariot of the sun or to some aspect of the sacrifice. See Horsch 1966, 192–3.

14 *Prajāpati . . . creatures*: on the sequence food, semen, and creatures, see BU 6.2 n.

QUESTION 2

1 *deities*: as vital faculties, see BU 1.3.9 n.

become manifest: I take *prakāśayante* (causative: 'they illuminate') to be used irregularly for the simple verb *prakāsante* ('they become manifest').

2 *reed*: here refers to the body. This image works well with the view that the body is kept alive by the passage of wind (breath) through its inner tubes.

3 *Don't delude yourself*: on the debate about the relative superiority of the vital functions, see BU 1.3.2–6 n.

dividing myself into five parts: see BU 1.5.3 n.

4 *he started to set off*: many translators take the particle *iva* here to mean that breath was pretending to or acting as if he were about to set off. No pretence is, however, intended (see Brereton's (1982) essay on *iva*); the meaning appears to be that breath actually took off but did not completely depart from the body, just as a queen bee would rise above the hive, hover there, and settle down again in the hive.

settled down: on the irregular formation here of the verb *prātiṣṭhante*, see Salomon 1991, 65–70.

queen bee: ancient Indians thought the queen to be a male, and hence the Sanskrit calls it a 'king bee'.

11 *lone seer*: see MuU 3.2.10.

you are the eater . . . household: read differently, this phrase may be translated: 'you are the eater, the true lord of all', or 'you are the eater of all, the true lord'.

you are our father, Mātariśvan: this may also be translated: 'you are the father of Mātariśvan' (see Salomon 1982, 51 n. 10 and parallel in AV 11.4.15). In earlier mythology Mātariśvan is identified with fire, but later came to be viewed as wind.

QUESTION 3

1 *Lord, from what . . . within the body*: the last question relates to the names that lifebreath receives when it exists as entities outside the body, for example as the sun, earth, and wind (see PU 3.8), and as different breaths within the body (see PU 3.4). Question 1 is answered in § 3 (sentence 1); question 2 in § 3 (verse); question 3, in §§ 4–5; question 4 in §§ 6–7; and question 5 in § 8.

3 *As this . . . by the mind*: this verse is rather obscure and has been subject to diverse interpretations. Mine is an interpretation, rather than a literal translation. The traditional interpretation is that the lifebreath, within the process of rebirth, enters another body 'by a path created by the mind', that is, in accordance with a person's past deliberate actions. On the verse and on the problematic word *manokṛtena*, see Salomon 1982, 51.

5 *in-breath* [apāna]: in earlier literature this breath was viewed as inhalation. It is now identified as the breath in the lower parts of the belly responsible for evacuation and ejaculation.

lifebreath itself: here *prāṇa* as 'out-breath' is identified with *prāṇa* as the undifferentiated lifebreath.

link-breath: in this phonetic etymology, this breath 'makes alike' the food that is eaten, that is, homogenizes the different foods in the digestive process, just as fire burns everything to ashes (see also PU 4.4).

seven flames: see MuU 1.2.4; 2.1.8.

8 *the sun . . . within sight*: when the sun rises one can see, and in this the author detects the fact that the sun and sight are two forms of breath.

9–10 *The up-breath . . . conception*: this passage, I think, has been misunderstood by the native interpretive tradition; hence, the misleading numbering of the paragraphs. I have assumed that the term *bhavam* in the expression *punarbhavam* is a later gloss interpreting the term *punar* as referring to rebirth. I take *punar* ('again') as qualifying the verb *āyāti* ('comes' or 'returns'), and the whole statement as referring to the dying person's entry into the lifebreath at the moment of death. The lifebreath then leads the dead person to this next birth.

12 *entrance*: I take *āyati* as standing for *āyāti*; see the second question at PU 3.1 (Horsch 1966, 193–4). This verse recapitulates the opening questions of this chapter.

QUESTION 4

3 *fort*: see BU 2.5.18 n.

householder's fire: on the three vedic fires mentioned here, see CU 2.24.3 n.; Fig. 3, p. xliii.

4 *link-breath*: on the etymology see also PU 3.5 n.

5–6 *this deity*: probably refers to the mind (see § 2). When the mind becomes overpowered by heat or fire, that is, by the up-breath which is equated with fire (PU 3.9), it sees no dreams.

9–11 *This intelligent . . . world indeed*: the prose passages and the verse alike pose many difficulties: see Salomon 1991, 59–60; Horsch 1966, 194.

QUESTION 5

6 *The three . . . not tremble*: I follow the emendations suggested by Horsch 1966, 195. The meaning of 'external, internal, and in between' is unclear; they may refer to the way the phonemes are pronounced: loud, soft, and medium. If that is the meaning, then 'performances' would mean the pronunciation of the syllable.

7 *With Ṛg . . . the supreme*: this verse also appears to be corrupt: see Horsch 1966, 196.

QUESTION 6

1 *sixteen parts*: listed in PU 6.4; see also BU 1.5.14 n.

3 *Who is the one . . . settle down*: see PU 2.3–4.

5 *Now, take . . . the ocean*: on this simile, see MuU 3.2.8; CU 6.10.1.

6 *In whom . . . disturb you*: on the interpretation of this verse, see Horsch 1966, 196–7; Salomon 1991, 54–6.

Māṇḍūkya Upaniṣad

1 *OṂ . . . simply OṂ*: see the parallels in CU 1.1.1; 1.4.1.

2 *Whole*: see BU 1.4.9–10n.

four quarters: see BU 4.1.2–7; CU 3.18; 4.5–8.

3 *The first . . . gross things*: on these states of awareness, see BU 4.2–4. The meanings of 'seven limbs' and 'nineteen mouths' are uncertain. The commentator Śaṃkara refers to CU 5.18.2 with reference to the seven limbs, but there a total of eleven parts are enumerated. He identifies the nineteen mouths as the five organs of perception, the five organs of action, five breaths, together with mind, reason (*buddhi*), ego-sense, and intellect (*citta*).

9–11 *The first . . . destruction*: on the use of phonetic etymologies, see BU 1.2.1n.

10 *The second . . . lineage*: the meaning appears to be that he will bring to a heightened level the lineage of knowledge (i.e. the line of men of learning into which he is born). The meaning of 'common' is less clear; it may mean that he will enjoy inclusion among both (opposing?) parties or that he will act as a mediator between them, which would accord with *ubhayatva* (lit. 'state of being both').

LIST OF NAMES OF GODS, PEOPLE, AND PLACES

FOR more detailed information about the humans, gods, and sages, as well as the place names mentioned in the Upaniṣads, the reader may consult the comprehensive index prepared by Macdonell and Keith (1912) and Macdonell's (1898) survey of vedic mythology. For the location of many of the places, consult Fig. 2 on p. xxxviii. The reader should consult the Index for a complete listing of occurrences of these names in the Upaniṣads. The following list does not include individuals mentioned solely in the long lists of teachers and pupils appended to several Upaniṣads.

Abhipratārin Kākṣaseni. A person of royal descent among the Kurus who appears in several ancient texts as engaged in theological discussions. The JB (3.156) reports that his sons divided his property while he was still alive.

Aditi. A female deity, the mother of several gods, including Varuṇa and Mitra. In later mythology she is made the mother of gods in general. Sometimes she is identified with the earth. See KaU 4.7; Macdonell 1898, 120–3.

Ādityas. Literally the son(s) of Aditi, the term in the plural refers to a group of gods, including some prominent ones such as Varuṇa, Mitra, and Indra. Early texts give their number as eight, but the Brāhmaṇas already show their number as twelve, which has remained the norm ever since. Together with the Vasus and the Rudras, they constitute the three major classes of gods (see CU 3.16). In the singular, the term Āditya refers to the sun.

Ajātaśatru. A king of Kāśi, not to be confused with a king of the same name, the son of Bindusāra, recorded in the Buddhist texts.

Āṅgirasa. The name of a class of priests closely associated with another group called Atharvan. The name is also used with reference to a group of sundry divine beings and is an epithet to several gods, especially the fire god Agni.

Āruṇi. The patronymic of Uddālaka Āruṇi.

Aśvala. Little is known about him, apart from the fact recorded in BU 3.1.2 that he was the Hotṛ priest of Janaka of Videha.

Aśvapati Kaikeya. Known only from the episode, recorded both in SB 10.6.1.2 and in CU 5.11.4, of his instructing several Brahmins about the self. He was a king of the Kekayas, a people located in the north-western region.

Aśvins. Twin deities described as young, beautiful, fond of honey, and expert in medical knowledge. They are the physicians of the gods.

Atidhanvan Śaunaka. A teacher appearing in CU 1.9.3; little else is known about him other than that he was the teacher of Udara Śāṇḍilya.

Āṭikī. The wife of Uṣasti in CU 1.10.1.

Bāka Dālbhya. A Brahmin from the Kuru-Pañcāla region, who is credited in the JB (1.9.2) with constraining Indra. His only appearance in the Upaniṣads is in the humorous tale of dogs at CU 1.12.

Bālāki. *See* Gārgya Bālāki.

Barku Vārṣṇa. Appears as a teacher who is at odds with Yājñavalkya. He is portrayed in a poor light both in SB 1.1.1.10 and BU 4.1.4.

Bhaga. This word means 'dispenser', and this 'dispenser of wealth' is counted among the twelve Ādityas.

Bhārgava Vaidarbhi. A learned Brahmin who questioned Pippalāda in the PU 2.

Bhuju Lāhyāyani. A Brahmin contemporary of Yājñavalkya; he attended a major sacrifice celebrated by Janaka of Videha (BU 3.3). Little else is known about him.

Brahmadatta Caikitāneya. Appears as a teacher in BU 1.3.24; JU 1.37; 1.59. Little else is known about him.

Brahmaṇaspati. Literally 'the lord of brahman(s)', the term is an epithet of Bṛhaspati.

Bṛhaspati. A deity closely linked to the fire god and to sacred speech, who is wise and is the lord of speech and eloquence. He is regarded as the priest of the gods and the source of wisdom. Later tradition identifies him with the planet Jupiter and ascribes to him, now considered a seer, texts of religious law and politics.

Buḍila Āśvatarāśvi. Also called Vaiyāghrapadya (CU 5.16), he was a rich Brahmin said to have been a contemporary of the kings Janaka of Videha and Aśvapati Kaikeya, as well as of Uddālaka Āruṇi. He is depicted as somewhat confused and ignorant.

Caikitāyana Dālbhya. Both names appear to be patronymics and occur elsewhere in vedic literature with reference to other individuals (see e.g. Bāka). Dālbhya was a Brahmin who took part in a discussion with and is subsequently instructed by Pravāhaṇa Jaivali on the meaning of the High Chant (CU 1.8–9).

Citra Gāṅgāyani. Appears in KsU 1.1 as a king and a contemporary of Śvetaketu and Uddālaka Āruṇi. He teaches the latter a doctrine similar to that taught by Pravāhaṇa Jaivali in BU 6.2 and CU 5.3–10; they are probably versions of the same story with a change of the royal character.

Cūla Bhāgavitti. Nothing is known about this teacher besides what is found in BU 6.3.9–10.

Dadhyañc Ātharvṇa. A seer who is famous for having revealed to the Aśvins the place of honey (see BU 2.5.17 n.).

Dhātṛ. A minor god connected with creation. In later texts, he is identified with the major creator gods Prajāpati and Brahmā.

Dṛptabālāki Gārgya. *See* Gārgya Bālāki.

Gandhāra. A region in the extreme north-west of the Indian subcontinent (see Map).

Gandharva. In the early vedic literature Gandharvas appear as a class of divine beings alongside the gods and the forefathers. They are associated with the Soma drink and are said to be fond of females. They are often associated with the celestial nymphs, Apsarases. In later literature, especially the epics, the Gandharvas are depicted as celestial singers and are associated with music.

Gardabhīvipīta Bhāradvāja. He is a teacher who is said to have told Janaka of Videha that *brahman* consists of the power of hearing (BU 4.1.5).

Gārgī Vācaknavī. One of the few learned women mentioned in the vedic literature, she went head to head with Yājñavalkya twice (BU 3.5, 8). Her position among the other disputants was strong enough that, once she realized that Yājñavalkya had defeated her, she in effect told them to shut up.

Gārgya Bālāki. Also called Dṛptabālāki ('Bālāki the Proud'), he comes from a distinguished family; Gārgyas are mentioned as teachers of liturgy and grammar. The episode of his attempting to teach King Ajātaśatru of Kāśi, who shows up his ignorance, is recorded both in BU 2.1 and in KsU 4.1–20, where he is depicted as a man who had travelled widely.

Gautama. The same as Uddālaka Āruṇi.

Ghora Āṅgirasa. Appears as the teacher of Kṛṣṇa Devakīputra in CU 3.17.6. Macdonell and Keith (1912, i. 250–1) regard him as a figment representing the dark side of Atharvavedic magical practice.

Glāva Maitreya. A Brahmin connected with Bāka Dālbhya in the story of the dogs (CU 1.12).

Gośruti Vaiyāghrapadya. Little is known about him, except that he appears as a pupil of Satyakāma Jābāla in CU 5.2.3 and SA 9.7.

Hāridrumata Gautama. Known only from his appearance in CU 4.4.3 as the teacher of the more famous Satyakāma Jābāla.

Himavat. The Himalayan mountains personified; the father of Umā in KeU 3.12.

Hiraṇyanābha. The name of a prince of Kosala mentioned in PU 6.1.

Iḷā. The personification of the milk and ghee offerings poured into the fire, she is said to be the mother of the fire god.

Indra. The most famous of the vedic gods, Indra is called the king of the gods. He is powerful and loves to drink Soma. His claim to fame is his victory over Vṛtra, a combat that is given cosmogonic significance. In the Vedas Indra is closely associated with rain, and prominence is given to his weapon, the Vajra, conceived of as the thunderbolt. In some of the Upaniṣads, Indra comes to be identified with the ultimate self (*ātman*).

Indradyumna Bhāllaveya. One of a group of men who went to receive instruction from Aśvapati Kaikeya about the self (CU 5.11) and about the Vaiśvānara fire (SB 10.6.1.1).

Īśāna. The term means 'lord' and is an epithet of various gods, especially of Rudra. Īśāna is also considered an independent god and is counted as one of the Rudras.

Jana Śārkarākṣya. Mentioned in the same episodes as Indradyumna.

Janaka of Videha. Perhaps the most famous and prominent of the kings mentioned in the Upaniṣads, Janaka appears already as a renowned king of a distant time in the episodes of Ajātaśatru of Kāśi (BU 2.1.1; KsU 4.1). Videha being to the east of the Kuru-Pañcāla country, the home of the major figures of the Upaniṣads, Janaka represents the growing importance of the eastern regions from which the new religions of Buddhism and Jainism would emerge some centuries later. Janaka is presented in the SB and the BU as very learned and able to debate the most learned of the Kuru-Pañcāla Brahmins. Although in the BU he usually learns from Yājñavalkya, in one episode of the SB (11.6.2) he teaches him the meaning of the daily fire sacrifice.

Jānaki Āyasthūṇa. Presented as a pupil of Cūla Bhāgavitti in BU 6.3.10.

Jānaśruti Pautrāyaṇa. A rich and pious man, possibly a king, who is taught the doctrine of the gatherer (*saṃvargavidyā*) by Raikva at CU 4.1.

Jāratkārava Ārtabhāga. One of the Brahmins attending Janaka's sacrifice who is defeated in debate by Yājñavalkya (BU 3.2), he is also mentioned as a teacher in SA 7.20.

Jātavedas. An epithet of the fire god, Agni.

Jitvan Śailini. He is mentioned in BU 4.1.1 as teaching Janaka that Brahman is speech, a view refuted by Yājñavalkya.

Kabandha Ātharvaṇa. The name of a Gandharva who possessed a woman in BU 3.7.1. In another version of the story (BU 3.3.1) the Gandharva is identified as Sudhanvan Aṅgiras.

Kabandhī Kātyāyana. A learned Brahmin who questioned Pippalāda in the PU 1.1.

Kahola Kauṣītakeya. Mentioned in several texts as a contemporary and rival of Yājñavalkya (SB 2.4.3.1; BU 3.5.1).

Kāśi. The old name of the city later known as Vārānasi (Benares). Kāśi is often connected with the kingdom of Videha.

Kātyāyanī. One of the two wives of Yājñavalkya and depicted as having only 'womanly interests' (BU 2.4.1; 4.5.1–2).

Kauravyāyaṇī. Her son is mentioned at BU 5.1.1.

Kausalya Āśvalāyana. A learned Brahmin who questioned Pippalāda in the PU 3.

Kauṣītaki. Patronymic of a teacher or a line of teachers. The name and the doctrines ascribed to him are prominent in a number of ancient texts (e.g. SA 2.17; 15.1) and two texts, the Kauṣītaki Brāhmaṇa and the KsU are named after him. A Kauṣītaki is also mentioned in CU 1.5.2, although it is unclear whether it refers to the same individual.

Kosala. The region east of Videha and closely associated with it and corresponding roughly to eastern Uttar Pradesh and western Bihar.

Kṛṣṇa Devakīputra. Mentioned in CU 3.17.6 as a pupil of Ghora Āṅgirasa. Although some have identified this Upaniṣadic figure as the Kṛṣṇa of the epics, the connection between the two is very doubtful.

Kumārahārīta. Mentioned as a teacher in BU 6.4.4. Nothing else is known about him.

Kuru. The name of a people and a region in the upper reaches of the Yamunā and Sarasvatī rivers, what is today eastern Punjab and Haryana. The Kurus are regularly associated with the Pañcālas.

Madhuka Paiṅgya. Mentioned as a teacher in SB 11.7.2.8, and as a pupil of Yājñavalkya in BU 6.3.8.

Madra. A region located towards the west of Kuru-Pañcāla around the upper tributaries of the Indus (i.e. in today's Punjab).

Maghavan. Literally 'bountiful', an epithet frequently ascribed to Indra.

Māhācamasya. A teacher mentioned in TU 1.5 and credited with adding *mahas* to the three Calls (CU 2.23.2 n.).

Mahāvṛṣa. A region located toward the north-west of Kuru-Pañcāla in what is today's Punjab.

Mahidāsa Aitareya. The teacher after whom the Aitareya Brāhmaṇa, Āraṇyaka, and Upaniṣad are named. His longevity is pointed out in CU 3.16.7 and JB 4.2.11, according to which he lived to be 116.

Maitreyī. One of the two wives of Yājñavalkya, who is presented as interested in theological matters. Her conversation with her husband, repeated twice, is one of the more important sections of the BU (BU 2.4.1; 4.5.1–2).

Manu. The first man and the progenitor of all humans, he plays the central role in the Indian myth of the flood. Later legends make him also the first lawgiver, and an important collection of ancient Indian laws is ascribed to Manu.

Maruts. A group of gods connected with the wind and thunderstorm, and thus associated with Indra's exploits. They are called the sons of Rudra and are often referred to in the plural as 'the Rudras'.

Matsya. A region to the south-west of Kuru-Pañcāla.

Maudgalya. Patronymic of one Nāka mentioned as a teacher in BU 6.4.4 and TU 1.9.1.

Mitra. A solar god regularly associated with Varuṇa.

Mṛtyu. Literally 'death', he is associated with the god of death Yama. In the Upaniṣads, the term has a range of meanings: death, Death personified, and the god Mṛtyu.

Naciketas. The son of Uśan Vājaśravas, who give him over to death. He is the main character in the KaU.

Naimiṣa. The name of a specially sacred forest. It may have been located somewhere along the river Sarasvatī.

Naka. *See* Maudgalya.

Nārada. This ancient seer is mentioned already in the AV. He attains great importance in later times and is regarded as a son of Brahmā, a divine seer (*devarṣi*), and a messenger between gods and men.

Paiṅgya. A famous teacher frequently mentioned in the Kauṣītaki Brāhmaṇa as an authority. His views are cited in KsU 2.2.

Pañcāla. The central region of vedic civilization, around the Yamuna and Ganga rivers, corresponding to the western Uttar Pradesh. The Pañcālas are closely associated with the Kurus.

Pārikṣitas. The patronymic of Janamejaya, the king of Kurus (AB 7.27, 34; 8.11). In the plural, the name probably refers to him and his brothers, Ugrasena, Bhīmasena, and Śrutasena, and more generally to the royal family of the Kurus. It appears that a serious scandal was associated with them and that they had atoned for it by means of a horse sacrifice. The disappearance of this once famous royal family may be associated with the conquest of the Kurus by the Salvas (Witzel 1989, 236). See also Horsch 1966, 253–5.

Parjanya. The god of the rain cloud, his main function is to shed rain. He is therefore associated with fertility, and the earth is said to be his wife.

Patañcala Kāpya. Mentioned in two similar episodes of BU 3.3 and 3.7 in which his wife or daughter is possessed by a spirit. He taught the sacrifice in the north-western country of the Madras.

Pauruśiṣṭi. The patronymic of one Taponitya mentioned in TU 1.9.

Pippalāda. The sage whose answers to six questions comprise the PU. His name connects him to the Paippalāda recension of the Atharvaveda.

Prācīnayogya. The patronymic of Satyayajña Pauluṣi, although it is applied to a variety of teachers (see TU 1.6.2 and the list of teachers at BU 2.6.2).

Prācīnaśāla Aupamanyava. One of the group of Brahmins who received instruction from Aśvapati Kaikeya (*see also* Indradyumna).

Prajāpati. Literally 'lord of creatures', he is the creator god *par excellence* in the Brāhmaṇas and the Upaniṣads. He is the father of the gods and the demons (*asura*), as well as of all creatures. See Gonda 1986.

Pratardana Daivodāsi. Mentioned in the KsU 3.1 as going to Indra's world after his death in battle, his patronymic 'descendant of Divodāsa' connects him to the famous Ṛgvedic king Sudās, the son or descendant of Divodāsa. Pratardana is also mentioned as a king in other vedic texts.

Prātṛda. Mentioned in an episode in BU 5.12.2, where he poses a question to his father. The name is a patronymic of a teacher named Bhālla in the JB 3.31.4.

Pravāhaṇa Jaivali. King of Pañcāla who appears in BU 6.2 and CU 5.3–10 teaching the famous doctrine of the five fires that explains the process of rebirth, and in CU 1.8.1 teaching the meaning of the High Chant.

Pūṣan. Closely associated with the sun god, he is viewed as the one who knows the paths and conducts the dead safely to the world of the fathers.

Raikva. A somewhat comical figure from the north-western region of Mahāvṛṣa who sat scratching his itch under a cart when he was discovered. He taught the doctrine of the gatherer to Jānaśruti at CU 4.1–3.

Rāthītara. The patronymic of one Satyavacas mentioned in TU 1.9.

Ṛjīṣin. Literally 'receiving the residue of Soma', this is an epithet of Indra.

Rudra. Generally regarded as a storm god, Rudra has an ambivalent personality. He is fierce and feared. He is also a healer, the one who averts the anger of gods. In his benign aspect he is referred to as *śiva*, 'the benign one', an epithet which becomes the name of the later god Śiva, with whom Rudra is identified.

Rudras. In the plural, the term refers to a group of eleven gods, who, together with the Ādityas and Vasus, constitute the three classes of gods. The Rudras are associted with the Maruts; both of these groups are ruled by Rudra.

Sādhyas. A group of somewhat ill-defined deities, said to occupy a region above that of the gods.

Śaibya Satyakāma. A learned Brahmin who questioned Pippalāda in the PU 5.

Sāmaśravas. A pupil of Yājñavalkya in BU 3.1.2.

Sanatkumāra. He, together with Sanaka, Sanandana, and Sanātana, are the mind-born sons of the creator god Brahmā. They are reputed for their knowledge and for lifelong celibacy.

Śāṇḍilya. He is one of important teachers of the fire ritual in the SB, to whom is ascribed a famous doctrine bearing his name, 'Śāṇḍilya-doctrine' (*śāṇḍilyavidyā*), in SB 10.6.3 and CU 3.14. There is some confusion, however, in the literature, because this patronymic may have belonged to several teachers (*see* Udaraśāṇḍilya). Although Śāṇḍilya is associated with texts belonging to the eastern regions, Witzel (1989, 204) has pointed out that the Śāṇḍilya tradition may have had its origins further west and spread later to the east.

Sarasvatī. The most celebrated river of the vedic age (although its identity in the early period is not altogether certain), it is personified as a goddess. In the Brāhmaṇas she becomes identified with speech and the goddess of speech, and in later mythology Sarasvatī is the goddess of eloquence and wisdom (BU 6.4.27).

Satvan. A region located around the southern tributaries of the Yamunā River and associated with the land of Matsya (KsU 4.1).

Satyakāma Jābāla. In one of the most moving stories of the Upaniṣads, Satyakāma's mother, Jabālā, confesses to her son that he was born out of wedlock and that she does not know who his father is. She asks him to call himself the 'son of Jabālā' (Jābāla), thus adopting a matronymic. This open truthfulness impresses his teacher, Hāridrumata Gautama, that he initiates him into vedic study (CU 4.4–9). Satyakāma appears as a teacher in several other vedic texts (e.g. BU 4.1.6), and he is said to be a pupil of Jānaki Āyasthūṇa in BU 6.3.11.

Satyayajña Pauluṣi. Also called Prācīnayogya, he is one of the group of Brahmins who receive instruction from Aśvapati Kaikeya (*see* Indradyumna).

Śaunaka Kāpeya. Śaunaka is a common patronymic applied to a variety of teachers (MuU 1.1.3). Kāpeya is mentioned in connection with Abhipratārin Kākṣaseni in CU 4.3.5, and the JB (3.1.21; 1.59.2) identifies him as the latter's domestic priest.

Sauryāyaṇī Gārgya. A learned Brahmin who questioned Pippalāda in the PU 4.

Savitṛ. The god associated with the stimulating power of the sun. He is the deity invoked in the most celebrated of vedic verses, the Gāyatrī or the Sāvitrī (RV 3.62.10).

Śilaka Śālāvatya. Nothing more is known about this teacher except for what is contained in CU 1.8.1, where he is depicted as a contemporary of Pravāhaṇa Jaivali.

Sinīvālī. Together with Rākā, she is a goddess associated with the phases of the moon. Rākā is connected with the full moon and Sinīvālī with the first day of the new moon.

Soma. A sacrificial drink pressed from a plant, a drink that apparently had mind-altering qualities. The drink is personified as a god and later identified with the moon. Thus the term often simply means the moon (see BU 1.3.24n.).

Sudhanvan Aṅgiras. The name of a Gandharva who possessed a woman in BU 3.3.1, while in another version of the story (BU 3.7.1) the Gandharva is identified as Kabandha Ātharvaṇa.

Sukeśa Bhāradvāja. A learned Brahmin who questioned Pippalāda in the PU 6.

Śuṣkabhṛṅgāra. We know him only from KsU 2.6, where he teaches that *brahman* is Uktha (BU 1.6.1 n.), indicating that he was possibly a teacher of the Ṛgvedic tradition.

Śvetaketu Āruneya. Son of the famous teacher Uddālaka Āruṇi, his dialogue with a king, variously identified as Pravāhaṇa Jaivali (BU 6.2; CU 5.3–10) and Citra Gāṅgāyani (KsU 1.1–2), sets the scene for the exposition of the important doctrine of the five fires and the theory of transmigration. Although he is made a contemporary of Yājñavalkya and Janaka of Videha in SB 11.6.2, this cannot be accepted at face value because his father is also a contemporary of these in BU 3.7. Śvetaketu is often depicted as a haughty young man contrasting sharply with the humility of his father. He is regarded as a wise sage and seer in later literature, but his late date is hinted at in the *Āpastamba Dharmasūtra* (1.2.5.4–6), which calls him a man of recent times.

Śvetāśvatara. The teacher of the doctrine presented in the SU, after whom the Upaniṣad is named.

Triśaṅku. A sage mentioned in TU 1.10, identified in later literature as a king of Ayodhya who desired to go to heaven with his body and became the southern cross constellation.

Tvaṣṭṛ. Described as a skilled workman, he is the father of Indra. He is a guardian of Soma, and thus attracts the hostility of his son, who wants to take possession of the drink. Soma is often called the 'honey of Tvaṣṭṛ', and it is in this capacity that he revealed to Dadhyañc the place of honey, i.e. Soma. This is the basis for the reference at BU 2.5.17.

Udaṅka Śaulbāyana. He is mentioned as a teacher already in the TS (7.5.4.2). At BU 4.1.3 he tells Janaka of Videha that *brahman* is the lifebreath.

Udaraśāṇḍilya. Little is known about him apart from what is mentioned in CU 1.9.3. He was the pupil of Atidhanvan Śaunaka.

Uddālaka Āruṇi. Also bearing the name Gautama, he was a famous teacher from the Kuru-Pañcāla region and the father of the equally famous Śvetaketu. Even though in BU 6.3.7 he is said to have been Yājñavalkya's teacher, elsewhere Yājñavalkya is presented as an equal of Uddālaka and as defeating Uddālaka in debate (BU 3.7). The entire sixth chapter of the CU is devoted to Uddālaka's exposition of the 'existent' (*sat*) as the source of all things, where he presents this novel doctrine rejecting the old view that the 'existent' emerged from the 'non-existent'.

Umā. The daughter of Himavat in KeU 3.12. In later mythology she is also called Pārvatī ('daughter of the mountain') and becomes the wife of Śiva.

Upakosala Kāmalāyana. Said to have been a pupil of Satyakāma Jābāla in CU 4.10.

Uśan Vājaśravas. The father of Naciketas in KU 1.1. He referred to as Gautama (KaU 1.10), and Naciketas is called the son of Uddālaka Āruṇi at KaU 1.11 (see, however, the note to this). If this is true, then Uśan is the same as Uddālaka, and Naciketas is the same as, or the brother of, Śvetaketu.

Uṣasta Cākrāyaṇa. Called Uṣasti in CU 1.10.1, he is there depicted as a learned but poor Brahmin who managed to outwit the priests of a sacrifice by his superior knowledge of the sacrificial chants. In BU 3.5, he is one of the Kuru-Pañcāla Brahmins who are defeated in debate by Yājñavalkya.

Uśīnara. The location of this region is uncertain, but it must have been near the heartland of Brahmanism of this period represented by Kuru-Pañcāla and Kāśi.

Vājaśravas. *See* Uśan Vājaśravas.

Vaiyāghrapadya. The patronymic of both Indradyumna Bhāllaveya (CU 5.14) and Buḍila Āśvatarāśvi (CU 5.16).

Varuṇa. One of the great gods in early vedic literature, he is viewed as the grand sovereign and upholder of the natural and moral order. He becomes increasingly associated with the waters, and his residence comes to be located within the ocean. In the period represented by the Brāhmaṇas and the Upaniṣads, Varuṇa's cosmic role fades with the emergence of Prajāpati as the supreme creator god.

Vasus. A group of eight gods distinguished from the Ādityas and Rudras, although their general character and specific identities remain rather vague.

Vidagdha Śākalya. A teacher who, according to the SB (11.6.3.3), volunteered to debate with Yājñavalkya on behalf of the assembled Brahmins (see BU 3.9). He is also reported to have told Janaka of Videha that *brahman* is the heart (BU 4.1.7).

Videha. A region located north-east of Kāśi and east of Kosala, with which it is closely associated. Corresponds roughly to northern Bihar.

Virocaṇa. The son of Prahlāda, who is viewed in the CU 8.7.2 as occupying a position among demons parallel to that of Indra among the gods. In later mythology both he and his father are viewed as pious and kind demons.

Viṣṇu. The great god of later Hinduism, who is a somewhat minor solar deity in the vedic literature. He is especially associated with his three steps with which he measured the three worlds, his third step being viewed as the highest heaven. These steps are connected in the SB (1.2.5) with Viṣṇu's assuming the shape of a dwarf and thus tricking a demon, who had conquered the world, into letting him have a small piece of land where he could lie down. Upon being granted the land,

Viṣṇu assumed his normal size and strode through the three worlds, securing them for the gods.

Viśvāvasu. A Gandharva who is regarded as fond of women and is a rival of the husband during the first night after the wedding.

Viśvedeva. Literally 'All-gods', the term came to be applied to a class of gods distinct from the Ādityas, Rudras, and Vasus. Their number is fixed as thirteen, and in later Brahmanical rites offerings to this group occupy a prominent place.

Vrātya. The term is used in ancient literature to refer to groups of people, at least some of whom appear to have led a wandering or a nomadic life. There is no consensus among scholars regarding the identity of Vrātya. Falk (1986*a*) has shown that the Vrātyas were probably 'poor, mostly young Brahmins and Kṣatriyas who in search of a 'start capital' form a dark, ominous sodality which demands ransom from the local, well-settled *gr̥hasthas* [householders] and even from the kings' (Witzel 1989, 235–6). Already in some vedic texts, however, the Vrātya is presented as a mysterious, powerful, and even divine person. In later times the term is used to refer to either mixed-caste people or to Brahmins who have not undergone vedic initiation. See also Horsch 1966, 401–20.

Yama. The Indian god of death from the most ancient period of vedic mythology until contemporary times. In ancient myths he is called king and divine characteristics are ascribed to him, but he comes to be identified with death itself (*see* Mr̥tyu) and many of the negative aspects of death become associated with Yama. Later myths associate him with judgement and punishment of the dead.

Yājñavalkya. He occupies a central position in the SB as an authority on ritual matters and in the BU as a teacher of esoteric doctrines. Traditionally credited with the composition of the White Yajurveda, his final settlement with his two wives, Kātyāyanī and Maitreyī, and his subsequent departure from home into possibly an ascetic way of life are narrated twice in the BU at 2.4 and 4.5. In the BU he appears as a humorous, sarcastic, and often irreverent figure.

INDEX

In several significant areas, this Index groups related terms under a single broad topic. Accordingly, all parts of a human or animal body are listed under *body, parts of*; all classes of society, such as Brahmins, under *social classes*; all colours, under *colour*; all the ritual fires and terms relating to fire, under *fire*; all grains such as rice and barley, under *grain*; all numbers, under *number*; all the various priests, under *priest*; all the directions such as north and south, under *quarters*; terms relating to the sacrifice, under *sacrifice*; all terms relating to the Sāman chants, under *Sāman*; all divisions of time such as day, month, and year, under *time*; all divisions of the Veda, under *Veda*; all vital powers such as breathing, sight, and hearing, under *vital functions*; all the various worlds, under *world*. Plurals are listed under the corresponding singulars. The four sacred sounds, *bhūr, bhuvas, mahas,* and *svar*, are listed under *Call*. The sign (n) after a reference indicates that the term is explained in the note to that passage. The numbers refer to the internal divisions of the Upaniṣads as described in the Note on the Translation (p. lix).

copper **CU** 4.17.7; 6.1.5
corpse, *see under* body
correspondence **BU** 6.1.4(n),14; 6.3.2; **CU** 5.1.4,14; 5.2.5
couch **KsU** 1.5(n)
counterpart **BU** 1.1.2(n); 4.1.2
cow, *see under* cattle
creation **BU** 1.2.1–7; 1.4.1–17; 1.5.21; 4.3.10; 5.5.1; 6.4.2; **AU** 1.1.1–2; 1.2.1; 1.3.1
creator **SU** 3.20; 4.14; 5.13; 6.16; **MuU** 1.1.1; 3.1.3
cremation **BU** 5.11.1; 6.2.14–16; **CU** 4.15.5; 5.9.2; 7.15.3; *see also* funeral
cripple **CU** 8.9.1–2; *see also* lame
crocodiles **SU** 1.4–5
crying, *see* weeping
cryptic **BU** 3.4.1–2; 3.5.1; 4.2.2; **AU** 1.3.14
crystal **SU** 2.11
Cūla Bhāgavitti **BU** 6.3.9–10
cultivated **BU** 6.3.13
curd **BU** 6.3.13; 6.4.15,24–5; **CU** 5.2.4; 6.6.1; **SU** 1.15–16
curse **BU** 6.4.12

Dadhyañc Ātharvaṇa **BU** 2.5.16(n),17–19; 2.6.3; 4.6.3
dance **KaU** 1.26
danger, *see* fear
darkness **BU** 1.3.28; 3.7.13; 3.8.8; 3.9.14; 4.4.10–11; **CU** 1.3.1; 3.17.7; 7.11.2; 7.26.2; 8.13.1; **IU** 3,9,12; **SU** 3.8; 4.18; **MuU** 2.2.6
dart **BU** 6.4.9
daughter **BU** 3.3.1; 6.4.17; **CU** 4.2.3; **KeU** 3.12
deaf **BU** 6.1.10; **CU** 5.1.10; **KsU** 3.3; *see also* hearing *under* vital functions
dear **BU** 1.4.8; 2.4.4–5; 4.1.3; 4.5.5–6
death (Death) **BU** 1.2.1–7; 1.3.9–16,28; 1.4.11,15; 1.5.21,23; 2.1.12; 2.4.12–13; 3.1.3; 3.2.10–13; 3.5.1; 3.6.2; 3.9.4,14,28; 4.3.7–8,35–8; 4.4.1–4,11,19; 4.5.13; 5.5.2; 5.9–11; 5.14.8; 6.2.2,13–16; 6.4.4,12; **CU** 1.2.9; 1.4.2–5; 1.10.4; 2.10.1,6; 2.22.3–4; 2.24.6,10,15; 3.14.1,4; 3.15.2; 3.16.7; 3.17.5–6; 5.3.2; 5.9.2; 5.10.8; 6.11.3; 7.26.2; 8.1.5–6; 8.3.1–2; 8.4.1; 8.6.4–5; 8.7.1–3; 8.8.5; 8.9.1–2; 8.12.1; **TU** 2.6; 2.8; 3.1–6; 3.10.4–5; **AU** 1.1.4; 1.2.4; 2.4,6; **KsU** 1.2; 2.8*a–b*,11–14; 3.3; 4.2,14; **KeU** 1.2; 2.5; **KaU** 1.4–29; 2.18,25; 3.15–16; 4.2,10–11; 5.6; 6.3,18; **IU** 3,11,14; **SU** 1.11; 3.8; 4.15; 6.15; **MuU** 1.2.7; **PU** 5.1,7; 6.6; see *also* birth, cremation, funeral, rebirth, Yama
  repeated death **BU** 1.2.7(n); 1.5.2; 3.2.10; 3.3.2; **KaU** 4.10–11
  rites before **BU** 1.5.17
deeds, *see* action
deity, *see* god
delusion **BU** 3.5.1; **KaU** 2.6; **SU** 1.4–5; 6.1; **MuU** 3.1.2
demon **BU** 1.1.2; 1.3.1(n),2–7; 5.2.3; **CU** 8.7.2; 8.8.4–5; **KsU** 4.20; **IU** 3
  competing with gods **BU** 1.3.1; **CU** 1.2.1–7
  offspring of Prajāpati **BU** 1.3.1; 5.2.1; **CU** 1.2.1
descendant **CU** 1.9.3; 4.11.2; 4.12.2; 4.13.2; **SU** 4.22
desire **BU** 1.2.4–7; 1.4.15–17; 1.5.3; 3.2.7; 3.5.1; 4.3.21; 4.4.5–7; 4.4.22; 5.14.7; 6.1.4; 6.3.1; **CU** 1.1.6–8; 1.2.13–14; 1.6.8; 1.7.6–9; 3.14.2–4; 3.17.6; 3.19.3; 4.10.3; 5.1.4; 7.10.1; 7.14.2; 7.16.1; 8.1.4–6; 8.2.10; 8.3.1–2; 8.7.1–3; 8.12.5–6; **TU** 2.1; 2.6; 2.8; 3.10.4; **AU** 2.6; 3.2,4; **KsU** 1.7; 2.14; 3.5–6; **KaU** 1.24–25; 2.3–4; 2.11,20; 4.2; 5.8,13; 6.14; **IU** 2; **SU** 1.11; 3.20; 6.13; **MuU** 2.2.1; 3.1.6,10; 3.2.1–2; **MaU** 9
Devakī **CU** 3.17.6
Dhātṛ **BU** 6.4.21
dice **CU** 4.1.4–6; 4.3.8; 7.3.1
dike **BU** 4.4.22(n); **CU** 8.4.1–2; **KaU** 3.2; **SU** 6.19; **MuU** 2.2.5
directions, *see* quarters
dish **BU** 5.15.1; 6.3.1; **IU** 15
disk **KaU** 1.16(n),17; 2.1; **SU** 2.14
diversity **BU** 4.4.19; **KsU** 3.8; **KaU** 4.10–11

THE WORLD'S CLASSICS

A Select List

HANS ANDERSEN: Fairy Tales
Translated by L. W. Kingsland
Introduction by Naomi Lewis
Illustrated by Vilhelm Pedersen and Lorenz Frølich

ARTHUR J. ARBERRY (Transl.): The Koran

LUDOVICO ARIOSTO: Orlando Furioso
Translated by Guido Waldman

ARISTOTLE: The Nicomachean Ethics
Translated by David Ross

JANE AUSTEN: Emma
Edited by James Kinsley and David Lodge

Northanger Abbey, Lady Susan, The Watsons, *and* Sanditon
Edited by John Davie

Persuasion
Edited by John Davie

WILLIAM BECKFORD: Vathek
Edited by Roger Lonsdale

KEITH BOSLEY (Transl.): The Kalevala

CHARLOTTE BRONTË: Jane Eyre
Edited by Margaret Smith

JOHN BUNYAN: The Pilgrim's Progress
Edited by N. H. Keeble

FRANCES HODGSON BURNETT: The Secret Garden
Edited by Dennis Butts

FANNY BURNEY: Cecilia
or Memoirs of an Heiress
Edited by Peter Sabor and Margaret Anne Doody

THOMAS CARLYLE: The French Revolution
Edited by K. J. Fielding and David Sorensen

LEWIS CARROLL: Alice's Adventures in Wonderland *and* Through the Looking Glass
Edited by Roger Lancelyn Green
Illustrated by John Tenniel

MIGUEL DE CERVANTES: Don Quixote
Translated by Charles Jarvis
Edited by E. C. Riley

GEOFFREY CHAUCER: The Canterbury Tales
Translated by David Wright

ANTON CHEKHOV: The Russian Master and Other Stories
Translated by Ronald Hingley

JOHN CLELAND:
Memoirs of a Woman of Pleasure (Fanny Hill)
Edited by Peter Sabor

WILKIE COLLINS: Armadale
Edited by Catherine Peters

JOSEPH CONRAD: Chance
Edited by Martin Ray

Victory
Edited by John Batchelor
Introduction by Tony Tanner

NORMAN DAVIS (Ed.): The Paston Letters

CHARLES DICKENS: Christmas Books
Edited by Ruth Glancy

Sikes and Nancy and Other Public Readings
Edited by Philip Collins

FEDOR DOSTOEVSKY: Crime and Punishment
Translated by Jessie Coulson
Introduction by John Jones

ARTHUR CONAN DOYLE:
Sherlock Holmes: Selected Stories
Introduction by S. C. Roberts

ALEXANDRE DUMAS *père*:
The Three Musketeers
Edited by David Coward

ALEXANDRE DUMAS *fils*:
La Dame aux Camélias
Translated by David Coward

MARIA EDGEWORTH: Castle Rackrent
Edited by George Watson

GEORGE ELIOT:
Felix Holt, The Radical
Edited by Fred C. Thompson

Middlemarch
Edited by David Carroll

Scenes of Clerical Life
Edited by Thomas A. Noble

Selected Critical Writings
Edited by Rosemary Ashton

GUSTAVE FLAUBERT: Madame Bovary
Translated by Gerard Hopkins
Introduction by Terence Cave

BENJAMIN FRANKLIN: Autobiography and other Writings
Edited by Ormond Seavey

ELIZABETH GASKELL: Cousin Phillis and Other Tales
Edited by Angus Easson

My Lady Ludlow and Other Stories
Edited by Edgar Wright

J. W. VON GOETHE: Faust, Part One
Translated by David Luke

OLIVER GOLDSMITH: The Vicar of Wakefield
Edited by Arthur Friedman

THOMAS HARDY: A Pair of Blue Eyes
Edited by Alan Manford

HESIOD: Theogony *and* Works and Days
Translated by M. L. West

E. T. A. HOFFMANN: The Golden Pot and Other Tales
Translated and Edited by Ritchie Robertson

HOMER: The Iliad
Translated by Robert Fitzgerald
Introduction by G. S. Kirk

THOMAS HUGHES: Tom Brown's Schooldays
Edited by Andrew Sanders

HENRIK IBSEN: An Enemy of the People, The Wild Duck, Rosmersholm
Edited and Translated by James McFarlane

HENRY JAMES: The Ambassadors
Edited by Christopher Butler

M. R. JAMES: Casting the Runes and Other Ghost Stories
Edited by Michael Cox

JOCELIN OF BRAKELOND:
Chronicle of the Abbey of Bury St. Edmunds
Translated by Diana Greenway and Jane Sayers

GWYN JONES (Transl.):
Eirik the Red and Other Icelandic Sagas

BEN JONSON: Five Plays
Edited by G. A. Wilkes

MADAME DE LAFAYETTE: The Princesse de Clèves
Translated and Edited by Terence Cave

WILLIAM LANGLAND: Piers Plowman
Translated and Edited by A. V. C. Schmidt

J. SHERIDAN LE FANU: Uncle Silas
Edited by W. J. McCormack

MIKHAIL LERMONTOV: A Hero of our Time
Translated by Vladimar Nabokov with Dmitri Nabokov

MATTHEW LEWIS: The Monk
Edited by Howard Anderson

MARCUS AURELIUS: The Meditations of Marcus Aurelius
Translated by A. S. L. Farquharson
Edited by R. B. Rutherford

KATHERINE MANSFIELD: Selected Stories
Edited by D. M. Davin

CHARLES MATURIN: Melmoth the Wanderer
Edited by Douglas Grant
Introduction by Chris Baldick

HERMAN MELVILLE: The Confidence-Man
Edited by Tony Tanner

Moby Dick
Edited by Tony Tanner

PROSPER MÉRIMÉE: Carmen and Other Stories
Translated by Nicholas Jotcham

MICHELANGELO: Life, Letters, and Poetry
Translated by George Bull with Peter Porter

MOLIÈRE: Don Juan and Other Plays
Translated by George Graveley and Ian Maclean

E. NESBIT: The Railway Children
Edited by Dennis Butts

EDGAR ALLAN POE: Selected Tales
Edited by Julian Symons

JEAN RACINE: Britannicus, Phaedra, Athaliah
Translated by C. H. Sisson

ANN RADCLIFFE: The Italian
Edited by Frederick Garber

THE MARQUIS DE SADE:
The Misfortune of Virtue and Other Early Tales
Translated and Edited by David Coward

SIR WALTER SCOTT: The Heart of Midlothian
Edited by Claire Lamont

ANNA SEWELL: Black Beauty
Edited by Peter Hollindale

TOBIAS SMOLLETT: The Expedition of Humphry Clinker
Edited by Lewis M. Knapp
Revised by Paul-Gabriel Boucé

ROBERT LOUIS STEVENSON:
Treasure Island
Edited by Emma Letley

ANTHONY TROLLOPE: The American Senator
Edited by John Halperin

GIORGIO VASARI: The Lives of the Artists
Translated and Edited by Julia Conaway Bondanella and Peter Bondanella

VIRGINIA WOOLF: Orlando
Edited by Rachel Bowlby

ÉMILE ZOLA: Nana
Translated and Edited by Douglas Parmée